# THE NEW CAMBRIDGE COMPANION TO RALPH WALDO EMERSON

While Emerson's place in American literary history has remained secure, *The New Cambridge Companion to Ralph Waldo Emerson* draws on a wealth of recent Emerson scholarship that has highlighted his contemporary relevance for questions of philosophy and politics, ecology and science, poetics and aesthetics, or identity and race, and connects these to the key formal and interpretive issues at stake in understanding his work. The volume's contributors engage the full breadth of Emerson's writing, developing novel approaches to canonical works like *Nature*, the essays "Self-Reliance" and "Experience," or to his poetry and journals, and bringing critical attention to his lectures and the long-overlooked texts of his later period. *The New Cambridge Companion to Ralph Waldo Emerson* thus both bears witness to the new Emersons that have emerged in the past decades and draws a new circle in Emerson's reception.

Michael Jonik is Professor of American Literature and Philosophy at the University of Sussex. He is the author of *Herman Melville and the Politics of the Inhuman* (Cambridge University Press, 2018) and coeditor of the *Oxford Handbook to Herman Melville* (Oxford University Press, 2025). He is Reviews and Special Issues editor for the journal *Textual Practice*.

*A complete list of books in the series is at the back of the book.*

AF148486

# THE NEW CAMBRIDGE
## COMPANION TO
# RALPH WALDO
# EMERSON

EDITED BY
## MICHAEL JONIK
*University of Sussex*

Shaftesbury Road, Cambridge CB2 8EA, United Kingdom

One Liberty Plaza, 20th Floor, New York, NY 10006, USA

477 Williamstown Road, Port Melbourne, VIC 3207, Australia

314–321, 3rd Floor, Plot 3, Splendor Forum, Jasola District Centre,
New Delhi – 110025, India

Cambridge University Press is part of Cambridge University Press & Assessment,
a department of the University of Cambridge.

We share the University's mission to contribute to society through the pursuit of
education, learning and research at the highest international levels of excellence.

www.cambridge.org
Information on this title: www.cambridge.org/9781009347761
DOI: 10.1017/9781009347747

First published 2026

*A catalogue record for this publication is available from the British Library*

*Library of Congress Cataloging-in-Publication Data*
NAMES: Jonik, Michael, 1979– editor
TITLE: The new Cambridge companion to Ralph Waldo Emerson /
edited by Michael Jonik.
DESCRIPTION: Cambridge ; New York, NY : Cambridge University Press, 2026. |
Series: Cambridge companions to literature | Includes bibliographical
references and index.
IDENTIFIERS: LCCN 2025040333 (print) | LCCN 2025040334 (ebook) |
ISBN 9781009347754 hardback | ISBN 9781009347761 paperback |
ISBN 9781009347747 ebook
SUBJECTS: LCSH: Emerson, Ralph Waldo, 1803–1882 – Criticism and
interpretation | Authors, American – 19th century – Biography |
Transcendentalists (New England) – Biography | Romanticism – United States |
United States – Intellectual life – 19th century
CLASSIFICATION: LCC PS1638 .N485 2026 (print) | LCC PS1638 (ebook)
LC record available at https://lccn.loc.gov/2025040333
LC ebook record available at https://lccn.loc.gov/2025040334

ISBN 978-1-009-34775-4 Hardback
ISBN 978-1-009-34776-1 Paperback

# CONTENTS

# CONTRIBUTORS

JENNIFER J. BAKER is Associate Professor of English at New York University, where she specializes in American literature, culture, and intellectual history of the eighteenth and nineteenth centuries. She is the author of *Securing the Commonwealth: Debt, Speculation, and Writing in the Making of Early America* (Johns Hopkins University Press, 2005) and, most recently, *American Romanticism and the Evolutionary Idea* (forthcoming from Stanford University Press). She is currently at work on a reception history of Melville's *Moby-Dick*, investigating how Cold War politics, academic culture, and changing literary taste propelled the once-obscure novel to fame and canonical status in the first half of the twentieth century.

PRENTISS CLARK is Associate Professor of English at the University of South Dakota and a past President of the Ralph Waldo Emerson Society (2022–23). She is the author of *Ralph Waldo Emerson: A Companion* (McFarland, 2022), and her essay "The 'Arch Abolitionist': Emerson, Love, and Social Justice" appears in the *Oxford Handbook of Ralph Waldo Emerson* (Oxford University Press, 2024). She has published articles in *Nineteenth-Century Literature*, the *Henry James Review*, and the *James Baldwin Review*, and her current project is a book on Emerson and James Baldwin titled *Jimmy & Waldo*.

LAURA DASSOW WALLS is Professor Emerita at the University of Notre Dame, where she taught American literature, particularly the American Transcendentalists, and the history and theory of ecological thought. Previously she taught at Lafayette College and the University of South Carolina. Her biography *Henry David Thoreau: A Life* (Chicago University Press, 2017) received Phi Beta Kappa's Christian Gauss Award and the *Los Angeles Times* Book Award for Biography. Her other books include the award-winning *Passage to Cosmos: Alexander von Humboldt and the Shaping of America* (University of Chicago Press, 2009), *Emerson's Life in Science: The Culture of Truth* (Cornell University Press, 2003), and *Seeing New Worlds: Henry David Thoreau and Nineteenth-Century Natural Science* (University of Wisconsin Press, 1995). Currently, she is working on a literary biography of the American writer Barry Lopez.

DANIELLE FOLLETT is Associate Professor (Maître de Conférences) in American literature at the Université Sorbonne Nouvelle in Paris, France. She specializes in nineteenth-century American literature and the history of ideas, particularly focusing on transcendentalism. She has published numerous articles on Emerson, Thoreau, and Poe, as well as on aesthetics and the history of the idea of chance. She coauthored the nineteenth-century chapter in *Figures of Chance: Chance in Literature and the Arts (16th–21st Centuries)* (Routledge, 2024).

SOPHIA FORSTER is Professor of English at California Polytechnic State University in San Luis Obispo. Her articles on nineteenth-century literature have appeared in such journals as *Modern Fiction Studies*, *ESQ*, and *J19*, among others.

PAUL GRIMSTAD is Senior Lecturer and Director of Undergraduate Studies at Yale University. He writes regularly for *The Believer*, *Bookforum*, *London Review of Books*, *The New Yorker*, *n+1*, *The Paris Review*, *Music and Literature*, *The New Republic*, and *Times Literary Supplement*, among other journals and magazines. His "Miles the Mercurial" was a notable selection for Best American Essays of 2021 (ed. Kathryn Schulz). His next book *Interested in Everything and Nothing Else: On the Polymath* is under advance contract with Princeton University Press and a novel, COLD FUSION, is out from Simon & Schuster in early 2027. He is the author of *Experience and Experimental Writing: Literary Pragmatism from Emerson to the Jameses* (Oxford University Press, 2013), which was recently the focus of a symposium in the journal *Nonsite*, and has contributed chapters to *The Oxford Handbook to Edgar Allan Poe* (Oxford University Press, 2019), *Melville's Philosophies* (Bloomsbury, 2017), *Stanley Cavell and Literary Studies* (Bloomsbury, 2011), *The Oxford History of the Novel* (Oxford University Press, 2016), and *The Jamesian Mind* (Routledge, 2023) as well as forthcoming chapters in *William James and Literary Studies* (Cambridge), *The Oxford Handbook to George Santayana* and "Baudelaire and America" in Yale French Studies. While an assistant professor of English at Yale, he received the Sarai Ribicoff '79 teaching prize for "instruction and character that reflect the qualities of independence, innovation, and originality." He has taught literature and philosophy at NYU, Columbia, and Yale.

NICHOLAS L. GUARDIANO is Alwin C. Carus Archivist and Associate Professor at Southern Illinois University Carbondale. His areas of research are American transcendentalism and pragmatism, metaphysics, aesthetics, philosophy of nature, semiotics, Neoplatonism, and nineteenth-century American art. Bringing together his interdisciplinary interests for a metaphysics of nature is his book *Aesthetic Transcendentalism in Emerson, Peirce, and Nineteenth-Century American Landscape Painting* (Lexington Books, 2017). At Southern Illinois University, he teaches broadly in the history of philosophy and oversees the philosophy collections at the Special Collections Research Center of Morris Library. He is also President of the Ralph Waldo Emerson Society (2026–27).

JEFFREY INSKO is Professor of English at Oakland University in Michigan, where he teaches courses in nineteenth-century American literature and culture and in the environmental humanities. He is the author of *History, Abolition, and the Ever-Present Now in Antebellum American Writing* (Oxford University Press, 2018). His essays have appeared in journals and collections such as *American Literary History, American Literature, ESQ: A Journal of Nineteenth-Century American Literature and Culture*, and *The Oxford Handbook of Ralph Waldo Emerson* (Oxford University Press, 2024).

MICHAEL JONIK is Professor of American Literature and Philosophy at the University of Sussex. He is the author of *Herman Melville and the Politics of the Inhuman* (Cambridge University Press, 2018) and coeditor of the *Oxford Handbook to Herman Melville* (Oxford University Press, 2025). He is Reviews and Special Issues editor for the journal *Textual Practice*.

DAVID LAROCCA is the author or contributing editor of twenty books, including *On Emerson* (Wadsworth, 2003), *Estimating Emerson: An Anthology of Criticism from Carlyle to Cavell* (Bloomsbury, 2013), *Emerson's* English Traits *and the Natural History of Metaphor* (Bloomsbury, 2013), Stanley Cavell's *Emerson's Transcendental Etudes* (Stanford University Press, 2003), *A Power to Translate the World: New Essays on Emerson and International Culture* (with Ricardo Miguel-Alfonso, Dartmouth College Press, 2016), and *The Bloomsbury Anthology of Transcendental Thought: From Antiquity to the Anthropocene* (Bloomsbury, 2017). Educated at Buffalo, Berkeley, Vanderbilt, and Harvard, he served as Harvard University's Sinclair Kennedy Traveling Fellow in the United Kingdom and, like Cavell before him, was honored with the Distinguished Achievement Award from the Ralph Waldo Emerson Society.

SEAN ROSS MEEHAN is Professor of English and Director of Writing at Washington College. He is the author of *A Liberal Education in Late Emerson: Readings in the Rhetoric of Mind* (Camden House, 2019) and *Mediating American Autobiography: Photography in Emerson, Thoreau, Douglass, and Whitman* (Missouri, 2008). He is the coeditor of *Approaches to Teaching the Works of Ralph Waldo Emerson* (MLA, 2018).

MARK NOBLE is Associate Professor of English at Georgia State University, where he teaches American literature and critical theory. He is the author of *American Poetic Materialism from Whitman to Stevens* (Cambridge University Press, 2015). His essays appear in *American Literature, Nineteenth-Century Literature, American Literary History, J19*, and various edited collections.

SPENCER TRICKER is Assistant Professor of English at Loyola University Chicago, where he specializes in Asian American and Pacific Islander literatures of the nineteenth and early twentieth centuries. His manuscript in progress, *The Wavering*

*Pacific: Literature, Empire, and Cosmopolitan Emotion*, examines the uses and abuses of cosmopolitanism in the writings of Asian, American, and Oceanian authors. His critical essays have appeared in *MELUS*, *Studies in American Fiction*, *American Literary Realism*, and two edited collections: *Crossings in Nineteenth-Century American Culture* (Edinburgh University Press, 2024) and *The Cambridge Companion to Nineteenth-Century American Literature and Politics* (Cambridge University Press, 2024).

JOSEPH URBAS is Emeritus Professor at the Bordeaux Montaigne University, where he taught American literature and Anglo-American philosophy. He is the author of *Emerson's Metaphysics: A Song of Laws and Causes* (Lexington, 2016) and *The Philosophy of Ralph Waldo Emerson* (Routledge, 2021). He is currently preparing a third book on Emerson's theory of justice.

JOHANNES VOELZ is Professor of American Studies at Goethe University Frankfurt, Germany. He is the author of *Transcendental Resistance: The New Americanists and Emerson's Challenge* (University Press of New England, 2010) and *The Poetics of Insecurity: American Fiction and the Uses of Threat* (Cambridge University Press, 2018). He is the co-director of "Democratic Vistas: Reflections on the Atlantic World," a research focus at Frankfurt's Institute for Advanced Studies, and he edits its book series, *Democratic Vistas/Demokratische Horizonte* (Transcript). He also directs the Research Training Group "Aesthetics of Democracy," an interdisciplinary doctoral program funded by the German Research Foundation.

TOM F. WRIGHT teaches at the University of Sussex, UK. He is the author of *Lecturing the Atlantic* (Oxford University Press, 2017) and the editor of *The Cosmopolitan Lyceum* (University of Massachusetts Press, 2013), *Transatlantic Rhetoric* (Edinburgh University Press, 2020), and *Oracy: The Politics of Speech Education* (Cambridge University Press, 2025). He broadcasts regularly about the history of ideas on BBC Radio 4.

DEVIN ZUBER is Associate Professor of American Studies, Religion and Literature at the Graduate Theological Union (GTU), Berkeley. He is the author of *A Language of Things* (UVA Press, 2020) and numerous essays dealing with religion and aesthetics, and environmental criticism.

# ACKNOWLEDGMENTS

I am grateful, firstly, to Ray Ryan, a senior editor at Cambridge University Press for his encouragement, guidance, and beatific patience, and to his excellent editorial support team. The volume's contributors opened my eyes to aspects of Emerson I had not recognized and taught me how to read him anew: Their insights will pay dividends across the years to come. I owe a special word of thanks to colleagues, friends, and keen Emerson readers who read and interacted with (or indirectly helped to shape) the material herein. Just a few of them are Cristina Alsina Rísquez, Rodrigo Andrés, Branka Arsić, Jennifer Baker, Christopher Bates, David Berry, Peter Boxall, Sharon Cameron, Kristen Case, Thomas Constantinesco, Sari Edelstein, Beatrice Fazi, Alice de Galzain, Merve Emre, Danielle Follett, Jennifer Greiman, Andrew Hadfield, Christopher Hanlon, Caroline Hildebrandt, Paul Hurh, Gabriel Josipovici, Wyn Kelley, Perpetua Kirby, Vesna Kuiken, Julien Nègre, Mark Noble, Mahon O'Brien, John Parry, Catherine Packham, Lloyd Pratt, Peter Riley, Cécile Roudeau, Nicholas Royle, Steven Sawyer, Francois Specq, Agatha Steeles, Antoine Traisnel, Johannes Voelz, Laura Dassow Walls, Rebecca Webb, Tom F. Wright, and Devin Zuber. The inspirational model of Ronald A. Bosco's editorial rigor and Emersonian perspicuity has guided this project. I am indebted to Cecily Brem for her diligent reading and copyediting of all the chapters and for adding her perspicuous insights throughout. Luiza Jonik kindly assisted me with the compilation of the index and textual apparatus. The chronology here builds on that of the previous *Cambridge Companion to Emerson*, edited by Joel Porte and Saundra Morris.

# CHRONOLOGY OF EMERSON'S LIFE

| | |
|---|---|
| 1803 | May 25: born in Boston |
| 1811 | May 12: father dies, age 42 |
| 1812 | Enters Boston Public Latin School; begins writing poetry |
| 1817 | Enters Harvard College |
| 1820 | Begins keeping a journal, a practice that continues into the 1870s |
| 1821 | Graduates from Harvard; teaches in Boston at his brother William's school for girls |
| 1822 | Continues to teach; publishes essay on "The Religion of the Middle Ages" in *The Christian Disciple* |
| 1825 | February: admitted to Harvard Divinity School; studies interrupted by eye trouble; teaches in Chelmsford |
| 1826 | Teaches in Roxbury and Cambridge; October 10: approbated to preach; lung trouble; November: voyages south to improve health |
| 1827 | June: returns to Cambridge; December: meets Ellen Tucker |
| 1828 | Brother Edward suffers from severe mental illness; December 17: Emerson engaged to Ellen, who is already ill with tuberculosis |
| 1829 | Ordained junior pastor of Boston's Second Church (Unitarian); September 30: marries Ellen |
| 1831 | February 8: Ellen dies, age 19 |

1832     Increasing ill health; decides he can no longer serve communion; resigns pastorate; December 25: sails for Europe

1833     Travels to Italy, France, and Great Britain; meets British literati, including Wordsworth, Coleridge, and Carlyle; back in Boston, begins career as lecturer with talks on "natural history"

1834     Continues to preach; spring: receives first half of Tucker inheritance; October: Edward dies

1835     Lectures in Boston on biography; August 15: buys home in Concord; September: marries Lydia Jackson

1836     Completes lecture series on English literature; May: brother Charles dies; July: Margaret Fuller visits; September: *Nature* published anonymously in Boston; October 30: Waldo born; winter: lectures on the philosophy of history

1837     July: receives final portion of Tucker estate; August: Thoreau graduates from Harvard, where Emerson delivers "The American Scholar" before the Phi Beta Kappa Society; fall–winter: lectures on human culture

1838     April: writes letter to President Van Buren protesting displacement of Cherokee people from their ancestral lands; July 5: delivers address at Harvard Divinity School that causes him to be banned from speaking at Harvard for many years; July 24: Dartmouth Oration ("Literary Ethics"); winter: lectures on human life

1839     January: preaches last sermon; February 24: Ellen born; winter: lectures on "The Present Age"

1840     July: first issue of Transcendentalist journal *The Dial*, edited by Margaret Fuller

1841     March: first series of *Essays* published; spring: Thoreau joins household; November 22: Edith born; winter: lectures on "The Times"

1842     January 27: Waldo dies; Emerson succeeds Fuller as editor of *The Dial*; September: takes walking trip with Hawthorne; December: delivers lecture series in New York, during which his "Poetry of the Times" is reviewed by Walter Whitman

| | |
|---|---|
| 1844 | July 10: Edward born; April: last issue of *The Dial*; October: *Essays, Second Series* published |
| 1845 | July 4: Thoreau moves to Walden Pond and builds cabin on Emerson's property; winter: lectures on "Representative Men" |
| 1846 | December: *Poems* published |
| 1847 | October: begins second trip to Europe; away ten months |
| 1849 | Lectures on "Mind and Manners in the Nineteenth Century"; *Nature; Addresses, and Lectures* published |
| 1850 | January: *Representative Men* published; July: Margaret Fuller Ossoli, returning from Italy, drowns with her husband and son off Fire Island, New York |
| 1851 | Excoriates Massachusetts senator Daniel Webster for supporting Fugitive Slave Law; winter: lectures on "The Conduct of Life" |
| 1853 | Mother dies, age 84 |
| 1854 | Lectures on "Topics of Modern Times" in Philadelphia; heavy lecture schedule throughout the country |
| 1855 | Antislavery lectures in Boston, New York, and Philadelphia; July 21: sends letter to Whitman praising first edition of *Leaves of Grass* |
| 1856 | August: *English Traits* published |
| 1860 | December: *The Conduct of Life* published |
| 1862 | Lectures on "American Civilization" in Washington and meets President Lincoln; May 6: Thoreau dies |
| 1864 | May 23: attends Hawthorne's funeral |
| 1865 | April: eulogizes the slain Lincoln |
| 1866 | Lectures in the West; receives Doctor of Laws degree from Harvard |
| 1867 | More lectures in the West; April: *May-Day and Other Pieces* published; named Overseer of Harvard College; delivers second Phi Beta Kappa address ("The Progress of Culture") |

1870     Writes preface to Plutarch's *Morals*; publishes *Society and Solitude*; lectures at Harvard on "Natural History of Intellect"

1871     April–May: travels to California by train; meets Brigham Young and John Muir

1872     Speaks at Howard University; July 24: house burns; October: sets out for Europe and Egypt with Ellen

1874     December: publishes *Parnassus*, an anthology of his favorite poetry, which omits Poe and Whitman

1875     December: *Letters and Social Aims* published, edited by James Elliot Cabot

1876     Fall: publishes *Selected Poems* with help of Ellen and Cabot

1882     April 27: Emerson dies of pneumonia in Concord; Whitman visits his grave and observes: "A just man, poised on himself, allloving, all-inclosing, and sane and clear as the sun."

Most references to Emerson's work in this *Companion* are to *The Collected Works of Ralph Waldo Emerson*, edited by Robert Spiller et al., Cambridge, MA: Harvard University Press, 1971–2013, and are cited parenthetically as *CW* with the volume and page number. Other commonly cited works by Emerson are abbreviated as follows:

*AW*      *Emerson's Antislavery Writings*, edited by Len Gougeon and Joel Myerson, New Haven and London: Yale University Press, 1995.

*CEC*    *The Correspondence of Emerson and Carlyle*, edited by Joseph Slater, New York: Columbia University Press, 1964.

*CS*      *The Complete Sermons of Ralph Waldo Emerson*, edited by Albert von Frank et al., Columbia and London: University of Missouri Press, 4 vols., 1989–93.

*EL*      *The Early Lectures of Ralph Waldo Emerson*, edited by Stephen E. Whicher, Robert E. Spiller, and Wallace E. Williams, 3 vols., Cambridge, MA: Harvard University Press, 1961–72.

*J*        *The Journals of Ralph Waldo Emerson*, edited by Edward Waldo Emerson and Waldo Emerson Forbes, 10 vols., Boston and New York: Houghton Mifflin, 1910–14.

*JMN*    *The Journals and Miscellaneous Notebooks of Ralph Waldo Emerson*, edited by William H. Gilman and Ralph H. Orth, et al., 16 vols., Cambridge, MA: Harvard University Press, 1960–82.

*L*        *The Letters of Ralph Waldo Emerson*, edited by Ralph L. Rusk and Eleanor M. Tilton, 10 vols., New York: Columbia University Press, 1939–95.

*LL*      *The Later Lectures of Ralph Waldo Emerson*, edited by Ronald Bosco and Joel Myerson, 2 vols., Athens: University of Georgia Press, 2001.

*PE*      *The Political Emerson: Essential Writings on Politics and Social Reform*, edited by David Robinson, Boston: Beacon Press, 2004.

*PN*      *The Poetry Notebooks of Ralph Waldo Emerson*, ed. Ralph H. Orth et al., Columbia: University of Missouri Press, 1986.

*PW*      *Emerson: Political Writings (Cambridge Texts in the History of Political Thought)*, edited by Kenneth Sacks, Cambridge: Cambridge University Press, 2008.

SL     *The Selected Lectures of Ralph Waldo Emerson*, edited by Ronald Bosco and Joel Myerson, Athens: University of Georgia Press, 2005.

TN     *The Topical Notebooks of Ralph Waldo Emerson*, edited by Ralph H. Orth et al., 3 vols., Columbia and London: University of Missouri Press, 1990–94.

W     *The Complete Works of Ralph Waldo Emerson*, edited by Edward Waldo Emerson, Boston: Houghton Mifflin, 12 vols., 1903–04.

MICHAEL JONIK

# Introduction

## *Emerson's Circles*

"Life wears to me a visionary face." Emerson, "Experience"
(*CW* 3: 48)

### Encounters

In the winter and spring of 1867, Ralph Waldo Emerson travelled westward on a speaking tour across a still war-weary America. He delivered lectures at lyceums, town halls, and churches in fast-growing cities like Detroit, Chicago, and St. Louis, as well as in smaller out-of-the-way towns like Battle Creek, Michigan; Lacon, Illinois; or Lawrence, Kansas. Although over sixty years old, he followed a rigorous schedule – he would deliver eighty lectures in 1867 across fourteen states – but extensive lecturing was not a new practice for Emerson.[1] Indeed, following his departure from the ministry in 1832, and notwithstanding the annual sum he was paid by his deceased first wife's estate, he had relied on lecturing as a primary means to earn his living. In so doing, he built an international reputation not only as an essayist and a poet, but as one of America's preeminent public intellectuals and literary figures, a reputation that has arguably only increased since his death in 1882.

But two stops during his winter 1867 western tour deserve special mention and can help orient this *New Cambridge Companion to Ralph Waldo Emerson*. First, across a frozen, snow-packed Midwest *en route* to St. Paul, he made a side trip to an encampment of Santee Sioux people (most likely to the Mdewakanton, a subgroup of the Isanti (Santee) Dakota (Sioux)) near Faribault, Minnesota. It is not clear whether Emerson headed there following the example of his friend and fellow Concord poet-philosopher, Henry David Thoreau. Thoreau had travelled to Minnesota in 1861 shortly before his untimely death in 1862 at forty-five years old, seeking to learn as much as he could about the local Indigenous peoples. For his part, Emerson made just a brief excursion, escorted by the grandson of the town's namesake and founder, Jean-Baptiste Faribault, whose family was of mixed French

Canadian and Dakota descent. In a letter dated February 1, 1867, Emerson describes the visit to his daughter, Ellen, to whom he wrote regularly during his lecture tours and who handled much of the day-to-day activities of his financial affairs:

> Here in a wild piece of timber for the Aborigines The warriors, they said, had been removed to Nebraska, or elsewhere, old Chief Opie or Opequa,[2] & his family occupied one, & old women & young men & and girls (& twice I mistook girls for young men) & their dogs, the others. Led by Faribault we lifted the skin curtain, & and entered one & another. Supper was all ready on a board on the ground in one, – the family all asquat on the earth, not looking at it, what I took for young men smoking their pipe. They said nothing, but looked cheerfully enough at Faribault who spoke Indian to them. In one tent we heard singing as we approached, but were silent on our entrance. I begged him to ask them to sing again, & and the girls got their book, – Indian psalms, – & sung very sweetly. I am sorry to say the light was not birch-bark nor pine-knot, but a kerosene lamp: but the fire in the middle of the tent was Monadnoc boughs. I inquired whether I could see such another Indian picture between that spot & Boston, & was assured I could not. (L 5: 493)[3]

There is, quite clearly, an element of staged spectacle or cultural-anthropological tourism at play here in Emerson's visit. The Santee Sioux people are seemingly on display for the touring preeminent white intellectual. Emerson's rhetoric in the letter, what is more, repeats stereotypical ways of describing Indigenous peoples, setting the "Aborigines" in a "wild piece of timber"; he admits to mistaking their gender twice; he begs for them to perform for him; and he laments the seeming inauthenticity of the "Indian picture" insofar as they use a modern kerosene lamp and not one of more "natural" birch-bark or pine-knot to light their living spaces. Furthermore, Emerson does not indicate here the extent to which he would have known the traumatic recent history of the people he was visiting. The "Dakota Wars" raged just a few years before in 1862 and were among the bloodiest confrontations between the US Army and North America's Indigenous peoples. The wars culminated in the largest mass execution in US history, when thirty-eight of three hundred Dakota sentenced to death were hanged by the government.[4] More would have died, but President Lincoln commuted the sentences of many of them, condemning the remainder to the gallows. Alexander Faribault, the father of Emerson's guide, served as translator for the Dakota and they were currently encamped on land he claimed as his own, but his family had also gained financially when the treaties he had helped to negotiate were broken.

We can only speculate on the extent to which Emerson knew of this violent context. His misrecognizing young women for young men runs against his awareness that many of the men had been removed to Nebraska, but he does not mention also that many had been killed in battle or later executed. But it is clear from the letter that, in the wake of these wars, on the lands of which they had been dispossessed, settler-colonial cities and towns and large-scale infrastructures – such as the railroads, communication networks, and industrial, commercial, and banking systems that made Emerson's trip possible – were being constructed rapidly. Yet there is also a tone of sadness in Emerson's muted registration of the fact that he could not see "such another Indian picture between that spot & Boston," a muted registration of forced removal and white settler-colonialist violence toward Indigenous peoples which had taken place for centuries, eradicating their presence almost completely. Emerson would have been attuned to the terminology of "removal," which he uses here in referring to the warriors having been "removed to Nebraska" as a consequence of the Dakota Wars. Thirty years before, in 1838, he had written one of the most powerful letters in American political history to President Martin Van Buren protesting the Cherokee Removal. In that letter, he calls removal "a crime" that "confounds our understandings by its magnitude, – a crime that really deprives us as well as the Cherokees of a country." Directly denouncing Van Buren in scathing terms, he concludes: "You, sir, will bring down that renowned chair in which you sit into infamy if your seal is set to this instrument of perfidy; and the name of this nation, hitherto the sweet omen of religion and liberty, will stink to the world."[5] This letter culminates Emerson's young commitment to fighting the injustice of Indigenous removal, begun as early as 1819 when as a student at Harvard he debated the question of whether "the conduct of the U.S. towards the Indians can be reconciled to the principles of justice and humanity?" – and to which he concluded it could not be.[6] Yet that the letter to Ellen Emerson in 1867 – which of course is a piece of private correspondence and not a political text – does not come close to this earlier heightened tone nonetheless points to Emerson's often contradictory politics. And what is more, as Drew Lopenzina and Laura L. Mielke have asked, to what extent did Emerson "speak for 'the Indian'" anyway, or imagine a real Indigenous presence?[7]

There is not space here to explore Emerson's complex and inconsistent relationship to US settler-colonialism and Indigenous peoples' removal and genocide in any great depth. But suffice it to say for the sake of introducing this new collection of critical texts on Emerson's life and work, that the letter raises key questions regarding how he advocated – or didn't advocate – for some of the pressing social and political causes of his day. Indeed, understanding the political dimensions of Emerson's thought in his own time – and for our time – is one of the key areas of Emerson's work that this *New*

*Cambridge Companion* seeks to explore. As such, its contributors engage questions related to Emerson's writings and lectures on democracy and race, antislavery and women's rights activism, Asian American immigration, and nature and ecology, and offer trenchant reconsiderations of Emerson's complex notion of the "times" in which he lived. The enduring question regarding Emerson's political involvements, that is, is always related to what he calls the question of how to live – how to conduct one's life – in one's own historical moment. As he says in his essay "Fate," "To me, however, the question of the times resolved itself into a practical question of the conduct of life. How shall I live?" (*CW* 6: 1).

Before I provide a fuller overview of some of the contributors' interventions, I would like to juxtapose Emerson's visit to the Santee Sioux (and the complex political Emerson it evokes) with a second scene, and with it a different, complex philosophical Emerson that also emerges from the same tour. Across the midwestern United States, Emerson delivered lectures called "Man of the World," "Social Aims," "Resources," "Inspiration," or "Eloquence" (many of which would appear, in one form or another, in his later books *Society and Solitude* (1870) and *Letters and Social Aims* (1875)). A few weeks after visiting the Santee Sioux, and after giving further lectures in Minneapolis, Fond du Lac, Des Moines, or Chicago, Emerson stopped in St. Louis to visit a group of philosophers who had taken up the banner of G. W. F. Hegel in America and would thus become known as the "St. Louis Hegelians." Emerson had come to St. Louis at the invitation of one of their leading figures, William Torrey Harris, who had founded the influential *Journal of Speculative Philosophy* in 1867 – a journal that would not only publish key translations and criticism on Hegel but also some of the early works of American pragmatist philosophers like William James and John Dewey. Emerson had also come at the urging of his friend and fellow Concord writer A. Bronson Alcott, who would later convene the Concord School of Philosophy, bringing Harris to Massachusetts in the 1870s.

Understanding Emerson's relation to Hegel – and his stop to visit the St. Louis Hegelians – can help give a sense of Emerson's relation to philosophy and his intellectual historical milieu more generally. To begin with, Emerson had encountered German philosophy through a variety of sources, and German Idealism, in particular, had played a profound, if understated, role in shaping the intellectual agenda of Emerson's nineteenth-century milieu. German Idealism was part of a larger American transformation of Anglo-European Romantic philosophies, and some of its central questions found sympathetic reformulations in Emerson's philosophy. In brief, these questions are centered on the problems of how to unify mind and nature, faith and knowledge, fate and freedom, and the conduct of life and the moral sentiment. Through his engagement with these questions, Emerson responded to the transcendental idealism of Immanuel Kant and to the "identity philosophy" of Friedrich Schelling, which he had absorbed from Samuel Taylor Coleridge, Thomas Carlyle, and the French eclectic philosopher Victor Cousin. And, as was the case with his close friend, editor, translator, writer, and intellectual Margaret Fuller, Emerson had strong affinities with the novelist, poet, and scientist Johann Wolfgang von Goethe (affinities expressed in his essay devoted to Goethe in his book *Representative Men* (1850)). Like that of Goethe, the keynote of Emerson's philosophy is, arguably, metamorphosis. To a large extent, Emerson's work could be said to be devoted to bearing witness to and celebrating nature's fluxes, transformations, and transitions; or, as he writes in his essay "Poetry and Imagination," the "endless passing of one element into new forms, the incessant metamorphosis" (*CW* 8: 7–8). In its totalizing claims, Hegel's Absolute Idealism purported to overcome the Cartesian and Kantian dualisms of mind and matter and the noumenal and phenomenal and thus to culminate German Idealism. Hegel's philosophy of nature, deemed "monstrous" by Goethe, offered a rigid conceptual system for thinking of metamorphosis as the rhythmic unfolding of nature and the passage of subjective spirit into objective spirit.[8]

In a journal passage dated 1866, the year before he visited St. Louis, Emerson noted the power of Hegel's thought:

> Hegel seems to say, "Look, I have sat long gazing at the all but imperceptible transitions of thought to thought, until I have seen with eyes the true boundary. I know what is this, and that. I know it, and have recorded it. It can never be seen but by a patience like mine added to a perception like mine. I know the subtle boundary, as surely as the mineralogist Hauy knows the normal lines of his crystal, and where the cleavage must begin. I know that all observation will justify me, and to the future metaphysician I say, that he may measure the power of his perception by the degree of his accord with mine." (*JMN* 10: 143)

Despite his recognition of Hegel's importance, Emerson was by no means an adherent of his philosophy. Indeed, his self-reliant thinking is marked by its aversiveness to philosophical systems or settled doctrines. And Emerson's knowledge of Hegel was for the most part gleaned from Hegel's commentators and summarizers rather than from direct and rigorous study of his texts and tenets. Emerson relied on conversations with his Concord contemporaries Emmanuel V. Scherb, Frederic Henry Hedge, James Elliot Cabot, and, indeed, W. T. Harris, and on philosophical compendia like J. B. Stallo's *General Principles of the Philosophy of Nature* (1848), Jean Chrétien

Ferdinand Hoefer's *Biographie universelle* (1852), and James Hutchinson Stirling's *The Secret of Hegel* (1865).[9] It was in this context, then, that, later in 1867, Emerson wrote to Harris requesting that he might teach him "the true value & performance of Hegel, who, at first sight is not engaging nor at second sight satisfying. But his immense fame cannot be mistaken and I shall read & wait" (*L* 5: 521).

His spring 1867 lecture to the St. Louis Hegelians differed from his other lecture stops on the tour, then, insofar as he came to St. Louis to learn from his auditors as much as to share his own philosophy with them. In a letter to his close friend Henry James Sr., Emerson remarked that it was a "true gratification to see Harris at St. Louis among the German Atheists." However, as he quickly added, "They did not wish to see or hear me at all, but that I should see and hear them" (*L* 5: 514). Emerson seemed more amused than offended, and, for his part, Henry James Sr. quipped that "It was very nice of you to cohabit with those St. Louis chickens."[10] As Emerson's twentieth-century biographer Ralph L. Rusk summarizes the visit in his *The Life of Ralph Waldo Emerson*:

> Emerson had a warm reception among the members of the Saint Louis Philosophical Society, founded little more than a year earlier and already the chief American center of Hegelian thought. He could only admire, not understand, the tireless talk of William Harris and his nineteen or so philosophers and propagandists. Harris and his men were glad enough to have him as their guest lecturer but were bursting with their own version of the gospel according to Hegel. His curiosity was deeply stirred again when, a little later, he received the opening numbers of the *Journal of Speculative Philosophy*, the Saint Louis society's remarkable publication that seemed to make the Missouri town for the moment the capital of all American philosophical studies. (Rusk 433)

Emerson's visit is noteworthy not merely as evidence of his continued status as a revered public intellectual in the postbellum period. It also shows him to be a lifelong student of the "transition of thought to thought" (*JMN* 10: 143) – and one who sought to be attuned to the emergence of new philosophies that might speak to new times. Emerson was never a static thinker. He was one ready to leave behind his previous suppositions, to shift his epistemological bases, to have his curiosity stirred. "Leave your theory," he urges us in "Self-Reliance" (*CW* 2: 33). "Who leaves all receives more," he advises in "Intellect":

> A new doctrine seems at first a subversion of all our opinions, tastes, and manner of living. Such has Swedenborg, such has Kant, such has Coleridge, such has Hegel or his interpreter Cousin seemed to many young men in this

country. Take thankfully and heartily all they can give. Exhaust them, wrestle with them, let them not go until their blessing be won, and after a short season the dismay will be overpast, the excess of influence withdrawn, and they will be no longer an alarming meteor, but one more bright star shining serenely in your heaven and blending its light with all your day. (*CW* 2: 203)

As such, his living mind is a leaving mind marked by such departures. He wrestles with Plato and Neoplatonism, Swedenborg and Kant, Coleridge and Cousin, and, finally, Hegel, and he lets them go.

So, despite a broad appreciation for Hegel, Emerson found Hegel's philosophical terminology largely "unintelligible" (see Wellek 55). And as one who claims he "reads for the lustres" (as he reminds us in his essay "Nominalist and Realist" (*CW* 3: 137)), Emerson characteristically devoted himself less to understanding the details of Hegel's system than to letting Hegel stir the fires of his imagination. So if Emerson was receptive to Hegel's thought, and if he indirectly contributed to his nineteenth-century Anglo-American reception, he would likewise leave Hegel behind in the name of finding his own thinking. As he writes in his journal:

The reason of a new philosophy or philosopher is ever that a man of thought finds he cannot read in the old books. I can't read Hegel, or Schelling, or find interest in what is told me from them, so I persist in my own idle & easy way, & write down my thoughts, & find presently that there are congenial persons who like them, so I persist, until some sort of outline or system grows. 'Tis the common course: ever a new bias. It happened to each of these, Heraclitus, or Hegel, or whosoever. (*JMN* 14: 189)

Across the last decades of his working life – and in his own "idle & easy" way – Emerson sought to outline his own system: what he called his "Natural History of the Intellect" project, a project that was ultimately unfinished. It would have been the culminating statement of the self-reliant, aversive thinking that Emerson had long celebrated, a nonsystematic poetic thinking of a wholly different philosophical character than Hegel's speculative system. So even if the idealist idea of the power of life is supposed to have found its fullest articulation in Hegel's Absolute Idealism, Emerson resists such a complete ordering of life as understood through the Idea (*der Begriff* – also "concept" or "notion"). Likewise, Hegel's formulations of questions of matter and mind, faith and knowledge, fate and freedom, and history and the evolution of natural forms would remain dissatisfying to Emerson. In his late lecture "Powers of the Mind," he declares that he hates "dialectics and logomachies" and seeks instead a metaphysics "perpetually reinforced by life" (*SL* 237). His living thinking is a thinking in transit and transition, a thinking of metamorphosis and change. Emerson thus prefigures later process philosophers who would likewise resist Hegel: his intellectual (and actual) godson William James, his great German reader Friedrich Nietzsche (who found in Emerson a "brother soul"[11]), as well as John Dewey, Alfred North Whitehead, and Gilles Deleuze. As a philosophical, religious, poetic, aesthetic, or political thinker, Emerson refused to synthesize his thought into digestible axiomatic formulas. Rather, it is in the ensemble of pulsating words that form into paratactic sentences, and in paratactic sentences that form into fluid essays, that Emerson's beauty and power lie.

### Transitional, Transnational Emerson

These were just two stops on a busy lecture tour. But his visits to the Santee Sioux and to the St. Louis Hegelians in 1867 nonetheless signal several important and complex aspects of Emerson's writing and reputation that this *New Cambridge Companion* seeks to capture and to explore further – aspects that set it apart from the earlier and still relevant *Cambridge Companion to Ralph Waldo Emerson* edited by Joel Porte and Saundra Morris in 1999. First, while the center of gravity of interest in Emerson's work remains his early lectures like "The American Scholar," his first book *Nature*, and seminal essays such as "Self-Reliance," "The Poet," "Experience," or "Fate," the *New Cambridge Companion* registers how critical attention to his work has expanded to include the whole of Emerson's lecturing and writing life, including his final phase of work. Critical attention to his later lectures and writings – nominally those following the publication of his 1860 *The Conduct of Life* – has been greatly facilitated by the publication of newly edited volumes in the Harvard Belknap's *Collected Works of Ralph Waldo Emerson*, namely *Society and Solitude* (2008; first published 1870), *Letters and Social Aims* (2010, first published 1875), as well as his *Poems: A Variorum Edition* (2011) and *Uncollected Prose Writings* (2013). And, thanks to the assiduous and dedicated editorial work of Ronald A. Bosco and Joel Myerson, we now have to hand curated collections of his later lectures, providing a more complete picture of how Emerson used the spoken forum to develop his thinking.[12] With this in mind, Christopher Hanlon's *Emerson's Memory Loss* (Oxford 2018) rereads Emerson's work retrospectively; he offers fresh interpretations of how Emerson's later texts, affected by his incipient dementia, were collaboratively curated (and even coauthored) – with figures like Emerson's daughter Ellen Emerson central and not incidental to their textual production.

So in addition to rethinking the first half of Emerson's career, this *New Cambridge Companion* seeks to put it into relief by engaging the full span of Emerson's work. This invites us to consider Emerson not only as the antebellum icon of the "American Renaissance" but, as his tireless schedule of speaking events in 1867 attests, also as a public intellectual active into the postbellum period and a transitional figure who maintained a finger on the pulse of American intellectual and political developments through the 1860s and 1870s. His westward travel, it is important to note, was facilitated by the contemporaneous development of American settler-colonial infrastructural networks. As the railroads pushed west and new cities emerged from the prairies, Emerson traveled to these places to lecture and to meet with groups like the Santee Sioux and the St. Louis Hegelians. Considering his relationship to the "times," then, as Jeffrey Insko argues in his chapter that opens the volume, is both to situate Emerson in intellectual and socio-political milieus in which he found himself and also to register the multiple and often conflicting ways of experiencing time that such new technologies and infrastructures in the nineteenth century brought to bear. Sean Ross Meehan's chapter, "Emerson's Late Styles," adds to this picture of the intellectual vitality of late Emerson. Meehan explores how Emerson's central rhetorical figurations of metonymy, analogy, and translation evidence his continued engagement in aesthetic, cultural, and philosophical matters beyond the 1850s, in works such as "Eloquence," "Poetry and Imagination," "Quotation and Originality," and his unfinished "Natural History of Intellect."

Reimagining Emerson as a tirelessly travelling lecturer crossing a still-fragmented post-Civil War America, and crossing new philosophical, intellectual, and political topographies, complicates the prevailing picture of him as a genius but aloof "Sage of Concord" busy penning odes to the powers of the intellect. That picture of Emerson has been caricatured by C. P. Cranch as a "transparent eyeball" or by Nathaniel Hawthorne as a "beacon [of intellectual fire] burning on a hill-top."[13] It is not just that Emerson channels the "vast flowing vigor" (CW 3: 42) of the universe he celebrates in his essay "Experience" into written literary form. Instead, it paints him as one who evolved his ideas in dialogue with public audiences across the US and abroad and endeavored to make a living by doing so. Orality and exchange also mark the form and content of his essays, which Tom F. Wright cannily explores in his contribution in this volume in terms of the concept of the "voiced essay." To be sure, one could catalogue the instances of reported speech in his essays, themselves a concert of quotations, a concert of consonant and dissonant voices. Often, too, we can note how Emerson was essaying (literally "trying out") his essays as lectures, a compositional practice that forms part of a larger organic process with his journal, notebook, and letter writing. One could certainly trace how ideas and phrases emerge in his notebooks and journals, find utterance in his sermons and lectures, and then achieve something of a finished form in his published essays and poems. Yet this was by no means an exclusively linear process. And even Emerson's published writing invariably retains a sense of dynamic irresolution, of process, of collaboration, of life. What he says of Montaigne's essays is true of his own living language: "Cut these words, and they would bleed; they are vascular and alive" (CW 4: 95).

This expanded sense of the span and geography of Emerson's work has us broaden his place in American literary and intellectual history. Of course, he is rightfully considered to be one of the lodestars of Transcendentalism, even as that moniker arguably obscures the diversity of literary, theological, philosophical, and political positions of its practitioners. Any sense of Transcendentalism as an exclusively autochthonous American movement – even given Emerson's own occasional literary nationalist pronouncements – likewise risks submerging its transnational dialogues with British and German Romanticisms.[14] But as Jennifer J. Baker explores here in Chapter 3, Emerson's calls for American literary or cultural independence were not in fact contrary to his pronounced admiration for (and adaptations of) the writing and thinking of Anglo-European Romantics like Goethe, Coleridge, Carlyle, or Wordsworth, but rather deepened and empowered the notions of genius and originality that underwrote the type of transnational "mode of perception" his work sought to inaugurate. As Devin Zuber's chapter examines, Emerson's lifelong sense of spirituality as living, felt, and guided by the moral sentiment was inflected by German theologians and philosophers such as Friedrich Schleiermacher, Johann Gottfried Eichhorn, or Ludwig Feuerbach (and, indeed, his brother William Emerson, who had encountered the German "Higher Criticism" while studying in Göttingen) – as well as by his eclectic readings in religious anthropology, Vedantic philosophy, Buddhism, or mystical Sufism. While David LaRocca critically examines transatlantic concepts of race and nationality in Emerson's 1856 book *English Traits*, Spencer Tricker, in his chapter "Emerson, Asia, and the 'Progress of Culture,'" looks the other direction to explore the complexities of Emerson's depictions of transpacific exchange. On the one hand, not unlike Zuber, Tricker argues that Emerson's cosmopolitan and universalist conceptions of Asian religion, art, and philosophy reinforce his Transcendentalist sense of morality. But at the same time, Emerson's geographical and historical representations of Asian cultures and peoples also complexly approach prevailing nationalist, imperialist, historically determinist, and racist views of Asian cultures and people. Nonetheless, as Tricker shows, Emerson's stylistic and epistemological inconsistency in representing Asia does not neatly reproduce the two sides of the stereotypical Orientalist coin. Rather, it offers a disunified and nonmonolithic "Asia" that subtly subverts Western notions of stadialist progress.

When the first *Cambridge Companion to Ralph Waldo Emerson* came out in 1999, scholars and graduate students were primarily reading him along the lines of the New Americanists. Since the turn of the millennium, one key shift in focus in Emerson studies has been away from historicist and biographically inflected criticism to one more attuned to philosophical approaches. These approaches built on landmark philosophical readings of Emerson by Stanley Cavell, who placed Emerson's aversive thinking in relation to Friedrich Nietzsche, Martin Heidegger, Ludwig Wittgenstein, and American pragmatism, and by Sharon Cameron, who further deemphasized Emerson's status as the proponent of "self-reliance" through her striking essays on impersonality in "Representing Grief: Emerson's 'Experience'" and "The Way of Life by Abandonment: Emerson's Impersonal," both later collected in her book *Impersonality: Seven Essays* (Chicago 2007). In her monumental *On Leaving: A Reading in Emerson* (Harvard 2010), Branka Arsić further explored notions of mourning and abandonment in Emerson and sounded new key tones in Emerson's writing in relation to vitalism and materialism. Together, Cavell, Cameron, and Arsić have influenced a generation of philosophical readers of Emerson, as well as scholars of ecocritical, posthumanist, and new materialist approaches. From other perspectives, John T. Lysaker's *Emerson and Self-Culture* (Indiana 2008); Jacques Rancière's *Aisthesis: Scenes from the Aesthetic Regime of Art* (Verso 2013); Thomas Constantinesco and Sophie Laniel-Musitelli's coedited volume, *Romanticism and Philosophy: Thinking with Literature* (Routledge 2015); Joseph Urbas's *Emerson's Metaphysics A Song of Laws and Causes* (Lexington 2016) and *The Philosophy of Ralph Waldo Emerson* (Routledge 2021); Herwig Friedl's *Thinking in Search of a Language* (Bloomsbury 2019); Benedetta Zavatta's *Individuality and Beyond: Nietzsche Reads Emerson* (Oxford 2019); Sharon Cameron's *The Likeness of Things Unlike: A Poetics of Incommensurability* (Chicago 2025); and Russell Goodman's *Emerson, the Philosopher of Oppositions* (Cambridge 2025) have likewise reoriented Emerson's work in exciting ways in relation to the history and future of philosophy. In *Writing Pain in the Nineteenth-Century United States* (Oxford 2022), Constantinesco examines the role of suffering in Emerson's metaphysics and ethics. Elisa Tamarkin, in *Apropos of Something: A History of Irrelevance and Relevance* (Chicago 2022), expansively explores Emerson as a philosopher of irrelevance and relevance.

Here, Michael Jonik's chapter "Life, Form, and Power in 'Experience'" builds on these philosophical studies of Emerson to sketch a genealogy of the concept of power in Emerson's writing. Power, a central leitmotif in "Experience," Jonik argues, nonetheless becomes increasingly important to Emerson's mature articulations of metaphysics and philosophy, nature and history, and politics and ethics in essays like "Power," "Success," or his lecture "Powers of the Mind." The impulsive, circulatory, transitory, depersonalizing, and yet aggrandizing modes of power that emerge in Emerson's thinking – the powers of the heart and the powers of the mind – find manifold articulation in his work as the creative potentialities of the imagination and the intellect, the deforming forces of love and loss, as well as the conditions that embolden individual selves to mastery, invention, and success. In turn, in her chapter "'Allied to all': Emerson and Ethics Beyond Self-Reliance," Prentiss Clark investigates how Emerson's ethical philosophy, in asking the question "How shall I live?," is nonetheless premised on a metaphysical and ontological interconnectedness rather than on an atomized individual self. Clark explores how Emerson's varied investments in ethics, aesthetics, religion, science, politics, or philosophy each make legible the intimacies that shape our shared existences.

William James or John Dewey have long been recognized as Emerson's philosophical heirs, and even the radically original Charles Sanders Peirce has reluctantly admitted in his essay "The Law of the Mind" to having caught some of Emerson's intellectual contagion:

> I was born and reared in the neighborhood of Concord – I mean in Cambridge – at the time when Emerson, Hedge, and their friends were disseminating the ideas that they had caught from Schelling, and Schelling from Plotinus, from Boehm, or from God knows what minds struck with the monstrous mysticism of the East. But the atmosphere of Cambridge held many an antiseptic against Concord transcendentalism; and I am not conscious of having contracted any of that virus. Nevertheless, it is probable that some cultured bacilli, some benignant form of the disease was implanted in my soul, unawares, and that now, after long incubation, it comes to the surface, modified by mathematical conceptions and by training in physical investigations.[15]

If Peirce posits that some of Emerson's influence entered him "unawares," William James avidly (though never uncritically) absorbed his ideas. James reacted against Emersonian monism, idealism, or transcendentalism, that is, but he also found these positions co-present with a richly suggestive philosophy of action, power, and experience, which, geared toward the common and the present, emboldened James's pragmatism. James translated some of Emerson's more abstract and idealist notions into his own key notions like psychic energy, intuition, and the stream of consciousness, and Emerson's distinctive voice finds echo in James's rhapsodic, hortatory prose. James celebrated Emerson in his address in Concord on Emerson's centenary,

"Emerson himself was a real seer. He could perceive the full squalor of the individual fact, but he could also see the transfiguration."[16]

Yet while Emerson's relationship to pragmatism is better documented than his relationship with American Hegelianism, and while his 1867 visit to the St. Louis Hegelians perhaps amounted to something of a nonencounter, more would still need to be done to fully explicate his relationship to late nineteenth- and twentieth-century philosophical history. As Joseph Urbas argues in his key chapter in this collection, "Writing Emerson into the History of American Philosophy" – and contrary to the influential claim by Stanley Cavell that Emerson's place in American philosophy had been repressed – Emerson's philosophical heirs are much more numerous and diverse than either the St. Louis Hegelians or the pragmatists. While Urbas critically resituates Emerson's influence on Dewey, James, Peirce, Royce, or Santayana, he also carefully recovers a "multiform" legacy of American Emersonians. These include, crucially, underrepresented female philosophers and educators such as Anna C. Brackett (1836–1911), Ellen M. Mitchell (1838–1920), Susan E. Blow (1843–1916), Mary Whiton Calkins (1863–1930), or Ella Lyman Cabot (1866–1934), the influential African American writer and thinker W. E. B. Du Bois (1868–1963), as well as a series of professional philosophers whose work shaped American institutional philosophy, such as Herbert W. Schneider (1892–1984), Charles Hartshorne (1897–2000), or Joseph L. Blau (1909–86).

Emerson's transitional, transnational placement in nineteenth-century cultural and philosophical history must also emphatically include his relation to science. In his lectures, essays, and journal meditations, we often find Emerson cataloguing scientific advances: the taxonomies of Linnaeus and the French botanists; the chemistry of Priestley, Lavoisier, and Faraday; the geology of Hutton, Playfair, and Lyell; the anatomical work of Buffon, Cuvier, and St. Hilaire; the investigations into speciation of Lamarck, Agassiz, and Darwin; the astronomy of Copernicus and Laplace; and the idealist conceptions of life in German *Naturphilosophie*. And, again, the poet-scientist Goethe's writings on plant morphology, osteology, or chromatics were exemplary for Emerson, as they modeled the "poetic perception of metamorphosis" (*CW* 8: 4). He celebrates the work of recent science in "Life and Letters in New England" as part of a reaction of the "general mind" against the "too formal science" of the eighteenth century: "there was, in the first quarter of our nineteenth century, a certain sharpness of criticism, an eagerness for reform, which showed itself in every quarter" (*CW* 10: 169). Natural scientists effectively rewrote geo-history, the development and durations of the physical earth, its perpetual forces, and its bloom into myriad different forms. As Michel Foucault famously details in

*The Order of Things*, at the threshold of the nineteenth century, conventional natural history was superseded by the emergence of a new discourse in the sciences of life, the discourse of biology. Emerson, too, was positioned on this threshold of the emergence of life. Systems of ordering and classifying the world were rebuilt and set in motion (the "record is alive," he declares in his essay on Goethe (*CW* 4: 151)). New attention was paid to internal organization, and processes of development began to be understood as constitutive of natural phenomena. Even the pseudo-sciences, as Emerson apologizes – Lavater's physiognomy, Gall and Spurzheim's phrenology, mesmerism – put science and knowledge "back in touch" with what is "human" or "genial." Each "affirmed unity and connection between remote points," and thus each provided "excellent criticism on the narrow and dead classification of what passed for science; and the joy with which it was greeted was an instinct of the people which no true philosopher would fail to profit by" (*CW* 10: 169). And Emerson undoubtedly reckoned himself one such "true philosopher." If German metaphysics provides him the philosophical vocabulary for his most perduring questions (of how we are to understand the forms and transitions of the physical world, of how humanity can create new worlds of meaning within its intellectual, material, moral, and spiritual life), it also gave Emerson the means to appraise the philosophical value of these gains in the sciences. As he says in a "formative journal entry"[17] for his "Natural History of Intellect" project: "the highest value of natural history & mainly of these new & secular results like the inferences from geology, & the discovery of parallax, & the resolution of Nebulae, is its translation into an universal cipher applicable to Man viewed as Intellect also" (*JMN* 10: 136).

Yet, as Mark Noble explores in his contribution to the volume, while Emerson was keenly attuned to scientific advances from his earliest writings until the end of his career, he also expressed an enduring ambivalence about the development of new scientific disciplines and empirical methods. Noble charts this ambivalence from Emerson's early epiphany at the Paris Muséum d'Histoire Naturelle in 1833 when he proclaimed, "I will be a Naturalist," through to his later essays and lectures, wherein Emerson continues to seek the unity of the empirical sciences' disparate modes of inquiry with philosophical intuition (viz., their "translation into an universal cipher applicable to Man viewed as Intellect also"). Similarly, Laura Dassow Walls's chapter "Nature, Ecology, Climate: Emerson's Ecopoetical Thought" challenges us to rethink how Emerson's conceptions of nature (also developed across his career) both render legible the contradictions of Western ideas of "nature" and an American modernity that disallows continuities between human and natural history. While, as Walls shows, Emerson's aesthetics seek to preserve the beauty and divinity of nature as a bulwark against modernity's incipient forms of destruction, Emerson nonetheless recedes as our contemporary even as his work discloses the emergence of the anthropogenic forms of climate destruction that increasingly threaten planetary life.

## "Adventuring on seas of thought"

All of this underscores how Emerson's complex relationships with his American contemporaries were themselves conjugated through the transnational movements in which he participated and which took place across the long *durée* of his intellectual life. Yet no matter where we find this transnational, transitional Emerson, he is admittedly never far from his Concord milieu, which he both profoundly affected and which profoundly affected him. As Hawthorne recalls in his "The Old Manse," and not without a touch of sarcasm, during his time living in Concord, "it was impossible to dwell in his vicinity without inhaling more or less the mountain atmosphere of his lofty thought, which, in the brains of some people, wrought a singular giddiness, – new truth being as heady as new wine." Yet while Hawthorne "admired Emerson as a poet, of deep beauty and austere tenderness," he concluded that he "sought nothing from him as a philosopher."[18] Henry David Thoreau's practical ecological philosophy developed in close but agonistic relation with Emerson's idealist conception of nature, and both of their later works explore the challenges to this conception posed by the emerging empirical sciences and materialism. Emerson, in his eulogy of Thoreau, cites his younger friend's "broken task" (CW 10: 431) but recognizes him as one who cultivated himself and strove, a latter-day Stoic or "Yankee Diogenes," to live fully, freely, and deliberately: "He declined to give up his large ambition of knowledge and action for any narrow craft or profession, aiming at a much more comprehensive calling, the art of living well. If he slighted and defied the opinions of others, it was only that he was more intent to reconcile his practice with his own belief" (CW 10: 414). When Emerson edited – if selectively – an early edition of Thoreau's correspondence (published in 1865 as Thoreau's *Letters to Various Persons*), he labeled it approvingly as a "perfect piece of Stoicism."[19]

Hawthorne and Thoreau were just a few of Emerson's neighbors in whom he found interlocutors, and indeed much has been said about his relation to A. Bronson Alcott, Theodore Parker, Jones Very, Frederic Henry Hedge, George Ripley, Orestes Brownson, and many others. But Emerson's work was fundamentally shaped by the diverse contributions of independent-minded female writers and intellectuals in his close circle: especially Margaret Fuller and his aunt and spiritual and intellectual advisor Mary Moody Emerson, but also myriad others such as Sophia Ripley, Elizabeth Hoar, Elizabeth Peabody, Caroline Sturgis, Louisa May Alcott, his wife Lidian Emerson, and, as we have seen, his daughter Ellen Emerson. Fuller, in particular, had a profound effect on Emerson's writing and thinking, and their intellectual and personal relationship was intense and mutually provocative. As Fuller puts it in a private letter to Emerson: "We are to be much to one another. How often have I left you despairing and forlorn. How often have I said, this light will never understand my fire; this clear eye will never discern the law by which I am filling my circle; this simple force will never interpret my need to manifold being." Or, as Emerson writes in an October 12, 1841 journal entry:

> I would that I could, I know afar off that I cannot, give the lights and shades, the hopes and outlooks that come to me in these strange, cold-warm, attractive-repelling conversations with Margaret, whom I always admire, most revere when I nearest see, and sometimes love, – yet whom I freeze, and who freezes me to silence, when we seem to promise to come nearest. (*JMN* 8: 109)

The relationship of these close friends and "beautiful foes"[20] eventually cooled, and Fuller left for New York and then for Europe. But it had yielded intense statements of proximity and division, marking the affective and intellectual itineraries of both of them. Following Fuller's untimely death in an 1850 shipwreck off Fire Island while returning from Italy, Emerson coauthored (with William Henry Channing and James Freeman Clarke) the *Memoirs of Margaret Fuller Ossoli* (1852), a work in which Emerson again selectively and complexly curated one of his friend's legacies.[21] Not only did he (with his co-authors) modify some of Fuller's passages, but in so doing, he both tenderly memorialized her and dispassionately minimized her singular expressions of feminist power, intellect, and desire, accusing her of "sentimentalism."[22]

Since the publication of the previous *Cambridge Companion to Ralph Waldo Emerson*, the lives and works of Emerson's female contemporaries like Margaret Fuller and Mary Moody Emerson have been extensively reexamined. Thanks to Phyllis Cole's seminal *Mary Moody Emerson and the Origins of Transcendentalism: A Family History* (Oxford 2002), as well as more recent interventions by Meg McGavran Murray, Christopher Hanlon, Noelle A. Baker, Maria Popova, Alice de Galzain, and David M. Robinson,[23] we now have a much clearer understanding of Emerson's attitudes toward the women of his mid nineteenth-century intellectual milieu and their own unique contributions to its creative ferment. Their work has also emphasized Emerson's inconsistent support for the women's rights movement. On the one hand, Emerson, in his 1855 "Address at the Women's

Rights Convention," remarked that "the times are marked by the new attitude of woman, urging by argument and by association, her rights of all kinds, in short, to one half of the world: the right to education; to avenues of employment; to equal rights of property; to equal rights in marriage; to the exercise of the professions; to suffrage" (*SL* 221). Yet on the other hand, Emerson had rejected three invitations to support the movement before this address (viz., in 1850 by Paulina Wright Davis to attend the Woman's Rights Convention in Worcester, Massachusetts; in 1851 by Lucy Stone to attend another convention in Worcester; and in 1853 by Wendell Phillips to use Emerson's name on a printed circular designed to secure signers for a petition to be laid before the constitutional convention). Even as he lent his support to women's rights activism, he still often relied on traditional representations of femininity and restricted his list of exemplary individuals to representative *men*, thus leading Leslie Elizabeth Eckel to label Emerson a "reluctant feminist."[24]

Emerson's hesitant advocacy for women's rights can be productively put into relation with his other reform and political work, including his antislavery writings and his attitudes toward race, his all-too-brief resistance to Indigenous American removal and genocide, and more generally, his understanding of democracy.[25] Here, in Chapter 8, "Labor, Slavery, and the Civil War," Sophia Forster returns to the question of the relation between Emerson's transcendentalism and his participation in the abolition movement but invites us to do so in the context of his varied and often paradoxical perspectives on social reform, labor, law, racial difference, and violence. In Chapter 9, Johannes Voelz, in turn, explicates how Emerson's multidimensional notion of democracy – conceived as a "way of life" – traverses official, state, or legal power relations and, crucially, has us rethink questions of individual and mass, equality and justice, abolitionism and the Civil War. David LaRocca's chapter focuses on Emerson's 1856 book *English Traits* to argue how Emerson's use of the term "race" relates to his concept of "nationality." Like Baker, LaRocca investigates Emerson's transatlantic relations. He argues, in contrast to less generous critics, that Emerson is indeed egalitarian, that his philosophy of the fluidity of identity brings him to a stance against definite identity distinctions, and that *English Traits* does not praise Saxon whiteness but poetico-sociologically investigates the nation of England.

Another recurrent theme in this *New Cambridge Companion to Ralph Waldo Emerson* is Emerson's remarkable influence in poetics and aesthetics, as felt in literary circles radiating outward from Concord to London, Paris, Rome, and beyond, and across the nearly 150 years since his death in 1882. While in intimate, complex conversation with Thoreau and Fuller, he was also in dialogue with many of the important literary and cultural figures of his time. Walt Whitman's sprawling accretive poetry answered Emerson's call in his essay "The Poet" to versify America's dazzling geography (see CW 3: 22). Upon receiving Emerson's approbation for the 1855 publication of *Leaves of Grass*, Whitman advantageously hitched his wagon to Emerson's star to help him gain national poetic notoriety. Emily Dickinson, who did not know Emerson directly, nonetheless drew from a thematically similar cultural, theological, and aesthetic canvas as did he, and her verse is in complicated and elliptical dialogue with his writing. If Hawthorne was less sanguine in their reactions to Emerson, Herman Melville celebrated Emerson as a deep "thought-diver" into the human condition; he nonetheless declared that he does not "oscillate in Emerson's rainbow,"[26] and caricatured Emerson's transcendentalism as ironically business-minded in the character of Mark Winsome in *The Confidence-Man* (1857). Edgar Allan Poe was outright hostile toward Emerson and his "Frogpondians," suggesting, infamously, that the editor of *The Dial* – Emerson, not Fuller – should be hanged. In his "Exordium to Critical Notices," Poe lambasted "Orphicism, or Dialism, or Emersonism, or any other pregnant compound indicative of confusion worse confounded."[27]

But while Emerson's expansive influence on American poetics is undeniable, the reputation of his own poetry, including his major books of original verse, his anthology of selected verse *Parnassus* (1875), and his translations of Persian poetry, has fared less well. Yet in her chapter "'Numbers Wild': Emerson's Poetry and Metaphysics," Danielle Follett defends Emerson's poetry from accusations that it is conventional or secondary, impenetrable or awkward. Rather, for Follett, Emerson's idiosyncratic poetic style, rhetoric, and prosody were thoughtfully wrought and consciously strained the conventions of meter and lyric form in a way that prefigures modernist innovation. Perhaps most crucial for Follett, however, is how Emerson's poetics were deeply embedded within his aesthetics and metaphysics, especially insofar as they sought a delicate balance of nature's symmetries and asymmetries, its consonances and dissonances, its regularities and irregularities – in short, as Follett borrows a phrase from Emerson's 1867 poem "May-Day," its "numbers wild" (CW 9: 327).

Similarly, Nicholas L. Guardiano emphasizes how Emerson's aesthetics, pervasive in his writing, stand in essential relation to his philosophy and are manifest in topics like perception, sensation, experience, creativity, and, especially, beauty. Placing Emerson's "metaphysically informed" aesthetics in a rich tradition from Plato and the Neoplatonists to Hume and Goethe and Dewey and Peirce, Guardiano compellingly explicates how beauty serves as an Emersonian ideal of human thought and action and compels us to know, to believe, to grow, and to create. On this basis, Guardiano claims one of Emerson's "most valuable (and under-appreciated) contributions to aesthetics" is in how he shows that "art shares in the inter-informing, polyphonic growth of a universe of signs."

Follett, Guardiano, and Meehan, respectively, in suggesting Emerson's poetic figurations as anticipating modernism, in placing Emerson's aesthetic figurations in relation to pragmatism, and in engaging the rhetorical figurations in Emerson's late styles, posit a transitional Emerson whose voice resounds beyond the limits of his own time. Whitman celebrates Emerson in *Specimen Days* "for his sweet, vital-tasting melody, rhymed philosophy, and poems as amber-clear as the honey of the wild bee he loves to sing"[28]; and, Henry James claims, like his brother William, an inherited eloquence from Emerson. But Emerson's voice undeniably inflects the writing of a multitude of authors, notably Sarah Orne Jewett, Edith Wharton, Willa Cather, Ralph Waldo Ellison, Pauline Hopkins, Gertrude Stein, Wallace Stevens, Jorge Luis Borges, and John Ashbery. Paul Grimstad, in his chapter "Emersonian Aesthetics in the Twentieth Century," likewise suggests Emerson's importance for subsequent artistic, literary, and musical experimentation and his role as a transitional figure from Romanticism to the modern and the contemporary periods. Whether in terms of the experimental writing of Marcel Proust, Ralph Ellison, or John Ashbery, or in the experimental music of Charlie Parker, Duke Ellington, Charles Ives, and Elliot Carter, Grimstad prompts us to find an Emersonian "self-reliant" art – an art emboldened to new independences, an art opened to complexities of movement and form, and an art that skates, surprises, dazzles, and swings.

Despite his deep resonances in the work of so many who have followed him, Emerson has often been taken to be aloof or distant. This is the case in Sarah Orne Jewett's short poetic recollection "A Sonnet on Meeting Ralph Waldo Emerson": "I met great Emerson, serene, remote, / Like one adventuring on seas of thought."[29] Similarly, Jorge Luis Borges, himself far away in Buenos Aires, paints an imaginative poetic portrait of a withdrawn Emerson:

> He thinks: I have read the essential books
> And written others which oblivion
> Will not efface. I have been allowed
> That which is given mortal man to know.
> The whole continent knows my name.
> I have not lived. I want to be someone else.[30]

Yet Emerson's readers – a vast and varied, multicultural and multiracial, national and global community – do not testify to such a serene remoteness or to a fame that longs to be someone else. Rather, they speak to an Emerson whose words and phrases, ideas and intuitions, modes of seeing and modes of living – the essential books he has read and the ineffaceable books he's written – have shaped our collective cultural life.

### "to draw a new circle"

The one thing which we seek with insatiable desire, is to forget ourselves, to be surprised out of our propriety, to lose our sempiternal memory, and to do something without knowing how or why; in short, to draw a new circle. Nothing great was ever achieved without enthusiasm. The way of life is wonderful: it is by abandonment.

(*CW* 2: 190).

While Emerson's place in American literary history has remained secure, the *New Cambridge Companion to Ralph Waldo Emerson* draws on a wealth of recent Emerson scholarship which has highlighted his contemporary relevance for questions of philosophy and politics, ecology and science, poetics and aesthetics, or identity and race, and connects these to the key formal and interpretive issues at stake in understanding his work. The volume's contributors engage the full breadth of Emerson's work, developing novel approaches to canonical works like *Nature* and the essays "Self-Reliance" and "Experience," or to his poetry and journals, and bringing critical attention to his lectures and to the long-overlooked texts of his later period. They range from explorations of Emerson's relationship to his contemporary moment; his religious and spiritual development and legacy; European and British Romanticism; nature, the environment, and climate; ethics and self-reliance; life, power, and form; political resistance and slavery; the "progress" of culture, US imperialism, and Sino-American relations; aesthetics, poetry, philosophy, and their expansive legacies in American culture, thought, and education. They bear witness to both Emerson's broad eclecticism and the many channels of influence and confluence that form the currents of his work, as well as its concussive and sometimes contradictory dissonances. The chapters in this *New Cambridge Companion to Ralph Waldo Emerson* thus both register the new Emersons that have emerged in the past decades and also point to new Emersons to come. They ask again the question of how are we to read him now and how might we continue to read him anew. They seek to draw another circle in Emerson's reception or prompt a movement outward into new futures for Emerson's work to take purchase.

At the end of his letter to Henry James Sr. regarding his visit to the St. Louis Hegelians, Emerson adds a note of gratitude, not for him but for his son, the young novelist Henry Jr.: "Thank your boy Harry from me for his good stories. I prize all your boys, and Alice, & send sympathetic regards to Mrs James. Yours ever, R.W. Emerson" (L 5: 514). In his 1888 *Partial Portraits*, Henry James Jr., in turn, expresses his gratitude to Emerson, putting him first among his sketches of influential writers. James contends that Emerson will assuredly remain enduring, "that he serves and will not wear out, and that indeed we cannot afford to drop him." This is because, as James summarizes:

> His instrument makes him precious. He did something better than any one else; he had a particular faculty, which has not been surpassed, for speaking to the soul in a voice of direction and authority. There have been many spiritual voices appealing, consoling, reassuring, exhorting, or even denouncing and terrifying, but none has had just that firmness and just that purity. It penetrates further, it seems to go back to the roots of our feelings, to where conduct and manhood begin; and moreover, to us to-day, there is something in it that says that it is connected somehow with the virtue of the world, has wrought and achieved, lived in thousands of minds, produced a mass of character and life. And there is this further sign of Emerson's singular power, that he is a striking exception to the general rule that writings live in the last resort by their form; that they owe a large part of their fortune to the art with which they have been composed. It is hardly too much, or too little, to say of Emerson's writings in general that they were not composed at all. Many and many things are beautifully said; he had felicities, inspirations, unforgettable phrases; he had frequently an exquisite eloquence.[31]

At the end of this passage, James adds a quotation from Emerson's "Divinity School Address": "O my friends, there are resources in us on which we have not yet drawn." This *New Cambridge Companion to Ralph Waldo Emerson* bears witness to this complex and multifarious Emerson, to this Emerson who has lived in thousands of minds, to this Emerson of singular power, to this Emerson of his time, of our time, and of times yet to come. It seeks to draw a new circle and to find in Emerson ever new resources on which we have not yet drawn.

## Notes

1. For biographical summaries of Emerson's 1867 trip, see Ralph L. Rusk, *The Life of Ralph Waldo Emerson* (New York: Columbia University Press, 1957), 432–33; John J. McAleer, Ralph Waldo Emerson, *Days of Encounter* (Boston: Little, Brown & Company, 1984) 582; Robert D. Richardson, Jr., *Emerson: The Mind on Fire* (Berkeley and Los Angeles: University of California Press, 1995), 555.
2. Most likely Chief Taopi (1813–69), of the Little Crow Band of the Mdewakanton Dakota.

3. See also Rusk, *The Life of Ralph Waldo Emerson*, 432–33; Richardson, *Emerson: The Mind on Fire*, 555.

4. See www.thenicc.edu/about/history/santee-sioux-nation.php; https://deathpenaltyinfo.org/death-row/native-americans

5. Ralph Waldo Emerson, "Letter to Martin Van Buren," in *Emerson's Anti-Slavery Writings*, ed. Len Gougeon and Joel Myerson (New Haven: Yale University Press, 1995), 3. For a compelling reading of Emerson's letter, see Branka Arsić, *On Leaving: A Reading in Emerson* (Cambridge, MA: Harvard University Press, 2010), 283, 288.

6. See Scott L. Pratt, *Native Pragmatism: Rethinking the Roots of American Philosophy* (Bloomington, IN: Indiana University Press, 2002), 215–22.

7. See Drew Lopenzina and Laura L. Mielke, "Speaking for 'the Indian,'" in *The Oxford Handbook of Ralph Waldo Emerson*, ed. Christopher Hanlon (Oxford: Oxford University Press, 2024), 161–76.

8. See Goethe's letter to Eckermann, as cited in Elaine P. Miller, *The Vegetative Soul: From Philosophy of Nature to Subjectivity in the Feminine* (Albany, NY: SUNY Press, 2002), 146.

9. In July 1865, Emerson had introduced Harris to Hedge as a "very good reader of Hegel" and that he has been "much gratified & a little surprised to receive from Missouri so sharpsighted a philosopher" (*L* 5: 422).

10. Qtd. in *L* 5:513n138.

11. Nietzsche, "Letter to Franz Overbeck" [1883], cited in Benedetta Zavatta, *Individuality and Beyond: Nietzsche Reads Emerson*, Alexander Reynolds (tr.) (Oxford: Oxford University Press, 2019), 187.

12. Ralph Waldo Emerson, *The Later Lectures of Ralph Waldo Emerson, 1843–1871*, ed. Ronald A. Bosco and Joel Myerson, 2 vols. (Athens: University of Georgia Press, 2001).

13. See Christopher Pearse Cranch, Illustrations of the New Philosophy: drawings, [ca.1837–39] (MS Am 1506). Houghton Library, Harvard University, Cambridge, MA. Nathaniel Hawthorne, "The Old Manse," in *Nathaniel Hawthorne's Tales*, ed. James McIntosh, 2nd ed. (New York: Norton, 2013), 314.

14. For discussion of Emerson's central place in transatlantic Romanticism, see *Romanticism and Philosophy: Thinking with Literature*, ed. Sophie Laniel-Musitelli and Thomas Constantinesco (London: Routledge, 2015).

15. Charles Sanders Peirce, "The Law of the Mind," in *Selected Philosophical Writings: Volume 1 (1867–1893)*, ed. Nathan Houser and Christian Kloesel (Bloomington, IN: Indiana University Press, 1992), 312–13.

16. William James, "Address at the Centenary of Ralph Waldo Emerson, May 25, 1903," in *William James: Writings 1902–1910* (New York: Library of America, 1987), 1125.

17. David Robinson, *Emerson and the Conduct of Life* (Cambridge: Cambridge University Press, 1993), 182.

18. Hawthorne, "The Old Manse," 315, 314.

19. See Robert D. Richardson, "A Perfect Piece of Stoicism," *The Thoreau Society Bulletin*, 153 (Fall, 1980), 1–5.

20. Fuller to Emerson, September 29, 1840, *The Letters of Margaret Fuller* (11:160).

21. See Christina Zwarg, *Feminist Conversations: Fuller, Emerson, and the Play of Reading* (Ithaca: Cornell University Press, 1995); Hanlon, *Emerson's Memory Loss*; Sonia di Loreto, "Margaret Fuller's Archive: Absence, Erasure, and Critical Work." *19: Interdisciplinary Studies in the Long Nineteenth Century*, 27 (2018); and Alice de Galzain, "Rewriting the Life of an 'Ultra-Radical': Margaret Fuller, Ralph Waldo Emerson, and *Memoirs of Margaret Fuller Ossoli* (1852)." Ph.D. diss., University of Edinburgh, 2023 and "'Woman [and] Artist': Margaret Fuller on Bettina Brentano-von Arnim and Friendship." *LIT: Literature Theory* 35:4 (2024): 285–303.

22. Ralph Waldo Emerson, W. H. Channing, and J. F. Clarke, *Memoirs of Margaret Fuller Ossoli*, vol. 1 [1852] (Boston: Roberts Brothers, 1875), 280.

23. In addition to the works listed in note 10, see also Phyllis Cole, *Mary Moody Emerson and the Origins of Transcendentalism: A Family History* (Oxford: Oxford University Press, 2002); Meg McGavran Murray, *Margaret Fuller, Wandering Pilgrim* (Athens, GA: University of Georgia Press, 2012); Noelle A. Baker, "'Let Me Do Nothing Smale': Mary Moody Emerson and Women's 'Talking' Manuscripts." in *Toward a Female Genealogy of Transcendentalism*, ed. Jana L. Argersinger and Phyllis Cole (Athens, GA: University of Georgia Press, 2014), 35–56; Maria Popova, *Figuring* (New York: Pantheon Books, 2019); David Robinson, *Transcendent Woman: Margaret Fuller's Art and Achievement* (Amherst: University of Massachusetts Press, 2025).

24. Leslie Elizabeth Eckel, "Emerson, Reluctant Feminist," in *The Oxford Handbook of Ralph Waldo Emerson*, ed. Christopher Hanlon (Oxford: Oxford University Press, 2024), 589–604. My thanks to Alice de Galzain for her essential recommendations to this section.

25. Len Gougeon asserts that "Emerson's involvement with the women's movement, though initiated at a later date, approximates the trajectory his experience with the antislavery movement"; see his "Emerson and the Woman Question: The Evolution of His Thought," *The New England Quarterly*, 71:4 (December 1998), 572.

26. Herman Melville, Letter to Evert A. Duyckinck, March 3, 1849, Herman Melville, *Correspondence*, ed. Lynn Horth (Evanston and Chicago: Northwestern University Press and The Newberry Library, 1993), 121.

27. Edgar Allan Poe, "Exordium to Critical Notices," in *Edgar Allan Poe, Essays and Reviews*, ed. G. R. Thompson (New York: The Library of America, 1984), 1031.

28. Walt Whitman, "Specimen Days," in *Complete Poetry and Collected Prose*, ed. Justin Kaplan (New York: Library of America, 1982), 902.

29. Included in a letter to Annie Fields (undated ca. 1886–90). See: www.sarahornejewett.org/soj/poe/ms-poe.html

30. Jorge Luis Borges, "Emerson," in *Selected Poems*, ed. and trans. Alexander Coleman. (New York: Penguin, 1999), 211.

31. Henry James, *Henry James: Literary Criticism* (New York: The Library of America, 1984), 270.

# I

JEFFREY INSKO

# Emerson's Times

"To-day is a king in disguise" (*CW* 1: 171), says Emerson in his 1841 "Lecture on the Times." Delivered at the Masonic Temple in Boston, Emerson's address represents one early instance of what was for him a career-long project: The attempt to understand and seize upon the historical moment, or what he often called "the present hour," in which he lived. That project was a central feature of his early public speaking. In 1836, four years before the "Lecture on the Times," Emerson had delivered a series of twelve lectures on "The Philosophy of History," one of which was titled "The Present Age" and another titled "The Times." The former phrase he also used as the general title of another series of lectures he gave in 1839–40. He continued to pursue the topic in the decades that followed. In 1850, he lectured in New York on "The Spirit of the Age." A decade later in "Fate," arguably the key essay in his 1860 collection *The Conduct of Life*, he begins with yet another meditation on "the Spirit of the Times" (*CW* 6: 1).

The challenge of the philosophical task he pursues in all of these writings is, as Emerson describes it in the 1841 lecture, to avoid misperception. "Let us unmask the king as he passes," he enjoins his audience, "Let us not inhabit times of wonderful and various promise without divining their tendency" (*CW* 1: 171). By "divining their tendency," Emerson means something like catching the drift of the historical present, determining its direction. "From what port did we sail?" he asks later in the lecture, "or to what port are we bound? No one knows" (*CW* I: 182). He echoes this sentiment in "Fate," stating there decisively, "we are incompetent to solve the times" (*CW* 6: 1).

What does Emerson's uncertainty entail here? On the one hand, as Thomas Constantinesco has shown, a desire "to detect and decipher the ominous signs of the times, to perceive and reveal the hidden truth of the age" was a prominent feature of American Transcendentalism and, more broadly, European Romanticism.[1] On the other hand, the unknowingness that characterized Emerson's particular version of that desire places him at odds with some of the period's prevailing ideas about history's "tendency." The stadialist model of history, for example, famously depicted in such works as Thomas Cole's series of paintings "The Course of Empire," understood historical movement as proceeding in stages, or cycles, from barbarism to pastoralism, agrarianism, and eventually industrial civilization before finally falling into decay and ruin. Although stadialism was developed by philosophers of history in Europe, the theory still had purchase in the early United States. But American historians also produced a more optimistic version of historical unfolding, one that did not necessarily end in ruin. The tradition of Romantic history in the US practiced by contemporaries of Emerson like George Bancroft and Francis Parkman promoted a vision of historical progress well suited to the ideological project of national growth and expansion. This tradition of Romantic historiography perceived the nation's future destiny, to use some familiar language, as "manifest." Whatever their differences, however, both of these traditions conceived of history as an orderly teleological process, in which time moves steadily forward.

Emerson's relation to models of historical progress is a fraught one.[2] But his ideas about *where* his own historical present was headed are perhaps less important than his preoccupation with *how* it was headed, its speed, and its pace. Or to put this differently, Emerson's interest in "the Times" was also, fundamentally, an interest in *time*. We can examine "Emerson's times," then, in this dual sense: His abiding investments, philosophical, social, and political, in the historical present – the time of *now* – and in its temporalities – the *time* of now. Emerson's commitment to the present as the bedrock of historical experience and the sphere of ethical action was shaped by the new conceptions of time and the new temporal experiences afforded by the technological, scientific, and political developments of his era. Thus if the "practical question" with regard to "the times" was, as Emerson states it in "Fate," an immediate one – "how shall I live?" – that question was complicated, as we'll see, by the heterochronicity of the times (CW 6: 1).

## A New Celerity to Time

As a keen observer of the tendencies of his age, Emerson was attuned to and deeply interested in the many social, political, technological, and intellectual transformations taking place in the nineteenth-century United States. These changes he recorded in his journals and incorporated into his lectures and essays. He was particularly struck by his era's emergent temporal modes, three of which bear mentioning here: The shift from natural to mechanical timekeeping, the new experiences of velocity made possible by developments in transportation infrastructure (powered by coal and steam), and the expanded timescales brought forth by the fledgling science of geology. These developments reshaped social life, refashioned individual subjectivity, and forced new reckonings in historical understanding.

"The antebellum decades," as historian Michael O'Malley has shown, "witnessed a small crisis in the authority of time,"[3] as mechanical time-keeping gradually began to supplant other ways of telling time, such as by the sun and moon or by the changing of the seasons. Before the widespread appearance of mechanical time, most Americans' workdays were organized by natural rhythms: sunrise and sunset. Of course, clocks and watches had been crafted by artisans for centuries before the nineteenth century, but in the early United States, they remained primarily luxury items for the wealthy. The mass production of clocks began in 1807, the decade of Emerson's birth, with the clockmaker Eli Terry of Connecticut; and, from that point forward, mechanized time became increasingly prevalent in the form of public clock towers as well as household and individual time-pieces. This shift, variously embraced, resisted, and implemented unevenly across populations, brought with it new forms of social organization and, at times, conflicting experiences of time. As Thomas Allen puts it in his study *A Republic in Time: Temporality and Social Imagination in Nineteenth-Century America*, "the greater availability of clocks ... as consumer goods in fact produced a heterogeneous tapestry of quite different temporalities within individual American homes and other spaces."[4]

Emerson documents these proliferating temporalities across his writings. In "Self-Reliance," for example, he twice turns to watches to figure the illusion of technology-as-progress. "Society never advances," he insists, and while it is always changing, "change is not amelioration" (*CW* 2: 48). To illustrate the point, he contrasts "the well-clad, reading, writing, thinking American, with a watch, a pencil and a bill of exchange in his pocket" with "the Naked New Zealander, whose property is a club, a spear, a mat and an undivided twentieth of a shed to sleep under!" The former, Emerson insists, "has lost his aboriginal strength" (*CW* 2: 48), a strength that is tied to one's connection with essential things, rather than with external contrivances. "The civilized man," Emerson says, "has a fine Geneva watch, but he fails of the skill to tell the hour by the sun" (*CW* 2: 48).

In making this point, Emerson not only casts the shift to mechanical time-keeping as a sign of our estrangement from the real; he also emphasizes the nonidentity of the two forms of time. Both artificial and approximate, clock time is merely a representation of solar (or natural) time. Emerson makes a version of the point even more explicitly in *English Traits* (1856), writing that "The kitchen clock is more convenient than sidereal time"

(*CW* 5: 29). The clock has its uses, in other words, but we ought not to view it as "exact or final." Indeed, Emerson illustrates the insufficiency of clock-time yet again in his later essay "Progress of Culture" (1875), when he considers it in relation to still another of the new temporal forms emerging in the nineteenth century: geological time. "The old six thousand years of chronology," Emerson says, invoking the vast scale of time made legible by the new science of geology, "become a kitchen clock, no more a measure of time than an hour-glass or an egg-glass since the duration of geologic periods has come into view" (*CW* 8: 111). I'll return to the powerful effect the new deep time of geology had on Emerson's thought below, but for now I simply want to note Emerson's interest in what Lloyd Pratt has described as the "conflicts between different modalities of time" at play in the nineteenth-century United States.[5]

For Pratt, that temporal plurality worked against the consolidation of national identity, or as he puts it, it "forbid the homogeneously linear time whose emergence has sometimes been associated with early American nationalism."[6] Put differently, the forces that sought to homogenize time in the service of nation-building, whether by supplanting "natural" time with clocks and watches or, later, by establishing uniform measures of time to regulate labor with factory clocks and working hours or commerce with railroad schedules and standardized times across vast distances, never quite succeeded. Pratt shows instead how works of literature indexed "antecedent and nascent orders of time in addition to those already informing their [audience's] experience of daily life" and also "superadded specific literary temporalities" to them.[7] Pratt's focus on fictional genres as the vehicle for bringing forth this temporal heterogeneity, however, excludes Emerson, which may implicitly seem to align him, as scholars have often done, with the nationalist project. But perhaps paradoxically, it is when Emerson seems most invested in nation-building that he records most sensitively the new temporal experiences modernity produces. Mechanical timekeeping represented just one of a number of ways in which time, as well as the ways it was understood and felt, transformed over the course of Emerson's lifetime. Transportation infrastructure provided another.

Consider Emerson's abiding fascination with the railroad, the development of which, as O'Malley so carefully documents, played a central role in time consolidation (culminating in the creation of standard time zones in the year of Emerson's death, 1883). Emerson refers to the railroad frequently in his essays and addresses, often as a symbol of national promise. In his lecture "The Young American," for example, delivered before the Boston Mercantile Library Association in 1844, Emerson celebrates the role of infrastructural development in the country's westward expansion. Thanks to "road building," as well as the "the locomotive and the steamboat," he says, "space is annihilated," as swift movement across vast distances has become increasingly possible. Just as importantly, Emerson emphasizes how these new transportation infrastructures produce new temporal experiences. The railroad in particular, Emerson says, "has given a new celerity to *time*, or anticipated by fifty years the planting of tracts of land, the choice of water privileges, the working of mines, and other natural advantages" (*CW* 1: 226; emphasis original).

It can be easy for those of us accustomed to driving on freeways and flying in airplanes to forget what riding in a locomotive might have felt like in 1844, what disorienting and exhilarating bodily sensations this "new celerity to time" might have generated. But Emerson, who over the next three decades would spend a significant portion of his working life traversing the country in railroad cars, registered that experience repeatedly. In his journal, for example, he described his first railroad encounter, in England in 1833, as both "strange" and novel. "Strange proof how men become accustomed to the oddest of things!" he wrote, "the laborers did not lift their umbrellas to look as we flew by them" (184). A journal entry from 1860 captures even more vividly the terrifying excitement of railroad velocity. Outside the train as it hurtles forward,

> The fences were tormented; every rail & rider writhed & twisted past the window, the snowbanks swam past like fishes; & the speed seemed to increase every moment. The (land the) rocks, walls, the fields (were in violent motion) streaming like a mill-tail. The train tore on with jumps & jerks that tested the strength of oak & iron. The passengers seemed to suffer their speed. (*JMN* 14: 343)

Emerson here records how the sensation of speed can be frightening – a torment to fences and passengers alike – as well as how it can alter one's perceptions, as otherwise stable objects appear to be in motion, taking on a fluid quality, like liquid (the "mill-tail"). In doing so, he helps reveal how the affordances of the period's novel temporal experiences involved much more than the rhythms of everyday life, the regulation of work and leisure, or the management of social relations. Many of the new temporal experiences were experienced *affectively*, in the body, habituating people to new physical sensations and expectations (of, say, velocity), and thereby refashioning subjectivities. Emerson's friend Henry David Thoreau likewise recognized how railroad time generated both new social arrangements and new human behaviors: "The startings and arrivals of the cars are now the epochs in the village day," he wrote in *Walden*, "They go and come with such regularity and precision, and their whistle can be heard so far, that the farmers set their clocks by them, and thus one well-conducted institution regulates a whole country."[8] Such a differently regulated country, Thoreau continues perceptively, produced a new kind of citizen-subject: "Have not men improved somewhat in punctuality since the railroad was invented?," he asks, "Do they not talk and think faster in the depot than they did in the stage-office?"[9]

So far we have seen how some of the period's multiple temporal modes and challenges to entrenched ideas and experiences of time necessitated social adjustments (and produced resistance to such adjustments) and provided unique affective experiences. Other developments necessitated intellectual adjustments. In Emerson's case, this was no more evident than in his grappling with the challenge to historical time posed by the period's scientific developments. Emerson kept abreast of these changes, in particular the new conception of time posited by geological science, which both perturbed and shaped his thought and writings. This is evident in his remark on "the old six thousand years of chronology" (CW 8: 111) in "Progress of Culture" – a reference to the fact that by the end of the eighteenth century, paleontologists and geologists had established that the earth's existence extended millions of years beyond the six millennia adduced by Biblical chronology. The discovery of so-called deep time – that is, the vast expanses of time, measured in millions, not thousands, of years, that geological theory unearthed – secularized time, upended human timescales, and strained conventional notions of historical change.

Emerson's writings register these shifts and the adjustment in one's sense of historical time they demanded. In "Nature" from his *Essays: Second Series*, for example, he acknowledges that "Geology has initiated us into the secularity of nature, and taught us to disuse our dame-school measures, and exchange our Mosaic and Ptolemaic schemes for her large style" (CW 3: 105). Similarly, he wrote in his journal in 1856, that "geology introduces new measures of antiquity" (JMN 14: 42). And elsewhere in "Progress of Culture," he writes that "a science of forty or fifty summers, has had the effect to throw an air of novelty and mushroom speed over entire history." "The oldest empires," he continues, "now that we have true measures of duration, show like creations of yesterday" (CW 8: 111). Geological knowledge generated a time warp that made the old seem young and the young appear old. That is, measured on the scale of geological time, the "oldest empires" and the newest (i.e., America) suddenly appear coeval; "geology," as Emerson puts it "has effaced these distinctions" (CW 8: 111).

But if geological time tripped up Emerson's sense of the scale of history, its more important effect was to revise Emerson's understanding of historical change. As Allen describes it, deep time helped Emerson begin to reject "a providential [or linear, teleological] understanding of history in favor of one characterized by contingency."[10] But once again, a crucial question for Emerson – and for geological theory – involved the *pace* of change. Did alteration of the geological features of the earth take place slowly, the result of subtle forces like erosion? Or did change take place in short bursts, over short periods of time, as the result of violent actions like earthquakes? These questions divided geologists of the period, who became classed as either "gradualists" (sometimes also called "uniformitarians") or "catastrophists." The Scottish geologist Charles Lyell, for example, demonstrated in *The Principles of Geology*, first published in 1830, how the slow, subtle workings of geological forces over vast reaches of time produced changes in the surface of the earth. For Lyell, change occurred gradually and uniformly over time. Others, such as the French paleontologist Georges Cuvier, held that comparatively abrupt, globally powerful events (like the Biblical Flood) more decisively shaped the geological features of the earth and produced the extinction of species uncovered by the fossil record. For Cuvier, change took place in short, sporadic, epochal bursts.

As all the foregoing examples illustrate, Emerson's nineteenth century underwent a series of dramatic temporal transformations, producing a complex admixture of competing and colliding temporal modes. Emerson's times, we might say, witnessed a series of revolutions in time that asked him and his contemporaries to learn to keep, experience, and measure time differently. Emerson's writings, as we've already begun to see, index these changes and adjust to them. But as a number of scholars have shown, his adjustment to geological deep time may have been the most profound of these temporal engagements.[11] Both gradualism and catastrophism held appeal for Emerson. Gradualist theory might seem congenial to his idealist sense of historical (and individual) progress as a steady, linear process of melioration, while catastrophism could satisfy his philosophical predilection for spontaneity, experimentation, or what in "Circles" he calls "unsettling." Yet Emerson's ultimate preference for the latter developed in response to another key feature of his times: the politics of slavery.

### Gradualism and Immediatism: The Temporality of Abolition

During the antebellum decades, another temporal debate, likewise framed in terms of gradualism and catastrophism, played itself out in the public arena over the movement to abolish slavery. One of the primary divisions among antislavery advocates from the eighteenth century well into the nineteenth revolved, in part, around the question of speed: So-called gradualists argued for caution, working for the end of slavery by way of caution, deliberations (or one might say delay), and careful planning – a slow-moving process of incremental measures aimed toward amelioration with a minimum of disturbance to existing social, political, and economic structures. Immediatists, by contrast, called for emancipation *now*, adopting (often) a stance of impatience with the prudence and hesitation of the gradualists. Although gradualist and immediatist dispositions had always characterized attitudes toward the institution of chattel slavery itself – every enslaved person seeking freedom was in a very real sense an immediatist – historians have generally identified a shift or transition between eighteenth-century British antislavery advocacy and the rise of immediatism in the US in the 1830s. But the transition was far from universal, as the gradualist mindset remained widespread, and even dominant, at least until the passage of the new Fugitive Slave Law in 1850. Indeed, gradualists (antislavery moderates) often portrayed immediatists (abolitionist radicals) as catastrophists of sorts, reckless zealots whose fervor and haste would only lead to violence and upheaval. Emerson's brother Charles articulated these charges in an 1835 lecture he gave in defense of immediate emancipation. "The cry" of immediatism's critics, he says, "is this subject is of a delicate nature – not rashly to be meddled with. You are tossing fire on a magazine of powder."[12]

Strikingly, these antislavery positions developed and crystallized contemporaneously – almost precisely so – with the analogous positions in geological debates over alterations in the earth. Indeed, gradualists often drew upon geological metaphors to express their fears of what immediatist agitation might produce; they worried, as one writer put it that "the volcano will burst," and that as a result, "insurrection and servile wars will begin."[13] But while it may be little more than coincidence that the discourses of geological science and slavery politics spoke a similar language, the convergence does help reveal how attitudes toward the pace of *social* change, like theories of geological change, implied distinct theories of history. As the historian David Brion Davis has shown, gradualism had its roots in Enlightenment liberalism and a belief in "the slow unfolding of a divine or natural plan of historical progress," a faith that also bred "considerable fear of sudden changes or precipitous action that might break the delicate balance of natural and historical forces."[14] By contrast, Davis links immediatism to "the romantic sensibility" and its "belief that ideas, when held with sufficient intensity, can be transformed into irresistible moral action."[15]

It's easy to see, then, why immediatism would appeal to Emerson, whose writings hold fast to the power of individual moral perception and to the value of spontaneous impulses: "a man should learn to detect and watch that gleam of light which flashes across his mind from within" (CW 2: 27), he writes famously at the beginning of "Self-Reliance."

Despite this apparent affinity for the immediate, Emerson has not always been linked to immediatist abolitionism. Instead, he has sometimes been criticized for turning to abolitionism belatedly, hesitantly – a view that a number of more recent critics have challenged.[16] And indeed, in some moods, Emerson can seem like a conventional gradualist. "There is a tendency in things to right themselves" (*CW* 6: 135), he writes in *The Conduct of Life*. "Patience and patience, we shall win at last" (*CW* 3: 48–49), he says in "Experience." And in his 1844 address on West Indian emancipation, he similarly appears to take for granted that time will eventually solve the problem of slavery. "The stream of human affairs flows its own way," he says, "and is very little affected by the activity of legislators." Instead, "other energies" appear to Emerson to drive events: "the tendency of things runs steadily to this point," he says.[17]

But setting aside the question of Emerson's views of political activism and his apparent faith in the inevitability of slavery's eventual demise, he was always what we might call a philosophical immediatist, one who extolled, to borrow Davis's phrase, "direct, intuitive consciousness."[18] This accent on immediate consciousness and the priority of one's spontaneous impressions entails an allegiance to the present moment, to the time of *now*. As he puts it in the essay "Behavior" (1860), "The thought of the present moment has a greater value than all the past" (*CW* 6: 99). Similar statements can be found across his essays. In "Self-Reliance," he insists upon the power of action in the present, for "divine wisdom," he says, "lives now, and absorbs past and future into the present hour" (*CW* 2: 38). "Be it how it will," he says earlier, "do right now" (*CW* 2: 34). Similarly, in "Experience," he writes, "the only ballast I know is a respect to the present hour" (*CW* 3: 35). And in the essay, "Works and Days," he states emphatically, "an everlasting Now reigns in Nature" (*CW* 8: 88).

Such an allegiance to the present and the time of now also forms the starting point of his lecture on "The Present Age." "The best use of History," he states there, "is to teach us to value the Present" (*EL* 2: 157). Yet he also often lamented that his contemporaries had failed to learn this lesson. "Our age is retrospective," he says in the opening sentence of Nature (1836), "it builds the sepulchres of the past" (*CW* 1: 7). He repeats the sentiment in "The Present Age": "Nothing is so disesteemed as the present," he explains. "Men's eyes seem bewitched. They blink the present. They look back or look forward" (*EL* 2: 157). Later in the lecture, Emerson likens this retrospective tendency to what abolitionists, drawing upon Henry Wadsworth Longfellow's "A Psalm of Life," frequently described as the "dead past," which they contrasted with the "living present" of moral action. "Reason exists in an eternal Now," Emerson states in his variation on this theme, "it creates evermore; it exists only whilst it creates; the stark and stiffened corpse is the emblem of the past; to Reason all things are fluid, plastic, and new" (*EL* 2: 158).

## Shocks and Ruins: The New

The crucial point regarding Emerson's conception of the present is that, in contrast to the past, it is *live* – always in motion, always moving, swirling, transforming, or, as he puts it in "The Present Age" lecture, "fluid, plastic, new." Such an understanding of the present not as a fixed and static point along a linear continuum but as something constantly in flux must have derived in part from Emerson's lived experience, from the tangle of temporal modes at play in his lifetime, as well as the novel sensations and upturning of ossified ways of knowing and perceiving that the heterochronicities and the technological and scientific developments of the day generated.

The key term for Emerson's devotion to the present is "new," which perhaps more than any other word in his philosophical lexicon binds his early to his late work, from the "new men, new land, new thoughts" (*CW* 1: 7) at the beginning of *Nature* (1836) to the "new convictions" (*CW* 8: 122) at the conclusion of "Progress of Culture," published in *Letters and Social Aims* (1875). Emerson's conception of newness entailed what in social and political contexts might seem to be a reckless embrace of sudden and unexpected transformations; after all, as we've seen, the prospect of violent social upheaval committed many of Emerson's fellow citizens to slow, cautious gradualist modes of reform. By contrast, and drawing upon the language of nineteenth-century geology, we might say that there was always a seemingly perilous element of catastrophism in Emerson's embrace of the new. "The new continents are built out of the ruins of the old planet," he writes exultantly in "Circles," "the new races fed out of the decomposition of the foregoing. New arts destroy the old" (*CW* 2: 180). Ruin, decomposition, destruction: These images invariably attend Emerson's invocation of the new. For instance, he writes later in the essay that upon the sudden appearance of the new, "all that we reckoned settled shakes and rattles; and literatures, cities, climates, religions, leave their foundations and dance before our eyes" (*CW* 2: 184). Emerson's celebration here of what otherwise looks like catastrophe echoes, in certain ways, the experience he recorded in his journal of locomotive speed: Hurtling forward in a headlong rush is frightening and dangerous. But it's also thrilling.

Here, by way of conclusion, we might return to "Fate," where Emerson at first seems to sidestep "the question of the times," turning instead to "the conduct of life" and more specifically the question, "how shall I live?" It's worth recalling that "Fate" was first delivered as a lecture in 1851 during the same period in which Emerson gave fiery orations in response to the Fugitive Slave Law. So the question that animates the essay is inevitably charged by the one question of the times that can't be skirted: slavery. And while the essay does not take up that topic explicitly, preferring instead to adhere, as Lawrence Buell hypothesizes, to the "temporizing convention of steering away from hot political topics in lyceum lectures,"[19] it does frame its central questions in terms familiar to debates over the abolition of slavery. Which is not just to say that an essay about human freedom, however abstractly considered, can't *not* speak to the social and material conditions that invariably form part of the essay's context. It's also to note how "Fate" is also an essay about historical unfolding, about how to contend with a world that is undergoing abrupt, frightening, and catastrophic change.

In this way the essay offers a timely – one might say prescient – meditation on how to respond to such a world and how to thrive under conditions of disaster. Emerson establishes those conditions in the essay's opening paragraphs. "Nature is no sentimentalist," he warns his audience. "We must see," he continues, "that the world is rough and surly" (CW 6: 3). To illustrate the point, he provides a series of vivid images of what he calls "the disasters which threaten mankind" (CW 6: 4). It's an eerily familiar list, comprised of extreme weather events, environmental destruction, disease, and pandemic:

> The planet is liable to shocks from comets, perturbations from planets, rendings from earthquake and volcano, alterations of climate, precessions of equinoxes. Rivers dry up by opening of the forest. The sea changes its bed. Towns and counties fall into it.... The scurvy at sea, the sword of the climate in the west of Africa, at Cayenne, at Panama, at New Orleans, cut off men like a massacre. Our western prairie shakes with fever and ague. The cholera, the small-pox, have proved as mortal to some tribes as a frost to the crickets. (CW 6: 4)

Some of the disasters Emerson enumerates are sudden and catastrophic, like "the shocks from comets, perturbations from planets, [and] rendings from earthquake and volcano." Others, such as "alterations of climate" or "precessions of equinoxes," are slow and gradual. In either case, such a state of affairs, Emerson warns, may be met with resignation – an acceptance of Fate – or with action – an embrace of freedom. Emerson of course urges the latter. The argument of "Fate" thus echoes both Emerson's response to the speeding locomotive in his journal and the earth-shaking arrival of the new in "Circles": Recognize the fright, but embrace the thrill. In "Fate," Emerson calls this particular disposition toward the world "fatal courage" (CW 6: 13).

Or to cast this in slightly different terms, "Fate" urges action over torpor and extols power over passivity. Fate is for Emerson, after all, just another word for "limitation." "Whatever limits us," he says, "we call Fate" (CW 6: 11). The acceptance of such limitation is what prevents both action and its precondition, the recognition of human agency in the face of overwhelming external forces. "Fate is immense," Emerson concedes, but nevertheless insists, "so is Power" (CW 6: 12). Thus, in his view, "every calamity is a spur and valuable hint" (CW 6: 19), less an insurmountable obstacle than an opportunity to exercise one's power. Man is and ought to be what Emerson calls "a stupendous antagonism." "The lightning which explodes and fashions planets, maker of planets and sun," he says, "is in him" (CW 6: 12).

Lightning, too, was among the powerfully destructive phenomena that in Emerson's time helped to figure the prospect of social upheaval and internecine violence generated by antislavery antagonism. The Fugitive Slave Law, Emerson told a Concord audience in 1851, "had the illuminating power of a sheet of lightning at midnight. It showed truth."[20] That speech, like "Fate," was Emerson's attempt to rouse his audience from slumber, to enjoin them finally to choose swift action over cautious temporizing, come what may. Emerson's reckonings with the variety of temporal changes of his era, tempered perhaps by his belief in the "Beautiful Necessity" he leans on at the conclusion of "Fate," had taught him how to view the uncertain results of action in the present with buoyant expectancy rather than with trepidation and apprehension. By contrast, a great many of his fellow citizens must have viewed the prospect of such radical change as something more terrifying than exhilarating, preferring the safety of reliance on the slow drift of history (Providence, Fate) to the dangerous locomotive rush of sudden transformation. And yet almost 200 years later, Emerson's times seem still to be our own times and we find ourselves once again witness to ongoing racialized violence and the urgent need to rouse ourselves to address social injustice. We find ourselves confronting, too, all-too-visible planetary shocks and ruins, as alterations of the climate have produced a world on fire, as more and more rivers dry up and sea beds change and towns and counties around the globe are poised to tumble into them. Under these conditions, Emerson's call for fatal courage seems more urgent than ever.

## Notes

1. Thomas Constantinesco, "*The Dial* and the Untimely 'Spirit of the Times,'" *American Periodicals* 28:1 (2018): 22.

2. For more on Emerson's conception of history and historical progress, see Jeffrey Insko, *History, Abolition, and the Ever-Present Now in Antebellum American Writing* (Oxford: Oxford University Press, 2018).

3. Michael O'Malley, *Keeping Watch: A History of American Time* (Washington, DC: Smithsonian Institution Press, 1990), 8.

4. Thomas M. Allen, *A Republic in Time: Temporality and Social Imagination in Nineteenth-Century America* (Chapel Hill, NC: University of North Carolina Press, 2008), 64.

5. Lloyd Pratt, *Archives of American Time: Literature and Modernity in the Nineteenth Century* (Philadelphia, PA: University of Pennsylvania Press, 2011), 3.

6. Ibid.

7. Ibid.

8. Henry David Thoreau, *Walden*, ed. J. Lyndon Shandley (Princeton, NJ: Princeton University Press, 1971), 117.

9. Ibid., 118.

10. Allen, *A Republic in Time*, 193.

11. In addition to Allen, see also Jennifer J. Baker, "Emerson, Embryology, and Culture," *J19: The Journal of Nineteenth-Century Americanists* 2:1 (2015): 15–39, and, especially, James Guthrie, *Above Time: Emerson's and Thoreau's Temporal Revolutions* (Columbia, MO: University of Missouri Press, 2001).

12. Charles's address is housed at the Houghton Library, Harvard University, and is dated April 29, 1835 (MS AM 82.6).

13. Catherine Beecher, *An Essay on Slavery and Abolitionism, with Reference to the Duty of American Females* (Philadelphia: H. Perkins, 1837), 83.

14. David Brion Davis, "The Emergence of Immediatism in British and American Antislavery Thought," *Mississippi Valley Historical Review* 49 (Sep. 1962): 214.

15. Ibid., 212, 230.

16. On Emerson's so-called conversion to abolitionism, see especially Len Gougeon, *Virtue's Hero: Emerson, Antislavery, and Reform* (Athens, GA: University of Georgia Press, 1990).

17. Ralph Waldo Emerson, "An Address ... on ... the Emancipation of the Negroes in the British West Indies, 1 August, 1844," in *Emerson's Antislavery Writings*, ed. Len Gougeon and Joel Myerson (New Haven: Yale University Press, 1995), 28.

18. Davis, "The Emergence of Immediatism in British and American Antislavery Thought," 209.

19. Lawrence Buell, "Emerson's Fate," in *Emersonian Circles: Essays in Honor of Joel Myerson*, ed. Wesley T. Mott and Robert E. Burkholder (University of Rochester Press, 1997), 22.

20. Ralph Waldo Emerson, "Address to the Citizens of Concord on the Fugitive Slave Law, 3 May, 1851," in *Emerson's Antislavery Writings*, ed. Len Gougeon and Joel Myerson (New Haven: Yale University Press, 1995), 36.

# 2

DEVIN ZUBER

# Spiritual Laws
## Religion and Rainbows

### In Rainbows

When Ralph Waldo Emerson entered Harvard University in 1817, and ultimately fell into studying theology at the Divinity School, he was the seventh Emerson over five generations of his family to matriculate there. On his mother's side, eight generations of clergy had preceded Waldo; on his father's side, seven generations back, his Puritan forefathers had been part of the original settlers of the Massachusetts Bay Colony. As if this spiritual pedigree were not overbearing enough, his middle name – his preferred nomenclature, more so than Ralph – derived from the Waldensians, the medieval heretical sect that later colored the Protestant Reformation. Their historical resonance also lent its name to the beautiful Concord pond, where the Emerson family owned property, land on which Thoreau would live and later turn into his most popular book. Institutional religion and theocratic law surrounded Waldo, quite literally. When Emerson moved into the ancestral home known as the Old Manse in 1834, to live with his mother, step-grandfather, brothers, and Aunt Mary Moody Emerson, the garret attic and study bookshelves were crammed with the journals, sermons, and sundry treatises of Emerson's many progenitors. Nathaniel Hawthorne later rented the house from the Emersons and described the lugubrious presence of this "vast folio body of 'divinity … bound' in black leather, exhibiting precisely such an appearance as we should attribute to books of enchantment" in the opening of his short story collection, *Mosses from an Old Manse* (1846): A work that, much like Emerson's own parallel projects, enacts a conversion of this Puritan heritage into Romantic literary aesthetics.[1]

Emerson's later takes on religion were not anything like the heavy folios of divinity penned by his forefathers, and in many regards, owed more to his immersion in the scientific discourses of his day than to any traditional Christian doctrines. In what has become one of his most signal essays for modern criticism and philosophy, "Experience" (1844), which was written out of a whirl of grief precipitated by the death of his beloved five-year-old son (also named Waldo), Emerson famously describes the shifting, dream-like quality of life as "a train of moods like a string of beads, and, as we pass through them, they prove to be many-colored lenses which paint the world their own hue, and each shows only what lies in its focus" (CW 3: 30). If we were to turn these moody, many-colored lenses toward the vexed question of Emerson's relationship with religion, we get an according rain-bow of different, and sometimes apparently contradictory, interpretations of the Sage of Concord. Was Emerson a free-thinker who dipped his "pen in the blackest ink" of doubt, as Emerson writes in *Worship* (CW 6: 106–28) – his last major published essay on the topic of religion – who can be claimed as a major secularizing force on American culture? Or was he rather a rosy harbinger of the New Age, whose self-reliant do-it-yourself spiritual-ity was popularized by the New Thought and Mind-Cure movements, and their so-called religion of healthy mindedness that William James came to value? What about the related green line that runs from Emerson's inau-gural *Nature* (1836) essay into the wilderness ethos of John Muir, and the consequent appearance of an American "nature religion" tradition? Or, conversely, did, the gospel of "Self-Reliance" lead not to spiritual liberation, but right into the Fordist factory line? Was Emerson rather the "prophet of piratical industrialism" (Allen Tate), capitalism's favorite "poet philos-opher" (Thomas Hughes), or, by extension, did he help give birth to more recent destructive neoliberal ideologies?[2]

Within contemporary philosophy, following Stanley Cavell, Emerson is seen as emphatically provisional, modeling a mode of skepticism and detach-ment which anticipates Nietzsche – "we may well give skepticism as much line as we can," Emerson had advised, after all, at the start of his *Worship* essay (CW 6: 107) – while at the same time, Emerson continues to be read as an inveterately idealist thinker who never abandons the fundamental, eth-ical unity between mind and matter.[3] Still others, like Harold Bloom, have insisted that Emerson's spiritual concerns inaugurate an "unofficial religion" of modern America, a form of "post-Christian" devotion with broad civic and democratic implications. Emerson's repeated insistence that practically anything was capable of emanating numinous, spiritual significance – such that common farm fields could become "mute gospels," "sacred emblems," as he memorably describes it in his *Nature* debut – makes him "our greatest philosopher of making the irrelevant count"; according to Elisa Tamarkin, "Nothing [for Emerson] is too old, obscure, or boring to have fresh mean-ing; nothing is too ordinary to feel like a kind of revelation."[4]

With such democratic universalizing of revelation, there would seem to be as many varieties of Emersonian religious experience as there are colors in the rainbow (or different glass beads strung out on a string): Emerson as an ecstatic mystic; a perennial skeptic, dipped in the blackest ink; a green pantheist; an ecclesiastical iconoclast who smashed the sepulchers of his Puritan forefathers; the all-American antinomian; an Orientalist who dabbled in Asian religions but couldn't keep his Buddhism straight from Hinduism; or finally, "a traveling salesclerk for the spirit" whose lecturing about the energetic transfers of the Oversoul anticipated contemporary practices of New Age trance channeling (according to Catherine Albanese).[5] In his own day, Emerson often faced public accusations of being an "infidel," as the prominent theologian Andrews Norton accused him of, after Emerson had affronted the Harvard Divinity School with his punk-style commencement address – a serious charge that dangerously skirted public prosecution for blasphemy in the state of Massachusetts.[6] "The Church seems to totter to its fall, almost all life extinct," Emerson prognosticated to the shocked students and faculty; they needed to cast behind themselves "all conformity," and to rather trust their own hearts (and not, ostensibly, the Harvard divinity curriculum, which was still tinged with Calvinist anxieties over what depravities might lie in human hearts) (CW 1: 84, 90).

Years later, fully comfortable with his public reputation as the doyen of the new Transcendentalism, Emerson ended up sitting for a portrait by the Scottish artist David Scott, a deeply religious painter who much admired Emerson. Although Emerson ultimately declined to purchase Scott's painting, it is a notable likeness, showing both Emerson's characteristic lecturing stance – right hand clenched into a self-reliant fist – and behind this gesture of power, a bright full-spectrum rainbow. The rainbow forms a multicolored aura around Emerson's head, glowing in the darkness (Emerson would write twelve years later, in an essay that appeared in *The Conduct of Life*, how "in youth, we clothe ourselves with rainbows") (CW 6: 22). Scott was playing with the rainbow as a classic icon of hope, keying the spirit of cosmological optimism that infuses so many of Emerson's essays, as Emerson's son Edward later remembered. Scott was also surely attuned to the deep valence of the rainbow as a Romantic symbol of the fusion of spirituality with science, epitomized by Johann Wolfgang von Goethe's influential theory of color and visual perception – the *Farbenlehre* – which Emerson had begun reading in the early 1840s.[7] In Emerson's own writing, rainbows, prisms, and crystals often flicker around his frequent troping on the optical dimensions of religious experience: His favorite representative mystic, Emanuel Swedenborg, with his thought like a "gigantic crystal," was ultimately "staggered under the trance of delight," a "glory too bright for his eyes to bear" (CW 4: 81).

For Emerson, religion was a bit like the phenomenon of a rainbow, painted behind him in this portrait by Scott: Both were manifestations of immaterial forces ultimately explicable through the universal laws of nature, decoded with the aid of natural sciences, such as optics and astronomy (Goethe had poeticized in his *Faust* how the rainbow is a "perfect symbol – ponder this well to understand more clearly / that what we have as life is many-hued reflection.").[8] In Emerson's central early essay on religion, "Spiritual Laws" (from *Essays: First Series*, which Emerson once contemplated alternatively titling "Forest Essays"), Emerson works to redeem spirituality from the "deadweight" of religious tradition and institutional dogma, relocating the impulse to believe as an inherent principle akin to other so-called universal laws of nature, like gravity, light, and electrical polarity. The essay concludes with an astonishing, complex metaphor for the human mind that mixes Emerson's readings in science and optics, including nascent photography, together with his parallel immersion in occult and esoteric discourses. In terms of our innate human grasping for the immateriality of the spiritual, Emerson writes, "we are the photometers, we the irritable goldleaf and tinfoil that measure the accumulations of the subtle element. We know the authentic effects of the true fire through every one of its million disguises" (CW 2: 96).

Comparing human perceptivity to both the goldleaf and tinfoil of the alchemist as well as to the photometer, a scientific instrument used for measuring the intensity of the sun's light – and especially, in the nineteenth century, essential for studying hues in the rainbow not otherwise visible to the naked eye, such as infrared – "Spiritual Laws" underscores how Emerson consistently naturalized religion into a sort of universal force, akin to the physics of light, at the same time that he wished to retain forms of premodern, gnostic wisdom: our "irritable," impulsive capacity for perceiving the "true fire" of invisible spiritual forces flowing around us.[9] "There is a soul at the centre of nature," he writes, "and over the will of every man, so that none of us can ever wrong the universe. It has so infused its strong enchantment into nature, that we prosper when we accept its advice, and when we struggle to wound its creatures, our hands are glued to our sides, or they beat our own breasts" (CW 2: 81). This chapter aims to add some contextual colors to the full spectrum of Emerson's spirituality, to explore how a leading scion of Puritan-descended clergy could come to feel that the spiritual laws of the cosmos were best explained not by theology, or by reading and interpreting one's Bible, but by the twinned, enchanting activities of science and poetics as forms of social praxis, a communal making of beauty and truth.[10] Given the perhaps surprising "return of religion" to our public spheres in the new millennium – be it via the resurgence of religion as a political force following 9/11, or the more recent (and alarming) global spread of various forms of Christian ethno-nationalisms – Emerson's unsettled relationship to religion might yet offer some salient insights for the problems and discontents of our still (post)secular age, especially when it comes to the challenges of religious pluralism.[11]

## Sepulchers of the Fathers

In his philosophical debut, *Nature*, when Emerson complains of being stuck in a retrospective age that "builds the sepulchres [sic] of the fathers" (*CW* 1: 7), the text is performing a kind of exorcism of Emerson's complex personal history. By the time Emerson published these words, kick-starting the first phase of New England Transcendentalism into high gear, he had traveled far from the theologically inclined youth who had followed in the footsteps of his father and grandfathers into the ministry. Emerson lasted a little over three years as an ordained clergyman in the Unitarian church, serving the Second Church of Boston congregation (his father, William, had served at the First), though Emerson would continue to preach as a guest minister in various pulpits up through 1839. Thanks to Emerson's inveterately copious journal habits, scholars can track Emerson wrestling with Christian theology and the related spiritual crises brought on by personal tragedies and recurrent illness, particularly the loss of his first wife, Ellen Tucker, in 1831 to tuberculosis. One of the most chilling moments in the thousands of pages of Emerson's journals is certainly his laconic observation on March 29, 1832, thirteen months after Ellen had been buried, that he "visited Ellen's tomb & opened the coffin" (*JMN* 4: 7). The rotting, decayed remains of his wife shook Emerson's eschatological certainty, and he was furthered disturbed that he could not feel any subsequent presence of her spirit: "She never comes to me," he despairs in his journal, in broken blank verse, "Sits never by my side / I never hear her voice / She comes not even to my dreams / O Ellen" (*JMN* 3: 285). Emerson's final sermon for his congregation delivered shortly later articulated why he could no longer believe, and faithfully administer in good conscience, that ultimate symbol of the Christian transformation of bodies into spirit, the Holy Supper.

Emerson's so-called Lord's Supper sermon nevertheless contains a core conviction that Waldo carried into all subsequent reflections on religion and spirituality, no matter how far he came to drift from traditional Christian strictures: That the essence of religion was not in dogma or creed, and the attendant institutionalization of belief, but in the felt experience of one's own inner feelings. "It is of the greatest important," Emerson told his congregants, "that whatever [religious] forms we use should be animated by our feelings; that our religion through all its acts should be living and operative" (*CS* 4: 192). This vital "fact of feeling," in Joan Richardson's phrasing, was gleaned by Emerson from several places, including, crucially, his absorption of the ideas of radical German theologians and biblical critics who were often lumped together by English-speaking Romantic readers as constituting the "Higher Criticism."[12] Emerson's humanistic, earthy Jesus in the "Lord's Supper Sermon," with Christ's "natural feeling and beauty" who was a "friend to his friends," echoes and parallels how Friedrich Schleiermacher, Johann Gottfried Eichhorn, and, later, Ludwig Feuerbach, all respectively developed their controversial religious anthropologies (CS 4: 187). Emerson encountered some of these radical theologies second-hand, via their diffusion in Anglo-thinkers such as Samuel Taylor Coleridge – the first American edition of Coleridge's *Aids to Reflection*, brought out by James Marsh in 1829, was particularly important to a young Emerson – but he also learned about them directly from his older brother William, who had studied in Göttingen, then the epicenter of the Higher Criticism's new disruptive energies. When William returned to America from Germany in 1825, shaken by religious doubts brought on by his time spent studying under Eichhorn, he renounced his plans to join the ministry and pursued instead a career in law (casting aside Goethe's personal advice to William that he should, more or less, just fake it in the ministry, even if he didn't believe in what he was doing).[13] Waldo, thus, was not the first Emerson boy who would come to reject the expected family profession. Unlike William, however, Waldo did not wholly abandon a ministerial calling, but rather transmuted its impetus into a different modality, of lecturing and writing to a widening and multifarious American public. As Robert Richardson puts it, while Emerson objected to Communion with a capital C – "something to be required of all Christians forever" – he devoted the remainder of his career to communion with a small c, communing and creating bonds between people.[14]

This vocation was not so clear in the immediate traumatic aftermath of Ellen's death and Emerson's resignation from the Unitarian church; Emerson would later articulate in "Spiritual Laws" the very idea of vocational calling as a process of unfolding abandonment.[15] When Emerson set sail for Europe on Christmas Day that year, sickly and underweight – his journals take note of him anxiously taking stock of his pounds – he had only the vaguest of ideas of what he was to do with his life. The eight-month sojourn through Italy, France, and England ended up being catalytic, life-changing; in addition to meeting Romantic writers who had been very formative for him, such as William Wordsworth and Coleridge, and striking up what was to become a life-long kindred friendship with Thomas Carlyle, Emerson underwent what can only be described as a sort of second birth, a spiritual epiphany in Paris – a revelation that took place not in a church or in the sublime solitude of the mountains or forest but in the museum displays of the cabinets of natural history at the city's Jardin des Plantes. Observing the sequence of arranged crystals, metal plates, hazy butterflies, carved shells, "birds, beasts, fishes, insects, snakes," Emerson detected a profound kinship not only between these disparate natural species but also with himself:

> the upheaving principle of life everywhere incipient in the very rock aping organicized forms. Not a form so grotesque, so savage, nor so beautiful but is an expression of some property inherent in man the observer, – an occult relation between the very scorpions and the man. I feel the centipede in me – cayman, carp, eagle, & fox. I am moved by strange sympathies, I say continually "I will be a naturalist." (*JMN* 4: 199–200)

This journaled declaration has been interpreted by various critics as the seminal turning point, where Emerson casts off any lingering allegiance to institutional Christianity and embraces new intellectual (and spiritual) horizons afforded by the natural sciences and their vitalistic attention to biological life.[16] What has sometimes been neglected in attention to this signal moment is how deeply religious Emerson's new awakened perception nevertheless remains, his "occult relation" between scorpions and man that is felt, full of "strange sympathies." What stirs Emerson to ecstasy here is not the objects and species in themselves but the "ray of relation" between them instigated by the scientific displays of the museum. In a weird way, as Laura Dassow Walls observes, this meant these cabinets of natural history were for Emerson, "more natural even than nature itself, more real than reality," because every specimen appeared "purified to the idea of itself."[17] The shells, crystals, and butterflies functioned as modes of spiritual instruction, hieroglyphic keys into the soul. Emerson's dissolving wonder in this moment of perception resurfaces shortly later in *Nature*, when he tells the reader in the first chapter how "the greatest delight which the fields and woods minister, is the suggestion of an occult relation between man and the vegetable" (*CW* 1: 10) – a de-light which, as always in Emerson who so often turns and tropes on the optical, is related to his understanding of the prismatic refraction of light, and our (photometric) receptivity to it.

"Occult" is the recurrent signifier in these relational chains delightfully linking human to scorpions and vegetables, a multivalent word for Emerson, indicating his interest in esoteric kinds of thought that his Puritan forebears would have immediately condemned as blasphemous, as well as astronomical phenomena (the occulting of planetary bodies, whereby a larger celestial body occludes and hides a smaller one).[18] At the same time Emerson was embarking on a new path shaped by natural sciences, he continued to read deeply and broadly in heterodox religious traditions. He took note of the "mystic night of Germany" of Madame de Staël and Goethe, as well as theosophists such as Jakob Böhme and Emanuel Swedenborg, among other representatives of "enthusiasm" and "Transcendentalism," two signal terms he began playing around with as organizing rubrics in his journals (*JMN* 3: 70). When Emerson returned to America after this first European trip (healthier and heavier, having regained his weight and good spirits), his post-church lecture career began with important public talks on "The Uses of Natural History," "The Naturalist," and topics like "Water." Emerson's esoteric readings are never very far behind these parallel surveys of contemporary natural sciences, such as geology; however, in "The Uses of Natural History," Emerson invokes a quote from Swedenborg how the natural world is but the "dialplate" of the spiritual, declaring that "the whole of Nature is a metaphor or image of the human mind. The laws of moral nature answer to those of matter as face to face in a glass" (*EL* 1: 25). Shortly later, Emerson recycled these lines into the published text of *Nature*, transposing an original eighteenth-century mystical source into the earthy, geological concerns of nineteenth-century natural history, which then flowers into the prose of one of America's most significant Romantic manifestoes (in addition to Swedenborg here, Emerson's "face to face in a glass" echoes both the Bible – 1 Corinthians 13 – as well as Jakob Böhme's recurrent metaphors of the world as reflective glass).[19]

Emerson absorbed and wrestled with the unsettling tendencies of the sciences in his era, as the episteme of an older natural philosophy tradition further fractured into emergent fields of geology, biology, and physics, among others; he particularly tracked, according to Walls, theories of evolutionary transmutation, concerns with race and species, and statistics and probability.[20] Stunned by the contemporary astronomy of John Herschel and Mary Somerville, Emerson felt that science "corrects our theology"; even prior to his well-known epiphany in the Jardin des Plantes, on the long sea journey over to Europe, Emerson had marveled at the winter stars, experimented with reading the night sky with a quadrant and declared that "another voyage would make an astronomer of me" (*JMN* 4: 107). Metaphysical concerns and questions were emphatically on the retreat from these new domains of knowledge; in many ways, Emerson's keenness on evolutionary theories echoes and anticipates the work of Charles Darwin, as Emerson was also one of Darwin's early American enthusiasts, and devoured *Origin on the Species* when it finally appeared with much controversy in 1860. How to account, then, for the religious persistence of Emerson's "occult" kinship between his interior subjectivity and the "upheaving principle of life everywhere"? It is perhaps even more surprising if we recall the claims for the secular made by the philosopher Charles Taylor, and how the slow leak of teleology out of different scientific domains led to new, modern constructions of the human self: One that was "buffered" from supernatural influences, in contrast to earlier, more enchanted eras when selves were more "porous," fluid, and open to the numinous and transcendent.[21] The well-known "transparent eyeball" moment in *Nature*, where Emerson, crossing the winter commons, glad to the brink of fear, dissolves into "nothing; I see all; the currents of the Universal Being circulate through me; I am part or particle of God" is a porous place where modernity's ostensibly buffered self gets cracked open by occulting forces; it is also a moment of rainbow optics, again, with Emerson's extended metaphors of transparency, the section ending with "especially in the distant line of the horizon, man beholds somewhat as beautiful as his own nature" (*CW* 1: 10).

## Correspondences

The spiritual connectivity holding this kinship together was not only figured as a universal law of nature, like gravity or the wave diffraction of light; Emerson also deployed his esoteric readings to conceive of his perceiving self, embedded in nature, as linguistic signs in a dynamic semiotic field, that it was all a kind of language, as one of the chapters in *Nature* was entitled: "it is not words only that are emblematic, it is things which are emblematic. Every natural fact is a symbol of some spiritual fact. Every appearance in nature corresponds to some state of mind" (*CW* 1: 18). Here, Emerson was drawing primarily on Swedenborg's vaunted "doctrine of correspondences" – in some places in the "Language" chapter of *Nature*, Emerson repeats word-for-word material from a French Swedenborgian, Guillaume Caspar Lencroy Oegger – but Jakob Böhme also became relevant here, via his idea of "signatures" of the Divine that were to be found "in and by all creatures, even in herbs and grass."[22] Swedenborg's correspondences and Böhme's signatures permitted Emerson to move language beyond the dry, rational models that his generation had inherited from John Locke and his followers, which had thoroughly desiccated the Unitarian theology of Emerson's day and further circumscribed language as solely a human capacity, arbitrarily determined by social conventions.[23] Correspondence reconnected words to things, but it also allowed, in a kind of chiasmus, those very things of nature – be they scorpions, vegetables, butterflies, or shells – to signify as words, even as *the* Word, filled with divinity and revelation. Though Swedenborg and Böhme had remained within the Christian pale themselves, heterodox and controversial as they were in their own Protestant moments, their respective amplifications of what Hans Blumenberg later termed "*die Lesbarkeit der Welt*," the "readability of the world," a discursivity about books-as-the-world and the world-as-book, expanded the so-called second book of God in such a way that the primacy of the first, the text of written revelation, was consequently displaced.[24] This became all the more acute as the philological tools of the Higher Criticism continued to pulverize the perceived unity of the Judeo-Christian scripture into fragments of different, sometimes contradictory texts. If such unity was chimerical in the biblical Word, it was to be holistically found – by the poetic perceiver, if they were attuned to it – within the boundless book of nature. The tension between these two poles of natural theology is sounded immediately at the start of Emerson's *Nature*: "Why should we not also enjoy an original relationship to the universe? Why should we not have a poetry and philosophy of insight and not of tradition, and a religion by revelation to us, and not the history of theirs?" (*CW* 1: 7).

The formative historian of New England Puritans, Perry Miller, was one of the first modern critics to ponder how strange it was that Emerson (and Thoreau) "should have had to go to Emanuel Swedenborg for a doctrine of 'correspondence,' since something remarkable like it had been embedded in their own tradition for two hundred years."[25] Miller was indicating the Puritan practice of typology, a habit of scriptural allegorical interpretation that, within certain writers, such as Jonathan Edwards, tended to slide off the pages of the Bible and become a means for describing the "images or shadows of divine thing" in various natural phenomena. While Miller's speculative connecting of the Puritan Jonathan Edwards all the way to Emerson – contending that a radical and ecstatic visionary tradition had more or less persisted within New England's intellectual landscape over the centuries – has been robustly criticized in more recent years, it is certainly true that Emerson had a living embodiment of Puritan mysticism quite close at hand, sometimes under his roof, in the figure of his Aunt Mary Moody Emerson.[26] If Emerson consistently contemned his father's generation as retrograde, it was wholly another story with his father's brilliant sister, who exerted an enormous influence on Emerson's thinking about religion and spirituality. A sort of "American Jacob Böhme" – as Robert Richardson calls her – Aunt Mary carried on extensive epistolary conversations with the Emerson boys throughout their adolescence, advising and mentoring the development of their thought, and lived for various periods in the same house as Waldo.[27] She was obsessed with her own mortality, slept in a bed shaped like a coffin, and when she traveled further distances from her home, she often wore burial shrouds as her travel clothes, just in case she happened to die while on the road. Her many letters, papers, and journals were treasured by Emerson, which he consistently organized, indexed, and mined for his own lectures and essays – some of Emerson's late and final reflections on religion, including remarks in the "Natural History of the Intellect" project, deploy his aunt's singular aphorisms. Privately despairing in his journal on the stultifying theological curricula at Harvard and elsewhere, Emerson appreciatively notes in 1837

> how much happier was my star which rained on me influences of ancestral religion. The depth of the religious sentiment which I knew in my Aunt Mary imbuing all her genius & derived to her from such hoarded family traditions, from so many godly lives & godly deaths of sainted kindred at Concord, Malden, York, was itself a culture, an education. (*JMN* 5: 323–24)

Aunt Mary cleaved from Emerson, however, when it came to his attraction to "occult" sources, such as Swedenborg, and his growing appetite for non-Christian religions. She advised Waldo to "avoid the dull heaven and silly loves" of Swedenborg, and when Emerson excitedly shared with her a copy of a Swedenborgian tract by Sampson Reed, she found it too full of trite "Swedishness" for her tastes (Emerson responded, "but what, in the name of all the fairies, is the reason you don't like Sampson Reed?").[28] Aunt Mary came to live with the Emersons in the Old Manse during the heady, early spinning days of Transcendentalism, as Waldo worked on drafts of *Nature*, and a growing crowd of family and friends started orbiting around Waldo's rising star. But eventually, especially after the death of Emerson's brother Charles Chauncy in 1836 (to tuberculosis, just like Ellen), her disagreements with her favorite nephew, now straying so far from Christianity, were strong enough that she left the Old Manse and moved back to her home in Maine (a steady stream of letters would continue for many more years).

## Other Worlds

In spite of being perturbed by all this "Swedishness" and orientalizing, Aunt Mary was also a critical, early conduit for Emerson to encounter something like comparative religions, modelling how one could use Idealist philosophy as a way to bring together disparate theological traditions. As Phyllis Cole has helped bring to light, Mary sent several letters to Emerson while he was a nineteen-year-old student at Harvard, describing her excitement at having met someone from India who told her about Rammohan Roy, the great Bengali reformer who had written important works in comparative theology in the 1820s. These included Roy's *The Precepts of Jesus: The Guide to Peace and Happiness* (1820), a Hindu appreciation for Gospel teachings that was electrifying Unitarians across the Anglophone world (Mary misunderstood Roy's comparative work, like many other Unitarians, as a case of Christian conversion). In another letter, Mary included a poem by the Sanskrit translator William Jones, "Hymn to Narayena," which distilled various parts of the Bhagavad-Gita into panegyric English. Emerson carefully copied the poem into his journal under the heading "IDEALISM," suggesting how young Waldo was already conceiving of Vedantic religions as a countercultural resource against his growing discontent with Unitarian theology and contemporary materialism.[29] The well-known end of Emerson's *Nature* essay, in "Prospects," with its enthusiastic imperative for the reader to go out and "build, therefore, your own world" (*CW* 1: 45), has been read by some critics as inculcating a sort of Manifest Destiny ideology, an enjoinder to the violence of Jacksonian democracy's expanding frontier.[30] This may be; and yet, certainly another way to understand these lines is in their troping relation to religion's problematic "building" on the tombstones of its Christian fathers, with which the essay commences. "Build your own world" becomes, then, an invitation to create one's own spirituality and an openness to religious practices beyond the ostensible boundaries of Christianity.

By the time Emerson came to define, somewhat defensively, what this new American Transcendentalism was all about in a crucial lecture he gave in 1842 ("The Transcendentalist," first delivered at the Boston Masonic Temple), he had fully marshalled eastern religions into this new generational zeitgeist that was concerned with miracle, the openness to influx, inspiration, and ecstasy. "The oriental mind has always tended to this largeness," Emerson claimed, "Buddhism is an expression of it ... The Buddhist ... is a Transcendentalist" (*CW* 1: 205). Anticipating (and informing) the later Beatnik appropriation of Buddhism in the 1950s into a defiant stance of cool detachment, Emerson heralds how the American relationship to Asian religions, Buddhism in particular, was initiated as a mode of aesthetic translation, the conversion of metaphysical principles into forms of countercultural art.[31] Some of these sorts of claims were already percolating in sundry reflections in *The Dial*, the Transcendentalists' major periodical, which began publication in 1840 (under the editorial supervision of Margaret Fuller and later Emerson himself). In the pages of *The Dial*, readers found the unusually titled "Ethnical Scriptures" series – underscoring how constructs of race and ethnicity could undergird the (American) construction of world religions in the antebellum period – which featured rotating selections of non-Christian sacred scriptures, from Confucius to Vedantic sources. Most notably, it was here in the Ethnical Scriptures that a Buddhist text – the Lotus Sutra – first appeared on American soil in the English vernacular, in a translation from the French undertaken by Elizabeth Palmer Peabody (and not Thoreau, as has often been contended).[32]

Does Emerson's blithe, eclectic borrowing from a smorgasbord of eastern religions come to taint his work with something like "cultural appropriation," one of the cardinal sins for criticism and art in our own era? Certainly, Emerson made use of a "structure of attitude and reference" about texts related to the Orient and a system of (cultural) translation that was inherently entangled in unequal power relations during a period of brutal colonization (and genocidal western expansionism, in the United States), to follow Edward Said's concerns.[33] And yet, as Wai Chee Dimock argues, tracking the *longue durée* of religion across these transcultural encounters of reading and adaptation can draw a different sort of map, one that doesn't necessarily center the West as a "gigantic ideological factory" of cooptation and brutal conquest. Instead, unpacking Emerson's deep sustained readings in Islam, Buddhism, and Hinduism lets "American literature burst out of the confines of the nation-state, becoming a thread in the fabric of world religion."[34] Rather than extending Harold Bloom's grandiloquent claim that "Emerson IS American literature," in Dimock's reading, Emerson's sustained engagement with translating the Sufi poetry of Hafiz and Saadi (from the German) – Hafiz was among the last poets Emerson cites before he stops writing at the end of his life – renders Emerson as yet another commentator in a long strand of Islamic interpretation, stretching back centuries and across continents, multiple languages, and cultures. Just as Emerson's natural philosophy could be said to have decentered traditional Protestant emphases on the primacy of the Biblical revelation, Emerson-as-Sufi exegete revealed Christianity to be "not unique, but one variant of truth of which other religions are also variants."[35] There remain valid concerns here for how Emerson nevertheless participated in the construction of a kind of wider, nineteenth-century universalism, which, while subsuming under it a figure of pluralistic world religions, also reified simultaneously ethnocentric assumptions about monotheism, the progress of western civilization, and proffered a sort of unity-in-diversity that is predicated on the secularizing presence of the modern nation state and its arbitrating powers.[36] Here, Emerson's universal pluralism might end up being as impossibly blank and (ethically) blind as his transparent eyeball, as such an eyeball, if we take this metaphor from *Nature* to its fullest extent, actually lacks the necessary opacity and the means to refract light waves and would thus not be able to perceive what it was seeing: The light would simply pass through it. Curiously, Emerson's transparent eyeball of *Nature* thus looks toward his later troping on how mysticism, etymologically, was a kind of blindness, a closing of the eyes to the world, a "getting out of their bodies to think" (*CW* 4: 55).

By his own admission, in an essay that begins with eyes – "the eye is the first circle" – Emerson claims simply to be an experimenter when it comes to religion: "No facts are to me sacred; none are profane; I simply experiment, an endless seeker, with no Past at my back" (*CW* 2: 179, 188). This moment in "Circles" is one of the earlier instances, as Leigh Eric Schmidt points out, where "seeker" becomes a self-identified term for a new form of modern spirituality (one indubitably premised on a kind of iconoclasm).[37] Within a few decades, Emerson's construction of a kind of spirituality that moved across and through world religions had formatively influenced the appearance of comparative religions as an academic field within the United States.[38] While it might be easy to extend the individualistic ethos of Emerson's spiritual seeker here forward into the consumerist marketplace of the New Age – sampling a little bit of this, just a little bit of that – and to construe accordingly Emerson's model of world religions as something akin to global capitalism, if we were to tarry longer with Emerson's respective entanglements with Buddhism, Hinduism, and Islam, other kinds of selves might emerge, ones that chafe against Taylor's "buffered self" of modernity and perhaps its problematic corollary, the shopper in the marketplace of decontextualized religion. In Emerson's poem "Hamatreya," for example, first published in 1847, the title loosely indicates a passage in the Vishnu Purana that Emerson's poem departs from. "Hamatreya" begins by indicating the hubris of various property owners ("Minnott, Lee, Willard, Hosmer, Meriam, Flint") who claim personal ownership of the earth. The earth then responds in the second half with an "Earth Song" that dissolves "the lawyer's deed" and "the lawyer, and the laws,/and the kingdom,/Clean swept herefrom" (CW 9: 69–70). The poem concludes with a remarkable quatrain, especially when one recalls it was written by a man who had once exhumed his dead lover's corpse:

> When I heard the Earth-song
> I was no longer brave;
> My avarice cooled
> Like lust in the chill of the grave. (CW 9: 70)

Emerson's ethical coordinates here are not drawn from his Calvinist heritage, with its trepidations about the fallen world; it rather come from where his painful, private experience of death meets the metaphysics of Vedanta, which informs this flower-song from the green world: "Earth laughs in flowers, to see her boastful boys/Earth-proud, proud of the earth which is not theirs" (CW 9: 69). The poem performs an undoing of the modern link between personhood and private property, dissolving its attendant spaces of the "lawyer, and the law." In our twenty-first century, as the climate crisis shows no sign of abating anytime soon – and it sure is getting hot down here – these kinds of moments in Emerson remain salient, trenchant places for thinking about how encounters with religious others can productively decenter selfhoods and suggest alternative kinds of relations with one another and with the planet. Indeed, many of the tensions that colored Emerson's prismatic, pluralizing approach to religion in the nineteenth century are ones that continue to trouble our own twenty-first. In the "shipwreck" of meaning commenced by the pulverizing of traditional religion, Emerson was clear about where he felt one could nevertheless find mooring: "Many opinions conflict as to the true centre. In the shipwreck, some cling to running rigging, some to cask and barrel, some to spars, some to mast; the pilot chooses with science, — I plant myself here; all will sink before this; 'he comes to land who sails with me'" (CW 4: 81). Nevertheless, Emerson's science remained profoundly Transcendental, filled with a reverence and wonder at the numinosity of the phenomenal world, his undying conviction that spiritual laws followed the selfsame principles as gravity and light.

## Notes

1. Nathaniel Hawthorne, *Tales and Sketches* (New York: Library of America, 1996), 1135–36.
2. There is a long critical tradition of claiming Emerson as a secularist; see, for example, George Kateb, *Emerson and Self-Reliance* (New York: Rowman & Littlefield Publishers, Inc., 2002), 81–83. Emerson's influence on alternative American spiritual currents such as New Thought have been variously addressed by Catherine Albanese, *A Republic of Mind and Spirit: A Cultural History of American Metaphysical Religion* (New Haven: Yale University Press, 2007), Leigh Eric Schmidt, *Restless Souls: the Making of American Spirituality* (Berkeley: University of California Press, 2012), and by John Haller, *History of New Thought: From Mind Cure to Positive Thinking and the Prosperity Gospel* (West Chester: Swedenborg Foundation Publishers, 2012). The "dark green nature" spirituality that dilates out of Emerson, through Thoreau, and onto John Muir and later figures such as Edward Abbey is the focus of Bron Taylor, *Dark Green Religion: Nature Spirituality and the Planetary Future* (Berkeley: University of California Press, 2010), as well as Devin Zuber, *A Language of Things: Emanuel Swedenborg and the American Environmental Imagination* (Charlottesville: University of Virginia Press, 2020). Allen Tate's memorable reading of Emerson as the blinded "Lucifer of Concord" is in Allen Tate, *Reactionary Essays on Poetry and Ideas* (New York: C. Scribner's Sons, 1936), 7; Emerson as capitalism's poet-philosopher is in Thomas P. Hughes, *Human Built World: How to Think about Technology and Culture* (Chicago: University of Chicago Press, 2005), 38.
3. Herwig Friedl usefully observes how the "stubbornly recurring" claims for Emerson as an Idealist is symptomatic of a "more conservative and traditionalist" line of readings, one that continues to obscure Emerson's indebtedness to a disruptive line of Platonic skeptics, such as Heraclitus and Sextus Empiricus. Herwig Friedl, *Thinking in Search of a Language: Essays on American Intellect and Intuition* (London: Bloomsbury Academic, 2019), 41–43.

4. See Stanley Cavell, *Emerson's Transcendental Etudes* (Stanford: Stanford University Press, 2003), an approach furthered by Joan Richardson, Branka Arsić, and Friedl, among others. For Bloom's idiosyncratic take on Emerson's "religious criticism," see Harold Bloom, *The American Religion: The Emergence of the Post-Christian Nation* (New York: Simon and Schuster, 1992), and *Agon: Towards a Theory of Revisionism* (New York: Oxford University Press, 1982), 145–78. Emerson as the great philosopher of the (ir)relevant is in Elisa Tamarkin, *Apropos of Something: A History of Irrelevance and Relevance* (Chicago: University of Chicago Press, 2022), 62.

5. Catherine Albanese, *The Delight Makers Anglo-American Metaphysical Religion and the Pursuit of Happiness* (Chicago: University of Chicago Press, 2023), 83.

6. The same spring (1838) Emerson offended Norton with his "Harvard Divinity School Address," the Massachusetts Supreme Court convicted freethinker Abner Kneeland for blasphemy. See Phillip Gura, *American Transcendentalism: A History* (New York: Hill and Wang, 2007), 110.

7. Robert Richardson, *Emerson: The Mind on Fire* (Berkeley: University of California Press, 1995), 346; Emerson purchased a fifteen-volume set of Goethe (in English translation), in 1836, and excitedly told his brother William that he "read little else than his books lately." Ronald A. Bosco and Joel Myerson, *The Emerson Brothers: A Fraternal Biography in Letters* (New York: Oxford University Press, 2005), 100–12.

8. Johann Wolfgang Goethe, *Faust I & II*, edited and translated by Stuart Atkins (Princeton: Princeton University Press, 1984), 123.

9. Branka Arsić thinks Emerson is specifically keying photography at the end of "Spiritual Laws." But given Emerson's substantial engagement with the scientist John Herschel (son of William, the discoverer of Uranus), who pioneered advancements in astronomical optics, the photometer as a specialized instrument to measure the light spectrum is certainly being implied. Branka Arsić, *On Leaving: A Reading in Emerson* (Cambridge, MA: Harvard University Press, 2010), 138.

10. Emerson's pursuit of truth was not a solitary endeavor but participated in a collaborative "moral economy of knowledge" with others, as Walls puts it. Laura Dassow Walls, *Emerson's Life in Science: The Culture of Truth* (Cornell: Cornell University Press, 2003), 15.

11. The "return of religion" announced at the turn of the twenty-first century by Peter Berger (*Desecularization of the World*), Jürgen Habermas, and others and has continued in the wake of Talal Asad's influential critique of various theories of secularization; see Talal Asad, *Formations of the Secular: Christianity, Islam, Modernity* (Stanford: Stanford University Press, 2003), 13–14.

12. Joan Richardson, *A Natural History of Pragmatism: The Fact of Feeling from Jonathan Edwards to Gertrude Stein* (New York: Cambridge University Press, 2007), 62–97.

13. Richardson, *Emerson*, 64–65.

14. Robert Richardson, *Three Roads Back: How Emerson, Thoreau, and William James Responded to the Greatest Losses of their Lives* (Princeton: Princeton University Press, 2023), 9–10.

15. See *CW* 2: 83.

16. The best account of Emerson's Paris "conversion" is still Lee Rust Brown, *The Emerson Museum: Practical Romanticism and the Pursuit of the Whole* (Cambridge, MA: Harvard University Press, 1997).

17. Walls, *Emerson's Life in Science*, 90.

18. See Versluis, *The Esoteric Origins of the American Renaissance* (New York: Oxford University Press, 2001), 124–46.

19. "This formed world has manifested itself with the motion of all forms with this visible world, as with a visible likeness, so that the spiritual being might be manifest in a corporeal comprehensive essence; as the desire of the inward forms has made itself external, and the internal being is in the external; the internal holds the external before it as a glass, wherein it beholds itself in the property of the generation of all forms; the external is its signature." Jakob Böhme, *The Signature of All Things: Signatura Rerum* (New York: Cosimo, 2007), 12.

20. Walls, *Emerson's Life in Science*, 167.

21. Charles Taylor, *A Secular Age* (Cambridge: Belknap Press, 2007), 37–42.

22. Böhme qtd. in PD Ouspensky, *Tertium Organum: The Third Canon of Thought, A Key to the Enigmas of the World*, translated from the Russian by Nicholas Bessaraboff and Claude Bragdon (Philadelphia: Emergence Education, 2022), 280.

23. Phillip Gura, *The Wisdom of Words: Language, Theology, and Literature in the New England Renaissance* (Middletown, CT: Wesleyan University Press, 1985), 20–21, 88.

24. Hans Blumenberg, *Die Lesbarkeit der Welt* (Berlin: Suhrkamp, 1981), 214–66.

25. Perry Miller, *The New England Mind: From Colony to Province* (Cambridge, MA: Harvard University Press, 1983), 213.

26. Miller, "From Edwards to Emerson," in *Errand into the Wilderness* (Cambridge, MA: Harvard University Press, 1984), 184–203.

27. Richardson, *Emerson*, 23.

28. Mary Moody Emerson qtd. in Phyllis Cole, *Mary Moody Emerson and the Origins of Transcendentalism: A Family History* (New York: Oxford University Press, 2002), 288; Emerson's reply is qtd. in Clarence Hotson, "Sampson Reed, A Teacher of Emerson," *New England Quarterly* 2 (April 1929): 251.

29. Cole, *Mary Moody*, 169–70; see also Alan Hodder, "Emerson, Rammohan Roy, and the Unitarians," *Studies in the American Renaissance* (1988): 133–35.

30. For an astute discussion of how many so-called "New Americanist" critics have read Emerson as imperialist, see Johannes Voelz, *Transcendental Resistance: The New Americanists and Emerson's Challenge* (Hanover: Dartmouth College Press, 2010), 175–204.

31. See also Rob Wilson, *Be Always Converting, Be Always Converted* (Cambridge, MA: Harvard University Press, 2009).

32. See the important correction of the record here in the updated edition of Thomas Tweed, *The American Encounter with Buddhism, 1844–1912: Victorian Culture and the Limits of Dissent* (Chapel Hill, NC: The University of North Carolina Press, 2000), xvi–xvii.

33. Edward Said, *Culture and Imperialism* (New York: Vintage Books), 1994.

34. Wai Chi Dimock, *Through Other Continents: American Literature Across Deep Time* (Princeton: Princeton University Press, 2009), 32.

35. Ibid., 36.

36. See also Asad, *Genealogies of Religion*, and Tomoko Masuzawa, *The Invention of World Religions: Or, How European Universalism was Preserved in the Language of Pluralism* (Chicago: University of Chicago Press, 2005), although neither author explicitly deals with Emerson.

37. Schmidt, *Restless Souls*, 228–29. See also Tracy Fessenden's discussion of Emerson amidst the American nineteenth century's "spiritual turn" which "starts and pivots from the materiality of death." Tracy Fessenden, "Haunted America: Reading the Spiritual Turn" in *Above the American Renaissance: David S. Reynolds and the Spiritual Imagination in American Literary Studies*, ed. Harold K. Bush and Brian Yothers (Amherst: University of Massachusetts Press, 2018), 24.

38. Gura, *American Transcendentalism*, 267–94.

# 3

JENNIFER J. BAKER

# Emerson and Transnational Romanticism

In what is often described as ironic, Ralph Waldo Emerson drew inspiration from European Romanticism in his call for American cultural independence. But was his embrace of these literary and philosophical works actually at odds with the project of creating a new national culture? Emerson reserves the right to contradict himself, of course, but his intellectual debts were never inconsistent with his vision of cultural independence. This complex relation to European Romanticism becomes evident when considering several key Romantic concepts in Emerson's works: most notably genius, idealism, and originality. Because Emerson understood the genius to be a teacher who empowers his students to reject him, he could imagine any reliance on Coleridge, Wordsworth, or Carlyle as ultimately enabling independence. Moreover, the philosophical idealism that was so essential to Emerson's call for cultural independence was not, in his view, fundamentally English or even German but, rather, a mode of perception that defied national categorization and, hence, did not threaten the distinctive US culture he hoped to inaugurate. Finally, Emerson began to clarify in his later writings a concept of originality that involved the adaptation of inherited forms rather than the invention of new ones; in this way, he envisioned borrowing as a precondition for innovation.

## *Nature* as Romantic Manifesto

The Romantic encounters that shaped Emerson's intellectual development have been well documented by scholars.[1] Central to this story are German and English Romantic concepts of selfhood and subjectivity, which led Emerson out of a period of crisis following his resignation from the Unitarian ministry and catalyzed the writing of his first book, *Nature* (1836). *Nature* describes humans in a state of crisis. Although the book presents the crisis as a universal one, Emerson has in mind the white, college-educated New England men he felt had become spiritually and intellectually deadened by

Unitarianism. In his account, humans are alienated from – or as Wordsworth said, "out of tune" with – the natural world and no longer alive to its wonders.[2] This alienation correlates with another: "man is disunited with himself," Emerson laments, psychically divided between his essential self and the self that performs according to society's expectations (CW 1: 43). Emerson urges readers to return to nature and regain a sense of its wondrousness, but also to return to – and trust in – their essential natures. As it turns out, full maturation involves, paradoxically, never fully abandoning the insouciance of childhood. The "lover of nature is he whose inward and outward senses are still truly adjusted to each other," Emerson declares, "who has retained the spirit of infancy even into the era of manhood" (CW 1: 9). This man-boy and lover of nature will lead the way to new culture, new laws, and new traditions.

At the heart of *Nature* is a question that had preoccupied Kant and post-Kantian thinkers: Does the material world determine the mind's perceptions or vice versa, does consciousness determine the material world? Emerson drew assistance from Coleridge, who himself had borrowed liberally from Friedrich Wilhelm Joseph von Schelling in formulating his own answer: "During the act of knowledge itself," Coleridge concludes in the *Biographia Literaria*, "the objective and subjective are so instantly united, that we cannot determine to which of the two the priority belongs."[3] The mind perceives the world independently, and the world exists independent of the mind, and yet human perceptions perfectly match that material reality. The laws of nature and the laws of mind are commensurate; hence, to study nature is to study oneself. As Emerson writes in "The Over-Soul," "the act of seeing and the thing seen, the seer and the spectacle, the subject and the object, are one" (CW 2: 160).

Emerson is not, however, always resolved about this commensurability. In the "Idealism" chapter of *Nature*, he admits a "noble doubt" that outward nature even exists because there is no way for a mind to verify nature's independent existence. In the end, it does not matter whether "nature enjoy a substantial existence without, or is only in the apocalypse of the mind," he writes. "Be it what it may, it is ideal to me, so long as I cannot try the accuracy of my senses" (CW 1: 29). Whether or not a material world exists independently, in other words, does not matter because all a mind can ever know is what exists in the realm of ideas. Whether outward nature exists and conforms to the mind's perceptions or whether that nature does not exist at all, one key fact remains: the mind is not constrained by the material world and so freely determines the objects of its perception. Coleridge's distinction between Understanding and Reason, a reworking of Kant's earlier distinction, is essential to this concept of freedom. Understanding, a lower faculty that handles sense data, is constrained by the material world, but Reason, a faculty that affords unmediated insight into what lies beyond it, is intuitive and requires no external proof or logical maneuvers. The "dependence of the understanding on the representations of the Senses" contrasts with the "independence and antecedency of Reason," Coleridge concludes in *Aids to Reflection*.[4]

Drawing on Romantic theories of subjectivity, Emerson saw the exercise of the mind's freedom as the mark of a healthy self that was capable of development. In essays such as "Self-Reliance" and "The American Scholar," Emerson draws from the gestational imagery used in English and German Romantic writing to talk about this cultivation of the self and mind. This literary construction of selfhood was also mutually involved with Romantic life science, which located power in internal growth rather than in external force. In the transformation of a seed from germ to adult form through cell differentiation, Romantic poets and scientists alike saw confirmation of the creative and expressive capacities of both the natural world and the human mind. Indeed, Emerson's attraction to Romantic dynamism would make him all the more receptive to theories of biological evolution.

This concept of the mind's freedom carried political implications. As Ian Copestake explains, *Nature* provided a "metaphysical justification" for the rejection of traditional authority exemplified by the French and American Revolutions.[5] Central to Emerson's project of transferring authority from tradition to the self was his creation of various outlier figures – the genius, the poet, the madman, the child – who followed their own conscience rather than the laws of the state or public consensus. That this so-called higher law was available to everyone was a Romantic conviction that held particular appeal for the Transcendentalists. In his 1833 review of *Aids to Reflection*, Frederic Henry Hedge praised Coleridge for placing "common opinions and general experience of mankind" on a "scientific basis." Emphasizing the egalitarian implications of this theory of conscience, Theodore Parker declared, "the *first man* knew this *moral* law, as well as the last shall know it. Here at least all men are equal."[6]

Emerson's healthy self is an "aboriginal Self" – wild, natural, nonconformist – a figure that draws from the "noble savage" trope of European Romanticism as well as Americanized versions found in James Fenimore Cooper's Leatherstocking tales and sentimental representations of Native Americans by writers such as Lydia Maria Child and Lydia Sigourney (*CW* 2: 37). Grounding the self's authority in its essential naturalness both echoed European Romantic environmental writing and provided a foundation for the American environmental movement. As James C. McKusick notes, Emerson believed in the necessity of "wildness," which was a feature of natural surroundings but also a state of mind and "quality of human perception." In nature's presence "a wild delight *runs* through the man, in spite of real sorrows," Emerson writes, "[i]n the woods is perpetual youth" (*CW* 1: 10). Although Emerson does not voice urgent concerns about land-clearing and species extinction, his insistence that the human spirit depends upon restorative wildness would shape Thoreau's conviction that "in Wildness is the preservation of the World." For the thousands of "tired, nerve-shaken, over-civilized people," John Muir would write at the dawn of the next century, "wildness is a necessity."[7] The wild individual answers to no authority but his own, and yet he is a figure born of European Romantic tradition and reflects Emerson's lifelong engagement with European culture. *Nature* demands for Americans their "own works and laws and worship," but Emerson will devote considerable energy to thinking about how to forge those new traditions by adapting, rather than rejecting outright, those of the past (*CW* 1: 7).

## Beyond *Nature*

Emerson's Romanticism was indispensable to the reconstruction of American literary history in the twentieth century. Winfried Fluck notes that Americanist scholarship, beginning with F. O. Matthiessen's *American Renaissance*, identified the Romantic celebration of intuition as the major catalyst for the "original, aesthetically innovative forms of culture" that constituted America's first literary flowering in the mid nineteenth century. In turning to intuition, the story goes, American writers learned to trust themselves, overcome their "cultural inferiority," and shed the nation's "provincial culture." Crucially, moreover, it was through intuition that the writer could represent the American populace. The "immediate intuition into the divine mind" brought literature closer to an absolute truth, Matthiessen wrote, but because this intuition was also an "outwelling from the universal mind," it made that literature more responsive to common concerns. Emerson's intellectual growth, according to Matthiessen, was fostered "not merely by the renascence of idealistic philosophy, but likewise by his eager apprehension of the possibilities of American democracy."[8]

Emerson's Romanticism is often conceived as something transplanted, but the metaphor can falsely suggest that Romanticism was a static import, a set of settled principles that crossed the ocean and took hold in US soil. What Emerson encountered in English and German Romantic works, in fact, was as much debate as doctrine, and the exact nature of the idealism that Emerson formulated as a result of those encounters is not easy to pin down. In her 1838 review of *Nature*, Elizabeth Peabody acknowledged that readers might be frustrated with Emerson's characterization of the "relation between mind and matter" as the "yet unsolved problem" despite attempts at a solution by a great many thinkers. Peabody stressed, however, that Emerson's goal is not to "give his own solution of the enigma" but, rather, to tell us "the condition of solving it ourselves."[9] The transplantation metaphor is especially misleading if it suggests that *Nature* proposed simply another version of post-Kantian idealism. *Nature* was certainly inspired by this idealism, as it was transmitted through the works of Coleridge and Carlyle as well as reviews and critical histories by Hedge, James Marsh, Victor Cousin, and Germaine de Staël, but, as Thomas Constantinesco explains, the book emerged, in fact, from a "tangled reception" of these ideas along with several other philosophical strands, including Platonism, Neo-Platonism, and Scottish Common Sense philosophy. Emerson considered the Platonic doctrine of ideas to be the root of his own era's Transcendentalist thought, declaring that the German Romantics were "semi-Greeks" (*CW* 5: 142). Prior to his discovery of Coleridge, his aunt Mary Moody Emerson and the French Eclectic Victor Cousin also introduced Emerson to Dugald Stewart's Common Sense argument that truth arose from the mind's constitution rather than sensory experience. This conviction about the mind's creative power was also reinforced by readings in Eastern philosophy, Emmanuel Swedenborg's correspondence theory, and the natural philosophy of practicing naturalists who aimed to discover a metaphysical unity underlying nature's biodiversity. For this reason, Constantinesco cautions that Emerson's "customary syncretism" and "loose practice of quotation" make it "difficult if not impossible to exactingly parse his philosophical borrowings."[10]

While *Nature* is Emerson's most emphatic statement of Romantic idealism, it is not, of course, characteristic of all his thinking. Stephen E. Whicher's 1953 account of Emerson's inner life, which charts a trajectory from confidence to skepticism, has powerfully shaped how scholars understand Emerson's departure from Romanticism in his later writings.[11] Although Romantic concerns do not disappear entirely, his understanding of mind-matter relations certainly changes. In works such as "Experience," "Nominalist and Realist," "The Method of Nature," and the 1844 essay "Nature," the natural world eludes human understanding and is no longer imbued with readily perceptible meaning as it had been in *Nature*. Both David Jacobson and Jonathan Levin, in fact, identify the 1844 "Nature" as a key rejection of the commensurability of mind and nature. Jacobson has characterized the essay as an antihumanist text that stresses nature's indifference to the mind's perceptions, and Levin has described the work as a meditation on the limits of human cognition.[12]

Whereas in *Nature* Emerson takes the "issue of skepticism as solvable or controllable," Stanley Cavell writes, "thereafter he takes its unsolvability to be the heart of his thinking." *Nature*'s core question about subject-object relations seem to lose its urgency in the later writings. These writings become "antirepresentationalist," Cary Wolfe argues, as Emerson comes to conclude that "neither does thought determine reality, nor … does reality determine thought."[13] The later writings also bear the hallmarks of a distinctly American form of pragmatism that contrasts notably with the idealism of *Nature*. Ideas in Emerson's late writing are not universal truths so much as catalysts for subsequent thought. "The retrospective value of each new thought is immense," Emerson declares in a late lecture titled "Powers of the Mind," "'Tis like a torch applied to a long train of powder" (*LL* 2: 78). In these influential readings of Emerson's career, Romanticism is a brief phase, only a prelude to his more mature philosophy.

There are scholars who do not see Emerson's career in stark bifurcated terms. Joseph Urbas, for example, has argued that there is more continuity in Emerson's philosophical positions than Cavell acknowledges. In particular, Urbas finds that Emerson's conception of human "moral sentiment" as a manifestation of nature's laws – and hence the grounds for linking the self and the world – was "something Emerson emphasized consistently throughout his career."[14] Urbas also joins Douglas R. Anderson in reading Emerson's shifts in thinking not as rupture but as dialectical method: an effort to arrive at a vision of reality that includes both Platonic unity and the varieties of experience.[15]

Despite distinctive changes in the later writing, there is also never a clean break with Romanticism in Emerson's thought. Romantic preoccupations with genius, self-culture, and poetic imagination persist, and even the later antirepresentational and pragmatic sensibilities can be traced back to a particular strain of Romantic thought. While the later Emerson abandons his trust in the permanent essence of words, symbolic meaning, and the metaphysical unity of nature, he turns from Romanticism only in the sense that he gives up a Romantic longing for "original relation," seeing instead a world that is continually in flux – imagining poetry, in Barbara L. Packer's words, as a "perpetual play of tropes." But if, as Packer argues, Emerson finally weans himself from the "concept of origins that had tantalized him for so long," we should remember that flux itself was also a lesson of European Romantic thinking, which posited that the universe and mind were always growing and changing.[16] Emerson's intense fascination with metamorphosis, in fact, was fostered by his readings in German *Naturphilosophie* and Romantically inflected natural history.

If the aesthetic philosophy of *Nature* does not represent the entirety of Emerson thought, it also does not represent the entirety of Romantic literary practice in the mid nineteenth-century United States. Americans read, enjoyed, and took inspiration from European Romantic works in various ways. Through the writings of Wordsworth, Coleridge, William Blake, Percy Shelley, and Lord George Byron, American readers absorbed ideas about the primacy of the self, the rejection of tradition, and the recreation of the world, but they did not necessarily associate those ideas with the question of subject-object relations central to *Nature*. Even among early Transcendentalists, Packer notes, readers read Byron and Walter Scott with "uncritical delight" and did not necessarily concern themselves with epistemology. Moreover, Alfred Bendixen has shown that many popular US poets practiced "varieties of romanticism that are quite different from the Transcendentalist tradition." Bendixen credits Emerson for introducing Americans to the liberating possibilities of Romantic modes, but he also argues that American Romanticism has its "real beginnings" not in New England but in New York. In the decade prior to *Nature*, he notes, the poems of Hudson River School painter Thomas Cole lamented the loss of wilderness and contemplated the powers of the human imagination in its encounters with nature.[17]

Making Emersonian Romanticism synonymous with American Romanticism yields a skewed picture of Romantic literary practice in the United States, particularly because much of Emerson's embrace of Romanticism was rooted in disenchantment. Emerson and like-minded New Englanders were unhappy with Unitarianism, which, in throwing off the superstitions of Puritanism, had become a "corpse-cold" religion (*JMN* 9: 381). They were unhappy with the Harvard curriculum and its emphasis on rote learning and Lockean empiricism. They were unhappy with William Paley and a rational Christianity that did not attempt to move its followers so much as convince them through arguments. Compounding these frustrations was a concern that the United States had left unfinished the work of the Revolutionary Age. Copestake describes Emersonian Romanticism, in fact, as a "critique of America's institutionalized failure" to live up to the ideals of the nation's founding, and Richard Gravil reads American Romanticism more generally as a "sustained effort" to redeem the political tentativeness of their English precursors.[18]

This understanding of Romanticism as a response to dissatisfaction is thoroughly ingrained in Emerson scholarship – reinforced by the common understanding of European Romanticism itself as a reaction to Enlightenment rationalism, industrialization, or modern science. And yet dissatisfaction does not necessarily account for the Romantic inclinations outside Emerson's circle. William St. Clair's history of book publishing in the Romantic era, for example, points to other possible explanations for Romanticism's rising popularity in the United States in the 1830s and 40s.

Examining the "processes by which the texts reached the hands, and there-fore potentially the minds," of readers, St. Clair charts how Romantic ideas gained, sustained, and lost popularity. Following the passage of the US Copyright Act of 1790, which excluded foreign authors from copy-right protection in the United States, American publishers flooded the book markets of New York, Boston, and Philadelphia with cheap reprints of works by Byron, Scott, Wordsworth, Coleridge, Austen, and the Shelleys. New stereotyping techniques allowed them to use cloned plates for decades, and these plentiful, inexpensive editions fueled the popularity of English writing at a time when US authors were calling for a national literature. According to St. Clair, Romantic works circulated among more economically diverse readers in the United States than had ever been possible in England.[19]

New literary circles and professional associations also contributed to Romanticism's vogue in the United States. David O. Dowling has detailed how these groups originated to provide aspiring authors with training and financial support so they could compete in the literary marketplace. Romantic intellectuals like Elizabeth Peabody and Horace Greeley acted as proto-literary agents, promoting these writers' works and disseminat-ing the "foundational principles of Romanticism" to the wider public, and Emerson himself served as a patron to younger writers – most notably Margaret Fuller and Henry David Thoreau – and shaped them in his image. The commercial and collaborative orientation of these professional groups could ironically be at odds with Romanticism's celebration of the solitary genius and its critique of the commodification of art, but these organizations nevertheless played a vital role in fueling Romanticism's popularity.[20]

## *English Traits* and Literary Independence

In *Atlantic Double-Cross* (1989), a study that owes much to Harold Bloom's theory of the anxiety of influence, Robert Weisbuch characterizes the nineteenth-century American writer as always struggling against his lit-erary forebears. This writer "begins from a defensive position" because the "achievements of British literature and British national life are the chief intimidations against which he, as American representative, defends him-self." A similar understanding of Anglo-American literary relations informs the introduction to the more recent anthology *Transatlantic Romanticism*, in which editors Lance Newman, Joel Pace, and Chris Koenig-Woodyard write that the Romantic era's "transatlantic cultural exchange" took place "within the defining structure of Britain's imperial and cultural dominance."[21] English Romanticism, they argue, is a form of aesthetic imperialism that was particularly vexing for a new nation trying to rid itself of all traces of dependence.

For many scholars, Emerson exemplifies this defensive posture. An oft-cited case in point is the opening chapter of *English Traits*, in which Emerson recollects his disappointing encounters with Coleridge and Wordsworth. Visiting the older poets in 1833, Emerson is struck by the "hard limits" of Wordsworth's thoughts and Coleridge's tendency to "commonplaces." Emerson acknowledges that literary celebrities generally disappoint in face-to-face encounters because the "conditions of literary success are almost destructive of the best social power" (*CW* 5: 2, 7, 12). However, rather than see this disappointment as the logical consequence of unrealistic, or even naïve, expectations, Weisbuch, Gravil, Julie Ellison, Leon Chai, Patrick Keane, and David LaRocca, among others, have argued that Emerson emphasizes this disillusionment in order to disavow his literary idols. Keane finds that Emerson needs to be "disappointed in order to preserve the autonomy of his own 'aboriginal Self.'" LaRocca concurs, arguing that English influence places Emerson in a paradoxical relation to origins: "the achievement of being original, in this sense – free to seek the aboriginal Self, to have an original relation – demands a denial of origins." Ellison argues that Emerson "has to deny that he stands in an imitative relation to European culture" and so he concludes that "Europe stands in an imitative, or false, relation to the soul, of which he is the representative."[22] In these arguments, Emerson's disdain is at times a conscious performance to cover up his private adoration of English writers, and at other times, it is an unconscious rationalization that helps him resolve his conflicted relationship with Europe. Either way, these scholars assume that Emerson's debts to English culture are intolerable, prompting him to "protect his autonomy," as Ellison puts it, by diminishing the "Old World's power through criticism." Emerson erases signs of "learned ideas," Weisbuch concludes, effectively "covering his tracks in the New England snow" because he cannot "acknowledge the history of European romantic poetics and philosophy as a chief presence in his thought."[23]

There is, however, a different way to read Emerson's disavowal. According to Emerson, a true genius teaches students to value their *own* thoughts, and this instruction ultimately brings about their independence. Far from mere "tuition," the work of genius inspires by making possible the recognition of "majesty." Encountering such works, students learn "to abide by [their] spontaneous impression with good-humored inflexibility" (*CW* 2: 27). Although they learn self-trust and insist on their own intuitions, they never deny the initial value of the encounter – if anything, rejection is the fitting *culmination* of a productive relationship. While "overinfluence" stifles independence, a healthy influence enables it (*CW* 1: 57). Given this understanding of genius, why would Emerson ever feel a need to "cover his tracks" and deny any earlier admiration of English poetry and thought?

Another problem with these readings of *English Traits* is that the Romanticism that inspired Emerson decades earlier is never presented in that book as English *per se*. *English Traits* aligns Englishness with those qualities and attitudes that have generated the English nation's power: practicality, materialism, mercantilism, imperialism, and industry. Emerson has mixed feelings about this Englishness. As Elisa Tamarkin notes, he appreciates the English people's plain-dealing and adherence to "things as they are," but, as Wesley T. Mott observes, he also praises those traits "only to expose these virtues as noxious when exaggerated, stagnant, ossified."[24] Such English traits can only enable transformative ideas once they are properly elevated. "The Saxon materialism and narrowness, exalted into the sphere of intellect, makes the very genius of Shakespeare and Milton," Emerson writes. "When it reaches the pure element, it treads the clouds as surely as the adamant. Even in its elevations materialistic, its poetry is common sense inspired; or iron raised to white heat." Using metaphors of distillation, purification, and elevation, Emerson proposes that English materialism enables its own transcendence, producing, in fact, a mindset that is very much at odds with mainstream English culture. For this reason, Emerson writes, "there is at all times a *minority* of profound minds existing in the nation, capable of appreciating every soaring of intellect and every hint of tendency" (*CW* 5: 132, 145 my emphasis). According to Philip Nicoloff, Coleridge and Carlyle exemplified this iconoclasm, positioning themselves against the grain of English culture and becoming for Emerson – at least in their younger days – "apostles of an international freedom and caustic critics of their native contemporaries."[25]

The title of *English Traits* is misleading, for although it aims to define English national character, it also insists on a "soaring of intellect" that transcends the nation (*CW* 5: 145). The book's central project is informed by a Romantic concept of national identity rooted in climate, geography, language, culture, and heredity. In this respect, it bears the influence of Johann Gottfried Herder's theory of folk culture as well as studies of the Germans by de Staël and Carlyle, both of whom celebrated travel, translation, and border-crossing while still keeping the nation intact. Although this Romantic nationalism is often understood as a break with the Enlightenment concept of universal belonging, it co-existed, in fact, with a Romantic cosmopolitanism that was closely tied to poetic imagination. The Romantic poet, as Johannes Voelz explains, "belonged to a select group of kindred spirits defined solely by their shared access to a higher realm of ideas" and hence was "not subject to social conventions and geographical boundaries."[26] In the essay "History," Robert D. Richardson, Jr., notes, Emerson extends this concept to all individuals, arguing that each person is already an incarnation of a universal mind and so never "determined by earlier, or stronger, influences."[27]

Ideas or art that might seem to be merely derivative, then, could actually be the reflection of this higher realm. Recalling his encounters with European architecture, Emerson writes in *Nature*, "The American who has been confined, in his own country, to the sight of buildings designed after foreign models, is surprised on entering York Minster or St. Peter's at Rome, by the feeling that these structures are imitations also, – faint copies of an invisible archetype" (CW 1: 40). Weisbuch reads this moment as an attempt by Emerson to diminish European culture by making the original an unbodied ideal rather than the brainchild of England or Italy. Emerson's point, however, is that a single truth finds different permutations over time and space, and therefore to follow "foreign models" is not mere copying but, rather, tapping into a universal. Seen this way, the use of foreign models would not prompt the kind of rationalization or defensive posture that Weisbuch discerns in the passage.

The archetype Emerson describes is *original* because it is primeval. For Emerson, however, true art is also innovative – *original* in its late eighteenth-century sense of being new and distinctly expressive of the individual artist. In "The Poet," Emerson celebrates the poet as never imitative, and yet he also declares that "poetry was all written before time was." Poets produce the "songs of the nations" because their finer organization allows them to hear the "primal warblings" and "write down these cadences more faithfully" (CW 3: 5–6). Emerson's conception of art as *both* old and new shapes how he understands American cultural independence vis-à-vis Europe. Because Emerson believed each nation and age could leave its own mark on inherited ideas, he saw America's intellectual debts to European Romanticism as part of an adaptive process through which the US would ultimately contribute to world culture.

## Adapting Tradition in *Representative Men*

Understanding Emerson's relationship to European Romanticism requires understanding how he conceived originality itself. As a number of scholars have shown, Emerson's later writings, particularly *Representative Men* (1855) and the essay "Quotation and Originality" (1859), posit a version of originality that does not involve wholesale creation. According to Packer, Emerson's exposure to textual source studies – German Higher Criticism of the Bible and scholarship on Shakespeare and Homer – led him to reject theories of literary origins and conclude, instead, that "'originality' is simply the compliment we pay" to poets skilled in theft and compilation. Christopher Newfield finds that the later Emerson comes to define originality as a "communal tradition," one that is at odds with possessive individualism because the poet's greatness actually derives from "achieving some identity with the masses."[28]

The Romantic concept of natural flux dramatically shaped Emerson's depiction of the genius's relation to earlier traditions. According to this model of creation, new forms derive from prior ones through a process of adaptation, distinguishing themselves incrementally through small but crucial variations that over time add up to notable change; likewise, the genius works by quoting, borrowing, and adapting earlier models. The economy of writerly production, which "argues a very small capital of invention," Emerson writes in "Quotation and Originality," does not depend on a large stock of newness (CW 8: 94). The genius does not reject earlier traditions in favor of creating *ex nihilo* but, rather, creatively modifies what has come before. In his essay on Goethe in *Representative Men*, Emerson borrows a term from natural history to describe literary works as "second creations." Whereas God's "prime creation" of the universe is the original act of creation, it is through "second creations" (say, the generation of new species or rock formations) that nature continually remakes that primeval form over vast stretches of time. The writer who possesses "exalted powers for this second creation" does something similarly adaptive: Shakespeare, for example, lays a "finer stratum" on the "original rock." Just as biological or geological adaptations are products of their particular environment, these literary "second creations" are consistent with the time and place in which they are produced. The power of the genius "throws him into natural history, as a main production of the globe, and as announcing new eras and ameliorations" (CW 4: 112, 122, 152).

Juxtaposing the history of great men with the history of life-forms, Emerson writes, "great men exist that there may be greater men. The destiny of organized nature is amelioration, and who can tell its limits?" (CW 4: 20). Emerson imagines a succession of great men akin to the succession of ever-complex life-forms, each making possible the rise of a successor who subsequently supplants the first. The book is structured chronologically, beginning with a study of Plato and then turning to Swedenborg, Montaigne, Shakespeare, Napoleon, and Goethe, thus providing readers with a narrative chronicling how each genius owes his thought to prior ones.

In "Plato," the first essay in *Representative Men*, Emerson writes that St. Augustine, Copernicus, Newton, Swedenborg, and Goethe all formulated ideas that derived from this great "exhausting generalizer." It is "fair to credit the broadest generalizer," he writes of Plato, "with all the particulars deducible from his thesis." But even Plato derived his ideas from Socrates and a host of other pre-Socratic thinkers, Emerson reminds us. And in his discussion of Swedenborg, he notes that the manner in which many other men posited ideas roughly similar to those of the Swedish philosopher and mystic, making Swedenborg "another example of the difficulty, even in a highly fertile genius, of proving originality." Emerson's conviction that all geniuses have shared access to a higher realm of ideas works against the notion of a single intellectual progenitor. Perhaps most notably, his chapter on Shakespeare mocks the "petulant demand" of the nineteenth century for originality and the quest by antiquaries and the Shakespeare Society to search for the bard's sources, scouring dirty and tattered manuscripts to see who wrote what play first; Emerson concludes finally that we cannot know, and hence "no man can any longer claim copyright" (CW 4: 23, 60, 111, 113).

Many scholars have seen Emerson's late understanding of originality as a turn away from Romanticism (even if ironically it frees him to embrace his Romantic precursors). This conclusion, however, equates Emerson's early Romanticism exclusively with a longing to return to a numinous and absolute origin: that is, his interest in metamorphosis is understood as a rejection of the Romantic fixation on the primeval. It is important to note, however, that even in *Nature* what Emerson longs for is "original *relation*," not a return to origins *per se* (CW 1: 7, my emphasis). The metamorphosis posited by Romantic natural history, and later by Charles Darwin, always bears a relation to the original creation because its new forms bear the traces of prior forms; originality and metamorphosis, in other words, are not mutually exclusive. Such an "original relation," combining new and old, is strikingly evident in the Whitmanian self:

> I find I incorporate gneiss, coal, long-threaded moss, fruits, grains,
>     esculent roots,
> And am stucco'd with quadrupeds and birds all over,
> And have distanced what is behind me for good reasons,
> But call any thing back again when I desire it.[29]

Whitman's evolving self has left behind the original creation but can always return to it because he embodies the very vestiges of natural history. Metamorphosis, moreover, connects one to the original creation by reenacting the process that brought about the natural world in the first place. As Thoreau wrote after reading Darwin's *Origin of Species*, the "development" involved in speciation is "equivalent to a sort of constant *new* creation."[30]

Rather than see Emerson's interest in original relation as at odds with his interest in metamorphosis – the former Romantic and the latter post-Romantic – we should consider, instead, how Emerson imagined them as equally central to the same process of natural change. The genius's artistic and intellectual productions register a quality of the natural world: namely its propensity for constant "melioration." These creative works occupy an advanced position on the timeline of inheritance, adaptation, and improvement, making them both derivative and innovative, both vestiges of an original form and the product of flux. In the chapter on Goethe in *Representative Men*, Emerson frames the relationship between a writer and his literary forebears in terms of a Romantically inflected natural history. This chapter is one of Emerson's many meditations on the poet-naturalist and his famous studies of plant morphology. Goethe's *Metamorphosis of Plants* had argued that a single common plant structure produces leaves, branches, and flowers as a seed grows into a seedling and then a mature plant. Goethe's theory of replication and differentiation explains his own emergence as a thinker who improves upon his borrowed Platonic ideas (here Emerson emphasizes availing oneself of a usable past rather than creating anew). The "narrative" of human progress is not a narrative of continuous replication (what he calls restamping the "print of the seal") because nature always strives upward, producing a "new and finer form of the original" (*CW* 4: 151).

The invocation of natural history also helps us understand Goethe as a higher-order form that contains within him all traditions that have come before – a form not unlike the Whitmanian self. Emerson concludes the Goethe chapter, and indeed concludes the entire book, by declaring that "Man is the most composite of all creatures" (the simple wheel-insect is at the other extreme), and "[w]e shall learn to draw rents and revenues from the immense patrimony of the old and the recent ages" (*CW* 4: 166). Individual history is embedded in a larger human genealogy, which is, in turn, embedded in a larger genealogy of all life forms, and what makes Goethe a genius is not simply that he borrows and borrows well from his inheritance, but that he will not be beholden to that inheritance. Reversing his earlier stance against the encumbrances of tradition in the 1836 *Nature*, Emerson celebrates the unapologetic adaptation of prior works: Whereas in *Nature*, he had lamented that his age was "retrospective," in *Representative Men* he declares that "every thinker is retrospective" (*CW* 1: 7, 4: 114). As he writes in the conclusion of "Quotation and Originality," "The divine gift is ever the instant life, which receives, and uses, and creates, and can well bury the old in the omnipotency with which Nature decomposes all her harvest for recomposition" (*CW* 8: 107).

American writers adapted European Romanticism to their own intellectual needs, following what Thomas Constantinesco calls a "logic of difference and repetition" in their reception of European works and ideas.[31] Theorizing that adaptive process by way of Romantic natural history and theories of biological development, Emerson predicted that the United States would be on the vanguard of a cultural evolution. "When there is something to be done, the world knows how to get it done," he declares in "Fate," and just as plants and animals produce new structural adaptions, the planet produces individuals capable of advancing world culture. "Dante and Columbus were Italians, in their time: they would be Russians or Americans to-day. Things ripen, new men come. The adaptation is not capricious" (CW 6: 21). For Emerson, the nineteenth century would be America's moment, but the nation's innovations would be inextricably tied to past forms.

## Notes

1. See Robert E. Spiller, "Critical Standards in the American Romantic Movement," *College English* 8 (April 1947); Julie K. Ellison, *Emerson's Romantic Style* (Princeton: Princeton University Press, 1984); Robert Weisbuch, *Atlantic Double-Cross: American Literature and British Influence in the Age of Emerson* (Chicago: University of Chicago Press, 1986); Leon Chai, *The Romantic Foundations of the American Renaissance* (Ithaca: Cornell University Press, 1987); Russel B. Goodman, *American Philosophy and the Romantic Tradition* (Cambridge: Cambridge University Press, 1990); Richard Gravil, *Romantic Dialogues: Anglo-American Continuities, 1776–1842* (New York: St. Martin's Press, 2000); Patrick J. Keane, *Emerson, Romanticism, and Intuitive Reason: The Transatlantic "Light of All Our Day"* (Columbia: University of Missouri Press, 2005); Barbara L. Packer, *The Transcendentalists* (Athens: University of Georgia Press, 2007); David Greenham, *Emerson's Transatlantic Romanticism* (New York: Palgrave Macmillan, 2012).
2. William Wordsworth, "The world is too much with us; late and soon," in *Wordsworth's Poetry and Prose*, ed. Nicholas Halmi (New York: W.W. Norton, 2014), l.8, 403.
3. Samuel Taylor Coleridge, "Biographia Literaria," in *Coleridge's Poetry and Prose*, ed. Nicholas Halmi, Paul Magnuson, and Raimonda Modiano (New York: W.W. Norton, 2004), 467.
4. Samuel Taylor Coleridge, *Aids to Reflection, in The Collected Works of Samuel Taylor Coleridge*, ed. John B. Beer (Princeton, NJ: Princeton University Press, 1993), 236.
5. Ian D. Copestake, "American Romanticism: Approaches and Interpretations," in *Encyclopedia of the Romantic Era, 1760–1850*, ed. Christopher John Murray (New York: Routledge, 2003), 17.
6. Frederic Henry Hedge, "Coleridge's Literary Character," in *Transcendentalism: A Reader*, ed. Joel Myerson (Oxford: Oxford University Press, 2000), 89; Theodore Parker, "Conscience and the Moral Law," Theodore Parker Papers,

Andover-Harvard Theological Library, qtd.," in *Romantic Reformers and the Antislavery Struggle in the Civil War Era*, ed. Ethan J. Kytle (Cambridge: Cambridge University Press, 2014), 47–48.

7. James C. McKusick, *Green Writing: Romanticism and Ecology* (New York: St. Martin's Press, 2000), 123; Henry David Thoreau, "Walking," in *Wild Apples and Other Natural History Essays*, ed. William Rossi (Athens: University of Georgia Press, 2002), 75; John Muir, *Our National Parks* (New York: Houghton, Mifflin and Co., 1901), 1.

8. Winfried Fluck, "Antebellum Period and Romanticism: Definitions and Demarcations," in *Handbook of American Romanticism*, ed. Philipp Löffler, Clemens Spahr, and Jan Stievermann (Berlin: de Gruyter, 2021), 14; F. O. Matthiessen, *American Renaissance: Art and Expression in the Age of Emerson and Whitman* (Oxford: Oxford University Press, 1941), 42n5, 135, 13.

9. Elizabeth Palmer Peabody, "Nature – A Prose Poem," *The United States Magazine and Democratic Review* 1 (February 1838), 323, 324.

10. Thomas Constantinesco, "Romanticism and European Philosophy, or 'Idealism as It Appears in 1842'" in *Handbook of American Romanticism*, ed. Philipp Löffler, Clemens Spahr, and Jan Stievermann (Berlin: de Gruyter, 2021), 123, 125.

11. Stephen E. Whicher, *Freedom and Fate: An Inner Life of Ralph Waldo Emerson* (Philadelphia: University of Pennsylvania Press, 1953).

12. David Jacobson, *Emerson's Pragmatic Vision: The Dance of the Eye* (University Park, PA: Penn State University Press, 1993), 107; Jonathan Levin, *The Poetics of Transition: Emerson, Pragmatism, and American Literary Modernism* (Durham: Duke University Press, 1999).

13. Stanley Cavell, "Finding as Founding," *This New Yet Unapproachable America* (Chicago: University of Chicago Press, 2013), 79; Cary Wolfe, "'The Eye Is the First Circle': Emerson's 'Romanticism,' Cavell's Skepticism, Luhmann's Modernity," in *The Other Emerson*, ed. Branka Arsić and Cary Wolfe (Minneapolis: University of Minnesota Press, 2010), 277.

14. Joseph Urbas, "Cavell's 'Moral Perfectionism' or Emerson's 'Moral Sentiment'?" *European Journal of Pragmatism and Philosophy* 2:2 (2010): 41–53, 43.

15. Joseph Urbas, *The Philosophy of Ralph Waldo Emerson* (New York: Routledge, 2021), 7; Douglas R. Anderson, *Philosophy Americana: Making Philosophy at Home in American Culture* (New York: Fordham University Press, 2006), 188–205.

16. Barbara L. Packer, "Origin and Authority: Emerson and the Higher Criticism," in *Reconstructing American Literary History*, ed. Sacvan Bercovitch (Cambridge, MA: Harvard University Press, 1986), 87, 88.

17. Barbara L. Packer, "Romanticism," in *The Oxford Handbook of Transcendentalism*, ed. Joel Myerson, Sandra Harbert Petrulionis, and Laura Dassow Walls (Oxford: Oxford University Press, 2010), 84–101, 85; Alfred Bendixen, "The Emergence of Romantic Traditions," in *The Cambridge History of American Poetry*, ed. Alfred Bendixen and Stephen Burt (Cambridge: Cambridge University Press, 2014), 178.

18. Copestake, "American Romanticism"; Gravil, *Romantic Dialogues*, xvii.

19. William St. Clair, *The Reading Nation in the Romantic Period* (Cambridge: Cambridge UP, 2004), 1. See, in particular, the chapter "North America."

20. David Dowling, "Antebellum Literary Culture: The Institutions of Romanticism," in *Handbook of American Romanticism*, ed. Philipp Löffler, Clemens Spahr, and Jan Stievermann (Berlin: de Gruyter, 2021), 36.

21. Weisbuch, *Atlantic Double-Cross*, xii; Lance Newman, Joel Pace, and Chris Koenig-Woodyard, Introduction, *Transatlantic Romanticism: An Anthology of British, American, and Canadian Literature, 1767–1867* (New York: Pearson Longman, 2006), 14.

22. Keane, *Emerson, Romanticism, and Intuitive Reason*, 85; David LaRocca, *Emerson's* English Traits *and the Natural History of Metaphor* (New York: Bloomsbury, 2013), 203; Ellison, *Emerson's Romantic Style*, 67–68.

23. Ellison, *Emerson's Romantic Style*, 68; Robert Weisbuch, "Post-Colonial Emerson and the Erasure of Europe" *The Cambridge Companion to Ralph Waldo Emerson*, ed. Joel Porte and Saundra Morris (Cambridge: Cambridge University Press, 1999), 206-07.

24. Elisa Tamarkin, *Anglophilia: Deference, Devotion, and Antebellum America* (Chicago: University of Chicago Press, 2008), 274; Wesley T. Mott, "Britain," in *Ralph Waldo Emerson in Context*, ed. Wesley T. Mott (Cambridge: Cambridge University Press, 2014), 26.

25. Philip Nicoloff, *Emerson on Race and History* (Columbia University Press, 1961), 13.

26. Johannes Voelz, "Transnationalism and Nineteenth-Century Literature," The Cambridge Companion to Transnational American Literature, ed. Yogita Goyal (Cambridge: Cambridge University Press, 2017), 92.

27. Robert D. Richardson, Jr., "Emerson on History," in *Emerson: Prospect and Retrospect*, ed. Joel Porte (Cambridge, MA: Harvard University Press, 1982), 57.

28. Packer, "Origin and Authority," 88; Christopher Newfield, *The Emerson Effect: Individualism and Submission in America* (Chicago: University of Chicago Press, 1996), 159, 160.

29. Walt Whitman, "Song of Myself," in *Leaves of Grass: A Textual Variorum of the Printed Poems*, vol. 1 of *Collected Works of Walt Whitman*, ed. Sculley Bradley et al. (New York: New York University Press, 1980), 41, l.670–73.

30. Henry David Thoreau, October 18, 1860, *Journal*, vol. 14 of *The Writings of Henry David Thoreau*, ed. Bradford Torrey (Boston: Houghton Mifflin, 1906), 147.

31. Constantinesco, "Romanticism and European Philosophy," 120.

# 4

LAURA DASSOW WALLS

# Nature, Ecology, Climate
## Emerson's Ecopoetical Thought

When it comes to Emerson and nature, one of the persistent puzzles is how someone who openly doubted "whether nature outwardly exists" (*CW* 1: 29) could nevertheless become one of the founding figures of ecopoetical thought – a *poiesis* or making, that is, that sings the nonhuman world into being in human terms, whether in formal poetry or lyric essays.[1] This puzzle points to an enduring conflict evidenced in Emerson between natural history and humanist philosophy: nature as a realm of both scientific inquiry and sensual delight most certainly exists, as he knew perfectly well. Nevertheless, intellectual doubt in the "real" existence of nature is fundamental to Western thought from Plato to René Descartes, a doubt updated for Emerson's generation by Immanuel Kant's insistence that while *noumenal* nature – the thing-in-itself, outside and independent of our mental operations – does exist, we cannot *know* it. What we can know is only *phenomenal* nature, the veil of appearances that masks the real reality. Thus natural objects, as Emerson reflects, are like stars in the night sky, always present but "always inaccessible" (*CW* 1: 9). No matter how closely we approach, "Nature is still elsewhere"; "There is in woods and waters a certain enticement and flattery, together with a failure to yield a present satisfaction. This disappointment is felt in every landscape" (*CW* 13: 111).

The paradox of Emerson, then, lies in his internal war between intellect and affection: the mind warns that nature doesn't really exist, or if it does, lies forever out of reach – until suddenly there it is, beauty blooming all around. If we still, as Eduardo Cadava elaborates, live in the "climate" of Emerson, then his paradox is also ours, such that examining the genealogy of Emerson's ecopoetical thought will help us understand both his limitations and our own.[2]

## Ways of Making: Nature, Ecology, Climate

Curiously, the tangled nature of "nature" does not prevent us from using the word readily and often, in full confidence we know what we mean.

As the environmental historian Joachim Radkau says, "for lovers of nature there is nothing more bewildering than the philosophical history of nature," which is "highly contradictory and muddled," a confusion that only increases "as the modern era progresses."[3] The confusion is worsened by the Western tendency to define "nature" discursively as the opposite of some human-centered entity or value: nature versus man, or spirit, or culture; the wild as against the civilized. Emerson himself opens his ground-breaking essay *Nature* (1836) in this dualistic tradition when he asserts, "Philosophically considered, the universe is composed of Nature and the Soul." This assertion activates a whole train of relational oppositions by setting the "ME," or Soul, against all that is "NOT ME, that is, both nature and art, all other men and my own body," which "must be ranked under this name, NATURE" (*CW* 1: 8). This very framework builds in Emerson's doubt, for how can the "ME" know that which is separate from "ME"? Just as Descartes famously declared back in 1637, we can't. All we can *know* is that we can *think*: *Cogito, ergo sum*. And so Emerson is left wondering whether nature truly enjoys "a substantial existence without, or is only in the apocalypse of the mind," leaving us to regard the material world "as a phenomenon, not a substance" (*CW* 1: 29–30).

But how can this be? The instant Emerson divides Soul from Nature, he mounts a revolt in the name of "common sense," according to which "*Nature* ... refers to essences unchanged by man; space, the air, the river, the leaf." Essences are, of course, abstractions; one doesn't get wet in the essence of a river, nor rake the essence of autumn leaves. And so, he continues, we mix our will with these essences, "as in a house, a canal, a statue, a picture" (*CW* 1: 8), generating from nature, that abstract idea, a warm and living material world, a second nature that completes and humanizes the first. Thus, as soon as Emerson doubts nature's very existence, he immediately recoils: "I have no hostility to nature, but a child's love to it. I expand and live in the warm day like corn and melons. Let us speak her fair. I do not wish to fling stones at my beautiful mother, nor soil my gentle nest" (*CW* 1: 35–36). One must, then, find the middle ground, a way, as he says, "to respect the perfection of this world, in which our senses converse," "to subdue and enjoy it" – until, that is, the moment when the mind opens and "reveals the laws which traverse the universe, and make things what they are, then shrinks the great world at once into a mere illustration and fable" of the human mind. In short, while the senses link us to nature through our bodies, once the mind opens, we realize that what we venerate in nature is more truly our own, our *human* nature (*CW* 1: 76).

Was ever a word more complex than this? Raymond Williams tracks the unfolding complexity of "nature" through the millennia of Western thought

by tracing its two basic dimensions: first, *nature* means *that by which something is what it is* – the inborn traits that define its inner "essence" (in Emerson's words). While Emerson relies on this meaning, which dates back to ancient Greece, he also imbues it with its more recent, Christian dimension, which specifies *the formative force of God* as the *author* of all being. The body of nature is, then, the sacred manifestation of God's creative power – a power that Emerson identifies as the innermost truth of *human* nature, for God is within every human being, the holy fire that is the essence of the human. Thus, in each one of us "will God go forth anew into the creation" (*CW* 1: 44).[4]

Second, the word *nature* points to *that which is external to whatever humans are*, a dualism through which Christianity defined the separation of nature from humanity – "Nature" from "Soul" – by God's infusion of *super*natural grace, that holy fire, into humans, and humans alone. Early modern scientists layered onto this ancient Christian dualism the modern meaning of nature as *universal natural law*, as in the pioneering work of Descartes, who identified as universal "laws of nature" those inviolable laws instituted by God as a divine legislator, inbuilt laws that nature, like a machine, cannot help but obey. These are, in Emerson's phrase, "the laws which traverse the universe" (*CW* 1: 76), laws which man can know, but nature cannot. As he reminds us in his original epigraph to *Nature* (attributed to Plotinus), "Nature is but an image or imitation of wisdom, the last thing of the soul; nature being a thing which doth only do, but not know" (*CW* 1: 286). This is why, paradoxically, Emerson can abandon this dumb, beautiful nature, "painfully accumulated, atom after atom, act after act, in an aged creeping Past," to exult in the realm of pure spirit, "one vast picture, which God paints on the instant eternity, for the contemplation of the soul" (*CW* 1: 36).[5]

Emerson plays confidently across the entire range of the meanings of nature, secure in the knowledge that, as he tells us, "the inaccuracy is not material; no confusion of thought will occur" (*CW* 1: 8). Remarkably, he's right: only the most attentive reader will notice the way nature shape-shifts throughout his pages, for we instantly recognize all the meanings he triggers without pausing to notice how utterly incoherent our modern, Western thinking about nature has become. Emerson therefore helps us see something important: by shifting so easily across these many meanings of nature, we use each one as a compensatory resource for what the others exclude, with no awareness of our logical absurdity. This one word can invoke, simultaneously, nature without humans and innermost human nature; nature as God's created plenitude of all species and as the impersonal, imperious realm of natural law, which traverses all species and commands all,

even humans, to obey; the fragile and beautiful beings and phenomena of a world we didn't make and now endanger; and the inviolable essence of all beings, which humanity can never disturb, no matter how much we remake them in our own image.

As Radkau remarks, "It is very easy to deconstruct nature as a norm and as philosophical category. The only puzzling thing is how indestructible this ideal is and how the concept of nature reemerges from every maelstrom of confusion and returns to original meanings." Nature is, finally, more than the mere product of discourse: as in Emerson's delicious line about expanding in the sun like corn and melons, it names our own human origins in biological nature as well as our sensual, bodily, animal being and our joy in the biological and ecological world we share, humans and nonhumans, in common. The confusion that frustrates the philosopher is meat and drink for the historian, for it opens to us the great realm of historical understanding and literary expression. This is Timothy Morton's point in *Ecology without Nature*, where he "takes nature out of the equation by exploring the ways in which literary writing tries to conjure it up": where the word "nature" smooths out and abstracts all this uneven history, the word "ecology" will summon it up, allowing us to see that nature is not ahistorical at all but another word for history itself, for the constant "arising and cessation" of ecological systems. Similarly, Bruno Latour points to the political work done by the hoary word "nature," a collective noun authorizing "the hierarchy of beings in a single ordered series" – helping us see Emerson's habit of using "nature" to teach a political lesson in order, hierarchy, and natural law. Here, too, what "nature" unifies, "ecology" pluralizes, allowing us to take into account whatever the word "nature" has been used to externalize.[6]

This makes it difficult to address Emerson as ecological. He's well aware of what he externalizes when he speaks of nature as against "Soul," but, as *Nature* demonstrates, that's exactly what he wishes to do. As we have seen, purifying the categories of nonhuman "Nature" against human/divine "Soul" allows him, in his next move, to celebrate the power of humanity in mixing the two, as in house, canal, statue, and picture. As Emerson declares a few pages later, "Thus is Art, a nature passed through the alembic of man" (*CW* 1: 17). Nor does he find this mixing the least bit alarming, for the world's "serene order is inviolable by us" (*CW* 1: 38–39); man's "operations taken together are so insignificant, a little chipping, baking, patching, and washing, that in an impression so grand as that of the world on the human mind, they do not vary the result" (*CW* 1: 8). In an era of ecological turmoil, even as the industrial revolution was rewriting natural systems worldwide, Emerson could reassure himself (as well as all of America) that nature cannot be harmed by human art or industry, for essences are eternally given in the mind of God: after every tree is gone, the eternal essence of the leaf remains. This conviction distinguishes Emerson as an important architect of what Bruno Latour has called "the modern constitution," by which modernity multiplies our human impact on the planet precisely to the extent of our collective conviction that nothing humans can do to nature will alter the essential purity of those distinct "ontological zones," humans and culture versus nonhumans and nature. Hence, to put this perhaps too baldly, the calamities we face in the Anthropocene were committed under the name of Emerson's Nature; they can be recognized and combatted today only in the name of ecology.[7]

Yet herein still lies a problem that Emerson also allows us to see: ecology is nothing anyone can *experience*. One will not expand and live in its warm day. In this, *ecology* is like the word *climate*, which, as climate scientists remind us over and over, cannot be seen or touched or experienced – what we do experience is *weather*. "Climate," as in our now-ubiquitous phrase "climate change," is a technological accomplishment, a collective understanding abstracted from massive layers of instrumentation and generations of empirical, inductive observation combined with centuries of deepening understanding of the laws of physics and chemistry. This accomplishment, a branch of what today is called Earth System Science, was just getting underway during Emerson's day in the paradigm-shaping work led by Alexander von Humboldt, the pioneer of ecological thinking. Humboldt's initiative was the outgrowth of yet *another* meaning of "nature," one that Lorraine Daston has named "local natures" (note the plural), which are integrative models of all that distinguishes a particular place and creates of it a coherent community. This study, too, has ancient roots, dating all the way back to the Greek historian Herodotus. During Emerson's day it was being dramatically updated by the vast planetary scientific research program initiated and promoted worldwide by Humboldt's voluminous popular and technical writings. One early outgrowth of this program was Humboldt's identification of distinct planetary climate zones, what Emerson called "this striped coat of climates" (CW I: II); another was the coining of the word "ecology" by one of Humboldt's followers, giving a name to the intuition that shaped all his work.[8]

The difference between Emerson's "nature" and Humboldt's "ecology" is profound. Emerson never relinquished his deistic commitment to a nature designed and mastered by an immense and impersonal Intelligence; Humboldt disallowed any theological commitments to build, instead, a bottom-up, empirical understanding of living nature as an emergent system of systems, including our planet as a self-creating open whole evolving across deep geological time through the reciprocal interactions of natural forces and beings, both organic and inorganic.[9] While "nature" and "ecology" are both abstractions, ways of addressing in a single collective noun the relational systematicity of things, they are abstractions of a different kind. *Ecology*, like *climate*, is not, pace Cadava, an analogical literary figure for history but a dynamic set of scientific generalizations reached by long, unbroken networks of reference that connect, step by step, the grounded materiality of the local event – a particular experience of this local marsh, or that snowfall, or heat wave – to the resulting forms by which abstractions, freed of the weight of their material referents, can circulate around the world.[10] By contrast, *Nature*, just as Emerson says, cannot be *reached* at all, by any means. The abstraction that is nature exists not on the mutable ground but only in the gathering mind. Yet it is precisely in its muddled and shape-shifting abstractness that Nature serves as a connective matrix – a high-level synthesis, as Radkau says, "of long collective experience and reflection; an abstraction, to be sure, but one that time and again takes on concrete form," including lived experiences that connect our intimate sense of well-being with the flourishing of the natural world: the gravity of granite, the sliding of rivers, the fleeting beauty of all green beings, the flash of wings bent on purposes other than our own, the way a forest knits together into wholes without closure.[11] With or without Emerson's help, "nature" seems here to stay.

## Ways of Breaking: Iconoclasm

How is it that Emerson can walk down two paths at once? – one path leading to a meadow "spotted with fire and gold in the tint of flowers," and another to "the kingdom of man over nature ... a dominion such as now is beyond his dream of God"? (CW 1: 45, 76). Emerson formed his ideas of nature in an era of religious crisis with deep roots in Calvinist Puritanism. In his study of Anglo-American iconoclasm, James Simpson reminds us that New England was founded during the long century when Reformation England legislated the destruction of religious images, turning iconoclasm into a weapon of radical modernity. The Puritan colonists who settled Massachusetts rejected the idolatrous materiality of the conventional Church by defining the true church as placeless, given that God is everywhere and all places are equally holy – separating "ideal Church from material Church," and driving a wedge of disgust between the ideal and the material worlds. Thus the Emerson who inherited and practiced his faith preached not in a "church" but in a classic New England "meeting house," designed to repudiate traditional church architecture by homogenizing space, removing all images, painting the interior white, and installing transparent, imageless glass.[12] Given that all space is equally the church of God, Emerson's opening revelation in *Nature* – "I become a transparent eye-ball. I am nothing. I see all. The currents of the universal Being circulate through me; I am part of particle of God" – takes place exactly where it must, on "a bare common, in snow puddles," with nothing "special" to recommend it. His "transparent eye-ball" transposes the one image allowed by the Puritan church, the all-seeing eye of God, into his own all-seeing eye-ball, a fusion with God that expands the self into the realm of the absolute while shrinking common, ordinary material relations into meaninglessness: "The name of the nearest friend sounds then foreign and accidental. To be brothers, to be acquaintances, – master or servant, is then a trifle and a disturbance" (*CW* 1: 10).

Emerson thus inherits and plays out what Simpson calls the profound drama of American modernity: "a drama of equality, but an equality produced by our equidistance from a single, unmediated, non-represented source of power."[13] In this "art on the edge of democracy," intercession, image, and representation all disappear under the power of abstraction; as Emerson says, "the universe becomes transparent, and the light of higher laws than its own, shines through it" (*CW* 1: 22). The proper goal of the seer, then, is to become one not with the law's subjects but with the law-giver: hence, as God's eye and the human eye become one, "material forms" are revealed to "preëxist in necessary Ideas in the mind of God," and earthly mortality is cast off like the "scoriae" – the slag or excrement – of the spirit (*CW* 1: 22–23).

The Emerson who arrived at this "apocalypse of the mind" (*CW* 1: 29) had trained at Harvard's Divinity School, where the center of dissension was the status of the Bible itself. German Higher Criticism had persuaded Harvard's careful scholars that this sacred Book was, when read according to scientific principles, not at all the word of God but merely the product of history – an anthology of human voices, riddled with errors and inconsistencies. Authority could not, then, consist in any inherited religious institution but only in the internalization of a "critical conscience," which constitutes the scholar as both inscribed by, and the proper judge of, all institutional forms. Emerson's own critical conscience concluded that a historicized Bible could no longer be sacred, and inherited religious objects and rituals – above all the bread and wine of the Eucharist – were nothing more than worthless relics from an historical past. Once this insight hit home, he resigned from the ministry, in December 1832, and set off on a quest for the true fountain-head of sacred power.[14]

Emerson found his fountainhead in nature. Seven months after his resignation, while touring the Paris Museum of Natural History, he experienced a vision that he himself dignified as a conversion. What staggered him, as he looked "along this bewildering series of animated forms – the hazy butterflies, the carved shells, the birds, beasts, insects, fishes, snakes" – was not the diversity of this vast assemblage of natural beings but the single "upheaving principle of life" they all shared: "Not a form so grotesque, so savage, nor so beautiful but is an expression of some thing in man the observer.... I am moved by strange sympathies. I say continually, 'I will be a naturalist.'"[15] What he had in mind, as he would later explain in *Nature*, was not the detailed, empirical study of natural history, which he dismissed as "this half-sight of science" (*CW* 1: 41), but rather "the *metaphysics* of conchology, of botany, of the arts, to show the relation of the forms of flowers, shells, animals, architecture, to the mind, and build science upon ideas" (*CW* 1: 40). Immediately on returning home, Emerson began working out his breakthrough insight through a series of lectures on "Natural History," which culminated in the publication of *Nature* in 1836. As his thinking evolved, he shifted in the 1840s away from the earlier essay's *subjective* idealism, in which the mind projects reality onto nature – as he said, "Build, therefore, your own world" (*CW* 1: 45) – to a form of *objective* idealism, a metaphysics in which the objects of Nature, rightly read, could securely fasten his references to spirit.[16] As he wrote in his remarkable 1841 address "The Method of Nature," "Nothing solid is secure; everything tilts and rocks" (*CW* 1: 121). Security in a world of tilt and flow, formation and dissolution, can be found not by studying nature, but by studying *mind in* nature, whence we learn that all of nature "is unbroken obedience" (*CW* 1: 124) to the metaphysical cause of nature, which knows "neither palm nor oak, but only vegetable life" as it sprouts into forests and festoons the globe with a garland of grasses and vines (*CW* 1: 125). "I draw from nature the lesson of an intimate divinity," Emerson rhapsodizes; the "solicitations of this spirit ... woo and court us from every object in nature," asking of us only that we "enact our best insight. Instantly we are higher poets and can speak a deeper law" (*CW* 1: 136).

In his 1844 essay "Nature," Emerson continues mining this vein of ecstasy, celebrating the beauties, enchantments, and ministrations of nature, before abruptly calling a halt: "It is very easy to outrun the sympathy of readers on this topic, which schoolmen called *natura naturata*, or nature passive. One can hardly speak directly of it without excess." (*CW* 3: 103). Proper homage belongs not to outward nature but rather "to the Efficient Nature, *natura naturans*, the quick cause, before which all forms flee as the driven snows" (*CW* 3: 104). "The world is mind precipitated," he concludes, the "incarnation" of "a volatile essence," a power that "makes the whole and the particle its equal channel ... and distills its essence into every drop of rain." Death in such a world loses its meaning; "Here is no ruin, no discontinuity, no spent ball. The divine circulations never rest nor linger" (*CW* 3: 113). In *Nature*, Emerson used poetic prose to describe a mystical fusion with God; here, poetry is itself a mystical experience, a way of conjuring nature, as Morton says, after "external nature" has failed us – as it always will. Hence the poet ever finds that "The pine-tree, the river, the bank of flowers before him, does not seem to be nature. Nature is still elsewhere" (*CW* 3: 111). As Richard Grusin has remarked, Emerson sacrifices the dead means for the living end; paradoxically, then, the true office of nature is to teach us how to leave her behind.[17]

Simpson stresses a crucial point that allows us to understand this dynamic: The work of iconoclasm is never done. Images are full of energy. To crush them only reactivates their power, and to attack them is not to destroy or silence them but to evoke what Simpson calls "their spectral presence," even their "personhood"[18] – just as Emerson did in *Nature*, when, having wished the external materiality of nature into nonexistence, he recoils and calls it back as "his beautiful mother." This typical movement – a destruction that reactivates the power of the destroyed – sets off what Simpson calls the "kinesis of iconoclasm," in which "the more actively one demolishes the idolatrous monument, the more energetically does it resurface."[19] There is, however, a way to stabilize the ongoing revolution of kinesis, and it is the way that Emerson follows: erect "an idol capable of disguising and disowning its status as idol." Often, Simpson observes, the resulting "animate monuments are books, living acts" that transfer the animacy of the idolatrous "stocks and stones" of the material world to the life-giving pages of books that disguise their own status as material objects.[20]

Thus it is, as Emerson says, that the book transmutes life into truth, "dead fact" into "quick thought" (*CW* 1: 55) – but, true to form, he immediately does a volte-face to warn against making the book itself, *any* book, into a new idol: "Instantly, the book becomes noxious. The guide is a tyrant," as the book congeals into yet another dogma that must be smashed, just as "love of the hero corrupts into worship of his statue." (*CW* 1: 56). What Simpson says of Milton is equally true of Emerson: "The iconoclast artist will be committed to originality and to the absolute purgation of tradition."[21] As Emerson announces in the first words of *Nature*: "Our age is retrospective. It builds the sepulchres of the fathers.... Why should not we also enjoy an original relation to the universe?" (*CW* 1: 7). True to the logic of iconoclasm, the originality of Emerson's own "relation to the universe" lies in converting it to language; as Cadava says, "Nature is in fact always another name for writing in Emerson."[22] Note, however, that this scriptural figure cuts two ways: in Thoreau, as in Humboldt, nature *writes itself*, resulting in a far more profoundly ecological poetics; in Emerson, the true author is not nature, but God, who by writing *through* nature warrants that "Nature is the symbol of spirit" (*CW* 1: 17). The reader must recognize that "the whole of nature is a metaphor of the human mind," which "is not fancied by some poet, but stands in the will of God, and so is free to be known by all men" (*CW* 1: 22). Even as "the fundamental law of criticism" is that "every scripture is to be interpreted by the same spirit which gave it forth," so will "a life in harmony with nature" turn all the world into "an open book," in which "That which was unconscious truth, becomes, when interpreted and defined in an object, a part of the domain of knowledge, – a new weapon in the magazine of power" (*CW* 1: 23). Emerson's nature, newly weaponized into language, need never escape the kingdom of humanity.

### Ways of Remaking: Emerson's Poetics

Nature reimagined as the language of God offers a way to stabilize another emerging crisis: the widening division between science as the locus of power and art as the expression of feeling. Emerson's poetics resisted this division, starting with his youthful engagement with the writings of Francis Bacon, the Anglican philosopher and crown-appointed Lord Chancellor who laid the foundations for modern science. Through Bacon's work, Emerson verified that the truth to which nature consents is not a statement *about* the world, one that must be demonstrated empirically (and so could be refuted, in the way of science, by nature's refusal to consent), but a truth *already in* the world, legislated there by the same Mind that is within us and therefore legible to the human mind. But reading this truth requires strict discipline lest the beauty of nature lead one astray. Simpson observes that for Bacon, error itself became the idol that must be destroyed, and so he ruled that "the seeker after science must above all exercise suspicion, especially with regard to 'whatever ravishes and possesses his intellect; and with such matters should be all the more careful to keep his intellect impartial and pure.'"[23] Emerson, echoing Bacon, frets in "The Method of Nature" that "the nature of all things" is to "seek to penetrate and overpower," to "woo and court the eye of every beholder," "to fascinate and possess, to pass into his mind, for they desire to republish themselves in a more delicate world than that they occupy." As Emerson continues, evoking the ancient myth of a reptile so venomous it kills with a glance, "These beautiful basilisks set their brute, glorious eyes on the eye of every child, and if they can, cause their nature to pass through his wondering eyes into him, and so all things are mixed." Emerson's warning against the alluring power of these "beautiful basilisks" also echoes Bacon: "Therefore man must be on his guard against this cup of enchantments, and must look at nature with a supernatural eye. By piety alone, by conversing with the cause of nature, is he safe and commands it" (*CW* 1: 131).[24]

This warning is essential because, as Emerson repeats, the mixing of all things with human will is what makes possible all human production: "It is a conversion of all nature into the rhetoric of thought, under the eye of judgment, with a strenuous exercise of choice" (*CW* 2: 199). By the time Emerson wrote the essay "Fate," in 1860, this rhetoric of thought had become militant, for Nature had become Fate itself, all that limits and constrains human power: "The book of Nature is the book of Fate" (*CW* 6: 8). As Emerson elaborates, "If Fate follows and limits power, power attends and antagonizes Fate. We must respect Fate as natural history, but there is more than natural history.... Man is not order of nature, sack and sack, belly and members, link in a chain, nor any ignominious baggage, but a stupendous antagonism, a dragging together of the poles of the Universe," on one side a thick-skulled and fishy animal, on the other "the lightning which explodes and fashions planets" (*CW* 6: 12). Knowledge, Bacon famously said, is power; even so, responded Emerson. The fatality of nature must be met with the power of intellect to convert us from subjects to rulers: "We are as lawgivers; we speak for Nature; we prophesy and divine" (*CW* 6: 14).[25]

Whence, then, the appealing eyes of those "beautiful basilisks"? For despite all the power of iconoclasm, the alluring siren songs of nature's beautiful beings still have not been entirely silenced – nor should they be, as Emerson and his generation learned from the aesthetic theories of Immanuel Kant. For what the intellect sunders, affection must rejoin; only through the appreciation of nature's beauty can those terrible "poles of the Universe" be dragged together, cultivating in us a sense of both the animal limitations that bind us to nature and our human potential for spiritual transcendence.[26] "Beauty," said Emerson, "is the mark God sets upon virtue" (*CW* 1: 15). It follows that only cultivation of moral virtue will develop the proper judgment that allows us to see, in each beautiful being, the unique way it, too, manifests the power of universal Mind. Thus, what Baconian science subdues as an instrument, Kantian aesthetics rescues as an end in itself, making of natural beings not a tool or resource for human use, but an art for art's sake. As Emerson tells the beautiful blooming Rhodora in his eponymous poem, "Tell them, dear, that if eyes were made for seeing,/ Then Beauty is its own excuse for being" (*CW* 9: 79). What higher end such beauty might serve cannot be grasped by the understanding, the chop logic of the poem's "sages," but only by the light of the imagination, which can intuit the harmony made manifest in nature's beauty without, by virtue of the cultivated moral intuition within. Thus the human soul sees in nature a true reflection of the order whose origin lies within ourselves. As Emerson says, "The light by which we see in this world, comes out from the soul of the observer." His name for this light is "Wisdom with his solar eye," the key that opens both scientific knowledge and poetic imagination – given that both arise from the same higher Source and are practiced by the same cultivated sensibility (*LL* 2: 76, 82).[27]

Emerson both exercised his cultivated sensibility and demonstrated it to others in his blank-verse poem "The Adirondacs: A Journal," based on his landmark adventure in American ecotourism in 1858, when he joined seven men, with eight guides, in a wilderness excursion to New York's Adirondack region.[28] Here any threat that the sublime power of wild nature might enchant and possess the poet is held under firm control by the poem's amused and "sophisticated mock-heroic tone" (*CW* 9: 343). Indeed, the only incursion of the sublime occurs when a visitor announces the successful completion of the transatlantic telegraph, a radical technological advancement "Urging astonished Chaos with a thrill/To be a brain, or serve the brain of man." With this, Emerson's conversion of nature into rhetoric is complete. The very lightning itself is mastered and schooled "to learn his verb and noun, ... Spelling with guided tongue man's messages/Shot through the weltering pit of the salt sea" (*CW* 9: 351). Yet there is still, of course, a wild remainder, as "through all creatures in their form and ways/Some mystic hint accosts the vigilant,/Not clearly voiced, but waking a new sense/Inviting to new knowledge, one with old" (*CW* 9: 349). This is the Emerson who inspired John Muir, whose intense theology of wild nature inspired the creation of wilderness as a sanctified zone, the protected site of humanity's spiritual re-creation – an antidote all the more necessary in a century given over to the "turbulent heyday" of the cities from which Emerson's hardy band of urban elites had, temporarily, fled (*CW* 9: 349, 352). Muir's inspiration in Emerson suggests how wilderness was originally constituted as a literary form by which the kinesis of iconoclasm could safely reanimate, in a quarantined space, all that it sought to destroy in the common world.

It's interesting in this context to contrast Emerson with Thoreau. While Thoreau in the 1850s was moving ever deeper into nature's materiality, pacing every part of the planet within reach of his doorstep and immersing himself in the distribution of material seeds and the ramifying networks of human/natural ecological interactions, Emerson was moving into an even more radical form of modernist abstraction, one that used cutting-edge physics to license insights into laws of nature derived from Christian theology. Emerson's proclamation in *Nature* that "the axioms of physics translate the laws of ethics" (*CW* 1: 21) suggests why, during his trip to England in 1848, he attended the lectures of the British physicist Michael Faraday, who was even then laying the groundwork for quantum mechanics and Einstein's theory of relativity. Faraday taught Emerson that, sure enough, there truly is no materiality in nature: as Emerson announced (in a lecture on poetry), "Faraday, the most exact of natural philosophers, taught, that when we should arrive at the monads or primordial elements, the supposed little cubes or prisms of which all matter was built up, we should not find cubes, or prisms, or atoms at all, but spherules of force." Emerson duly translates this axiom of physics into a law of ethics: "Power and purpose rides on matter to the last atom.... The ends of all are moral" (*LL* 1: 299).[29] As he had earlier said, "moral justice can no more be defied or evaded than Gravitation."[30] During the darkest days of the Civil War, Emerson used Faraday to rally the flagging energies of the Union, arguing that victory over the South was written into the atomic structure of matter itself. As he writes in the lecture "Perpetual Forces": "the iron of iron, the fire of fire, the ether and source of all the elements, is moral force. It is a fagot of laws, and that band which ties them together is Unity, is Universal Good," such that, "if we should really come down to atoms ... we should not find little cubes or atoms at all, but only spherules of forces, a fagot of forces, a series of currents in which all things are forced to run; – a series of threads, on which men, and animals, and plants, and brute matter are strung as beads; – those forces only exist" (*LL* 2: 300–1). At the far end of Emerson's exultation that "moral force" is written into the very atoms themselves will be the splitting and harnessing of Faraday's atomic "spherules of force" into the ultimate weapon – the atomic bomb that exploded over Hiroshima in 1945. As Latour reminds us, we have never left this righteous state of war, never stopped looking ahead to "the land where atoms and particles flow – otherwise we would have to despair of humanity. The victory of peace is just around the corner."[31]

Is there never, anywhere, an outside to Emerson's self-mirroring conception of Nature? Perhaps. There's a haunting moment, at the end of his essay "History," when Emerson acknowledges the alien animation of the otherness of nature – a disturbance that points to the fracture he cannot heal: "Hear the rats in the wall, see the lizard on the fence, the fungus under foot, the lichen on the log. What do I know sympathetically, morally, of either of these worlds of life? As old as the Caucasian man, – perhaps older, – these creatures have kept their counsel beside him, and there is no record of any word or sign that has passed from one to the other." The thought puts Emerson in an unusual mood: "I am ashamed to see what a shallow village tale our so-called History is. How many times we must say Rome, and Paris, and Constantinople! What does Rome know of rat and lizard?" (*CW* 2: 22). It is almost as if Emerson intuits the proposal of the historian

Dipesh Chakrabarty, in *The Climate of History in a Planetary Age* (2021), "that anthropogenic explanations of climate change spell the collapse of the age-old humanist distinction ... between natural history and human history." Chakrabarty's painstaking quest to make sense of the crisis of the Anthropocene highlights the flaw in Emerson's reasoning – a flaw that now leaves us all in "the ruins of an enduring fable" that, beginning with Kant, "made a strict separation between our 'moral' and 'animal' (i.e., biological) lives, assuming that the latter would always be taken care of by the natural order of things."[32] Today, though, not only does the natural order of things no longer take care of our biological lives, but the entire domain of biological life is subjected to the vagaries of human moral life. Whatever "climate" we experience today, in the era of global warming, is not a figure for human history but a consequence of it. What tilts and rocks now is not everything *around* Emerson, but everything *including* Emerson – all his works and days, all his kingdom of man over nature, all the modernity he helped us build, all his consequences we must somehow face.

The importance of Emerson to us today lies in the understanding he provides of who we are and how we brought ourselves to this pitch. What we read when we read Emerson is nothing less than a playing out of the profound drama of American modernity, which refused, and refuses still, the collapse of human and natural history in order to protect the exceptional human-as-divine from an emergent vision of an ecological humanity embedded in all the social and ecological practices and relations that give earthly life its meaning. The day may come – may be coming soon – when we can no longer read Emerson as our contemporary, the necessary thinker who put America on the path to modernity. When that day comes, we will find ourselves living in a very different world – a world in which a broken Nature no longer speaks the reassuring language of a benevolent God, in which a broken humanity has finally begun the task of learning how to speak anew on, and to, a planet that has all along been conjuring a climate all its own. For now, we remain part of Emerson's climate, even as he helped create the climate that dooms us. The rats and lizards have returned, bearing 1,000,000 words and signs to a Rome that is at last starting to listen. Emerson may not have been able to hear them; but we must.

## Notes

1. See Mark Tredinnick, *The Land's Wild Music* (San Antonio: Trinity University Press, 2005), 236–39.
2. Eduardo Cadava, *Emerson and the Climates of History* (Stanford: Stanford University Press, 1997), xiii, 6.

3. Joachim Radkau, *Nature and Power: A Global History of the Environment*, trans. Thomas Dunlap (Cambridge: Cambridge University Press, 2008), 18.

4. Raymond Williams, *Keywords: A Vocabulary of Culture and Society* (New York: Oxford University Press, 1985), 219–21.

5. Williams, *Keywords*, 222–23. Lorraine Daston offers a three-part taxonomy of nature: "specific natures" (the inborn traits which define the essence, or "ontological identity card," of a thing or species); "local natures" (integrative models of all that distinguishes a particular place, to create of it a coherent community); and "universal natural law" (universal and inviolable "laws of nature" instituted by God). Lorraine Daston, *Against Nature* (Cambridge: MIT Press, 2019), 7–31.

6. Radkau, *Nature and Power*, 18; Timothy Morton, *Ecology Without Nature: Rethinking Environmental Aesthetics* (Cambridge, MA: Harvard University Press, 2007), 19, 21; Bruno Latour, *Politics of Nature: How to Bring the Sciences into Democracy* (Cambridge, MA: Harvard University Press, 2004), 25, 244–45.

7. Bruno Latour, *We Have Never Been Modern* (Cambridge, MA: Harvard University Press, 1993), 10–12.

8. Daston, *Against Nature*, 15–19. Emerson is alluding to Alexander von Humboldt's *Tableau Physique* (1807), a ubiquitous image in his day. See my book *Passage to Cosmos: Alexander von Humboldt and the Shaping of America* (Chicago: University of Chicago Press, 2009), 44–45 (*Tableau*); pp. 313, 327n12 (coinage of "ecology" by Ernst Haeckel in 1866).

9. Darwin followed Humboldt literally in voyaging to South America and figuratively in extending Humboldtian science to evolutionary theory; see Walls, *Passage to Cosmos*, viii–ix, 235–41.

10. Cadava, *Emerson and the Climates of History*, 22; Bruno Latour, "Circulating Reference," in *Pandora's Hope: Essays on the Reality of Science Studies* (Cambridge, MA: Harvard University Press, 1999), 24–79.

11. Radkau, *Nature and Power*, 18.

12. James Simpson, *Under the Hammer: Iconoclasm in the Anglo-American Tradition* (Oxford: Oxford University Press, 2010), 5, 41–45.

13. Simpson, *Under the Hammer*, 47.

14. Richard A. Grusin, *Transcendentalist Hermeneutics: Institutional Authority and the Higher Criticism of the Bible* (Durham: Duke University Press, 1991), 5, 71; Elisabeth Hurth, *Between Faith and Unbelief: American Transcendentalists and the Challenge of Atheism* (Boston: Brill, 2007), 24–30.

15. Quoted and discussed in Laura Dassow Walls, *Emerson's Life in Science: The Culture of Truth* (Ithaca: Cornell University Press, 2003), 84–91.

16. Hurth, *Between Faith*, 113.

17. Grusin, *Transcendentalist Hermeneutics*, 50.

18. Simpson, *Under the Hammer*, 48, 70–71.

19. Ibid., 13, 95.

20. Ibid., 85, 114. Simpson's quote from Milton is evocative of Emerson: "a good Book is the pretious life-blood of a master-spirit, imbalm'd and treasured up on purpose to a life beyond life" (114).

21. Ibid., 109.

22. Cadava, *Emerson and the Climates of History*, 3.

23. Simpson, *Under the Hammer*, 12 (quoting Bacon).
24. For Emerson and Bacon, see Walls, *Emerson's Life in Science*, 33–42.
25. Compare Alfred North Whitehead's trenchant observation: "Fate in Greek Tragedy becomes the order of nature in modern thought." See *Science and the Modern World* [1925] (New York: Simon and Schuster, 1967), 10.
26. As Emerson said in "Intellect and Natural Science," "Affection blends, Intellect disjoins the subject and object." Ralph Waldo Emerson, *The Later Lectures of Ralph Waldo Emerson, 1843–1871*, ed. Ronald A. Bosco and Joel Myerson, 2 vols. (Athens: University of Georgia Press, 2001), (Herein *LL* 1: 66).
27. See Emerson's "Powers of the Mind," *Later Lectures* 2:76, 82. For more on Emerson's "solar eye," see Walls, *Emerson's Life in Science*, 199–203.
28. This trip has been famously captured in a painting by James Stillman (who also organized the adventure), "The Philosopher's Camp," on display in the Concord Free Public Library.
29. For Emerson and Faraday, see my essay "'Every truth tends to become a power': Emerson, Faraday, and the Minding of Matter," in *Emerson for the Twenty-first Century: Global Perspectives on an American Icon*, ed. Barry Tharaud (Newark: Delaware Press, 2010), 301–17.
30. Emerson, "The Spirit of the Times," *Later Lectures* 1:123.
31. Latour, *Politics of Nature*, 218.
32. Dipesh Chakrabarty, *The Climate of History in a Planetary Age* (Chicago: University of Chicago Press, 2021), 26, 134.

# 5

PRENTISS CLARK

# "Allied to all"
## Emerson and Ethics beyond Self-Reliance

> Nothing past but affects *you*. Nothing remote but through some
> means reaches *you*. Every superficial grain of sand may be considered
> as the fixed point round which all things revolve, so intimately
> is it allied to all
> – Sermon CLXIX (CS 4: 232)

"You asked me if I liked Mackintosh's Ethics," Emerson wrote to his
brother William in 1832, "Assuredly. It is the most important work on the
most important science" (L 1: 348). Though ethics, for Emerson, is "the
most important science," it is equally, and always, the practice of everyday
living – he calls it in *Nature* (1836) "the practice of ideas, or the introduction of ideas into life" (CW 1: 35) – as much a matter of daily conduct as
a subject of philosophical investigation. The "question of the times," he
writes at the beginning of "Fate" (1860), "resolved itself into a practical
question of the conduct of life. How shall I live?" (CW 6: 1). A question
for crises and a question for every hour, this ethical question informs his
thinking from first to last. It grows out of his sense that every individual,
like "Every superficial grain of sand," exists "allied to all" in a universe
saturated with moral law. As he writes in *Nature* (1836), "The moral law
lies at the centre of nature and radiates to the circumference. It is the pith
and marrow of every substance, every relation, and every process" (CW
1: 26). For Emerson, human life is through and through a matter of moral
consequence, which necessitates constantly assessing one's relationships –
to self, fellow persons, nation, nature, God – and what these relationships
mean and require.

Emerson's writing formalizes this ethical practice. "What is *my* relation to Almighty God? What is *my* relation to my fellow men? What am
I designed for? What are my duties? What is my destiny?" (CS 4: 215) he
asks in Sermon CLXV; "I propose to look philosophically at the conduct
of life" (JMN II: 294) he resolves in his journal; "Well, & what do you

88

project?" he wonders in his journal, "Nothing less than to look at every object in its relation to Myself" (*JMN* IV: 272); "It is with the design of attempting a more just survey of man's relations that I have invited this audience" (*EL* 2: 7) he announces in his *Philosophy of History* (1836–37) lecture series. One sees in these sentences Emerson living his ethics and his sense that investigating this "most important science" entails the method of a poet who "re-attaches things to nature and the Whole" (*CW* 3: 11). The following essay traces this method across Emerson's oeuvre and beyond the concept of "self-reliance," which has long been a focus, if not a point of departure, in studies of Emerson's ethics. More specifically, this essay shows how Emerson's ethics begin in the perception of individuals "allied to all," a perception enabling us to better see kinships between ethics, aesthetics, religion, science, and politics, and to consider ethics a practice of observing the intimacies in which we exist and in which the ethical question "How shall I live?" begins living in us.

"Two caricatures of Emerson," in Susan Dunston's terms, "have framed discussions of his ethics: the intellectual and the poet." Unsurprisingly, she writes, "Each version of Emerson has drawn ardent adherents, hostile critics, and conciliatory apologists but neither one sufficiently describes his ethics. Thinking of him as living preferentially in the mind casts his ethics as ethereal principle; thinking of him as living passionately in the moment casts his ethics as entirely relativist."[1] Furthermore, these versions of Emerson and their attendant disciplinary paradigms maintain the kinds of false divisions that Emerson's work as a whole – and his thinking about ethics in particular – variously contest. The most canonical instance, from *Nature* (1836), might be his correcting "the half-sight of science" with poetry, which offers a "hint to explain the relation between things and thoughts" and can show "that wonderful congruity which subsists between man and the world" (*CW* 1: 40, 41). Or as he reflects in Topical Notebook *PY*, "Science is false by being unpoetical. It assumes to explain a reptile or mollusk, and isolates it; – which is hunting for life in graveyards. Reptile or mollusk, or man or angel, only exists in system, in relation" (*TN* 2: 265). "Is not the poetic side of science entitled to be felt and presented by its investigators? Is it quite impossible to unite severe science with a poetic vision?" ("Humanity of Science" *EL* 2: 36). A fuller engagement with Emerson's ethics requires attending to the way he attempts just this: uniting "severe science with a poetic vision" that reveals the way "Our life is consentaneous and far-related" ("Fate" *CW* 6: 20).

In other words, a poetic angle of vision that sees the world "in system, in relation" – the way "All are needed by each one; / Nothing is fair or good alone" ("Each and All" *CW* 9: 14) – is the substance of Emerson's ethics and his method of investigation. "I am in all my theories, ethics & politics, a poet" (*L* III: 18), he wrote to his wife Lidian in 1842. "That," he declared seven years earlier, "is my nature & vocation," and though he considered his "singing" "very 'husky'" and "for the most part in prose," he nevertheless insisted, "Still am I a poet in the sense of a perceiver & dear lover of the harmonies that are in the soul & in matter, & specially of the correspondences between these & those" (*L* 1: 435). Crucially, being a poet, for Emerson, means perceiving and seeking to express the "correspondences" between self and world, between the "matter" of the world and the "soul" which animates all, an endeavor embodied in his "theories, ethics & politics" alike. "What does all this love for signs denote," he asks in his 1841 lecture "The Poet," "if not that the relation of man to these forms in nature is more intimate than the understanding yet suspects" (*EL* 3: 354). "[R]elation and connection are not somewhere and sometimes, but everywhere and always," he observes in "Fate," "no miscellany, no exemption, no anomaly, – but method, and an even web" (*CW* 6: 117).

Emerson's oeuvre brims with similar sentences, each an attempt to recount human existence within a web of innumerable and often inexplicable interconnections and all demonstrating the poetics of ethics: the way this "most important science," in thinking and in living, is a matter of being "allied to all," to human and nonhuman forms of life, to what can and cannot be known, even to what might be unintelligible. Ethical investigation thus involves not only "enumerating the values of nature and casting up their sum" but also, and equally, "untaught sallies of the spirit," "a continual self-recovery," and "entire humility" (*Nature, CW* 1: 39). Emerson's writing, accordingly, takes the form of sketching, describing, essaying, and celebrating. He does not, in John Lysaker's terms, "report a grasp of imperatives, normative principles, or regulative ideals, though such things might lie within the harmonies he hears," but rather, he "claims to apprehend moments when values are immanently evident within facts, that is, when self and world are in harmony with themselves and one another."[2] The most ordinary "facts" of existence, for Emerson, are alive with meanings and values that call for an account.: "What is summer? What is woman? What is a child? What is sleep?" (*CW* 1: 44). So rather than abstract from the world "imperatives, normative principles, or regulative ideals," he observes and would express the way "a fact is true poetry" (44), bearing significance for how one lives. "What we have ... to say of life," he concludes in "Considerations by the Way" (1860), "is rather description, or, if you please, celebration, than available rules" (*CW* 6: 131).

Scholarship on Emerson and ethics, like Emerson scholarship as a whole, ranges widely and often between poles. He has been championed and castigated for promoting individualism, which either threatens democratic society or contributes to the common good. He has been read as a Transcendentalist whose idealism enables or undermines social justice. He "is celebrated as an originator of our virtues," in Wesley Mott's summation, "and damned for releasing our vices."[3] A "Philosophical Proteus," in Herwig Friedl's terms, he has been read as an antifoundationalist, skeptic, moral philosopher, process philosopher, proto-pragmatist, and democratic theorist.[4] Conversations on Emerson and ethics, more specifically, variously focus on "self-reliance"; on Emerson's lifelong interest in character; on his faith in the "moral sentiment"; on his holistic sense of what living well entails; and on connections between his philosophy and various traditions of ethical thought. Stanley Cavell, for example, situates Emerson within a Western tradition of moral perfectionism – "the self is always attained, as well as *to be* attained" – and shows how "Emersonian perfectionism" is the ongoing task of defining, questioning, and taking responsibility for one's self and a task "essential to the criticism of democracy from within" (*Conditions* 12, 3). Lawrence Buell suggests that Emerson's "basic persuasion looks less like either of the two dominant traditions of western ethical theory – Benthamite moral utilitarianism and Kantian deontology or duty ethics – than like what is now called 'virtue ethics'" (212). Joseph Urbas finds that Emerson gives us "an ethics *with* ontology, an ethics grounded in being and the causal power of the universe" (*Metaphysics* 191). Susan Dunston shows how Emerson's work is "a significant philosophical antecedent and contributor to contemporary environmental ethics," weaving together "intellectual strains as diverse as ecology, Indigenous science and ethics, Sufi poetry, feminism, and systems thinking" (*Environmental* xvi). Most generally, scholars might be said to agree that "his question is not 'What can I know?'" as Robert Richardson puts it, "but 'How should I live?'" (16). Or in Gustaaf Van Cromphout's terms, "How one should live is the fundamental question of ethics" and "Among the questions that confronted Emerson in the course of his long life, none was more important and insistent than 'How shall I live?'" (1).[5] This question presses with special force – with "the force of a personal address" (*CS* 4: 215) – during Emerson's crisis of vocation, and marks not only what would be his departure from the ministry but also the beginnings of a poetic project rooted in, and finding forms beyond, what he called "the perception of … this infinitude belonging to every man" (*CS* 4: 216).

Sermon CLXV, delivered in 1833 when Emerson returned to the United States from his formative first trip to Europe, voices "a revolution of religious opinion taking effect around us" and its ethical implications:

... men have begun to feel and to inquire for their *several sake* in the joy and suffering of the whole. What is *my* relation to Almighty God? What is *my* relation to my fellow men? What am I designed for? What are my duties? What is my destiny? ... The questions are now again presented, because the wonder of the surrounding creation begins to press upon the soul with the force of a personal address. (*CS* 4: 215, Emerson's emphases)

This passage asks us to take account of ourselves; to experience ourselves consequentially placed as moral agents within "the joy and suffering of the whole." In other words, it presents in condensed form the Emersonian themes of moral agency, integrity, duty, and "an original relation to the universe" (*Nature CW* 1: 7), "a personal relation," Susan Dunston says, "at once ontological, ethical, and aesthetic."[6] When the sermon goes on to ask, "And what is the answer?," one encounters the radical theological perspective from which Emerson's career would unfold.

Man begins to hear a voice in reply that fills the heavens and the earth, saying, that God is within him, that *there* is the celestial host. I find that this amazing revelation of my immediate relation to God, is a solution to all the doubts that oppressed me.... It is the perception of this depth in human nature – this infinitude belonging to every man that has been born – which has given new value to the habits of reflexion and solitude. (*CS* 4: 215–16, Emerson's emphasis)

If ethics, as Emerson put it, is "the practice of ideas, or the introduction of ideas into life" (*CW* 1: 35), then one might say the practical form this revelation takes is Emerson's departure from the ministry in order to preach the "one doctrine" – often quoted yet arguably misunderstood – he says he teaches "In all [his] lectures": "the infinitude of the private man" (*JMN* VII: 342). In effect, this infinitude is the way every individual partakes of the "one mind common to all individual men" ("History" *CW* 2: 3), "not diverse from things, from space, from light, from time, from man, but one with them" ("Self-Reliance" *CW* 2: 37). It means "each being," regardless of station, "allied to all" (*CS* 4: 232) and all returning to the "unbounded soul of [the] World" ("Self-Possession" *LL* 2: 119), bears the obligation of moral agency with consequences both immediate and beyond measure.

Emerson's reception history within and outside academia often frames this "infinitude of the private man" as a brand of individualism incompatible with the pursuit of democracy. David Marr, for instance, finds Emerson inaugurating an American "tradition" that "teaches us to picture human experience without history, freedom without politics, authority without community" (210). Similarly, an emphasis on the "imperial" self, Quentin Anderson argues, amounts to an "overextension of the significance of individual claims"[7] compromising civic life. Yet when reading the "infinitude of the private man" within the broader context of Emerson's oeuvre – and beyond the concept of "self-reliance" often yoked to it – one sees how it names and celebrates a metaphysical and ontological fact at the heart of Emerson's ethics.[8] "[W]hat is this Admiration to which we would excite the soul?" he asks in Sermon CLXIX, "What is it but a perception of a man's true position in the universe and his consequent obligations? This is the whole moral and end of such views as I present" (*CS* 4: 234). For Emerson, ethics begins in perceiving this "position in the universe," this "wonderful congruity which subsists between man and the world" (*Nature CW* 1: 40), the way "[w]e first share the life by which things exist" ("Self-Reliance" *CW* 2: 37), and the way human "life is intertwined with the whole chain of organic and inorganic being" ("History" *CW* 2: 20). "This ontological fact," Dunston reminds us, "must shape our answer to 'the practical question of the conduct of life. How shall I live?' (*CW* 6: 1), for we, and the world, co-constitute those relations and connections."[9] Emerson everywhere marvels at this fact. "[W]hy is it," he asks in "Address on Education," "that this complex net of personal relations is woven round him? Why does he work with so many companions? Why must he face so many enemies? … Why, but to learn the laws of Ethics – the law of moral agents in the universe, – in other words, the moral constitution of his own mind?" (*EL* 2: 201). This "complex net of personal relations" that cheer as well as chagrin is, for Emerson, a necessary and ongoing education in ethics, a metaphysical fact extant in everyday life and revealing "the moral constitution" of one's mind. Accordingly, far from egocentrism, or what Yale president A. Bartlett Giamatti called "contempt for restraining or complex connections,"[10] Emerson's proposal "to look at every object in its relation to Myself" (*JMN* IV: 272) here becomes an ethical practice of accounting for oneself together with "every object"; that is, observing what "every object," when brought near to oneself, means and requires.

In fact, he insists in the lecture "Ethical Writers" (1836) that "The law which Ethics treats is that we mean by the nature of things; the law of all action which cannot yet be stated, it is so simple … and yet is fully exemplified in all its height and depth in the private life of every man" (*EL* 1: 370). Consequently, he goes so far as to say in "Love" that "All that is in the world that is or ought to be known, is cunningly wrought into the texture of man, of woman" (*CW* 2: 108). Similarly, in all his engagements with his era, one sees him turn from "The Spirit of the Times" (1848) or "the theory of the Age" ("Fate" *CW* 6: 1) to the persons who constitute it. The law "which cannot yet be stated," in other words, might be seen and shown, and when Emerson opens his *Philosophy of History* (1836) by announcing his "design of attempting a more just survey of man's relations" – a survey seeking to reclaim "the variety and reach of [man's] affinities" (*EL* 2: 19) – one might say he comes nearest to describing the design uniting his sermons, journals, lectures and essays: following the method of the poet who "re-attaches things to nature and the Whole" ("The Poet" *CW* 3: 11), correcting the "half-sight" of science with metaphors, analogies, anecdotes, and musings that make intimate the world "in system, in relation" (*TN* 2: 265) and the "conspiring reception" ("The Method of Nature" *CW* 1: 122) it requires of us.

Put differently, the substance of Emerson's ethics and his methods of investigation converge in a body of writing that makes an argument for rediscovering the intimacies in which we exist. "I would to God I might awaken the attention of every torpid hearer," he persists, "till he apprehended the intimate connexion which can subsist between himself and God, when his own heart shall beat pulse for pulse in harmony with the universal whole" (*CS* 1: 290). The vocabularies and paradigms of theology, aesthetics, science, and ethics variously and only incompletely approach this "intimate connexion" between individuals and the "universal whole"; approximate it, yet never systematize it, and rightly so.[11] For example, another way Emerson describes this "connexion" is to call it "The fundamental fact in our metaphysic constitution," which "is the correspondence of man to the world, so that every change in that writes a record in the mind" ("Success" *CW* 7: 152).[12] Or take the poem "Woodnotes II," in which a pine tree, through song, calls an orphaned listener back into the "perfect tune" of the universe: "Come learn with me the fatal song/Which knits the world in music strong … Not unrelated, unaffied, / But to each thought and thing allied, / Is perfect Nature's every part, / Rooted in the mighty Heart" (*CW* 9: 109). Again and again, Emerson emphasizes this radical interconnectedness that is at once a metaphysical fact and a fact realized in the practice of everyday life.

Even, and perhaps especially, in "Experience," an essay that seems to leave us at the furthest extremes of skeptical alienation, Emerson shows how here too we find ourselves in an immediate, morally consequential relationship to the world. "Illusion, Temperament, Succession, Surface, Surprise, Reality, Subjectiveness" are the "lords of life," and though Emerson "dare not assume to give their order" or "compile a code," he nevertheless concludes, "I name them as I find them in my way" (*CW* 3: 47) – a deliberate act of observing where he finds himself and choosing to live accordingly. In other words, human partiality in all its forms does not diminish our participation as moral agents in the world but requires it all the more: "Without any shadow of doubt, amidst this vertigo of shows and politics, I settle myself ever firmer in the creed, that we should not postpone and refer and wish, but do broad justice where we are, by whomsoever we deal with, accepting our actual companions and circumstances, however humble or odious, as the mystic officials" (*CW* 3: 35). While one might not be able to state as a law "the nature of things" or "give ... order" to the "lords" that largely shape human life, one can make an ethical commitment to "do broad justice where we are" and to the future that right action now will realize. "[T]here never was a right endeavor, but it succeeded. Patience and patience, we shall win at the last ... there is victory yet for all justice" (*CW* 3: 48–49). These sentences capture how the "fundamental fact in our metaphysic constitution" equally informs Emerson's transcendentalist faith and his pragmatic response to "our actual companions and circumstances."

The "Divinity School Address" (1838) perhaps offers the most explicit narrative of how one encounters this "fundamental fact" and how it brings home the meaning of ethical obligation.

> Behold these infinite relations, so like, so unlike; many yet one. I would study, I would know, I would admire forever ... A more secret, sweet, and overpowering beauty appears to man when his heart and mind open to the sentiment of virtue. Then he is instructed in what is above him ... *He ought.* He knows the sense of that grand word, though his analysis fails entirely to render account of it. (*CW* 1: 76–77, Emerson's emphasis)

This felt experience of one's being amid "infinite relations," an aesthetic awareness of receiving instruction from the universe, makes possible a living yet inexplicable knowledge of "that grand word" *ought*. In effect, Emerson here teaches divinity students the lesson he articulates later in "Success" (1860): "it is not propositions, not new dogmas and a logical exposition of the world, that are our first need; but to watch and tenderly cherish the intellectual and moral sensibilities ... and woo them to stay and make their home with us" (*CW* 7: 152). As Joseph Urbas explains, Emerson "wanted moral distinctions as *felt realities* grounded in something outside of human nature but continuous with it" (italics in original).[13] "Morals coeval with existence" was a phrase Emerson borrowed from his Aunt Mary Moody, and in his lecture "Ethics" (1841) he explains how "Self-Trust" is "not a faith in a man's own whim or conceit as if he were quite severed from all other beings and acted on his own private account, but a perception that the mind common to the Universe is disclosed to the individual through his own nature" (*EL* 2: 151). Accordingly, the "Divinity School Address" exhorts students to "cast behind [them] all conformity" (*CW* 1: 90) and to observe "the sentiment of virtue" – the "moral sentiment" – as it emerges within the course of daily life and thought.

Akin to, and informed by, the "moral sense" first proposed by the third Earl of Shaftesbury and Francis Hutcheson and developed by Scottish

Common Sense philosophers such as Thomas Reid and Dugald Stewart, the moral sentiment, as Emerson defines it, is the "main, central, prominent power of the soul ... the Conscience, the distinguisher of right and wrong" (Sermon IX *CS* 1: 116). More, though, than an individual's conscience, this "old Sovereign sentiment" (*TN* 3: 276) has an independent existence. "It is alive," Emerson says, "and maketh alive ... It is wholly impersonal; it passes through my whole being, and I cannot think without being affected by it, – but it refers me to all the world; and is present to every other creature, as to me. It is the law of soul, and not of my soul. It melts all things into itself, for it is itself their ground of being" ("Holiness" *EL* 2: 345). In Urbas's assessment, it is Emerson's "core principle of causal, ontological, and moral continuity" and "the foundation" of his ethics.[14] "We are made of it," Emerson says, "the world is built by it, things endure as they share it; all beauty, all health, all intelligence, exist by it" ("Perpetual Forces" *LL* 2: 300). The moral sentiment is the "bedrock of consistency" in Emerson's thought, David Robinson argues, "the most important point of continuity in his thinking from first to last."[15] The moral sentiment reveals, and is the experience of, the fact that one exists within innumerable intimacies of immediate moral consequence. It "puts us at the heart of nature, where we belong; in the cabinet of Science and Causes; there, where all the wires terminate which hold the world in magnetic communication, and so converts us into universal beings" ("Morals" *LL* 2: 132–33). An operative ethical sense, "*He ought*," an awareness of one's position "at the heart nature" inspiring and guiding one's conduct of life, "the moral sentiment ... lies at the foundation of society" (*CW* 1: 79). While the "Divinity School Address" stirs divinity students to see how "[i]n one soul, in your soul, there are resources for the world" (89) – specifically, resources for revitalizing "a decaying church and a wasting unbelief" (88) – the essay "Self-Reliance" (1841) extends this provocation to a broader audience, boldly charting the practical consequences, for individuals and for society, of estrangement from our universal being at the "heart of nature."

Though the canonical essay "Self-Reliance" has long been considered a declaration of individualism, the ethics it calls for depends on a renewed intimacy with existence. In other words, in response to alienation from moral life, a state in which "There is the man *and* his virtues" (*CW* 2: 31) and a condition evident, for instance, in "conformity" and "foolish consistency" (33), the essay would reacquaint readers with "that deep force, the last fact behind which analysis cannot go; [where] all things find their common origin" (37). Variously named "the aboriginal Self," the "cause," the "life by which things exist" (37), and the "relation of the soul to the divine spirit" (38), this fact in "Self-Reliance," as elsewhere in Emerson's work, is the metaphysical and ontological basis of his ethics, an ethics committed to engaging one's world in "a new and unprecedented way" (42). "If any man considers the present aspects of what is called by distinction *society*," Emerson presses, "he will see the need of these ethics. We are afraid of truth, afraid of fortune, afraid of death, and afraid of each other" (43). Against conformities that "make [individuals] not false in a few particulars, authors of a few lies, but false in all particulars" (32), a "greater self-reliance must work a revolution in all the offices and relations of men; in their religion; in their education; in their pursuits; in their modes of living; in their association; in their property; in their speculative views" (44). This "greater self-reliance" means deliberately living the condition of being everywhere individually implicated in "the joy and suffering of the whole" (*CS* 4: 215), fated to the freedom and obligation of moral agency. "Ethical self-reliance," in Dunston's reading, "ultimately rests on the great fact of relational identity that Emerson experienced with others."[16] It "entails not a narrow selfishness or even just cultivation of one's self but an empathy with all selves," Alan Levine and Daniel Malachuk suggest, "not only an ethical commitment to the active 'reform' or 'cultivation' of one's self but also to a political democracy where all other individuals are able to do the same."[17] Alone accountable for what one takes to be "right" and "wrong," the self-reliant individual works in integrity and wholehearted commitment to this freedom and obligation – "There is a great responsible Thinker and Actor working wherever a man works" (*CW* 2: 35) – a way of life not justified in advance by given forms and explanations but tested and amended in the process of living.

Decades later, in his posthumously published *Natural History of Intellect* (1893), Emerson will say, "Metaphysics must be perpetually reinforced by life, must be the observations of a working man on working men; must be biography, – the record of some law whose working was surprised by the observer in natural action" (*W* 2: 1250). His most ambitious attempt to gather the lessons of these lifelong observations, to arrange them into a single study uniting "severe science with a poetic vision," is *Natural History of Intellect*. A vital yet understudied text, pursued for decades and posthumously compiled and published by his daughter Ellen Emerson and literary executor James Elliot Cabot, *Natural History of Intellect* is a "compelling philosophical project," David Robinson asserts, that despite its "state of incompletion" is "significant as a point of reference for Emerson's attempt to correlate knowledge with ethical action."[18] A "nearly forty-year endeavor to construct a unique model of philosophy replete with its own internally consistent poetics, ethics, history, and science," in Ronald Bosco's terms, it is the "largest long-term intellectual project of his career" ("Historical Introduction" to *CW* 8: lxxii, lxx). This project doesn't have the completeness of "systematic form" (or even the completeness of a final draft prepared by Emerson) but rather, the completeness of conceptual coherence.[19]

"I cannot myself use that systematic form which is reckoned essential in treating the science of the mind," he begins,

> But if one can say so without arrogance, I might suggest that he who contents himself with dotting a fragmentary curve, recording only what facts he has observed, without attempting to arrange them within one outline, follows a system also, – a system as grand as any other, though he does not interfere with its vast curves by prematurely forcing them into a circle or ellipses, but only draws that arc which he clearly sees. (*W* 2: 1250)

In effect, the project propositionalizes the method and attitude of the poet that underwrites Emerson's engagement with the "most important science" ethics. "Metaphysics is dangerous as a single pursuit," he cautions, "We should feel more confident in the same results from the mouth of a man of the world. The inward analysis must be corrected by rough experience.... I think metaphysics a grammar to which, once read, we seldom return" (*W* 2: 1250). In some ways his description of the project is more notable than the project itself because it casts light back on his oeuvre, recasting earlier observations as deliberate methods. For instance, the reflection at the end of *Nature*, "It were a wise inquiry for the closet, to compare, point by point, especially at remarkable crises in life, our daily history, with the rise and progress of ideas in the mind" (*CW* I: 44), becomes formalized in *Natural History of Intellect*: "What I am now to attempt is simply some sketches or studies ... *Memoires pour servir* toward a Natural History of Intellect" (*W* 2: 1251), "a sort of Farmer's Almanac of mental moods" (1249).[20] "If a true metaphysician should come," Emerson imagined in *Natural Method of Mental Philosophy* (1858), "he would accompany you through your mind, pointing at this treasure-crypt, and at that, indicating the wealth lying here and there, which the student would joyfully perceive" (71). *Natural History of Intellect* undertakes this journey, correcting and reinforcing metaphysics by "rough experience" and showing how "Ethics is the soul illustrated in human life" (*JMN* XII: 163); that is, the way raising and responding to the question "How shall I live?" finds form in our lives together.

"This insistence on the necessity for each person to undertake his or her own moral exploration is a key to the radical nature of Emersonian ethics," poet Ann Lauterbach writes, "it is almost beyond what we can imagine: that the public, one by one, can and will think outside of the proscriptions and prescriptions of political and social commerce and commentary; that each of us is both willing and able to find our way out of received ideas that govern so much of our discourse."[21]

To "find our way out of received ideas that govern so much of our discourse" requires each of us to undertake, in our own ways, the way of poets: rediscovering the "infinitude of the private man" – the way "Our life is consentaneous and far-related" ("Fate" CW 6: 20) – and what it necessitates and makes possible. For "We are all poets at last," in Emerson's view, "Each of us is a part of eternity and immensity" (EL 3: 365). Accordingly, his body of writing, with a unity not so much of completeness but of purposefulness, reconnects us to ourselves, fellow persons, the natural world, and beyond. "What is a day? What is a year? What is summer? What is woman? What is a child? What is sleep? To our blindness, these things seem unaffecting" (Nature CW 1: 44). "Why should not we also enjoy an original relation to the universe?" (Nature CW 1: 7). "What would we really know the meaning of?" ("The American Scholar" CW 1: 67). "Where do we find ourselves?" ("Experience" CW 3: 27). "How shall I live?" ("Fate" CW 6: 1). These seemingly simple yet incisive questions, vital for civic living and human existence, bring us face to face with what would seem to be matters already settled, as if Emerson wanted us to confront them anew and now more deliberately. "Settle everything anew for yourself especially where you suspect the customary judgements [or] things esteemed settled" (JMN III: 325).

Emerson's responses to the crises of his day embody this principle. The record of his relationship to abolitionism and, later, to women's rights, shows him persistently settling anew his position, engaging in what Jean McClure Mudge terms "a complex, prolonged inner dialogue," ultimately lessening the "conflict between [his] basic values and his unsettled attitudes on race and gender."[22] For example, he declared in "American Slavery" (1855) and elsewhere that he did "not cripple but exalt the social action," yet "the doctrine of the independence and inspiration of the individual" (LL 2: 11) remained his keynote: "no forms, neither constitutions, nor laws, nor covenants, nor churches, nor bibles, are of any use in themselves. There is no help but in the head, and heart, and hamstrings of a man" ("Fugitive" LL 1: 342). So while he acknowledges the need for organized reform and legislation – he publicly celebrated the Emancipation Proclamation, an act that "compels the innumerable officers ... of the Republic to range themselves on the line of this equity"[23] – he holds that social change is equally, and crucially, a matter of ordinary ethics; a matter of how individuals conduct their daily lives together. "The subject of the Times," he emphasizes, "is not an abstract question. We talk of the world, but we mean a few men and women" ("Introductory Lecture" CW 1: 168). So too History, which, like Fate, when more nearly seen, is a matter of "all the relations of the human being" ("Introductory" EL 2: 18):

> If a man wishes to acquaint himself with the real history of the world, with the spirit of the age, he must not go first to the statehouse or the court room. The subtle spirit of life must be sought in facts nearer. It is what is done and suffered in the house, in the constitution, in temperament, in the personal history, that has the profoundest interest for us. (CW 7: 54)

Though "These facts are, to be sure, harder to read" (54), they largely constitute our lived social state; contribute to what makes it just and unjust, and inform how we define what these words mean to us, individually and collectively. "Certainly, 'the social state,' 'patriotism,' 'law,' and 'government,' all did cover ideas, though the words have wandered from the things" (LL 2: 11), he remarks in "American Slavery," a barbed reminder that estrangement from our words means estrangement from our lives. The consequences appear in every form of collective life: "in society, in education, in political parties, in trade and labor, in expenditure, or in the direction of surplus capital, you may see the credence of men; how deeply they live, how much water the ship draws" (7).

Not by chance, then, does Emerson open the essay "Fate" by turning from "the theory of the Age" to the "practical question of the conduct of life" (CW 6: 1). This question fates every individual to the freedom of being a moral agent "allied to all" and even beyond what can be known. In fact, "along with the civil and metaphysical history of man, another history goes daily forward – that of the external world, – in which he is not less strictly implicated" (CW 2: 20). Emerson does not offer precepts or blueprints for finding one's path. Instead, he exhorts, "Broader and deeper we must write our annals ... if we would truelier express our central and wide-related nature, instead of this old chronology of selfishness and pride to which we have to long lent our eyes" (23). His body of work attempts such annals, and recounts what he learns along his way.

> The secret of culture is to learn, that a few great points steadily reappear, alike in the poverty of the obscurest farm, and in the miscellany of metropolitan life, and that these few are alone to be regarded, – the escape from all false ties; courage to be what we are; and love of what is simple and beautiful; independence, and cheerful relation, these are the essentials, – these, and the wish to serve, – to add somewhat to the well-being of men. ("Considerations by the Way" CW 6: 148)

Provoked by this open secret, I wake "on a stair" in "a series of which we do not know the extremes" (CW 3: 27), bound to find myself amid the intimacies in which we exist and in which the ethical question "How shall I live?" begins living in us.

## Notes

1. Susan L. Dunston, "Ethics." in *Emerson in Context*, ed. Wesley T. Mott (Cambridge: Cambridge University Press, 2014), 172.
2. John T. Lysaker, *After Emerson* (Bloomington, IN: Indiana UP, 2017), 134.
3. Wesley T. Mott, "'The Age of the First-Person Singular': Emerson and Individualism," in *A Historical Guide to Ralph Waldo Emerson*, ed. Joel Myerson (Oxford: Oxford University Press, 2000), 62–63.
4. Herwig Friedl, *Thinking in Search of a Language: Essays on American Intellect and Intuition* (London: Bloomsbury, 2019), 7. For representative overviews of Emerson's reception history, see Sarah Wider's *The Critical Reception of Emerson* (2000), Lawrence Buell's "The Emerson Industry in the 1980s" (1984), Michael Lopez's "De-Transcendentalizing Emerson" (1988), and Randall Fuller's "Critics: 1948–2013" (2014). For scholarship on Emerson and individualism, specifically, see Charles E. Mitchell's *Individualism and its Discontents: Appropriations of Emerson, 1880–1950* (1997), Wesley Mott's "'The Age of the First-Person Singular': Emerson and Individualism" (2000), and James Albrecht's *Reconstructing Individualism: A Pragmatic Tradition from Emerson to Ellison* (2012).
5. For other approaches to Emerson and ethics, see Branka Arsić's *On Leaving: A Reading in Emerson* (2010), Michael Colacurcio's *Emerson and Other Minds* (2021), John Lysaker's *After Emerson* (2017), and David Robinson's *Emerson and the Conduct of Life: Pragmatism and Ethical Purpose in the Later Work* (1993).
6. Susan L. Dunston, *Emerson's Environmental Ethics* (Lanham, MD: Lexington Books, 2018), 1.
7. Quentin Anderson, *The Imperial Self: An Essay in American Literary and Cultural History* (New York: Knopf, 1971), 18.
8. For a comprehensive account of Emerson's metaphysics, see Joseph Urbas's *Emerson's Metaphysics: A Song of Laws and Causes* (2016).
9. Dunston, *Emerson's Environmental Ethics*, xiv.
10. A. Bartlett, Giamatti, "Power, Politics, and a Sense of History," in *The University and the Public Interest* (New York: Atheneum, 1981), 172.
11. "There is something of the heart of Emerson's message profoundly recalcitrant to the formulations of the discursive intelligence" (6), Jonathan Bishop observes.
12. Emerson defines egotism in equally metaphysical terms: "'Tis a disease that, like influenza, falls on all constitutions. In the distemper known to the physicians as *chorea*, the patient sometimes turns round and continues to spin slowly on one spot. Is egotism a metaphysical variety of this malady? The man runs round a ring formed by his own talent, falls into an admiration of it, and loses relation to the world" ("Culture" *CW* 6: 70).
13. Joseph Urbas, *The Philosophy of Ralph Waldo Emerson* (London: Routledge, 2021), 103.
14. Ibid., 99.

15. David Robinson, *Emerson and the Conduct of Life: Pragmatism and Ethical Purpose in the Later Work* (Cambridge: Cambridge University Press, 1993), 7.

16. Dunston, *Emerson's Environmental Ethics*, 173.

17. Alan M. Levine and Daniel S. Malachuk, "Introduction," in *A Political Companion to Ralph Waldo Emerson*, ed. Alan Levine and Daniel Malachuk (Lexington: University Press of Kentucky, 2014), 1–2.

18. Robinson, *Emerson and the Conduct of Life*, 182.

19. See Christopher Hanlon, *Emerson's Memory*, in which he describes the book as "a readerly and writerly convergence" (12) between Emerson, Ellen, and Cabot; a practice of "communal" thinking that unsettles what critics have taken to be Emerson's "earlier notions of an inviolate self-consciousness" (38, 39).

20. In Hanlon's terms, "Emerson pitches his investigation as an application of Yankee record-keeping, diurnal journaling, a *Walden* of the mind" (26). In David Robinson's reading, "The method of science never functions ... as a true methodology, but only as a scaffolding, discarded when Emerson's meditation on intellect becomes self supporting" (189).

21. Ann Lauterbach, "After Emerson: Of General Knowledge and the Common Good," in *New Morning: Emerson in the Twenty-first Century*, ed. Arthur S. Lothstein and Michael Brodrick (Albany, NY: SUNY Press, 2008), 196–208.

22. Jean McClure Mudge, "Actively Entering Old Age," in *Mr. Emerson's Revolution*, ed. Jean McClure Mudge (Cambridge: Open Book Publishers, 2015), 230, 231.

23. Emerson, *The Political Emerson: Essential Writings on Politics and Social Reform*, ed. David M. Robinson (Boston: Beacon, 2004), 180.

# 6

MICHAEL JONIK

# Life, Form, and Power in "Experience"

"The results of life are uncalculated and uncalculable."
Emerson, "Experience"
(*CW* 3: 40)

"Never mind the ridicule, never mind the defeat: up again, old heart! ...
there is victory yet for all justice; and the true romance which the world
exists to realize, will be the transformation of genius into practical power"
(*CW* 3: 49). Many readers of Emerson's seminal essay "Experience" have
taken this "uplifting peroration"[1] to offer an optimistic counterpoint to
the skepticism that emerges across the essay, the skepticism instilled from
not being able to mourn the death of his son Waldo, for not being able to
experience life directly but only by indirect blows, or for not being able to
foreclose the "discrepance" (*CW* 3: 48) between the world he thinks and the
world he sees. Yet the hopeful tone of the passage aside, what would it mean
for genius to be transformed into practical power? More generally, what
does power mean for Emerson? How does his unique poetico-philosophical
notion of power allow him to intervene in the long idealist tradition of
thinking about power? And as is crucial for understanding "Experience,"
how does power relate to concepts of life and form?

The interplay of life, form, and power is both central to the essay and
comes to mark Emerson's mature articulations of metaphysics and philosophy, nature and history, and politics and ethics. It is instantiated across
Emerson's relentlessly eclectic thinking – from the creative potentialities
of the imagination and the intellect, and the deforming forces of love and
loss, to the conditions that embolden individual selves to mastery, invention, and success. The impulsive, circulatory, transitory, depersonalizing,
and yet aggrandizing modes of power that emerge in Emerson's thinking –
the powers of the heart and the powers of the mind – point to a vitality
that not only appears as the content of his essays and lectures but is at
once stylistically performed by them. Like the living words he celebrates in

his homage to Montaigne, we might likewise say of Emerson: "Cut these words, and they would bleed; they are vascular and alive" (CW 4: 95).

## "Power ceases in the instant of repose"

One might rightly associate the question of power with Emerson's later works such as the essays "Fate" and (of course) "Power" in his book *The Conduct of Life,* or in lectures such as "Powers of the Mind," "Moral Forces," and "Perpetual Forces." But power is a consistent theme across Emerson's entire writing career. Even before "Experience," often taken to be his central philosophical statement, Emerson begins to develop a multimodal philosophy of power that traverses physical and metaphysical, idealist and materialist, or psychological and political domains.[2] His *Essays First Series,* to this end, offer an extended statement on the role that power plays in life. This role is most perspicuous, perhaps, in "Self-Reliance," in which Emerson asserts the importance of seizing the power that passes through each one of us in order to live most fully within ourselves. At first it might seem that power for Emerson is concentrated in an individual: "The power which resides in him is new in nature, and none but he knows what that is which he can do, nor does he know until he has tried" (CW 2: 28). But it is important to note that Emerson does not say that an individual *holds* power, but rather that power *"resides"* in an individual. Power is singular, or singularized, in its individual manifestation, and, like every singular life, manifests something new in nature. But power is not held, rather it is exercised: One's power is therefore only apparent when it is "tried." Already, then, we can see how there is a practical or action-oriented movement in Emerson's thinking of power, yet one that is not determinately focused on a given end. Power is *essayed,* and thus is part of life's ongoing processes of experimenting and experiencing. "Do the thing, and you shall have the power: but they who do not the thing have not the power" (CW 2: 67).

And as power is essayed, it changes the person who exercises it. Our life and vitality depend on our power to create ourselves anew or, better, to allow the power of life to recreate us. So, if power is at the seat of the "self" of self-reliance, it is not as a fixed foundation. Power is an active and creative force of self-othering. It is the power to say, after Arthur Rimbaud and Jon Fosse, "I is another." As a creative vitality, the power of life is antipathetic to any stasis or stagnation: "Life only avails, not the having lived. Power ceases in the instant of repose; it resides in the moment of transition from a past to a new state, in the shooting of the gulf, in the darting to an aim" (CW 2: 40). As transitional, power might be understood as *causal* – as the driving force of change that is life. "Causation," as Joseph Urbas puts it, "is the power of life"; it is "the vital, creative, transformative principle at the heart of creation," what philosophers call *natura naturans* or "nature naturing."[3]

Across his *Essays First Series*, Emerson's philosophy of power becomes expressed in several different modes. It is the power of love to overpower and depersonalize individuals, the power of friendship to deliver us to higher selves, or the power of "compensation" to open new vistas of life in the face of calamity and loss. The power of intellect is behind everything we do, Emerson asserts, as intellect "is the simple power anterior to all action or construction" (CW 2: 193). But power is also relentlessly forward-moving and upheaving. As Emerson writes in "Circles": "In the thought of to-morrow there is a power to upheave all thy creed, all the creeds, all the literatures, of the nations, and marshal thee to a heaven which no epic dream has yet depicted.... Step by step we scale this mysterious ladder: the steps are actions; the new prospect is power" (CW 2: 181). In "Compensation," Emerson makes a key claim about the immanence of power, one that works for both animate and inanimate nature, humans and nonhumans alike: "Every thing in nature contains all the powers of nature" (CW 2: 59). This claim unfolds across his thinking, in terms of how the part contains the whole, or how one's partial experiences nonetheless signal a kind of access to a unified or ideal experience. Emerson returns to this thought often, as he invites us to create our own "original" relation to the universe, to act in a way worthy of our present life, or to realize that new revelations are available to us – here, today, now.

Often his essays' heading poems offer powerful distillations of his thinking, and in the poem that opens "Compensation," Emerson writes:

> Laurel crowns cleave to deserts,
> And power to him who power exerts;
> Hast not thy share? On winged feet,
> Lo! it rushes thee to meet;
> And all that Nature made thy own,
> Floating in air or pent in stone,
> Will rive the hills and swim the sea,
> And, like thy shadow, follow thee. (CW 2: 54)

Power is both exerted by us and, in a sense, exerts us. Hast not thy share? If your share is not apparent, the power of nature is nonetheless available to you and will hasten to come to find you, if not follow you. As immanent in nature, it is both a potentiality floating in air and pent in stone, but it is also an actualized force of deformation that will rive the hills and swim the sea, or cling to you, abyssally close, "like thy shadow." In turn, "Spiritual Laws" offers a short treatise on power and insinuates how Emerson will also come to understand political power as in relation to the power of individuals. Yet as he celebrates the power of Caesar and Napoleon – and equally Shakespeare and an unnamed great mathematician – perhaps counterintuitively, he finds evidence of their power in nature and not "in them." How are they powerful? How can I be powerful too? Emerson advises: "Place yourself in the middle of the stream of power and wisdom which animates all whom it floats, and you are without effort impelled to truth, to right, and a perfect contentment" (CW 2: 81). It is this "balance" of power – between power as personal and individualizing and yet, at the same time, impersonal and de-individualizing – that will mark Emerson's thinking on power and its relation to his ideas of life and form.

## Power and Impersonal Life in "Experience"

"Experience," from his follow-up Essays: Second Series, further develops Emerson's thinking of power, to the extent that power becomes the keynote concept in the essay. But if, in "Compensation," we find power and power finds us, in "Experience," we are first met with the disorienting powerlessness evoked by the opening question of the essay, "where do we find ourselves" (CW 3: 27)? In keeping with this disorientation, there is what could be called an *atopos* of power in the essay: power is marked by its dislocation, power is everywhere and nowhere. Not only does Emerson assert that "I exert the same quality of power in all places" (CW 3: 43), but also more fundamentally, he says, "Like a bird which alights nowhere, but hops perpetually from bough to bough, is the Power which abides in no man and in no woman, but for a moment speaks from this one, and for another moment from that one" (CW 3: 34). Power is transitory and transitional rather than held; it is impersonal ("in no man and in no woman") and ephemeral ("speaking" for a moment here and a moment there).[4] In "The Poet," in many ways a companion essay to "Experience," Emerson calls this impersonal power "public power":

> beside his privacy of power as an individual man, there is a great public power, on which he can draw, by unlocking, at all risks, his human doors, and suffering the ethereal tides to roll and circulate through him: then he is caught up into the life of the Universe, his speech is thunder, his thought is law, and his words are universally intelligible as the plants and animals. (CW 3: 15–16)

We must stimulate not only our intellect but also our "instinct" to join this powerful flow, to let "circulate" through us "the life of the Universe."

We recalibrate our synapses so that we find "new passages are opened for us into nature, the mind flows into and through things hardest and highest, and the metamorphosis is possible" (16). If all people have access to this "extraordinary power" (16), poets are particularly receptive to it. They achieve what Emerson later in "Poetry and Imagination" calls the "poetic perception of metamorphosis" (CW 8: 4). And poets can, through their imaginative use of symbols, in turn enable others to become intoxicated with the flowing, joyful, and divine power of all entangled life.

In "Experience," Emerson characterizes the long traditions of mythology, theology, and philosophy as so many attempts to name this power – the "unbounded substance" or "vast-flowing vigor" that passes through and possesses all things:

> Fortune, Minerva, Muse, Holy Ghost, – these are quaint names, too narrow to cover this unbounded substance. The baffled intellect must still kneel before this cause, which refuses to be named, – ineffable cause, which every fine genius has essayed to represent by some emphatic symbol, as, Thales by water, Anaximenes by air, Anaxagoras by (*Nous*) thought, Zoroaster by fire, Jesus and the moderns by love: and the metaphor of each has become a national religion.... In our more correct writing, we give to this generalization the name of Being, and thereby confess that we have arrived as far as we can go. Suffice it for the joy of the universe, that we have not arrived at a wall, but at interminable oceans. Our life seems not present, so much as prospective; not for the affairs on which it is wasted, but as a hint of this vast-flowing vigor. (CW 3: 42)

As with Emerson's ontology of power in "Self-Reliance" or "Compensation," in "Experience" power is still to be found in the prospective dynamism of life, which is generalized in the Western philosophical tradition under the name "Being." As such, the question of "what is power?" is inseparable from the questions of "what is life?" and "what is Being?" In each case, while the answer is perhaps elusive and ineffable, Emerson's comportment of power, life, and Being is always toward the prospective: "Onward and onward!" And if life gives us hints of the vast-flowing vigor, it is in the very onwardness of the power of life that Being is self-evident. It shows itself as the ever-creative power of the new. If Emerson says that "life is full of surprises," the surprises themselves are the events of an unbidden and unsettling power passing through us, of the incalculability of life as it takes hold of us and sweeps us away into the new, even in the face of calamitous loss. "Once we lived in what we saw; now, the rapaciousness of this new power [given to us by a new picture of life] ... threatens to absorb all things, engages us" (43).

Even if this "new power" (or "new energy" as Emerson articulates it in "The Poet") is direct and unmediated in the sense that it doesn't need to explain itself, counterintuitively, perhaps, it is expressed in its indirectness:

"Direct strokes [nature] never gave us power to make; all our blows glance, all our hits are accidents" (*CW* 3: 30). Now, this indirectness is part of Emerson's initial mood of lament in "Experience," couched in terms of the "lord of life" he calls "illusion," and connected to how he will characterize the "evanescence and lubricity" of objects (*CW* 3: 29). But it adds another aspect to how he understands power more broadly as impersonal. Power is not a question of conscious agency, of personal choice, or of one's will, but "keeps quite another road than the turnpikes of choice and will, namely, the subterranean and invisible tunnels and channels of life" (*CW* 3: 39). Power is not what one can access directly; those that are powerful are only powerful insofar as they exercise power indirectly: "The most attractive class of people are those who are powerful obliquely, and not by the direct stroke" (39).

For Sharon Cameron, one of the most influential philosophical readers of "Experience," this "obliquity of power saturates the essay": "Power comes from the inability to nail it down anywhere. Power pervades the essay in the multiple instances of dissociation, as these succeed each other in a series of 'which we do not know the extremes, and believe it has none.'"[5] For Cameron, the obliquity of power in "Experience" "exists to empower the grief that the essay has marginalized" – or, in other words, obliquity allows Emerson neither to fully mourn the loss of his son, which frames the essay, nor to make it central thematically to its performance of "experience."[6] Rather obliquity, or marginalization, is how Emerson might preserve his grief as inaccessible in a proximal but nonintegrated psychic space. As such, Cameron implies that grief, though absent from the essay after its early invocation, remains its driving force. "Although some change occurs between the stupor of the essay's beginnings and determined energy of its final pages, this change does not take place prospectively in the essay's last sentence, though that is where Emerson speaks of a potential 'transformation of genius into practical power.'"[7] The "primary transformation" that the essay charts, then, is not from genius into practical power, but from a power over death that completed mourning might bring to a psychic space in which that power is not actualized but only fantasized.[8]

In ways similar to Cameron, Stanley Cavell and Branka Arsić have highlighted impersonal power in relation to the compensatory powers of a "way of life" as "abandonment" (*CW* 2: 190). In so doing, they stress power as a patient enduring of suffering and as a power to leave behind and to live again. Cavell, for his part, writes: "Emerson's, emphatic call to patience should threaten a familiar idea of Emersonian power [that he later outlines in 'Fate' or 'Power'], for Emerson, makes power look awfully like (from a certain platform, look exactly like) passiveness."[9] In her poetico-philosophical exploration of "Experience" in *On Leaving: A Reading in Emerson*, Arsić extends Cameron's and Cavell's understanding of impersonal power in terms of how power exposes us to deformation: "Very simply put," Arsić writes, "power would reside not only in the capacity to deform who we are, but also in our ability to suffer that deformation in order to change."[10] Power is the power to become other and to undergo change, even to suffer the loss of a son.[11] After Cavell, Arsić takes this ability to suffer deformation as the power of passivity and patience; or rather she understands power *as* passivity or patience. She writes: "Cavell's detection of the pervasiveness of passivity within Emerson's, thinking, is thus perhaps the most accurate diagnosis of what that thinking is predicated on."[12] Power's synonyms for Cavell and Arsić are not force, antagonism, or activity, but rather, patience, enduring, passivity, suffering, reception, or passion. As such, power is decoupled from any assertion of ego or personhood. Power is instead "understood as the suffering restlessness of the impersonal," which, for Arsić, is the "major argument not only of 'Experience' but also of 'The Transcendentalist,' [and] paradoxically enough, of 'Self-Reliance.'" Finally, that "power ceases in the moment of repose ... [and] resides in the moment of transition from a pass to a new state" is evidence for Arsić that power "belongs" to an impersonal, nonpositioned, and involuntary life; "Power, then, belongs to the 'it.' *It* is, *it* works, *it* thinks."[13]

## Power and Form

Emerson, while often rhapsodizing on this impersonal power as vitality, at the same time bears witness to what could be called a countervailing tendency within life. Like the counterpoint of freedom and fate he will describe in *The Conduct of Life*, already in "Experience," power as abandonment or deformation is offset by form: "Life itself is a mixture of power and form, and will not bear the least excess of either" (*CW* 3: 35). This thought is then recapitulated a few pages later in the essay: "Human life is made up of the two elements, power and form, and the proportion must be invariably kept, if we would have it sweet and sound" (*CW* 3: 38). How, then, are we to understand this mixture or proportion of power and form? First, in "Experience," Emerson articulates the seemingly anti-Hegelian formula that "life is not dialectics" (34); or, adapting another dissonant figure of thought, Emerson takes himself to "accept the clangor and jangle of contrary tendencies" (36). Life, then, is a volatile, ateleological mixture of power and form in a way that is not *per se* a dialectic of form and power, so much as a messy multiplicity of conflicting forces and contrary tendencies. In their readings of "Experience," Cavell and Arsić arguably downplay these contrary tendencies within Emerson's essay; for Arsić, form is what power undoes. Yet we should be careful not to understand form as a fixity in contrast to power as deformation, movement, or fluidity. As he states in many instances, form is itself fluid and fugacious, and signals flux or process. Indeed, in Emerson's thinking, form – as *morphe* – could be said to be given over to *metamorphosis*. Form is rendered as becoming and transformation: "Nothing is so fleeting as form; yet never does it quite deny itself," he writes in "History" (*CW* 2: 8). So life is not dialectics, but rather incessant metamorphosis; it is effectuated in messy mixtures of form and power, in ever-volatile balances of the two. Yet, at the same time as power has a modality of form, form has a modality of power. Form as *morphe* is not entirely given over to *metamorphosis* as the power of deformation (or becoming-other): "never does [form] quite deny itself." There remains *within* form an antagonist power to physical or metaphysical metamorphoses; that is, form also signifies a desire to endure in being, not unlike Spinoza's notion of the *conatus*, a power that maintains individuated form. This manifests itself in one way as a "fatalism" in the power of nature that does not merely propel us to new selves and to leave behind old ones.

Power is therefore also at the base of the assertive force of the personal. Emerson's ontological scenography outlined in "Experience," that is, suggests a play of powers that are unsettling to individual personhood and, yet, in conflicting ways, that also maintain, if not constrain, personhood. Emerson puts the constraining power in terms of temperament, the "veto or limitation-power in the constitution," and a "power which no man willingly hears any one praise but himself" (*CW* 3: 31).

> There is an optical illusion about every person we meet. In truth, they are all creatures of given temperament, which will appear in a given character, whose boundaries they will never pass: but we look at them, they seem alive, and we presume there is impulse in them. In the moment it seems impulse; in the year, in the lifetime, it turns out to be a certain uniform tune which the revolving barrel of the music-box must play. (31)

As part of the "system of illusions," temperament is perhaps not perceivable in moments of encountering others in the midst of an action, but rather in the longer timeframes of habitual actions. The power of temperament is in its drive toward the uniformity or conformity of action that works within persons, or which gives persons a legible "personality." Emerson, of course, speaks against the constraining power of habitual life in "Self-Reliance," in terms of the "terrors" of consistency and conformity (see *CW* 2: 33). But here, in his reportage of experience "from the platform of ordinary life"

(31), he names temperament as a self-controlling "lord of life." The illusion of temperament even applies to our friends, who "appear to us as representatives of certain ideas, which they never pass or exceed" (33).

This is not to say that this limitation-power of temperament for us or for others is absolute – what is in Emerson's thinking? – but, again, personality and temperament are in an antagonistic relation with the impersonal, deforming, and creative power. Emerson emphasizes this when he writes that "it is impossible that the creative power should exclude itself.... The intellect, seeker of absolute truth, or the heart, lover of absolute good, intervenes for our succor, and at one whisper of these high powers, we awake from ineffectual struggles" (32). We can sneak out of the glass prison of our identity by a hidden door, if only we can discover it. As Michael Lopez writes, power for Emerson thus seems to be an overcoming of powerlessness or a power struggle with the forces of constraint.[14] The key becomes not just to immerse ourselves in the ever-flowing vigor but also to find our power in the things that constrain us, in the invisible prisons of our temperament, in our shortsightedness, and in our skepticisms. This takes what Emerson calls "work" in his later thinking (and we might hear behind work the Greek notion of *energeia*). It takes courage to overcome our weaknesses, and its achievement is success, no matter how contingent success might prove in a world of relentless flux and change.

## The Powers of the Heart

In the passage that closes "Experience," the interjection "up again old heart!" is by no means insignificant. The transformation of genius into practical power is, in a sense, a matter of the heart. For Emerson, it is the heart that is the seat of power – not as power's centralization, but as its force of decentralization. The powers of the heart, like all power in Emerson, are in circulation. The heart is a metaphor for the healthy on-flow of life (the "health of body consists in circulation" (CW 3: 32)) and another Emersonian figure for ontological, affective, political, or physical manifestations of power. So even if we must keep a balance of form and power, Emerson nonetheless often celebrates this "superfluity of spirit for new creation" (CW 3: 27). The heart stands for the power of the impulses that drive us to resist both temperament's drive to uniformity (to act in the same way) and the will to conformity (to act according to the impulses of others). As he says in "Experience," pulsation and impulsivity are part of nature itself: "Nature hates calculators; her methods are saltatory and impulsive. Man lives by pulses; our organic movements are such; and the chemical and ethereal agents are undulatory and alternate;

and the mind goes antagonizing on, and never prospers but by fits" (3: 39). The power of life is less dialectical, then, than systolic and diastolic. The heart thus stands for the doubleness and undulations that character-ize the dynamism of Emerson's living thinking. The heart literalizes cour-age (the *coeur*, if you like, at the heart of courage); and, as he writes in "Courage," if there is courage in war and technics, there is also "courage of genius" in aesthetic creation: "courage gives the cutting edge of every profession" (*CW* 7: 135).

Power is pulse, pulsation, impulse, and, as if through an inadvertent lex-ical shift, "*plus*," or what Emerson calls a *plus life*—a "surcharged" life he details in his essay "Power" from *The Conduct of Life*. The *plus* life is to live in the fullness of one's being, in the fullness of one's beating heart. In his analyses of power, Emerson feels compelled to report on those individuals of the *plus* life – be they beatific or bellicose, divine or demonological – not for their politics of power, but for their ontologies of power:

> Men of this surcharge of arterial blood cannot live on nuts, herb-tea, and ele-gies; cannot read novels, and play whist; cannot satisfy all their wants at the Thursday Lecture, or the Boston Athenaeum. They pine for adventure, and must go to Pike's Peak; had rather die by the hatchet of a Pawnee, than sit all day and every day at a counting-room desk. They are made for war, for the sea, for mining, hunting, and clearing; for hair-breadth adventures, huge risks, and the joy of eventful living.... One comes to value this *plus* health, when he sees that all difficulties vanish before it. (*CW* 6: 36)

If problematically couched here in the American imperialist language of masculinist rugged individualism and adventure-as-violent-extraction, Emerson's more fundamental aim is to understand how impersonal power is put in the service of an assertion of personality. These are people who draw on the power of nature to extract from nature its power and who work with the powers of material-energy flows in order to master them.

This mastery is at the core of Emerson's understanding of practical power: It is a power that is husbanded in order to make and to do: "all difficulties vanish before it." But this logic of overcoming often recurs in Emerson's thinking. In the human inventiveness of the nineteenth century he celebrates in "Works and Days" or "Success" in *Society and Solitude*, it verges on a thermodynamics of power: through the energetic investments of thinking and working, that is, human ingenuity can meet and overcome the chal-lenges it faces. In another register, as Thomas Constantinesco has carefully detailed, this economy also watches over Emerson's understanding of pain and suffering, in which pain is converted or transferred into eventual power. Yet, as Constantinesco notes in terms of "Experience," even as we might then "court" or "crave" pain "as an object of desire" to provoke the type of self-growth only the sharp edges of reality can offer, it is not clear that this pain can ever fully be transformed or made impersonal. "The echo of pain persists," heard not only across the rest of his *Essays: Second Series* but also in the lingering discrepancy and clangor and jangle of contrary tendencies to which Emerson's essay, and oeuvre, attunes us.[15]

More generally, power increases through the overcoming of what Emerson calls "antagonist power" (*CW* 2: 20). Emerson outlines antagonist power as an impersonal power that drives personality to the fullness of its expression. To be powerful means to draw on and productively redirect the multiple conflicting forces and competing imperatives in which any person is enmeshed: "[A person's] power consists in the multitude of his affinities, in the fact that his life is intertwined with the whole chain of organic and inorganic being.... A man is a bundle of relations, a knot of roots, whose flower and fruitage is the world.... He cannot live without a world" (20). As imbricated in the causalities of organic and inorganic being, individual power, then, is not distinct, for Emerson, from his natural history and metaphysics of power. Yet the world that we cannot live without is the world that throws up impediments in front of us, and that dares us to act in the face of them. The *plus* life or a *plus* health marks a style of eventful living courageously and deliberately ("rough and ready"), and therefore can affirm both individual and collective life. Emerson's understanding of individual political power relies on this *plus* condition. Those who live a *plus* life are his representative individuals: "Each *plus* man represents his set, and, if he have the accidental advantage of personal ascendency ... all his coadjutors and feeders will admit his right to absorb them" (*CW* 6: 31). As charismatic, they are natural leaders, and are thus given to "success," which for Emerson is a key term in his later thinking and yet is rooted in the transformation of genius into practical power: "We say that success is constitutional; depends on a *plus* condition of mind and body, on power of work, on courage" (38). The politically powerful find their power in overcoming the antagonist powers that resist them. In a multi-layered pun, he chimes, "Power educates the potentate" (33).

The power that educates the potentate, not unexpectedly, finds its paradigmatic example in the figure of Napoleon, one of his representative men. As he writes in "History":

> Put Napoleon in an island prison, let his faculties find no men to act on, no Alps to climb, no stake to play for, and he would beat the air, and appear stupid. Transport him to large countries, dense population, complex interests and antagonist power, and you shall see that the man Napoleon, bounded that is by such a profile and outline, is not the virtual Napoleon. (20)

While Napoleon's power draws on the power of nature and of the world, it also needs the resistance of people and material forces to heighten its strength. Egypt, the Alps, Europe – their resistance only increases his power and expands his force of personality. Neither born to greatness nor having greatness thrust upon him, Napoleon rather achieves greatness as provoked by the challenges of complex interests and antagonist power. Yet even if the powerful "have the good nature of strength and courage," their "coarse energy" has its vices (CW 6: 34). Power, itself beyond good and evil, can be put to destructive ends. That such charismatic power of the *plus* life can be used to exploit or overpower others is well known: the "success" of an individual ego can expand to demoniacal proportions, unleashing misery, oppression, and violence on others. Napoleon typifies how the success of the powerful always runs this risk of excess, of destruction, and of eventual self-ruin. As Emerson writes in *Representative Men*, "Bonaparte was the idol of common men because he had in transcendent degree the qualities and powers of common men"; but at the same time, his "exorbitant" egotism only served to lay waste to Europe and to himself. Emerson mordantly asks: "And what was the result of this vast talent and power, of these immense armies, burned cities, squandered treasures, immolated millions of men, of this demoralized Europe? It came to no result" (CW 4: 147).

More generally, in Emerson's optimistic philosophy, the excesses of the *plus* life and of power can be meliorated by the force of culture and checked by the powers of the heart, or what he calls the force of the moral sentiment. The moral sentiment is another name in Emerson's thought for the heart's seeking absolute truth and moral harmony and for the power of moral perfectionism to work in individuals: "we have a certain instinct, that where is great amount of life, though gross and peccant, it has its own checks and purifications, and will be found at last in harmony with moral laws" (CW 6: 32). As instinctual, the moral sentiment is not *per se* a matter of personal volition but is more broadly consonant with nature and history themselves. "Nature knows how to convert evil to good" (CW 7: 147). Emerson goes so far as to say that the power of morality is immanent to matter itself. "Power and purpose rides on matter to the last atom.... The ends of all are moral" (LL 1: 299). Emerson's understanding of history's teleology likewise is based on a movement toward moral harmony, an arc that "bends towards justice," as his contemporary Theodore Parker articulated it, and Martin Luther King Jr. famously repurposed it.[16] It can be manifest as a "sacred courage" to render unnecessary the excesses of "beast-like men"; as such, it is courage that musters nature's "scope" to bring about the "secular melioration of the planet" (CW 7: 137–39). The powers of the heart, then, point to the "victory" to come "for all justice," a victory that is only achievable by allowing the moral sentiment to guide the transformation of genius to practical power. Harmony, unity, justice, and love – these are the virtues of Emerson's practical power. The powers of the heart, in turn, become synonymous with the power of love, the driver of this melioration, and would be at the basis of Emerson's ideal republic – even, as he laments at the end of "Politics," that "[t]he power of love, as the basis of the State, has never been tried" (CW 3: 128).

## The Powers of the Mind

As the heart names a living process of seeking absolute good, likewise the intellect is not a fixed attribute but names a nondialectical seeking of absolute truth. The powers of the mind lie parallel to the powers of the heart for Emerson and are given to the same laws. The mind pulses like a heart; it is undulatory and alternate: "the mind goes antagonizing on, and never prospers but by fits" (CW 3: 39). As with the antagonist power more generally, the mind gains greater strength through the resistances of the world, which it endeavors to think. The difference he describes at the end of "Experience" between the world of the mind and the world "in the city and in the farms" (CW 3: 48), then, is not an insoluble *aporia*. Nor does it reintroduce the Cartesian dualism between *res cogitans* and *res extensa*, or the Kantian dualism between *noumena* and *phenomena* that thinkers like Fichte, Schelling, and Hegel sought to unify. (Indeed, Emerson will often celebrate a one-to-one correspondence between mental and material substance in terms of power: "All power is of one kind, a sharing of the nature of the world. The mind that is parallel with the laws of nature will be in the current of events, and strong with their strength" (CW 6: 30). Or: "The mind yields sympathetically to the tendencies or laws which stream through things and make the order of nature" (LL 2: 75; cf. CW 7: 152)). Rather, the difference between mind and matter and, in turn, between thinking and living, can be thought of as this antagonizing, as the mind's restless striving toward the perfection of correspondence or expressiveness. Emerson's claim that he "observe[s] that difference" and "shall observe it" (CW 3: 48) positions him as a natural historian of the mind who bears witness to its ongoing invested struggling within the facticity of life.

In his 1858 lecture "Powers of the Mind" – in many ways a response to "Experience" – Emerson seeks to deepen his observations of this difference. This includes his doubts regarding previous metaphysicians' claims to have unified matter and mind. Despite being deeply influenced by Kant, Fichte, Hegel, Schelling, or Coleridge, he registers a lack in German metaphysicians' "transcendent abilities" – a failure to have found, despite what they might profess, "the hidden pass that leads from Fate to Freedom" (*LL* 2: 71). This impasse of German metaphysics is nonetheless not exactly the mood of despair that watches over "Experience," which Emerson attributes to the difficulty to know at all: "People disparage knowing and the intellectual life, and urge doing. I am very content with knowing, if only I could know" (*CW* 3: 48). In "Powers of the Mind," his "objection" to metaphysics instead "lies against the manner of the study, and not the knowledge itself" (*LL* 2: 72). That is, Emerson is not critical of all the epistemological advances of metaphysics, instead he criticizes the metaphysical method's inability to unlock the powers of the mind. If it were able to do so, it would, he says, achieve common fame. If, as he details, metaphysics "is dangerous as a single pursuit," Emerson's renewed metaphysics, by contrast, would take as its "proper counterparts" the German idealist thought, the rough experience of ordinary life, and the "reformed" physical sciences (72; 74). He calls for a "high analogic mind" to "charm us with disclosing mental structure, as the naturalist with his architectures" (74), and, as such, put metaphysics in tune with an animate theory of nature in all its multiformity, in all its power: a science of life that is simultaneously a science of the mind. He works to enumerate the "laws and powers of the intellect" as "facts in a Natural History" (*W* 12: 10) in the manner a naturalist would collect and classify natural facts or specimens, therefore underscoring his continued philosophical interest in the power of ordinary life – in encountering living facts in their movement and multiplicity.

For Emerson, understanding the powers of the mind does not entail constructing a logical, systemized metaphysics, but rather an analogic poetic philosophy receptive to the creative vitality of life itself. On this basis he celebrates poets and writers like Montaigne, Shakespeare, or Goethe over philosophers as the teachers of mental philosophy. Theirs is not merely the analytic power to dissect in order to know, but a synthetic power that constructs new worlds of thinking and living. The powers of the mind, while finding their fullest expression in high analogic minds and poets and writers, nonetheless lie dormant in every person. As he had written in "Intellect": "if the constructive powers are rare, and it is given to few men to be poets, yet every man is a receiver of this descending holy ghost, and may well study the laws of its influx" (*CW* 2: 202). Emerson thus restates his perennial idealist belief in the individual's subjective mental power: "the natural direction of the intellectual powers is from the within outward" (*LL* 2: 72). Or: "You cannot exaggerate the powers of the mind. All that the world admires comes from within: in other words, all our existence is subjective" (76). Every one of us has a tremendous yet dormant metaphysical energy, an "unfathomable power" (77), which, if we could only "come out of our egg-shell existence"

(77) and seek contemplative interlocutors, we could maximize our intellectual potential: "a mental power is awaiting us more excellent than anything that is now called philosophy; perceptions of an immense power native to the soul" (74).

The powers of the mind, although subjective in origin, are not given over to a solipsism of thought. They must be antagonized and magnified by one's interlocutors, and "the inward analysis must be corrected by rough experience" (72). The powers of the mind, and the metaphysical study of them, must find their purchase, and indeed their power, in ordinary life. Echoing "Experience," he claims, "Life itself is mixed.... And so metaphysics must be perpetually reinforced by life" (72). Life reinforces metaphysical thinking; metaphysics deepens our access to the powers of the mind. The mixed quality of life means thinking and practice are in a relationship of mutual, if messy, intensification: thinking intensifies practice, and practice opens new challenges for thinking. In the midst of life, a new thought can reorient us or disorient us, set us free, or destroy us. In proximity to Nietzsche, he writes, "A thought would destroy most persons whom we know" (80). Thoughts make insistent claims upon us, they hold us in their grip and demand actualization: "Our thoughts disdain us, if we do not put them into practice, – disdain us, and forsake us" (79). Emerson dares us to think – that hardest of tasks. The impersonal force of his writing is felt most intensely in its unsettling of our settled habits of thinking, and therefore of our habits of living. Metaphysics as reinforced by life is not dialectics, then, but "biography" (72): a life-writing of the intellect in the spontaneity of natural action. If Nietzsche would come to criticize metaphysics as negating life – that any thought that attempts to go beyond life denies life – the wager of Emerson's new metaphysics is that it be reinforced by the power and incalculability of life and guided by the laws of the moral sentiment. The powers of the mind work in parallel with the powers of the heart. On this basis, he reformulates the transformation of genius into practical power as a "just combining of the intellectual inquiry with practical life" (73).

### Epilogue: "and again, preparation and arrival"

In "Experience," Emerson famously names the "lords of life": Illusion, Surprise, Surface, Dream, Reality, Succession, Temperament. They offer a prismatic organization to the essay: a moving mosaic of moods through which it passes, as if to perform the multiplicity and flux of experience itself. Each of these lords of life evokes the tenuous balances of form and power that, for Emerson, define life: the illusions that hold us in place, that disorient us amid the flow of days, and the sheer incalculability of life; the power that we can only experience obliquely and cannot ourselves hold; and yet the power of deformation, of leaving and abandonment, and the power of form to self-organize, to endure, and to endue crescive selves. If "Experience" begins with a mood of lament before our "unhandsome condition" and our inability to fully feel the sharp edges of loss and grief, its deep affirmation of the "vast flowing vigor" in which we move, and which moves through us, promises the compensations of an ever-renewing life. To be sure, Emerson's ontology of power connects him to the long philosophical history of power – from Aristotle's notions of *energeia, entelechia,* or *dunamis* and the physics of power in Hobbes and Spinoza, to the idealist conceptions of power in Kant, Schelling, and Hegel; and in turn, to his ontological German nephew, Nietzsche, the philosopher of the will to power, and his pragmatist godson, William James, who likewise details the powers of the mind in light of the "powers" and "energies of men."[17] Yet Emerson's contribution to our understanding of power is unique in how it stresses everyone's unique ability to participate in the impersonal power that flows through us all and which shapes us all. His ontology of power marks every aspect of his thinking, providing it with its basic blueprint. It is a power that we cannot possess but which can possess us.[18]

In "Powers of the Mind," Emerson modifies and updates his list of the lords of life. He writes: "I invite you to the beholding and knowing of real gods, who work and rule forever and ever, – Memory and Vision; the Power of Imagination, the Poet Apollo; the Zodiackal Chain of Cause and Effect; Illusion, the Veil; and Transition, the Energy" (*LL* 2: 82). Like the lords of life of "Experience," again Emerson emphasizes the illusion that sometimes marks life, but the keynote here is that the power of life is synonymous with transition. He puts this as a compelling formula: "Transition is the attitude of power, and the essential act of life. The whole history of the mind is passage and pulsation, dark and light, preparation and arrival; and again, preparation and arrival" (*LL* 2: 91). Emerson's writing persistently invites us to bear witness to this thought of transition: the "ever-again" of preparation and arrival. It invites us to find ourselves in the pulsing, circulating powers of the heart and powers of the mind – the powers that antagonize us and that are ours to overcome, and that might yet set us free in a delicate and elusive transformation of genius into practical power.

## Notes

1. Jeffrey Stout, "The Transformation of Genius into Practical Power: A Reading of Emerson's 'Experience'" *American Journal of Philosophy and Theology*, 35:1 (January 2014), 4.

2. Recent critics have explored power in Emerson in a variety of ways, from his relation to philosophy of self-culture and of the conduct of life, to natural and science and causality. See Michael Lopez, "The Conduct of Life: Emerson's Anatomy of Power," in *The Cambridge Companion to Emerson*, ed. Joel Porte and Saundra Morris (Cambridge: Cambridge University Press, 1995), 243–66, and, *Emerson and Power: Creative Antagonism in the Nineteenth Century* (DeKalb, IL: North Illinois Press, 1995); John Lysaker, *Emerson & Self-Culture* (Bloomington, IN: Indiana University Press, 2008); Lee Rust Brown, *The Emerson Museum: Practical Romanticism and the Pursuit of the Whole* (Cambridge, MA: Harvard University Press, 1997); Laura Dassow Walls, *Emerson's Life in Science: The Culture of Truth* (Ithaca, NY: Cornell University Press, 2003); or Joseph Urbas, *Emerson's Metaphysics: A Song of Laws and Causes* (Lanham: Lexington Books, 2016) and *The Philosophy of Ralph Waldo Emerson* (London: Routledge, 2021).
3. Urbas, *Emerson's Metaphysics*, xxix.
4. As Eric Keenaghan succinctly summarizes: "If one cannot possess power, one simply is powerful, because one is possessed by, or articulates, power, and so exemplifies what it means to be alive and singular merely by living." Eric Keenaghan, "Reading Emerson in Other Times: On a Politics of Solitude and an Ethics of Risk" in *The Other Emerson*, ed. Branka Arsić and Cary Wolfe (Minneapolis: University of Minnesota Press, 2010), 184.
5. Sharon Cameron, *Impersonality: Seven Essays* (Chicago: University of Chicago Press, 2007), 73.
6. Ibid., 76.
7. Ibid., 73.
8. Ibid., 76.
9. Stanley Cavell, "Finding as Founding: Taking Steps in Emerson's Experience,'" in *Emerson's Transcendental Etudes*, ed. David Justin Hodge(Stanford: Stanford University Press, 2003), 137.
10. Branka Arsić, *On Leaving: A Reading in Emerson* (Cambridge, MA: Harvard University Press, 2010), 160.
11. Ibid., 160–62.
12. Ibid., 161.
13. Ibid., 162.
14. Lopez, "Conduct," 257.
15. Thomas Constantinesco, *Writing Pain in the Nineteenth-Century United States* (Oxford: Oxford University Press, 2022), 47, and 44–48 *in passim*.
16. Theodore Parker, "Justice and Conscience," in *Ten Sermons on Religion* (Boston: Crosby, Nichols, and Company, 1853), 84–85.
17. See William James's essays "The Powers of Men," and "The Energies of Men" in *Essays in Religion and Morality, The Works of William James*, ed. Frederick Burkhardt, et al. (Cambridge, MA: Harvard University Press, 1982).
18. See note 4 above.

# 7

TOM F. WRIGHT

# Emerson at the Lectern and the Voiced Essay

Staten Island, a winter's night in 1843. The Tompkins Lyceum is filled with a congregation assembled to hear America's finest essayist, Ralph Waldo Emerson, who is approaching the lectern to speak. After he had finished, one observer present wrote that something in the Transcendentalist's performance style had helped make his complex ideas easier to grasp for those in the audience:

> Commencing on a key, he would continue on the same up to the last word or two, and then drop into a deep musical tone which was very impressive. Occasionally at the end of a sentence he would suddenly stop, for what seemed like a long time, and, with his eyes uplifted upon his audience, looking like one inspired. Everyone in the audience seemed to stop breathing, as if afraid to mar the solemn impression produced.[1]

The Emersonian essay can be one of the most intimate of forms, offering a curiously confidential connection to an author's unfolding thoughts. But as this scene testifies, it was also a social art. In moments like the above, the essayist becomes not a mere writer but a charismatic presence, whose intent can be fully understood only by witnessing his words come to life, energized by the dynamics of a live assembly. Accounts like the above help us get closer to the experience of Emerson at the lectern. Since he was one of the transatlantic world's most prominent public intellectuals at a moment of exponential growth in print coverage, there are plenty of them to guide us back into those transfixed audiences.

For too long there was a tendency to take such scenes for granted. It was widely known that the supposedly otherworldly Sage of Concord in fact made his living in rustic rooms like those on Staten Island. But the culture of which the Tompkins Lyceum was a part was often dismissed as the milieu of uncomplicated middle-brow entertainment or as the mere financial necessity that underwrote his ability to write and think. In the last decade or two, as interest in the writer's place within his own public sphere has become more important, and as new digital archives have made historical reconstruction more possible, Emerson at the lectern has once again become a major preoccupation. We now have a much fuller understanding of Emerson's place within this crucial cultural marketplace, his impact on multiple networks of audiences of listeners and readers, and how this network of reception in turn impacted his writings.[2] Taking a clear view of Emerson at the lectern is one of the most important ways of confronting the meanings of an ambivalent figure who was at once an educator, a savvy influencer, a radical individualist, and a cultural entrepreneur. This is in fact far from a new argument. In the 1880s one of his earliest biographers wrote that "the essayist needs to be interpreted by the lecturer; for his voice and manner become a fine commentary on his written thought, giving to it new and unexpected meanings."[3] Attention to the lecture circuit context has been a muted concern in Emerson studies.[4]

This chapter makes the case that we can't understand Emerson or his work without placing ourselves back in moments like the above. However, rather than simply making another plea for attention to context, what follows uses the image of Emerson at the lectern to think more conceptually about the role of voice in his thought and his aesthetics. In what follows, I contend that we should read his work as an exemplary example of the nineteenth-century "voiced essay": a form explained not only by its didacticism or suggestively sermonic qualities but also by its engagement with orality on the level of style and idea. Like other essayists of this era, Emerson drew strength from "oratorical" styles, [re]imagining his readership as circles of listeners, and using tropes of ventriloquism and vocal orchestration. Looking back at his work through ideas of performance and speech reminds us that the Emersonian essay has never been solely introspective or intimate. And in a nineteenth-century moment of slippage between media forms and cultural registers, his form of the voiced essay took on a new social urgency as a form of displaced secular sermon.

## What was Emerson's Lectern?

In order to understand what made Emerson's career possible, we need to grasp the scale and importance of what became known as the lyceum circuit and the dense world of print that surrounded it. The idea of organized educational talks by notable figures before public audiences was a feature of the era throughout the Anglophone world but flourished most powerfully in the United States in the decades leading up to the Civil War, where it was often known as the "lyceum movement." By the middle of the century, the lecture circuit had become one of the nation's defining cultural forces. Especially for writers in the antebellum North, the popular lecture circuit had become a chief means of gaining exposure and supporting a life of letters. A diverse range of predominately male authors from across the literary spectrum found stints touring the republic's lecture halls a unique means of funding their writing, reaching wider audiences, and coming to know their own changing country. Lecturing played a key role in multiple social movements, helped energize cultural debates and political controversies, and became one of the lasting literary forms of the period. For Frederick Douglass, the figure of the public lecturer was "a modern invention called forth by the increasing demands of restless human nature."[5] For Henry David Thoreau, it was the institution "from which a New Era will be dated to New England, as from the games of Greece."[6]

When historians speak of the lyceum movement, they are often referring to two quite distinct phenomena.[7] In its earliest form, it was a network of adult education institutions devoted to debate, discussion, and invited talks from important local figures that began in the mid-1820s and spread from Massachusetts throughout the small towns of the North East. They were intended as ecumenical and nonpartisan spaces in which communities could learn from each other and useful knowledge could be circulated.[8] By the 1840s, however, this network had developed into something quite distinct. The "lyceum" now signified a series of loosely connected series of institutions that existed primarily to host lectures by prominent travelling speakers from across the nation, in seasons that ran from autumn to spring. The early lyceum had become a "lecture circuit," and its members were less participants than spectators. In 1855 a Boston paper observed that "every town or village of any sort of enterprise or pretentions has its annual course of popular lectures, while the cities support several courses."[9] The emphasis might still notionally be on education, useful knowledge, and training for commercial life, but there was a new impulse toward entertainment, and the most extravagant and charismatic speakers became national celebrities.

Lecture halls were both academy and playhouse, as much a part of performance culture as any other staged ritual, a hybridity that Margaret Fuller captured in the phrase "Entertaining Knowledge."[10] Just as with other forms of oratory, lyceum speakers were prized not only for their intellect but also for more intangible qualities the culture termed "manner." Similar to the theater, the popular lecture was also one of the most distinctive and hard-nosed cultural markets to emerge in nineteenth-century American culture. For an 1850s audience, the standard charge of twenty-five cents for an evening's entertainment made a night at the lecture an economic sacrifice. For speakers it promised a second and often arduous profession, involving constant movement, erratic transport and accommodation, inclement winter weather, and superficial sociality. But it could also pay well. As Beecher wryly put it, celebrity speakers were rewarded with "F.A.M.E." ("Fifty dollars, And My Expenses"), and during the late 1850s, the most popular might deliver upwards of a hundred lectures in a good season and earn $5,000 for three months' work.[11]

Crucially, it was a phenomenon that was made possible and sustained through reciprocity with print. Thanks to a proliferating culture of promotion, reportage, transcription, and commentary, the lyceum was a culture of performance experienced as much through page as auditorium and a phenomenon that generated new kinds of reading experiences, both public and private. Thanks to copious newspaper reportage, the most prominent talks in any given city were often also summarized and reviewed in the press, which created a large secondary audience. Moreover, a sizable market emerged for published lectures. When collected in book form, popular collections such as Henry Ward Beecher's *Lectures to Young Men: On Various Important Subjects* (1846) brandished their prior oral status. Branding what might otherwise have been mere essays as "lectures" provided public legitimacy, confirming prior communal consumption, and drawing off the glamour of oratory. In such form, these spoken words achieved a second life, and in some cases future audiences would anticipate the lecturers' words from familiarity with their published form.

### Emerson as Lecturer and Public Intellectual

Emerson was in just the right place at the right time to make the most of this new media world. Having abandoned a promising Unitarian preaching career in Boston in the early 1830s, he possessed the required combination of oratorical fluency and intellectual flair. The oral delivery of his evolving ideas became the defining feature of his artistic life. Beginning to lecture in earnest in the early 1830s, within ten years he had become one of the circuit's most celebrated speakers. By the end of his career in the 1870s, he had delivered almost 1,500 lectures across 22 states from Maine to California. His career was also part of what might be called the "transatlantic lyceum." Because of Emerson's growing fame and network of admirers in Europe, he also lectured throughout England and Ireland on his 1847–48 tour, and like fellow reformers, authors luminaries such as Frederick Douglass, William Makepeace Thackeray, and Lola Montez, he was a creature of what might be termed globalized lecture culture.[12]

One of the best ways to view Emerson at the lectern is to see the genre of the popular lecture as the solution to what F. O. Matthiessen called Emerson's "quest for form."[13] Turning his back on preaching in search of a less restrictive form of engagement, in the lyceum as he had landed on a secular medium whose versatility and breadth made immediate sense to him. In the 1830s, he often hailed the lyceum a "panharmonicon" in which "everything is admissible," and this fusion of sacred, secular, and political styles of thinking and speaking held enormous appeal for someone seeking to collapse boundaries between discourses.[14]

As one might expect, much of the pulpit still remained. When we look from Emerson's early sermons to his early lectures, the tone and approach are often similar. His friend Thomas Carlyle thought there was too much of this left, complaining in November 1844 that a new essay read as "a *sermon* to me, as all your other deliberate utterances are" (*CEC:* 134). In similar fashion, Emerson's first biographer noted that "his aim has always been that of the preacher, differing only in manner of treatment and in range of matter."[15] He also introduced other tonal notes: from poetry, from evocative descriptions of the natural world, but also from the more worldly fervor of political stump. The young fledgling lecturer's sensibility was formed not just by an admiration for Unitarian preachers such as Edward Taylor but also by Whig orators such as Senator Daniel Webster, and he strove to emulate aspects of their variously anecdotal and grandiloquent style in his writings.[16] Add to this a dash of the analytical college philosophical lecture, and we arrive at the recognizable tonal hybrid that defined Emerson's career.

In order to get an accurate sense of Emerson at the lectern, we need to approach the published works carefully. It is tempting to conflate the lecturer and essayist and assume that the words we read were those heard by his nineteenth-century audiences. But as the painstaking scholarship of Lawrence Buell and others has shown, the journey of Emerson's ideas was more complex than this.[17] Typically, Emerson's ideas took on their recognizable shape in the notebooks, were then auditioned before the public in constantly redrafted lectures, complete with his notorious tendency to seem to shuffle his pages mid-delivery, and were subsequently edited once more before their periodical or book publication. Some lectures remained simply lectures and never made their way to print; some topics and themes delivered as lectures ended up in print under quite different titles; quite often, eventual essays were composites of multiple lectures delivered at disparate times. Those eager to follow this process are now well-served by excellent editions of the lectures from across his career.[18]

Readers should also be careful not to romanticize Emerson's success on the lecture circuit. The selective record usually cited to explain his impact on his contemporaries often provides a misleading picture of a figure who was far from universally embraced. Some accounts have rightly become legendary, such as Walt Whitman's reflection on the life-changing experience of watching the Concord Sage deliver "Nature and Powers of The Poet" in New York in March 1842: "I was simmering, simmering, simmering; Emerson brought me to a boil."[19] But for every such converted disciple, there were far more baffled listeners who were left indifferent if not hostile. As one not untypical review from Cleveland, Ohio, in 1859 lamented that "we would quite as like to see a perpendicular coffin behind a desk as Mr. Emerson."[20]

Moreover, as prone as he was publicly to emphasize the idealistic side of lecturing, Emerson was also a hard-headed operator in an emergent culture industry. "Whenever I get into debt, which usually happens once a year," he wrote in January 1843, "I must take plunge into this great odious river of travellers into the dangerous precincts of charlatanism, namely lecturing."[21] Aware of the incongruity of what he found himself doing for a living, he self-deprecatingly referred to himself in a July 1841 letter to Carlyle as "an incorrigible spouting Yankee" (CEC: 340). The Emerson on the lectern stands as a fascinating symbol of the tenuous relationship between the scholar and the nascent capitalist system. By 1857 he was writing wearily to his wife that "I must find better ways to live" (L5: 56).

Nonetheless, Emerson at the lectern also remains one of the nineteenth century's most enduring symbols of the democratic public intellectual. As he wrote in "The Poet," "it is a secret that every intellectual man quickly learns, that beyond the energy of his possessed and conscious intellect ... beside his privacy of power as an individual man, there is a great public power" (CW 3: 15). The lyceum was Emerson's way of being public in two key respects. First, it allowed him to test his ideas constantly against public opinion. As one reviewer wrote of his late work Society and Solitude (1870), "these writings ... savor unmistakably of the lecture-room, and of the disciplining which they have undergone before hundreds of sharp, intellectual audiences."[22] Second, Emerson's annual route through the halls, towns, and auditoria of the early republic furnished him with rare insights into the maturing republic.

Contrary to his reputation as the hermetic Sage of Concord, the publicness of Emerson at the lectern supports the view of the writer as socially engaged commentator presented in the scholarship from the late 1990s onward.[23] Yet, as much as it was a way of offering himself to the service of the nation, it was a form of publicness that had its complications and limitations, often reticent and oblique on the primary issues of the day: public and yet strangely absent. And we can begin to understand these tensions by taking a closer look at how speech and audiences were imagined within his most famous work.

## Emerson's Oral Aesthetics

Many essays from earlier periods of the English tradition had been designed as spoken texts. But the nineteenth-century phenomenon was unprecedented in scale. The essayist and orator drew closer than ever before; theaters, temples, and town halls joined the coffee house as the spiritual home of the essay. The influence of this phenomenon, and of the kinds of scenes captured earlier, helped shape the aesthetic of Anglo-American essays, their subject matter, range of reference, and the ways in which essayists imagined and addressed their publics. In the Golden Age of Oratory, American audiences cultivated an understanding of voice and relished performance. They would have recognized and appreciated these features in prose. We can see these specifically with the tonal impact of the lecture form. The theatricalized pedagogy of the public lecture duly affected the texture of literary life, permeating not only the obvious locations of literary culture, such as the pages of Thoreau, Douglass, and Twain, but also the frenzied eclecticism of *Moby-Dick*, or the ironic intellectual soliloquies of Poe's narrators, where the supposedly staid pedantic lyceum "voice" is burlesqued as part of broader satirical agendas.

But in Emerson this attachment to spoken delivery went beyond the conventions and rhythms of lyceum prose into an overarching orality. From his earliest work to his latest, motifs of voice are a constant preoccupation right up to essays from *Society and Solitude* (1870), such as "Eloquence" and "Clubs," with its fixation on the idea of conversation. The orality of his writings was clear for perceptive readers. Matthew Arnold fancied that he heard a "voice oracular" addressing his "bodily ear" from Concord, Massachusetts: "to us at Oxford, Emerson was but a voice speaking from three thousand miles away."[24] Some saw this as part of his debt to the style of his friend Carlyle. As Emerson had written of his Scottish mentor, "he does not write in the written dialect of the day ... but he draws strength and motherwit out of the spoken vocabulary" (*LL*: 64). Upon receiving his copy of "The American Scholar" essay, Carlyle returned this vocal compliment, writing to Emerson that, "I could have *wept* to read that speech; the clear high melody of it went tingling through my heart." (*CEC*: 44). A laudatory 1850 piece on Emerson by his fellow Transcendentalist Theodore Parker had proclaimed that "such is the beauty of his speech ... that they lend him, everywhere, their ears, and thousands bless his manly thoughts."[25] From the 1860s onward, this quote became used as the pull quote for the Osgood and Company widely reprinted publicity adverts for their collection of Emerson's works. For late nineteenth-century readers who never had the chance to hear him lecture in person, it was Emerson at the lectern that was presented as the ideal way of consuming and conceiving of his words.

Emerson's stylistic links to spoken origins were most present in his lectures and writings of the 1830s and 1840s, where what Walter Ong influentially called "residual orality" was at its most prominent and pronounced.[26] Sometimes the oral context of the lectures is obvious, but even elsewhere it is clear that these texts were composed as much for the ear as the eye. As many readers have noted, his early essays rely heavily on sonic patterning, with a musical quality that turns the rippling euphony and anaphoric repetitions of moments such as this one from "The American Scholar" into a form of incantation, appealing to audience memory: "Every day, the sun; and after sunset, night and her stars. Ever the winds blow; ever the grass grows. Every day, men and women, conversing, beholding and beholden" (CW 1: 54). Often, the rhapsodic intensity of these earlier essays aspires to the metrical flow of verse. Take the exuberant pantheistic opening to the "Divinity School Address" (1838): "In this refulgent summer, it has been a luxury to draw the breath of life. The grass grows, the buds burst, the meadow is spotted with fire and gold in the tint of flowers. The air is full of birds, and sweet with the breath of the pine, the balm-of-Gilead, and the new hay" (CW 1: 76).

As Lawrence Buell has pointed out, moments like this "yield the most when they are not just scanned by the eye but also heard by the mind's ear."[27] Their effect relies on the tension between seductively alliterative rhythms and unexpected diction, and such moments are not simply musical but also thematic. With its insistence on the idea of "breath," its phonemic swell, and its vowel patterning, Emerson's language becomes an impassioned speech-song whose sensual qualities not only mimic that of the glories of nature but also sound a clarion call against what Emerson saw as modern Christianity's deafness to the natural sublime.

One motivation for this embrace of an oratorical style was Emerson's repeatedly stated desire to simulate something more vibrant and robust than a written essayistic argument. Emerson praised the essays of Montaigne on these grounds, proclaiming that, "I know not anywhere the book that seems less written" (CW 4: 95). In "The American Scholar," he had argued that while books are presented as backward artifacts that "pin" the reader "down," audiences "drink" the orator's words because "he fulfils for them their own nature." (CW 1: 63).[28] Yet sometimes the scenes of performance that Emerson conjured up for his readers were intentionally more specific. "The American Scholar" met its broader public through publication as the pamphlet *An Oration, Delivered before the Phi Beta Kappa Society at Cambridge* (1838), and even if the title of "The Divinity School" didn't speak for itself, the point was further underlined upon publication by being prefaced as "Delivered before the Senior Class in Divinity College ... July 15, 1838" (CW 1: 75). Such invocations of initial spoken context reconnected readers to a scene of original oral delivery, suggesting that to read them was to conceive oneself as part of a community of imagined fellow listeners. One encounters a more organic effect of presence in numerous comparable essays of the period, such as John Ruskin's 1857 "The Political Economy of Art," whose opening retains phrases ("I see that some of my hearers look surprised at the expression. I assure them, I use it in sincerity") that allow readers to imagine their presence in crowds such as his original English audience at the Manchester Athenaeum.[29] Thanks to moments like this, certain essays always remain contextually bound.

## Voiced Essays

The status of these essays as "social" was also a property of the newly public ambitions and political imagination of the texts themselves. One tradition of the literary essay tends to presume intimate communion: a conversation by a fireside, perhaps, or an intimate confession. As William Hazlitt put it, the experience of Montaigne's essays is one in which the reader is "admitted behind the curtain, and sits down with the writer in his gown and slippers."[30] In the mid nineteenth century, another tradition came to the fore: one more explicitly oratorical than conversational. In this distinctively Victorian lineage, essayists such as Ruskin, Arnold, or Thoreau often borrowed heavily from the rhythms of public speaking and preaching, placing as much emphasis upon rhetoric and persuasion as upon self-reflection. Perhaps more importantly, essayists in this tradition strove to emphasize the collective, with a focus on communal predicaments and shared solutions, with the essayist simulating not one-to-one intimacy but a triangular relationship between speaker, reader, and a wider audience often imagined as a crowd of listeners.

This Romantic yearning for preliterate expression not only suffused the poetry of the age, of course, but also influenced the essay form. Ivan Kreilkampf has described this tendency of the writing of the period to emulate public speech as an "ongoing romance with voice as a cure for print culture's ills," with the live speaker idealized as "a vanishing source of charismatic power, one freed from all the binds and compromises of bureaucratic knowledge."[31] In this way, readers of Emerson's essays respond not to poised rational argument nor the disinterested informality of the familiar essay, but to their cultivation of a persona whose rhetoric simulates the energies of oral encounter. And more subtly, as in the poetry of Walt Whitman, this was also a persona that relied upon allowing readers to feel that they were being spoken to *en masse*.

One critical tradition has been to see such essays as examples of "Sage" writing, or didactic nonfiction that chastises and instructs readers from a position of assumed wisdom and charismatic authority.[32] Yet we might also usefully see this as a tradition of the "voiced essay": a form explained not only by its didacticism or suggestively sermonic qualities but also by its engagement with orality on the level of style and motif. Along with Carlyle, Emerson is perhaps the most prominent example of this tradition. Both authors drew strength from "oratorical" styles, reimagining their readerships as circles of listeners and using tropes of ventriloquism and vocal orchestration in the service of quite distinct political visions. Thinking about Emerson's writings as multi-levelled charismatic vocal and social performances provides a new way of thinking about the essay and its audience at a historical moment of productive tension between competing forms of social authority.

In his greatest essays, such as "Self-Reliance" (1841), tropes of listening are also widespread, and his argument continually returns to the idea of what "the soul hears." (*CW* 1: 9). In an influential modern reading of Victorian fiction, Garrett Stewart has argued that direct address found in novels ("Dear Reader …") helped forge "the encoded presence of a reading consciousness to a narrative text."[33] Carlyle and Emerson's essays adopted a related but crucially different strategy by reversing the logic of print and encoding the complex presence of readers as listeners. Just as Carlyle's essays, for example, often invoked the presence of a live listener, "Self-Reliance" invokes not readers but "audience" when predicting that "I might not carry with me the feeling of my audience in stating my belief" (*CW* 1: 30). Emerson's pieces also went further in staging moments of two-way oral contact with imagined listeners. Perhaps the most memorable example occurs in the culminating moments of "Circles" (1841), where he confronts his "hearers" directly:

> O circular philosopher, I hear some reader exclaim, you have arrived at a fine Pyrrhonism, at an equivalence and indifferency of all actions … [But] let me remind the reader that I am only an experimenter. Do not set the least value on what I do, or the least discredit on what I do not, as if I pretended to settle anything as true or false. I unsettle all things. (*CW* 2: 201)

Speaker, reader, and hearer become partners here in a process of communicative action, with sequences such as this casting the "reader" as one who not only "hears" but whose inner voice is in turn heard by the composing speaker. In this way, the Emersonian essay regenerates its message from utterances that move toward what Mikhail Bakhtin called "answerability," not only inviting response but also folding imagined responses into the drama of the text.[34] In this way, the literary essayist addresses both an implied audience of like-minded readers and a live audience that is rhetorically oppositional.

Emerson saw his essays as attempts to create a figurative "circle of listeners" that transcended the social and racial exclusions of their actual performances. By embedding in print this triangular relationship between speaker, listener, and fellow attendants, Emerson helped strengthen what Benedict Anderson has called the "deep horizontal comradeship" of an abstract imaginary congregation: a sense of simultaneity that aimed to bring into being and solidify a circle of listeners that was at times both national and wider than the nation, aspiring to the limited but nonetheless broader "we" of Euro-American modernity.[35]

## Orchestrated Voices

Emerson's essay aesthetic also relied upon the dextrous juggling of a wide range of voices. He celebrated the discursive freedom of his new medium of the lecture-essay in terms of its vocal diversity, praising it as a form in which "everything is admissible, philosophy, ethics, divinity, criticism, poetry, humour, fun, mimicry, anecdotes, jokes, ventriloquism. All the breadth & versatility of the most liberal conversation ... all may be combined in one speech; it is a panharmonicon." (*LL*: 48). Like this panharmonicon, a nineteenth-century technological novelty that imitated the sounds of multiple instruments simultaneously, Emerson's essays hum with resonances of a series of synthesized voices. Most famously, they gave voice to the mute glories of nature, allowing it, in the words of one astute recent reading of his essays to "testify" for itself.[36] Blending pantheism and Swedenborgian mysticism, he promoted the literary essay as a form of ventriloquism and the channel through which nature could speak: the means by which to break what he called in "The Divinity School Address," "the never-broken silence with which the old bounty goes forward [that] has not yielded yet one word of explanation." (*CW* 1: 76).

Emerson's essays often read as tapestries of quotations brought to life and staged as moments of interaction. His essays tended to orchestrate imagined speakers, with "Self-Reliance" shifting into the voice of the "Caliph Ali" and *Nature* concluding in the persona of an "Orphic Bard." His most arresting method was the staging of dialogues in which the authorial voice confronts opposing views directly as heard speech. His gift for anecdote and narrative presents the world of ideas as a matter of demands, statements, and rejoinders. His verb choices are revealing, with "says" outnumbering "writes," and "tells" rivalling "wrote." He is often imagining and reporting back not textual exchanges but spoken interactions, presenting correspondence as dialogue, not lengthy or drawn-out epistolary communication but speech acts and confrontations that crackle with the spirit of oral repartee. Bearing in mind the widespread nineteenth-century custom of communal reading aloud, we might even imagine these voices rendered anew by readers obliged to adopt a range of accents and tones.[37]

Once again, "Self-Reliance" provides a perfect illustration of how this worked. The totemic line "A foolish consistency is the hobgoblin of little minds," in "Self-Reliance," for example, is countered swiftly as follows: "Ah, then, exclaim the aged ladies, you shall be sure to be misunderstood! Misunderstood! It is a right fool's word. Is it so bad then to be misunderstood?" (CW 2: 26). More elaborately, the essay's other well-known injunction – "Whoso would be a man must be a nonconformist" – generates the following imagined dialogue:

> I remember an answer which when quite young I was prompted to make to a valued adviser, who was wont to importune me with the dear old doctrines of the church. On my saying, What have I to do with the sacredness of traditions, if I live wholly from within? my friend suggested, – "But these impulses may be from below, not from above." I replied, "They do not seem to me to be such; but if I am the Devil's child, I will live then from the Devil." No law can be sacred to me but that of my nature. (CW 2: 30)

In this rare moment of personal intrusion, the essay articulates and closes off the alternate "impulse" with a stark statement of principle, leaving us with discordant voices raised in uneasy competition. This antiphonal chorus leads critics such as Sharon Cameron to read Emerson's essays as an erasure of personality, since at their heart is "anonymous voice, which is not a recognizable voice because not legible as a single person's voice."[38] In these ways, acts of citation and vocalization displace confession, resulting in a series of subtle tensions. Emerson promotes himself as chief listener, at times effacing himself as a narrative agent giving solace to harbored voices, at others rebuking them. Reading these essays presents a paradox to each reader. As we navigate these competing voices, do they weave together as part of a dialectical journey toward truth, or do they remain a chorus of unresolved cries?

Emerson's solution to the paradox of positioning himself at once as both speaker and listener was to turn the challenge back on his audience. A central metaphor of his writings was the claim that readers should trust their own inner voice. Drawn in part from Quaker imagery, this is the keynote of "Self-Reliance," where he urges readers to "listen to the inward voice and bravely obey" (*CW* 2: 30); it is also the theme of "Spiritual Laws" (1841) where he argues that "there is guidance for each of us" in listening to speech from within (*CW* 2: 110). This urge to listen to intuition also takes on a cultural nationalist aspect in "The American Scholar," where, having "listened too long to the courtly muses of Europe," the process of personal renovation necessary for American democratic individuality is figured in terms of giving voice to an "ill-suppressed murmur" of the national sublime (*CW* 1: 63). Emerson's classic essays therefore continue to urge readers to listen to themselves rather than solely to his own voice. It was a paradoxical form of essayistic authority, and one that his most famous poetic disciple, Whitman, saw as Emerson's key strength, in that this urging onwards of the essays "breeds the giant that destroys itself," as part of essays that foresaw their own obsolescence.[39]

Emerson saw great men as those that allowed will to flow through them. At the lectern on Staten Island we see an essayist figured more as a motivational speaker than a hero, merely claiming to model a habit of perception, casting a powerful gaze back upon the crowd, "eyes uplifted on the audience," and asking of listeners and readers alike that they trust not him but their own powers of comprehension.[40] His essays disperse meaning through a series of woven voices just as, in the terms he used in "Self-Reliance," "It must be that when God speaketh he should communicate, not one thing, but all things; should fill the world with his voice; should scatter forth light, nature, time, souls, from the centre of the present thought." (*CW* 2: 30)

## Epilogue: Voiced Essays in the Influencer Era

These lectern and voice-centric readings of Emerson also open up a role for his work in helping us understand the dynamics of far more recent media. I want to end with the thought experiment of imagining a *digital* Emerson and specifically asking what he might tell us about the personality-focused viral Web 2.0 video culture. The analogy is playfully anachronistic. But after all, Emerson did reassure us in "The American Scholar" that "science is nothing but the finding of analogy ... in the most remote parts" (*CW* 1: 54). One particular style of digital video seems an obvious inheritor of the lectern energies of Emerson's era. Dating from the 1980s but at peak popularity in the 2010s, the "TED talk" names an online video genre of short talks from invited luminaries from various walks of life offering condensed summaries of lessons learnt and worldviews, unfailingly delivered in uplifting fashion in front of eager paying audiences.[41] Videos have been streamed hundreds of millions of times on YouTube, Vimeo, and TikTok.

It has become something of a commonplace for scholars of the nineteenth century to jump at the resemblances of TED to the lyceum or to its successor format, the festival-like culture of education talks known as Chautauqua. In fact, this analogy holds more validity than we might realize, since the founders of the original TED conference in 1984 modeled their enterprise explicitly on the eclecticism and moral utility of these earlier forms.[42] In this way, the templates and career trajectories of figures like Emerson inspired and brought into being the media forms that came long after them and how they anticipated crucial elements of this Web 2.0 world. One resonance to the analogy is the misleading veneer of modernity. Along with the paradigm shift of the penny press that energized and sustained oral culture, users of the lyceum of the 1830s were just as self-conscious about taking part in something unprecedented as are the consumers of online influencers.[43] For the moment of its peak novelty, the Emerson of the lectern was the early adopter, cultural entrepreneur, and one-man influencer brand that exploited a communication network's potential for remarkable ends. Another resonance is the shared emphasis on embodied intimacy and the imagined relationship of audience to speaker, often in the form of an elaborate conversion experience. Influencers of the 2020s offer to many "followers" just the kind of paradoxically illicit and confidential relationship that individual readers of Emerson claim to have recreated by "hearing" the voice of the Sage at the lectern through his essays.

Above all, it is important to see platforms such as TikTok, YouTube, and Vimeo as not just visual but also "resurgent orality."[44] Emerson suggests something very similar about the "voiced essay," whose striving for oral qualities engaged not only textual but also other sensory resources. These multimodal ambitions would only be realized much later, when the broadcast media of phonographs, radio, audiobooks, and podcasts realized these aims. And as such, by deriving meaning from original live, participatory contexts, Emerson's essays themselves were predicated on a strange form of textual inadequacy, signaling their own insufficiency and incompleteness if read solely as silent and private. Whether in his study or at the lectern, Emerson was a creature of a new accelerated, highly connected age. Yet one who promised to be its antidote: The deep calm of his essays offered a space of slowing down, of focus, and benign coherence amid the melee of the public sphere. What I have been presenting as the "voiced essay" was crucial to this. Through a commitment to orality on the level of style and idea, Emerson tried to push the materially focused genre of the essay form toward larger, spiritual concerns through an engagement with "voice." By marrying secular, sacred, and oratorical rhythms, these essays attempt to teach us how to listen, presenting responsible citizenship as a matter of auditory perception.

# Notes

1. Anonymous, "a series of letters published in The Gazette of Stapleton, NY," qtd in George Willis Cooke, *Ralph Waldo Emerson: His Life, Writings and Philosophy* (Boston: Osgood & Co., 1881), 258.

2. Recent works on Emerson as lecturer include Bonnie Carr O'Neill, *Literary Celebrity and Public Life in the Nineteenth Century* (Athens, GA: University of Georgia Press, 2017); Tim Sommer, *Carlyle, Emerson and the Transatlantic Uses of Authority: Literature, Print, Performance* (Edinburgh: Edinburgh University Press, 2021); and my own *Lecturing the Atlantic: Speech, Print and an Anglo-American Commons* (Oxford: Oxford University Press, 2017). Important earlier work includes Mary Kupiec Cayton, *Emerson's Emergence: Self and Society in the Transformation of New England 1800–1845* (Chapel Hill: University of North Carolina Press, 1992); Thomas Augst, *The Clerk's Tale: Young Men and Moral Life in Nineteenth-Century America* (Chicago: University of Chicago Press, 2003), 114–57.

3. George Willis Cooke, *Ralph Waldo Emerson: His Life, Writings and Philosophy* (Boston: Osgood & Co., 1881), 256–69. This is the case also made in Joel Myerson and Ronald Bosco's eds. *Selected Lectures of Ralph Waldo Emerson* (Athens, GA: University of Georgia, 2005), ix: "To understand Emerson's writing … [we must see him] as a lecturer."

4. F. O. Matthiessen, *American Renaissance: Art and Expression in the Age of Emerson and Whitman* (Oxford: Oxford University Press, 1941), 23.

5. Douglass, "The Lecturers," *Frederick Douglass's Paper*, January 13, 1854.

6. Henry David Thoreau, *A Week on the Concord and Merrimack Rivers*, ed. Robert F. Sayre (New York: Library of America, 1985), 86.

7. For accounts of the lyceum, see Carl Bode, *The American Lyceum: Town Meeting of the Mind* (Oxford: Oxford University Press, 1956); Donald Scott, "The Popular Lecture and the Creation of a Public in the mid-Nineteenth-Century United States," *The Journal of American History*, 66:4 (1980), 791–809; Angela Ray, *The Lyceum and Public Culture in the Nineteenth-Century United States* (East Lansing: Michigan State University Press, 2005); Tom F. Wright ed., *The Cosmopolitan Lyceum: Lecture Culture and the Globe in Nineteenth-Century America* (Amherst: University of Massachusetts Press, 2013); Angela Ray and Paul Stob eds., *Thinking Together: Lecturing, Learning, and Difference in the Long Nineteenth Century* (University Park, PA: Pennsylvania University Press, 2018).

8. See Thomas Augst, *The Clerk's Tale: Young Men and Moral Life in Nineteenth Century America* (Chicago: University of Chicago Press, 2003).

9. "Popular Lecturers," *Boston Daily Evening Transcript*, October 29, 1855.

10. Fuller, "Entertainments of Past Winter," *The Dial*, July 1842.

11. Figures refer to Bayard Taylor's earnings for 1854, Bode, *American Lyceum*, 217.

12. This transatlantic career is explored in Sommer's, *Emerson, Carlyle and the Transatlantic Uses of Authority*; Wright, *Lecturing the Atlantic*; and in Daniel Koch, *Ralph Waldo Emerson: Class, Race and Revolution in the Making of an American Thinker* (London: Bloomsbury 2012).

13. F. O. Matthiessen, *American Renaissance: Art and Expression in the Age of Emerson and Whitman* (Oxford: Oxford University Press, 1941), 23.

14. "New England: Genius, Manners and Customs," in *The Later Lectures of Ralph Waldo Emerson, 1843–1871*, I, 48.
15. Thomas Carlyle to Jean Carlyle Aitken, May 6, 1840, Carlyle Letters Online Vol. 12: 134–37. http://carlyleletters.dukejournals.org/; George Willis Cooke, *Ralph Waldo Emerson: His Life, Writings and Philosophy* (Boston: Osgood & Co., 1881), 263.
16. See Lawrence Buell, *New England Literary Culture from Revolution Through Renaissance* (Cambridge: Cambridge University Press, 1989), 110.
17. Buell, *New England Literary Culture*, 116.
18. See Stephen Whicher and Robert Spiller, eds., *The Early Lectures of Ralph Waldo Emerson Vol 1.1833–36* (Cambridge: Belknap Press, 1959) and Stephen Wicher and Robert Spiller eds., *The Early Lectures of Ralph Waldo Emerson Vol 2: 1836–38* (Cambridge: Belknap Press, 1959); and Ronald A. Bosco, and Joel Myerson eds. *Selected Lectures of Ralph Waldo Emerson* (Athens, GA: University of Georgia, 2005) and Ronald A. Bosco and Joel Myerson eds. *The Later Lectures of Ralph Waldo Emerson, 1843–1871* (Athens: University of Georgia Press, 2010).
19. Walt Whitman to John Townsend Trowbridge, 1860, quoted in Matthiessen, *American Renaissance*, 523.
20. "Mr. Emerson on The Laws of Success," *Cleveland Plain Dealer*, January 21, 1859.
21. Quoted in James Elliot Cabot, *A Memoir of Ralph Waldo Emerson Vol. 2* (Boston: Houghton, Mifflin and Co., 1888), 474.
22. *Appleton's Journal*, May 28, 1870.
23. The two most influential of these are George Kateb, *Emerson and Self-Reliance* (New York: Sage Publications, 1995) and Stanley Cavell, *Emerson's Transcendental Etudes* (Stanford: Stanford University Press, 2003).
24. Matthew Arnold, "'Written in Emerson's Essays', (1849)," in *The Poems of Matthew Arnold* (Oxford: Oxford University Press, 1909); Matthew Arnold, "Emerson," in *Discourses in America* (London: Macmillan and Co., 1885), 144.
25. Parker, "Emerson," *Massachusetts Quarterly Review*, March 1850.
26. Walter Ong, *Orality and Literacy: The Technologizing of the Word* (Oxford: Oxford University Press, 1982), 41.
27. Lawrence Buell, *Emerson* (Cambridge, MA: Harvard University Press, 2002), 101.
28. "Divinity School Address," *Nature, Addresses, and Lectures*, 86.
29. John Ruskin, "The Political Economy of Art," in Lloyd J. Hubenka ed. *Unto This Last: Four Essays on the First Principles of Political Economy* (Lincoln: University of Nebraska Press, 1967), 1.
30. William Hazlitt, "On the Periodical Essayists," in *The Collected Works of William Hazlitt*, ed. A. R. Waller, Arnold Glover, and William E. Henley (London: J.M. Dent & Co, 1902), 7.
31. Ivan Kreilkamp, *Voice and the Victorian Storyteller* (Cambridge: Cambridge University Press, 2005), 70.
32. See John Holloway, *The Victorian Sage: Studies in Argument* (London: Macmillan, 1953) and George P. Landow, *Elegant Jeremiahs: The Sage from Carlyle to Mailer* (Ithaca: Cornell University Press, 1986).
33. Garrett Stewart, *Dear Reader: The Conscripted Audience in Nineteenth-Century British Fiction* (Baltimore: Johns Hopkins University Press, 1996), 12.

34. Mikhail Bakhtin, "Speech Genres," in *Speech Genres and Other Late Essays*, ed. Michael Holquist, Vern McGee, and Caryl Emerson (Austin: University of Texas Press, 1986), 139.

35. Benedict Anderson, *Imagined Communities: Reflections on the Origin and Spread of Nationalism* (London: Verso, 1991), 35.

36. Shari Goldberg, *Quiet Testimony: A Theory of Witnessing from Nineteenth-Century American Literature* (New York: Fordham University Press, 2013).

37. For the culture of reading aloud, see Carolyn Eastman, "Reading Aloud: Editorial Societies and Orality in Magazines of the Early American Republic," *Early American Literature* 54:1 (2019), 163–88.

38. Sharon Cameron, *Impersonality: Seven Essays* (Chicago: University of Chicago Press, 2007), 93.

39. Walt Whitman, "'Emerson's Books, the Shadow of Them' (1882)," in *The Complete Writings of Walt Whitman*, ed. Walt Whitman, Richard M. Bucke, Thomas B. Harned, Horace Traubel, and Oscar L. Triggs (New York: Putnam's, 1902).

40. Anonymous, "a series of letters published in The Gazette of Stapleton, NY," qtd. in George Willis Cooke, 258.

41. For the remit and history of the TED organization, see www.ted.com/about/our-organization/history-of-ted (Accessed on May 12, 2022).

42. For a discussion of Harry Marks and Richard Saul Wurman's debts to Chautauqua, see Megan Garber, "How TED Makes Ideas Smaller," *The Atlantic*, March 2012.

43. James Cortada, *All the Facts, History of Information in America* (Oxford: Oxford University Press, 2013)

44. Ong, *Orality and Literacy*, 21.

# 8

SOPHIA FORSTER

# Labor, Slavery, and the Civil War

On January 25, 1855, renowned abolitionist Wendell Phillips took a break from the annual meeting of the Massachusetts Anti-Slavery Society to attend a lecture on slavery by Ralph Waldo Emerson. Upon Phillips's return to the Anti-Slavery Society meeting, its proceedings state, he was "rapturously applauded" and "called upon for a speech." Phillips replied, however, that "he had nothing to say, but he had just been listening to a *great* speech by Mr. Emerson – one of the greatest and bravest ever made in the city of Boston, or of New England."[1] Abolitionists had not always believed that mid nineteenth-century America's most famous philosopher represented their concerns as well as they themselves could. In 1844, antislavery poet John Greenleaf Whittier had responded to Emerson's first oratorical entry into abolitionist politics, an address celebrating the anniversary of emancipation in the British West Indies, with the comment that "we had previously, we confess, felt half indignant that, while we were struggling against the popular current, mobbed, hunted, denounced, from the legislative forum, cursed from the pulpit, such a man as Ralph Waldo Emerson should be brooding over his pleasant philosophies, writing his quaint and beautiful essays, in his retirement on the banks of the Concord, unconcerned and 'calm as a summer's morning.'"[2] In just over a decade, abolitionists had gone from seeing Emerson as a belated and halting entrant to antislavery politics to viewing him as a prized exponent of the movement's values. Since the recovery of Emerson's antislavery work in the early 1990s, scholars have been preoccupied by the question of what, if anything, changed in Emerson's thought to lead him into abolitionism. Was antislavery activity always implicit in the "pleasant philosophies" Emerson expounded and published in the years leading up to the "Emancipation Address"? Or did his public participation in abolitionism, which would stretch through the Civil War, represent a departure from the transcendentalism of his earlier "quaint and beautiful essays?"

To answer this question requires examining Emerson's perspectives on a host of subjects, including social reform, labor, law, racial difference, and violence. On all of these topics Emerson's thought is fundamentally paradoxical. In this chapter, I argue that critics' sense of a conflict between Emerson's transcendentalist and political work is itself symptomatic of his ideas about key dimensions of abolitionism. Emerson, that is, engages the antislavery argument in terms that are by definition contradictory, as he both emphasizes and tries to reconcile a series of oppositions within transcendentalist principles. These include conflicts between self-reliance and social reform; between labor as a means of self-development and of economic development; between absolute moral law and temporal statute law; between teleological history and evolutionary history; and, finally, between the refusal of violence and the use of violence as a political expedient. Whether scholars see conflict or congruity between Emerson's transcendental and political work depends in large part on how they assess Emerson's own efforts to bridge the divide in his antislavery writings. When critics judge those efforts successful, they often pronounce Emerson a consistent abolitionist whose changing degree and manner of public engagement with antislavery reflect his perception of the situation's exigency; when critics judge those efforts unsuccessful, they generally offer a developmental narrative for his career, in which Emerson either falls from a powerful transcendentalist detachment into the vulgarities of contemporary politics or rises from the abstractions of transcendentalism to a powerful ethical posture. This chapter will address the complexities of Emerson's formulations of transcendentalist oppositions, showing how his various engagements with slavery can play out in counterintuitive ways. In the context of his views on "free labor" as developing an individual's unique faculties, Emerson's expressed resistance to a career as an abolitionist powerfully resists slavery by critiquing it as an economic system that prohibits the free choice of labor granted by capitalism. Conversely, in the context of his understanding of moral law as natural law, Emerson's abolitionist argument that slavery contravenes a "higher" law than statute law equivocally denounces slavery because it allows for the possibility that as a product of the natural development of humans, slavery cannot violate moral law. Finally, Emerson's defense of abolitionist violence, including the Civil War, likewise engages contradictory principles to unexpected ends, as the naturalization of such violence transforms physical force into moral force.

## Intellectual Labor, Slavery, and Capitalism

Considerations of the relationship between transcendentalism and abolitionism inevitably contend with Emerson's own sense of the conflict between his role as an intellectual and as a social reformer. What Whittier describes as Emerson's initial "unconcern" with abolitionism is expressed bluntly in his famous transcendentalist essay "Self-Reliance" (1841), as part of a philosophical stance that would seem to inhibit rather than encourage Emerson's entrance into abolitionism. In the course of elaborating his doctrine of nonconformity, Emerson notoriously suggests that rude rejection appropriately responds to "an angry bigot [who] assumes this bountiful cause of Abolition, and comes to me with his last news from Barbados" (CW 2: 30). Emerson's complaint here, at a moment when he had not yet publicly spoken out against slavery, hinges more on his sense of the hypocrisy of many social reformers, including abolitionists, rather than the pursuit of abolitionism per se.[3] A decade later, though, the opposition that Emerson constructs between his own practical act of speaking out against slavery and the famous essay's injunctions to nonconformity suggests the depth of his ambivalence. In two of his most significant antislavery speeches of the 1850s, Emerson opens with apparent admissions of the incompatibility of his intellectual and antislavery activities, using the language of "Self-Reliance" to overtly problematize his own participation in abolitionism. In his "Address to the Citizens of Concord" in 1851, Emerson begins by proclaiming that "The last year has forced us all into politics, and made it a paramount duty to seek what it is often a duty to shun."[4] The insistence on the general "duty to shun" the conventional ethical responsibilities that "politics" represents – presumably responsibilities to oppressed social groups – directly echoes Emerson's announcement, immediately following his denunciation of the abolitionist in "Self-Reliance," "I shun father and mother and wife and brother, when my genius calls me" (CW 2: 30). The use of this same language in 1851 suggests that for Emerson the demand to participate in politics has hitherto belonged to what he calls in the earlier essay the moral "reflex standard," which he claims that he may "neglect" in order to "absolve me to myself"; when hailed by his genius, he can "den[y] the name of duty to many offices that are called duties" (CW 2: 42). To be "forced" into politics as a "paramount duty," as Emerson claims to be in 1851, implies a violation of his will.

If the beginning of the 1851 speech reminds us that Emerson's philosophy often sets individual self-development and self-expression against the demands of a larger social world, the opening of his 1854 speech, "The Fugitive Slave Law," returns to the same thorny section of "Self-Reliance" to emphasize Emerson's seeming reluctance to enter the fray of antislavery politics. "I do not often speak to public questions," Emerson begins. "They are odious and harmful, and it seems like meddling or leaving your work" (AW, 73). Certainly, Emerson might here appear to refer to his own ostensibly unobjectionable advice from the earlier essay, where he urges his reader, "do your work, and I shall know you. Do your work, and you shall reinforce yourself" (*CW* 2: 32). But this 1841 injunction is not as innocuous as it seems, since it is just as embroiled as the 1854 comment in the question of one's own responsibilities to others. Emerson claims in "Self-Reliance" that commitment to doing his own work as a thinker and writer militates against participating in reform projects in general, on the basis that both the practitioners and objects of such reform are men who "do not belong to me and to whom I do not belong" (*CW* 31). By contrast, he says, "There is a class of persons to whom by all spiritual affinity I am bought and sold; for them I will go to prison, if need be" (31). It is significant that this statement occurs shortly after Emerson's explicit rejection of the call to participate in abolition in "Self-Reliance": Having just dismissed the problems of the enslaved person as not "belonging" to him because he does not "belong" to their group, Emerson proceeds to compare himself to an enslaved person ("bought and sold," literally "belonging" to another as property) in order to affirm the call to pursue one's own work, a metaphor that seems to trivialize the situation of those who are legally enslaved. Emerson revisits the contrast between imprisoned allies and socially oppressed populations in "The Fugitive Slave Law," saying, "I have my own spirits in prison, – spirits in deeper prisons, whom no man visits if I do not" (*AW* 73) – a statement that modifies his more blatantly offensive 1852 journal comment, "I have quite other slaves to free than those negroes, to wit, imprisoned spirits, imprisoned thoughts, far back in the brain of man."[5] This statement's clear prioritization of Emerson's intellectual work over the work of freeing enslaved people employs a metaphor related to the one he used in "Self-Reliance," as he seems to compare those interested in freedom from conformity, particularly intellectual conformity, to "slaves" for whose "free[ing]" he is solely responsible.

Emerson's problematization of his participation in the abolitionist movement suggests that he intended to advertise his reluctant departure from transcendentalism. Some scholars working in the decade immediately after the recovery of Emerson's political work, which began with Len Gougeon's book *Virtue's Hero* (1990) and the subsequent appearance of his coedited collection *Emerson's Antislavery Writings* (1995), have deemed transcendental philosophy and progressive politics, including antislavery politics, irreconcilable – a conclusion that generally leads to a disparagement of Emerson's philosophy as incapable of addressing social oppression.[6] But recent interpretations have been more generous to Emerson's repeated efforts to distinguish antislavery activity from his own work as a philosopher and artist. These suggest that what Emerson distrusted was not the cause of antislavery itself so much as the impetus that drew reformers to it: the desire, antithetical to self-reliance, to "act, and urge others to act, on the basis of something abstract and distant rather than present and directly experienced"[7] and the related tendency to use social reform as a substitute for self-reform.[8] As Peter Wirzbicki puts it, Emerson "was suggesting that, while abolition is a just cause ('bountiful'), many activists were attracted to such a pure moral crusade exactly because its obvious righteousness shielded them from their own anxiety, granted them a false moral pride that silenced the uneasiness in their souls"; the flip side of this argument was the conviction of many transcendentalists that abolitionism "was a 'partial' reform, aiming only to emancipate slaves and not to fully remake individuals by developing their true selves."[9] This more sympathetic reading of Emerson's work gathers strength from the fact that as the national crisis over slavery intensified in the 1850s, Emerson didn't slight antislavery activity; if anything, he intensified his participation in it even as he continued to write, present, and publish more conventionally philosophical texts. Not only did he shift from speaking on slavery primarily in Concord to delivering abolitionist speeches in New York and Boston as part of organized lecture series on the topic, but in the 1850s he threw his support behind the Boston Vigilance Committee, which sought to aid fugitive slaves, and John Brown, the fiery defender of Free-Soil settlers in Kansas following the Kansas-Nebraska Act of 1854. Meanwhile, Emerson made his only foray into the realm of organized politics during these years, using the 1851 speech to campaign for the antislavery congressman John Gorham Palfrey that spring.

Emerson's expressed reluctance to participate in abolitionism can in fact illuminate a key dimension of his antislavery views, for it is closely related to his critique of slavery as an economic institution. The growing urgency Emerson feels to address the political cause corresponds to his increasing need to emphasize how vexed that address feels in light of his own vocational commitments. I would argue that this is ultimately symptomatic of Emerson's somewhat idiosyncratic theory of "free labor," which he began developing in the late 1830s.[10] This framework, which governs Emerson's understanding of his own work, goes beyond what would become the standard Republican position in the 1850s, in which northern capitalism affords the laborer opportunities for moral and economic self-development absent in slavery. While Republicans emphasized both the intrinsic reward of individual self-discipline and the instrumental rewards of higher productivity, Emerson thought capitalism accommodated an experience of labor that expanded the self's innate faculties and capacities. In this context, Emerson's expressions of reluctance to enter politics can be seen as embodying an important aspect of his protest against slavery. Paradoxically, when

Emerson insists on raising the question of the relevance of abolition to him personally – positioning it as a call *away* from his proper work – he instantiates his critique of slavery as an economic system. Slavery, Emerson claims repeatedly in both his overtly political and his transcendental texts, annuls the possibility for specialized self-chosen labor that produces the distinctive form of self-development that Emerson's own career represents.

Emerson's address "Man the Reformer" (1841) represents a rare explicit consideration of the work of the intellectual in tandem with an analysis of the institutions of capitalism and slavery. Presented to the Mechanics' Apprentices' Library Association in the same year that "Self-Reliance" was published, the lecture addresses the importance of manual labor to the education of man. It allies the antislavery movement with a utopian project of return to such labor: If manual labor becomes the occupation of all, Emerson seems to suggest, it will no longer devolve to enslaved persons in faraway places. Near the opening of the essay, Emerson proposes that the reliance of "the general system of our trade"[11] on the labor of enslaved people in the West Indies makes northerners complicit in the institutions of slavery. "We are all implicated, of course, in this charge" of abuse in the economy, Emerson says, since "it is only necessary to ask a few questions as to the progress of the articles of commerce from the fields where they grew, to our houses, to become aware that we eat and drink and wear perjury and fraud in a hundred commodities" (*PE* 37). And because "[t]he sins of our trade belong to no class, to no individual," "none feels himself accountable" (*PE* 38). Emerson's emphasis on social responsibility here presents a stark contrast with his refusal in "Self-Reliance" to concern himself with the socially oppressed at the expense of those "to whom by all spiritual affinity I am bought and sold" (*CW* 31). Taken alongside Emerson's gestures in the address toward the necessity of universal participation in manual labor, these comments have been seen by some scholars to represent a powerful early critique of slavery on Emerson's part.[12]

But Emerson's utopian vision contains qualifications that reveal its shortcomings as a solution to the problem of slavery, as well as the disadvantages to intellectuals of ending capitalism's division of labor. When Emerson says that "we must begin to consider if it were not the nobler part to ... put ourselves into primary relations with the soil and nature," he voices the ideas of others whom he calls "many philanthropic and intelligent persons" (*PE* 39). Among these were, presumably, George and Sophia Ripley, whose Fourierist Brook Farm community Emerson had recently declined to join. Emerson himself offers a contrasting vision that emphasizes the value of the division of labor, claiming that the necessary phenomenon of men withdrawing themselves from "the labors of commerce, of law, of state" would last but a short time. This would be the great action, which always opens the eyes of men. When many persons shall have done this, when the majority shall admit the necessity of reform in all these institutions, their abuses will be redressed, and the way will be open again to the advantages which arise from the division of labor, and a man may select the fittest employment for his peculiar talent again, without compromise. (*PE* 39)

These advantages Emerson had enumerated at some length in a pair of 1837 lectures devoted explicitly to labor, using language that this passage echoes. In them Emerson singles out the power of the division of labor to create individual self-development through the engagement of each person's unique "faculty" with the external world. Emerson claims in "Trades and Professions" that "To the endless variety of substances is a match in the endless variety of faculty. To each man is his calling foreordained in his faculty."[13] In "Doctrine of the Hands" he similarly insists that "The calling of each man is prescribed for him by his peculiar faculty," adding that "We have scarcely observed the infinite variety of commodities which in every part of nature invite the hand of man before we are struck with a correspondence thereto in his faculty. As great as is the difference of products is the difference of aptitudes to avail themselves of these" (*EL* 2: 235). The assertion in "Man the Reformer" that in a capitalist system "a man may select the fittest employment for his peculiar talent ... without compromise" (*PE* 39) clearly draws on this earlier model of labor as a "calling" whose development of individuals' special "faculties" or abilities redounds to the benefit of society.

This endorsement of the capitalist division of labor does not necessarily mean that Emerson abandons his protest against slavery; he remains troubled by the structure of an economy based on enslaved labor. While Emerson does not finally believe that manual labor must be shared by everyone, he insists that every individual ought to *work* in some way. He makes this perhaps clearest in a rare pre-1844 public reference to slavery in the conclusion of "Doctrine of the Hands," where, after deriding the "fatal pride of idleness," he announces his hope that "New England will come to place its pride in being a nation of servants and not, like the planting states, a nation of served" (*EL* 2: 244). Emerson claims that this "service" constitutes the individual's participation in the varied work of the world, arguing that "Whilst every man can say, I serve; to the extent of my being I apply my faculty to the service of mankind in my especial place, he therein sees and shows a reason for his being in the world and is not a moth or an incumbrance [sic] on it" (*EL* 2: 244). For Emerson, those who don't labor at their "especial place" deprive themselves of self-development, in turn encumbering the rest of the body politic, which must compensate for their failure to contribute their own unique abilities. Although "Man the Reformer" begins by entertaining the idea that those involved in nonmanual labor might be part of the "nation of served" who participate in slavery by placing the burden of their needs on the enslaved, it eventually refigures that formulation, presenting an alternative that Emerson would continue to promote in his later antislavery work. While he insists on the value of manual labor to the "enervated" (*PE* 43) scholar, still Emerson says he doesn't want to insist that every man should be a farmer. Rather, "the doctrine of the Farm is merely this, that every man ought to stand in primary relations with the work of the world, ought to do it himself ... and for this reason, that labor is God's education" (*PE* 42). This passage makes it clear that "the work of the world" encompasses any labor that humans have deemed to be of value, including intellectual labor.

This doctrine reappears throughout the major antislavery addresses. In these, Emerson joins an emphasis on the ultimate "wages" of labor as the development of the faculties – even the selfhood – of the individual that freely chosen labor provides with praise for the monetary wages with which laborers are rewarded in a capitalist system of divided labor. In "An Address on the Emancipation of Negroes in the British West Indies" (1844), Emerson raises the same problem as in "Man the Reformer" of northern involvement in corrupt trade practices, saying that "It was or it seemed the dictate of trade to keep the negro down.... We found it very convenient to keep them at work, since, by the aid of a little whipping, we could get their work for nothing but their board and the cost of whips" (*AW* 20). But, Emerson insists, the demand of the "moral sense" "is found to be, in the long run, for what the grossest calculator calls his advantage.... It was shown to the planters that they, as well as the negroes, were slaves; that though they paid no wages, they got very poor work" and "needed the severest monopoly laws at home to keep them from bankruptcy" (*AW* 21). If slavery does not make economic sense because the work provided by those kept from choosing their own labor is inferior, it also degrades the very selfhood of those who remain idle. As Emerson notes in "The Fugitive Slave Law," "A man who steals another man's labor, (as a planter does,) steals away his own faculties" (*AW* 84–85). This strand of abolitionist argument reaches its climax in 1862's *Atlantic Monthly* essay "American Civilization," where Emerson describes the division of labor as "nothing but a large allowance to each man to choose his work according to his faculty," which "fills the State with useful and happy laborers, – and they, creating demand by the very temptation of their productions, are rapidly and surely rewarded by good sale: and what a police and ten commandments their work then becomes! So true is Dr. Johnson's remark, that 'men are seldom more innocently employed than when they are making money'" (PE 162). By contrast, the "conspiracy of slavery" involves "stealing [men's] labor and the thief sitting idle himself" (PE 169) in a context where "denying a man's right to his labor" represents a profound moral failure, since "the distinction and end of a soundly constituted man is his labor. Use is inscribed on all his faculties" (PE 168). In Emerson's own case, his ability to both choose and make a living from exclusively intellectual labor in the northern economy testifies to the contributions possible when a capitalist division of labor combines with a universal legal condition of freedom to allow one to find their occupational niche.

### "Higher Law," Natural Development, and Racial Difference

If Emerson believes that the capitalist division of labor must remain, what answer to the problem raised in "Man the Reformer" of the interpenetration of northern capitalism and southern slavery? The lecture finally lands on an ambiguous note, saying that "If we suddenly plant our foot, and say, – I will neither eat nor drink nor wear nor touch any food or fabric which I do not know to be innocent … we shall stand still" (PE 45). Instead, Emerson says, "we must not cease to *tend* to the correction of these flagrant wrongs, by laying one stone aright every day" (PE 45–46). We might read Emerson's own participation in antislavery activity as embodying precisely this effort. While it may be true, as Jack Turner claims, that this approach to reducing complicity "does not rise above clichés,"[14] Emerson's phrase "the correction of these flagrant wrongs" highlights the central point on which turn many of Emerson's subsequent arguments against slavery: the claim that it violates a "higher law" than those given in statute books, a law perceptible to everyone who looks inside themselves but also evident in natural history when studied at a sufficient distance. As with Emerson's resistance to social reform, this powerful claim is contradictory. In this case, though, it is Emerson's ardent support of abolitionism, rather than his reluctance to engage with it, which paradoxically manifests the opposite principle. Emerson's efforts to ground "higher" moral law in natural processes of development lead him uncomfortably close to the conclusion of some mid nineteenth-century theorists of evolution that as much as slavery is a natural outcome of human development, it necessarily expresses moral law. To counter this, Emerson explicitly attacks the use of evolutionary theory for racist ends by highlighting the irony of evolutionary racial science's association of Blacks with animality when slavery's existence implies the arrested moral development of whites.

The invocation of a higher moral law became an explicit part of the political conversation about slavery in March 1850, a few days after Massachusetts senator Daniel Webster delivered what many northeasterners saw as a perfidious address defending the Compromise of 1850 (the series of bills designed to balance the demands of the northern and southern factions around the expansion of slavery). Most notoriously, it contained the Fugitive Slave Law, which gave new teeth to the constitutional provision requiring the return of enslaved people who had fled their state. Four days after Webster's address, the antislavery senator from New York William H. Seward delivered a famous response, in which he declared that "there is a higher law than the Constitution."[15] If, as Albert von Frank notes, this seemed to echo the understanding of many abolitionists, particularly the followers of William Lloyd Garrison, "that the U.S. Constitution was a proslavery document," nonetheless, "[t]he idea of a 'higher law' superseding and governing human enactments ... had not been routinely a part of senatorial debate.... The discourse that it emphatically *did* belong to was that of New England Transcendentalism – rather more than to the often biblical and prophetic discourse of abolitionism."[16]

Indeed, alluding to the derision at Seward's speech expressed by Webster's supporters, Emerson told the audience of his 1851 response to Webster, "A few months ago, in my dismay at hearing that the Higher Law was reckoned a good joke in the courts, I took pains to look into a few law books" (*AW* 59). He finds there "that immoral laws are void" (*AW* 59) and that "a person ought not to obey such commands as are evidently contrary to the laws of God" (*AW* 60). In his earlier transcendental texts Emerson had, of course, translated this distinction between human and eternal law into that between conformity and self-reliance, where the former "loves not realities and creators," as the latter does, but rather "names and customs" (*CW* 2: 29). His antislavery speeches continue this argument. Laws' ontological status as customs, the ossified expressions of previous inspirations of genius, meant to Emerson that they should be subject to constant revision, based on the continuing development of the people whom they governed. In "Citizens of Concord," Emerson declares of statute laws that they "do not make right"; those which people are bound to uphold "are simply declaratory of a right which already existed," a right granted to individuals by higher moral law (*AW* 57). In 1855, Emerson suggested that a history of legal course corrections confirms this, insisting that the country's "abject regard for forms ... is an insanity which nothing will cure but great outrages, such as the Boston Port Bill and Stamp Act, in 1770, and the Fugitive Slave Bill and Nebraska Bill. These startle the common sense, and make us feel that we must put the Tea overboard, and hunt the slaveholder, – must destroy the law before the principle" (*AW* 135). And in 1856, Emerson addressed statute law's potential for injustice by highlighting the close relationship between that law and the individuals who enforce it, observing that when the Free Soilers in Kansas complain of intimidation and violence, the president tells them to go to the courts, "though he knows that when the poor plundered farmer comes to the court, he finds the ringleader who has robbed him ... unbuckling his knife to sit as his judge" (*AW* 114). Comments like these lead scholars to describe Emerson as holding an ideal of statute law as "a living code of justice,"[17] an instrument formed by a "creative process" of "extemporizing."[18]

Emerson's appeal to higher law in the context of abolitionism first appeared in "Emancipation," where he describes it not only as moral law but also as "natural" law. This connection between morality and nature strengthens the power of Emerson's higher law philosophy to oppose slavery by insisting that an individual's intuition of the violations of slavery – the fact that, as Frederick Douglass would hold, "There is not a man beneath the canopy of heaven, that does not know that slavery is wrong for him" – has the final ethical word. Emerson begins his lengthy account of the history of British antislavery with a discussion of the famous 1772 case in which Lord Mansfield pronounced the release of George Somerset, an enslaved man who fled the Scotsman by whom he had been purchased in Virginia upon their arrival in England. Emerson quotes from the conclusion of Mansfield's decision, which announces Somerset's discharge on the basis that "[t]he power claimed by this return [of Somerset to the man who bought him] was never in use" (*AW* 11) in England. Slavery, Mansfield follows, is "incapable of being introduced on any reasons, moral or political, but only by 'positive law'" – positive law which, he explains, is preserved by "[i]mmemorial usage ... long after all traces of the occasion, reason, authority, and time of its introduction, are lost; and in a case so odious as the condition of slaves, must be taken strictly" (*AW* 11). Tellingly, Emerson includes Mansfield's immediately following parenthetical comment that "tracing the subject to natural principles, the claim of slavery never can be supported" (11). Given that Emerson begins the next paragraph with the comment that the Somerset decision "established that principle that the 'air of England is too pure for any slave to breathe,' but the wrongs in the islands were not thereby touched" (11), we might surmise that his citation of Mansfield's words intends, above all, a rhetorical contrast between the limitations of statute law and the power of a higher moral law based on "natural principles." While positive law may suffice to end the right to enslave within England, achievement of a universally liberating effect falls under the purview of natural law. Indeed, later in the essay, Emerson circles back to the liberating power of the principles with which nature endows individuals. Although England is dominated by the "civility" of "a trading nation," the development of abolitionism there shows that "man is born with intellect, as well as with a love of sugar, and with a sense of justice, as well as a taste for strong drink. These ripened, as well as those" (*AW* 20–21). If natural principles make freedom the proper condition of Black as well as white men, they also make whites incapable of supporting slavery. Considering the Fugitive Slave Law in 1851, Emerson says, "all men that are born are, in proportion to their power of thought and their moral sensibility, found to be the natural enemies of this law" (*AW* 58). Emerson suggests that men will eventually innately oppose a law that is not based on moral principles.

Emerson's invocation of higher law as natural law has a more ambiguous effect on his abolitionism, however, when he presents that law as coextensive with the principles of natural science as well as with individual intuition. On one hand, the use of scientific metaphors reinforces his argument for humanity's inevitable rejection of slavery. Addressing the "absurd" (*AW* 60) charge that the development of abolitionism occasioned the Fugitive Slave Law, Emerson makes a powerful comparison between material and moral law: "Will you blame the ball for rebounding from the floor; blame the air for rushing to where a vacuum is made or the boiler for exploding under pressure of steam? These facts are after the laws of the world, and so is it law, that, when justice is violated, anger begins. The very defence [sic] which the God of Nature has provided for the innocent against cruelty, is the sentiment of indignation and pity in the bosom of the beholder" (*AW* 61). On the other hand, the understanding of natural history as coextensive with moral development had the potential to stymie an argument against slavery. When Emerson states in "Emancipation" that nature "deals with men after the same manner" (*AW* 31) as it does plants and animals, he downplays the role of abolitionism in "sav[ing]" the Black race, saying "[t]he anti-slavery of the whole world, is dust in the balance before" the fact that

> [w]hen at last in a race, a new principle appears, an idea; – that conserves it; ideas only save races. If the black man is feeble, and not important to the existing races not on a parity with the best race, the black man must serve, and be exterminated. But if the black man carries in his bosom an indispensable element of a new and coming civilization, for the sake of that element, no wrong, nor strength, nor circumstance, can hurt him: he will survive and play his part. (*AW* 31)

As Laura Dassow Walls points out, this pre-Darwinian survivalist vision implies that "[i]t is *nature* that has destined the black race for either success or failure, as if the white race bears no responsibility for blacks' oppression … or for their freedom."[19] Yet scholars have shown that these lines also point in a different direction. Ian Finseth parses this passage as showing that "the tension persisting between his Hegelian fetishizing of 'ideas' and 'principles,' which he believed defined a racial group's metaphysical identity, and his evident acceptance of the physical or phenotypic characteristics that defined a racial group in the first place"[20] allowed Emerson to escape biological determinism. Both scholars note the significance to Emerson's thought on race of his understanding that scientific knowledge was inevitably a function of human perspective, even if biology itself could not be altered by culture. In "Emancipation," immediately following the passage examined earlier, Emerson famously links the survival of the Black race to the emergence of "such men as Toussaint and the Haytian heroes, or of the leaders of their race in Barbados and Jamaica" – Gougeon makes a persuasive case that he also had Frederick Douglass in mind[21] – saying "here is the anti-slave; here is man: and if you have man, black or white is an insignificance" (AW 31). For Walls, this presents a perfect example of the way that Emerson balanced biological/material and cultural/spiritual realities: for Emerson "[t]he real 'fact,' then ... is the idea that has materialized in the body of the Negro but which points back to the principle of freedom in all men, black or white."[22] Yet it also remains true that by suggesting that Blacks' enduring contribution will be their very experience of overcoming subjugation, the passage leaves open the possibility that without the emergence of "leaders of their race," Blacks would have justly been "exterminated."

Despite this implication, Emerson denounced the use of evolutionary theory for racist ends. Drawing on the evolutionists' understanding of the erect posture of humans as a "progressive" adaptation, Emerson employs a philosophical trope that relates men's upright stance to moral rectitude to insist that whites prove their humanity – in Emerson's parlance, their "manhood" – by resisting slavery but also to suggest the irony of evolutionary racial science's association of Blacks with animality when their moral development had been constrained by the institution of slavery. As Adriana Cavarero explains, for the Western philosophical tradition, the so-called upright man "is literally a subject who conforms to a vertical axis, which in turn functions as a principle and norm for its ethical posture."[23] In "Citizens of Concord," Emerson evokes this trope when he describes white men's willingness to follow the Fugitive Slave Law as indicative of their "read[iness] to go down on all fours" (AW 56). Emerson suggests that unlike animals, who have literally lower material concerns, "men" are distinguished by the correspondence between their literal upright posture and their adherence to figuratively higher concerns of morality: "whilst animals have to do with eating the fruits of the ground," he says, "men have to do with rectitude, with benefit, with truth, with something which is, independent of appearances" (AW 58). Emerson insists, "every time a man goes back to his own thoughts, these angels receive him, talk with him, and ... in the best hours, he is uplifted in virtue of this essence, into a peace and into a power which the material world cannot give" (*AW* 58). For Emerson, a man's "own thoughts" are, of course, the ultimate ethical guide. In "Self-Reliance" he announces, "To believe your own thought, to believe that what is true for you in your private heart is true for all men" is "genius" (*CW* 2: 27) insofar as it embodies the highest moral standard: Evoking Christian eschatology, Emerson claims that "our first thought is rendered back to us by the trumpets of the Last Judgment" (*CW* 2: 27). In "Citizens of Concord," Emerson adds the suggestion of evolutionary verticality to his use of Christian imagery to describe individual "thought" as the basis of ethical behavior. As Caverero notes, for philosophers in the Western tradition, "man stands up and verticalizes himself in many different ways: by standing up on his feet, moving above beasts or even above his own species, raising himself toward the Most High, straightening himself up thanks to correct reason."[24] In this passage, Emerson evokes all of these: to rise from "all fours" is also to achieve "rectitude" as "thoughts" become the "angels" by which man is "uplifted." Many white men, hitherto taken to be "upright men, compotes mentis," have been rendered animalistic, Emerson implies, insofar as they see in abolitionism only "canting fanaticism, sedition, and 'one idea'" (*AW* 56) rather than the crowning achievement of a teleological process of evolution: the expression of men's communion with the angels of thought and thus true morality.

Emerson's use of the contrast between the white "man" who resists unjust laws and the animal who submits to them was not new to abolitionist discourse.[25] But Emerson advances the trope's function to a critique of the evolutionary racial science that supports slavery. At the end of the passage cited earlier, Emerson insists that "to pretend ... that the acquisition of property was the end of living" – the motive for slavery – is "to confound all distinctions ... to leave us in a grimacing menagerie of monkeys and idiots" (*AW* 59). While at one level the trope continues the denunciation of his fellow white northerners for sinking down to the level of mere animals, driven by material necessity rather than moral freedom, it does more than that, for the reference to monkeys also speaks to the scientific racism of the same period, some versions of which drew on evolutionary theory to distinguish humans of African descent by their relationship to primates, often based on the theory of polygenesis.[26] Emerson posits a relationship between the condition of Blacks and their treatment by animalistic whites, implicitly denying the racist association of Blackness with evolutionary backwardness. Emerson makes this critique even clearer in 1854, when he identifies the central question about slavery as that of whether "this system, which is a kind of mill or factory for converting men into monkeys, shall be upheld and enlarged" and claims that "Mr. Webster and the country went for the application to these poor men of a quadruped law" (*AW* 79). While scholars have generally understood Emerson's use here of the term "quadruped" to describe the law's character (a law that belongs to animals), it is important to note that it also describes the law's effect (a law that creates animals, or more specifically, a law that does not create humans).[27] Emerson suggests that Blacks are forced into a metaphorical inclined position by whites; they are made "into monkeys" by human law, rather than being an entirely different species or being arrested in their evolutionary development into "men." Later in the speech, Emerson explicitly calls out the racist use of evolutionary science by such men as George Glidden and Josiah Nott, who cemented belief in the theory of polygenesis in the United States during this period. Addressing the question of the status of people of African descent vis-à-vis whites, Emerson says, "The plea that the negro is an inferior race sounds very oddly in my ear from a slave-holder," and asserts the true relationship between enslaved people and enslavers: "when I hear the southerner point to the anatomy of the negro, and talk of chimpanzee, – I recall Montesquieu's remark, 'It will not do to say, that negroes are men, lest it should turn out that whites were not'" (*AW* 85). Emerson misquotes Montesquieu's words, whose various translations agree that they say that if Blacks are considered men, then whites might suspect themselves not to be "Christians." Emerson's revision omits Montesquieu's implied definition of "manhood" as coextensive with Christianity in order to center the category of "man" itself in the context of slavery's justificatory association of "negroes" with animality. He thus suggests that whites are quadrupeds specifically insofar as they have inhibited the evolutionary development of Blacks to moral rectitude.

## Abolitionist Violence as Moral Force

For Emerson, the greatest achievement of the Civil War would be to remove this impediment to Black development. In 1862, Emerson said of Lincoln's Emancipation Proclamation that "[i]t does not promise the redemption of the black race: that lies not with us: but it relieves it of our opposition" (*AW* 132). This was consistent with his celebration of West Indian emancipation almost two decades earlier: "I esteem the occasion of this jubilee to be the proud discovery, that the black race can contend with the white ... now let them emerge" (*AW* 31–32). What was less consistent was Emerson's support of the tremendous amount of violence required to produce this outcome. Larry J. Reynolds claims that Emerson moved from arguing that armed struggle and civilization were incompatible, which led him to elide the violent acts of abolitionists and overtly reject the legitimacy of political violence through the early 1850s, to rationalizing such violence under the influence of John Brown.[28] To do so, Emerson employed the same scientific imagery of natural forces he used to discuss the significance of racial difference and did so to similarly ambiguous ends, as he implied that the recourse to violence, unfolding as part of natural law, was a moral force. In a speech on John Brown following his death in the Harper's Ferry raid, Emerson recurs to the argument he had made in "Citizens of Concord" about the human sentiments of indignation and pity as forces of nature, insisting that "[n]othing is more absurd than to complain of th[e] sympathy" that people have for John Brown; one should "[a]s well complain of gravity, or the ebb of the tide. Who makes the Abolitionist? The Slaveholder. The sentiment of mercy is the natural recoil which the laws of the universe provide to prevent mankind from destruction by savage passions" (AW 123). Here, though, scientific metaphors yoke a moral motive to violent means, for Emerson was undoubtedly aware that Brown's mercy for the enslaved, described as a "natural recoil" from the slaveholder's "savagery" that is as inevitable as gravity or the tide, was manifested in the recoil of the Sharps rifles that were used to murder proslavery settlers – rifles procured with money raised by Brown's northeastern supporters through, among other things, speeches such as the one Emerson gave at a Kansas relief meeting in 1856.

Emerson presented the Civil War's violence as likewise inevitable because of its grounding in natural law, saying in 1862 that the war "existed long before the cannonade of Sumter and could not be postponed. It might have begun otherwise and elsewhere, but war was in the minds and bones of the combatants ... and you might as easily dodge gravitation" (AW 133) because the end of the war was a moral one: to "allow [Southern society's] reconstruction on a just and healthful basis. Then new affinities will act, the old repulsions will cease, and, the cause of war being removed, nature and trade may be trusted to establish a lasting peace" (AW 134). The following year Emerson unabashedly celebrated the advent of the war in "Fortune of the Republic," again using the image of gravity to insist that a political "revolution" such as was underway in the United States "is the work of no man, but the eternal effervescence of nature": he invited his audience to "[g]o push the globe, or scotch the globe, to accelerate or to retard it in its orbit. It is elemental. It is the old gravitation" (PE 204). But if the revolution wrought by antislavery is as inexorable as the earth's revolution around the sun, still Emerson affirms that individuals remain uncertain about their role in this movement. Immediately following the lines earlier, he warns, "Beware of the firing and the recoil! Who knows or has computed the periods? A little earlier, and you would have been sacrificed in vain. A little later, and you are unnecessary" (*PE* 204). Here the reference to the rifle is used to suggest that even as the ultimate outcome of history is surely moral, the necessity of violent action at any particular "period" is unknown to individuals. But human uncertainty is unavoidable, Emerson suggests, because "[c]ommittees don't manage revolutions. A revolution is a volcano, and from under everybody's feet flings its sheet of fire into the sky" (*PE* 204). If this metaphor performs the kind of elision of violence that Reynolds describes as characteristic of Emerson's antislavery writings, it does so by means that are also characteristic of those texts: the use of the larger sweep of a moral natural history to recontextualize all individual actions.

It is perhaps fitting that the final paragraphs of this speech, Emerson's final address on slavery, recapitulate a number of the paradoxical elements of his thought on the topic. First, his insistence on the inevitability of revolution is followed by the seemingly contradictory suggestion that it is a willed effort toward a chosen goal: "[t]he end of all political struggle, is, to establish morality as the basis of all legislation.... We want a state of things in which crime will not pay" (*PE* 204). He repeats this point in the last paragraph, but there he emphasizes the larger "guidance of events," saying that while he "could heartily wish that our will and endeavor were more active parties to the work," yet despite their inefficacy, "I see in all directions the light breaking" (*PE* 205). This implied metaphor draws on a different planetary revolution – that of the earth on its axis – to insist on moral progress. Meanwhile, the second-last paragraph collapses the contradiction between material "fact" and individual intuition, claiming that "The guiding star to the arrangement and use of facts, is in your leading thought" (*PE* 205). Given that, as we've seen, trusting one's own thought defines self-reliance, it makes sense that Emerson goes on to assure his audience, "You will have come to the perception that justice satisfies everyone, and justice alone. You will stand there for vast interests; North and South, East and West will be present to your mind, and your vote will be as if they voted" (*PE* 205). Individual perception will become universal, as individuals come to "arrange" and "use" facts in the same way. The final lines of the speech project nothing less than a fusion of the temporal human world and the ideal one as the outcome of this fusion of individual and social mass, as Emerson imagines that "trade and government will not alone be the favored aims of mankind, but ... every exercise of imagination, the height of Reason, the noblest affection, the purest religion will find their homes in our institutions, and write our laws for the benefit of men" (*PE* 205). At long last, Emerson declares, the eternal law intuited by all individuals will coincide with statute law.

Emerson himself would live long enough to realize that such would not be the case, at least not in the short term. It was perhaps in anticipation of this reality that when Emerson spoke at the dedication of the Soldiers' Monument in Concord in 1867, he framed the outcome of the conflict in terms of a much longer time scale, suggesting that the Civil War marked a single, albeit momentous, occasion in the moral development of the world. When war becomes a reality, Emerson says, "The secret architecture of things begins to disclose itself; the fact that all things were made on a basis of right; that justice is really desired by all intelligent beings; that opposition to it is against the nature of things; and that, whatever may happen in this hour or that, the years and the centuries are always pulling down the wrong and building up the right."[29] And so Emerson's public antislavery career ends on that same contradictory note that he had sounded throughout it: confidence that the "nature of things" – a reality beyond human understanding – would, in a world of "intelligent beings," eventually resolve even the most egregious of social crimes, that of slavery.

## Notes

1. *Proceedings of the Massachusetts Anti-Slavery Society at the Annual Meetings Held in 1854, 1855 & 1856* (Boston: Office of Massachusetts Anti-Slavery Society, 1856), 38.
2. Quoted in Len Gougeon, *Virtue's Hero: Emerson, Antislavery, and Reform* (Athens: University of Georgia Press, 1990), 91.
3. For analyses of the passage from "Self-Reliance" in context of the essay as a whole, see Gougeon, *Virtue's Hero*, 55–57; Martha Schoolman, "Emerson's Doctrine of Hatred," *Arizona Quarterly* 63:2 (2007): 1–26.
4. Ralph Waldo Emerson, *Emerson's Antislavery Writings*, ed. Len Gougeon and Joel Myerson (New Haven, CT: Yale University Press, 1995), 53. Hereafter cited parenthetically in text as *AW*.
5. Quoted in James H. Read, "The Limits of Self-Reliance: Emerson, Slavery, and Abolition," in *A Political Companion to Ralph Waldo Emerson*, ed. Alan M. Levine and Daniel S. Malachuk (Lexington, KY: University of Kentucky Press, 2011): 160–61.
6. See Christopher Newfield, *The Emerson Effect: Individualism and Submission in America* (Chicago, University of Chicago Press, 1996); John Carlos Rowe, *At Emerson's Tomb: The Politics of Nineteenth-Century American Literature* (New York: Columbia University Press, 1997); Anita Patterson, *From Emerson to King: Democracy, Race, and the Politics of Protest* (New York: Oxford University Press, 1997); and Jay Grossman, *Reconstituting the American Renaissance: Emerson, Whitman, and the Politics of Representation* (Durham, NC: Duke University Press, 2003).
7. Read, "Limits," 158.
8. Jack Turner, *Awakening to Race: Individualism and Social Consciousness in America* (Chicago: University of Chicago Press, 2012), 35.
9. Peter Wirzbicki, *Fighting for the Higher Law: Black and White Transcendentalists Against Slavery* (Philadelphia: University of Pennsylvania Press, 2021), 71, 72.

10. I have developed this argument in greater depth elsewhere. See Sophia Forster, "Peculiar Faculty and Peculiar Institution: Ralph Waldo Emerson on Labor and Slavery," *ESQ* 60:1 (2014): 35–73.

11. Ralph Waldo Emerson, *The Political Emerson: Essential Writings on Politics and Social Reform*, ed. David Robinson (Boston: Beacon Press, 2004), 37. Cited parenthetically as *PE*.

12. See Turner, *Awakening to Race*, 30–32; Martha Schoolman, *Abolitionist Geographies* (Minneapolis: University of Minnesota Press, 2014), 40.

13. Ralph Waldo Emerson, *The Early Lectures of Ralph Waldo Emerson*, ed. Stephen E. Whicher, Robert E. Spiller, and Wallace E. Williams, 3 vols. (Cambridge, MA: Harvard University Press, Belknap Press, 1959–72), 2, 113. Hereafter cited as *EL*, with volume and page number.

14. Turner, *Awakening to Race*, 39.

15. Quoted in Linck C. Johnson, "'Liberty is Never Cheap': Emerson, 'The Fugitive Slave Law,' and the Antislavery Lecture Series at the Broadway Tabernacle," *New England Quarterly* 76:4 (2003): 552.

16. Albert J. von Frank, *The Trials of Anthony Burns: Freedom and Slavery in Emerson's Boston* (Cambridge, MA: Harvard University Press, 1998), 96–97, 100.

17. von Frank, *Trials*, 102.

18. Gregg D. Crane, *Race, Citizenship, and Law in American Literature* (Cambridge: Cambridge University Press, 2002), 99.

19. Laura Dassow Walls, *Emerson's Life in Science: The Culture of Truth* (Ithaca: Cornell University Press, 2003), 167.

20. Ian Finseth, "Evolution, Cosmopolitanism, and Emerson's Antislavery Politics," *American Literature* 77:4 (2005), 735.

21. Len Gougeon, "Militant Abolitionism: Douglass, Emerson, and the Rise of the Anti-Slave," *New England Quarterly* 85:4 (2012): 629.

22. Laura Dassow Walls, "'As Planets Faithful Be': The Higher Law of Science in Emerson's Antislavery Lectures," *Nineteenth-Century Prose* 30:1–2 (2003), para. 8.

23. Adriana Cavarero, *Inclinations: A Critique of Rectitude*, trans. Amanda Minervini and Adam Sitze (Stanford: Stanford University Press, 2016), 6.

24. Cavarero, *Inclinations*, 67–68.

25. Wirzbicki points out that the more common and relevant contrast for both abolitionists and transcendentalists was between the authenticity of "manhood" and the instrumentality of becoming a "tool" of the slave power. See *Fighting*, 166–68.

26. See Melissa Stein, *Measuring Manhood: Race and the Science of Masculinity 1830–1934* (Minneapolis: Minnesota University Press, 2015), Chapter 1.

27. See Crane, *Race*, 97; Wirzbicki, *Fighting*, 201–2.

28. See Larry J. Reynolds, *Righteous Violence: Revolution, Slavery, and the American Renaissance* (Athens, GA: University of Georgia Press, 2011), Chapter 2.

29. Ralph Waldo Emerson, *The Complete Works of Ralph Waldo Emerson*, ed. Edward Waldo Emerson, 12 vols. (Boston: Houghton Mifflin, 1903–4), 354.

# 9

JOHANNES VOELZ

# Democracy

Speaking at the Emerson Memorial Meeting at the University of Chicago in 1903, on the occasion of Ralph Waldo Emerson's centenary, John Dewey predicted that "the coming century may well make evident what is just now dawning, that Emerson is not only a philosopher, but that he is the Philosopher of Democracy."[1] While Emerson's status as a philosopher continues to be tenuous 120 years after Dewey's lecture, his association with democracy is firmly established. Political theorists and philosophers like Judith Shklar, George Kateb, Cornel West, and Stanley Cavell have all interpreted his thought as pervaded by democratic commitments.[2] So have literary critics and historians, from the earliest days of the emergence of American Studies to the present day, including Vernon Louis Parrington, F. O. Matthiessen, Daniel Aaron, Richard Poirier, Len Gougeon, Lawrence Buell, Herwig Friedl, Donald Pease, and Branka Arsić.[3]

Yet, for all the conventionality it has accrued over time, the interpretation of Emerson as a democratic thinker and writer has a surprisingly large number of detractors. An early interpretation of Emerson by George Santayana, which would soon after be echoed by cultural nationalist critics like Van Wyck Brooks, bemoaned Emerson's apolitical individualism and claimed that "he was detached, unworldly, contemplative"[4] – a romantic thinker bereft of any sense of evil who "supplied nothing to supplant [the genteel tradition] in other minds."[5] Later revisionist critics like Sacvan Bercovitch, Quentin Anderson, and Christopher Newfield continued Santayana's line of interpretation, finding Emerson's writings either so individualist that they became apolitical or, in Newfield's case, so submissive to a higher authority that they didn't qualify as democratic.[6] At mid-century, Perry Miller, though of the opinion that Emerson was "a serious man" and "a great American," emphasized how ill at ease democracy made him.[7] This historically oriented interpretation continues to find new proponents as well, for instance in the recent work of Neal Dolan, Benjamin Park, and Daniel Malachuk.[8]

This chapter makes the case for Emerson as a democratic thinker and writer, and it aspires to do so by taking to heart the strongest arguments of the opposition. Making the case for Emerson the democrat requires a firmer grip of the meaning of "democracy." Here, democracy is approached not just as a form of government or even as a matter of politics but as what John Dewey liked to call "a way of life."[9] Enlarging democracy beyond politics is a concern that, in light of the various contemporary crises of democracy, has recently found renewed attention among political theorists. One fruitful proposition to update and further develop Dewey's notion of democracy as a way of life has been offered by Roberto Frega, who underlines that democracy "offers a standard for social interactions even outside official, state, or legal power relations [and] ... describe[s] the most appropriate way in which human beings can live together."[10]

Situating Emerson in democracy as a way of life requires a multilayered analysis that captures Emerson's engagement both within and beyond official, state, or legal power relations. It involves coming to terms with a broad range of Emerson's concerns, from his interpretation of democracy as a social structure and cultural dynamic to his own engagement of the democratic public by way of his profession as a freelance lecturer to, finally, the question of how he conceptualized the relation between democracy and the principles of justice. For this reason, I proceed in five steps: In the first section, I begin by reconstructing Emerson's misgivings about democratic mass society. Second, I contrast this critique with his embrace of what he once called, in his journal, the unfolding of "the democratic element" (*JMN* 5: 201), by which he meant something like the political materialization of reason and self-reliance. Third, I discuss Emerson's concept of the "representative" as an officiator of the unfolding of the democratic element and connect it to what Stanley Cavell famously called "Emersonian moral perfectionism." Fourth, bringing to bear Dewey's concept of democracy as a way of life on Emerson in the most literal sense, I consider democracy as an element not merely of his transcendentalist doctrine but of his *practice* as a writer, orator, and publicly engaged intellectual. And finally, I ask under what conditions Emerson's transcendentalism came into conflict with democracy as a *political* system and practice. This question became urgent after 1850 as Emerson committed himself to radical abolitionism. In particular, his approval of righteous violence, "*religious wars*" (*CW* 10: 351; emphasis in original), and Lincoln's state of exception brought to light what is at stake when the claims of the institutions and procedures of democracy are subordinated to the demands of a religiously inflected morality. Thus, the chapter ends by making explicit its intervention in an ongoing debate in recent Emerson scholarship on the question of whether his position really can be squared with democracy.

## Jacksonian Democracy

"Nothing would be easier than to collect from [Emerson's] *Journals* enough passages about the Democratic party to form a manual of Boston snobbery," Perry Miller quipped in 1953.[11] Indeed, Emerson didn't spare any venom commenting on President Andrew Jackson and the Democratic Party. During the presidential election of 1832, which brought Jackson a second term in office in a landslide, the twenty-nine-year-old Emerson remarked with notable disgust, "Yet seemeth it to me that we shall all feel dirty if Jackson is reelected" (*JMN* 4: 57). Emerson was in the company of the majority of his New England compatriots. In the rest of the nation, Jackson and his Democratic Party (at the time often referred to as "Democracy") were overwhelmingly popular. But Emerson could never warm to Jackson and his "Democracy." Ten years later, he still fumed, "I cannot for a moment permit these profligate Tammany Hall & Morning Post adventurers to represent the cause of humanity and love" (*JMN* 8: 288).

Emerson's main complaint of Jacksonian democracy held that it was a movement that appealed to selfishness rather than impersonal principles and values, and that it posed a threat of leveling downward anything that was high, excellent, and noble. Most explicit in this regard is a journal entry from 1843: "Democracy with us is charged with being malignant, and I think it seems aimless, selfish resistance, pulling down, & wild wish to have physical freedom, – but for what? only for freedom; not to any noble end" (*JMN* 8: 341). Critics like Neal Dolan notice "a profound streak of anti-popular aristocratic sentiment" in words like these,[12] and, indeed, in Emerson's bleak assessment of the psychosocial desires of the "masses," we can detect the nucleus of a theory of *ressentiment* that was later fleshed out by Friedrich Nietzsche, who, among Emerson's devoted readers, surely belongs to those most skeptical of democracy.

But in Emerson's revulsion against Jacksonian popular democracy, we can also find the building blocks of a critical theory of mass society and public opinion. "In this country," he wrote in 1839, "there is No Measure attempted for itself by legislatures but the Opinion of the people is courted in the first place & the measures are perfunctorily carried through as secondary" (*JMN* 7: 306). When the popularity of ideas rather than ideas themselves determines politics, society is on its way to becoming, as he put it in "Self-Reliance," a "joint-stock company in which the members agree for the better securing of his bread to each shareholder, to surrender the liberty and culture of the eater" (*CW* 2: 29). In a society driven by public opinion, "the virtue in most request is conformity" (*CW* 2: 29). And once conformity becomes pervasive, the self-commanding authority of moral principles is all but lost. Once "noble ends" are sacrificed to the claim of resentment clothed as freedom, freedom itself turns into the despotism of majority opinion.

Emerson's critique resonates with his contemporary critics of mass society, such as Alexis de Tocqueville and Harriet Martineau. A keen reader of Tocqueville's *Democracy in America* (1835–40), Emerson quoted liberally from the French aristocrat's interpretation of American democracy in his "New England" lecture series, delivered in the winter of 1843–44. From a chapter of the first volume of *Democracy* in which Tocqueville introduces his concept of the "tyranny of the majority," Emerson cites the following passage:

> In that immense crowd which throngs the avenues to power in the United States, I found very few men who displayed any of that manly candor and that masculine independence of opinion which frequently distinguished the Americans in former times, and which constitute the leading feature in distinguished characters wherever they may be found. It seems at first sight as if all the minds of the Americans were formed on one model, so accurately do they correspond in their manner of judging.
>
> A stranger does indeed sometimes meet with Americans who dissent from these rigorous formularies; with men who deplore the defects of the laws, the mutability and the ignorance of democracy; who even go so far as to observe the evil tendencies which impair the national character and to point out such remedies as it might be possible to apply: but no one is there to hear these things beside yourself, and you to whom these secret reflections are confided, are a stranger and a bird of passage. (Emerson *LL* 1: 55–56[13])

As Tocqueville sees it, in American democracy, independence of opinion has been drowned in the conformity of the crowd so that individual judgment accurately matches that of a generalized "model." At closer sight, Tocqueville suggests, it turns out that Americans haven't been turned into conforming automatons quite yet. In private they are still capable of articulating dissent. But the pressures of conformity forbid them to voice it except to the traveler from abroad (like himself), who does not have any impact on American public opinion because he remains "a stranger and a bird of passage."

Roughly one century later, Max Horkheimer and Theodor W. Adorno, in *Dialectic of Enlightenment* (1944), would quote from a passage from the same chapter of Tocqueville's book in which the characteristic sanction for violations of conformity is spelled out: "The sovereign can no longer say, 'You shall think as I do on pain of death;' but he says, 'You are free to think differently from me, and to retain your life, your property, and all that you possess; but if such be your determination, you are henceforth an alien among your people. [...] Your fellow-creatures will shun you like an impure being, and those who are most persuaded of your innocence will abandon you too, lest they should be shunned in their turn. Go in peace! I have given you your life, but it is an existence incomparably worse than death.'"[14]

Tocqueville, Emerson, and Horkheimer/Adorno all shared the view that ultimately individuals who consciously feared the sanctions of non-conformity because they amounted to a life "worse than death" stood at risk of internalizing this fear. And once the conformist pressures were fully absorbed, individuals lost the ability to think differently. As Emerson put it in his 1844 essay "Politics," "when a quarter of the human race assume to tell me what I must do, I may be too much disturbed by the circumstances *to see so clearly* the absurdity of their command" (*CW* 3: 125, emphasis added). Emerson here describes a dynamic of conformism in which individuals lose the ability to critically judge the demands of the masses, however absurd they may be. Seen in this broader context, Emerson's disgust at mass democracy, while clearly inflected by the sense of entitlement common to Federalist "natural aristocracy," contains other layers than the mere shoring up of class privilege: It anticipates a tradition of critiquing mass society that would come to fruition in the mid twentieth century in the work of Frankfurt and New York intellectuals.[15] Both circles of intellectuals writing against the specter of totalitarianism identified "mass society" as a structural enforcement of unfreedom, and both effectively continued a line of critique spearheaded by Tocqueville's and Emerson's complexly structured misgivings about popular democracy.

## The Democratic Element

Surprisingly, perhaps, Emerson occasionally was capable of adopting a more dialectical perspective of Jacksonian democracy. In 1834, for instance, he noted in his journal that "this rank rabble party, the Jacksonism of the country" – precisely because of its utter lack of culture – "may root out the hollow dilettantism of our cultivation in the coarsest way & the new-born may begin again to frame their own world with greater advantage" (*JMN* 4: 297). Thanks to its coarseness, really existing democracy had the potential for cleaning the slate and helping Americans "build, therefore, [their] own world," as Emerson demands at the end of his first book, *Nature*, from 1836 (*CW* I: 45).

But on what grounds could Emerson expect that the new world would differ from the old? What would keep the world built by Americans from descending into the self-dwarfing conformity characteristic of the popular democracy Emerson so abhorred? The answer lies in Emerson's belief in a divine moral law, the heeding of which would lead to melioration, enlargement, generalization, and the recognition of a Platonic identity permeating all forms of life. Understanding Emerson's two takes on democracy first requires a closer look at his dialectics of form, a figure of thought central to his writings. "Nothing is so fleeting as form; yet never does it quite deny itself," Emerson explains in "History" (*CW* 2: 8). Thus, while individual forms are mere representatives of a higher spiritual instance – "be it called morals, religion, or godhead, or what you will," as Emerson would put it nonchalantly in 1851 (*AW* 58) – that higher plane of being always takes a particularized form. Put differently, individual forms are fleeting, but higher reality, infused with moral and religious sentiment, becomes accessible only through these fleeting forms. "Other world! there is no other world," Emerson would later scoff. "God is one and omnipresent: here or nowhere is the whole fact" (*LL* 2: 269). In his reading of Emerson's aesthetics, Jacques Rancière captures well this mixture of idealism and immanent materialism: "One could call [the poetry envisioned by Emerson] idealist, for it strives to define the spiritual potential hidden in the diversity of things and material activities. One could call it materialist, for it does not concede any world of its own to spirituality – it recognizes it only as the link that unites sensible forms and activities."[16]

Emerson applied this dialectic of idealism and materialism to politics in such a manner that democracy appeared on both sides of his not-quite-Platonic divide between appearance (form) and higher reality (Oneness expressed in the succession of forms). Thus, on one level, democracy was a particular political and social form that, while characteristic of its time, was not in itself superior to any other political form. Accordingly, Emerson, in 1840, noted that "Man of genius belongs to monarchy, aristocracy, & democracy equally" (*JMN* 7: 336). And in his essay "Politics" – which is the primary text in which he developed this dialectic – Emerson emphasized the merely historical nature of the democratic system of government: "Democracy is better for us, because the religious sentiment of the present time accords better with it. Born democrats, we are nowise qualified to judge of monarchy, which, to our fathers living in the monarchical idea, was also relatively right" (*CW* 3: 121). Emerson's notion of a "relative right" ought not to be misunderstood as the modern concept of cultural relativism. Different political forms, such as monarchy and democracy, were "relatively right" insofar as they each gave form and expression to an absolute right – an absolute that could only be glimpsed in historically specific, variant forms. The flip side of this relativism is that for Emerson, each form expressed the higher principle of right only imperfectly, which in turn meant that while monarchy and democracy were "relatively right" in accordance with what Emerson called their respective "spirit of the age" (*CW* 3: 121), they were also relatively deficient in as much as they expressed,

and gave form to, only a particular aspect of higher reality. "[Our] institutions [...] have not any exemption from the practical defects which have
discredited other forms. Every actual State is corrupt. Good men must not
obey the laws too well" (CW 3: 121–22). In short, as a political and social
form, democracy deserved to be taken with a grain of salt: from a prospective view, democracy, like monarchy before it, was a form destined to
wither away.

As "Politics" makes also clear, however, political systems also had their
place on the other – call it metaphysical – side of his dualistic equation. On
this level, it was the qualities of particular political systems that reappeared
as tropes for describing higher reality. Thus, Emerson was confident to say
that "Nature" – a loaded term for Emerson that could either mean material forms, the higher principles running through them, or, as here, both at
once – "is not democratic, nor limited-monarchical, but despotic" because
of the merciless flux destroying all established forms (CW 3: 118). By the
same token, that same principle of never-ceasing metamorphosis expressive
of the unity of Being could also be described in terms of democracy and thus
provide democracy with moral authority.

Looking back, in 1836, over the past century, Emerson mused in his
journal about the historical unfolding of what he called "the democratic
element": "the political changes of the time which have unfolded [...] the
democratic element have shown the nullity of those once highly prized circumstances & given a hollow sound to the name of king & earl & lord"
(JMN 5: 201). Emerson spelled out an affinity, indeed an inner link, between
his concept of metamorphosis that expressed the connectedness of all things
in the unity of Being and the de-hierarchizing and informalizing trajectory
of democracy. "What is good goes now to all. What was good a century ago
is written under the manifest belief that it was as safe from the eye of the
common people as from the Tartars. The Universal Man is now as real an
existence as the Devil was then" (JMN 5: 203). Emerson's "democratic element" goes beyond treating democracy as a mere metaphor for the unfolding of the spirit. Rather, in metonymic fashion, he fuses social and political
egalitarianism with the spiritual enlargement that comes with receptiveness
to the moral law.

"The Universal Man" is universal in two senses, then. We might think of
them in terms of a vertical and a horizontal axis. On the vertical axis, the
democratic element renders the individual universal in the sense that the
individual grows into the impersonal, generalized sphere of higher Being.
On the horizontal axis, the democratic element puts individuals on an equal
plane, extending "the good" to "the common people." Here the universal
tends to pertain to the entirety of all humanity.

The unfolding of the "democratic element," Emerson insisted, had to be sharply differentiated from the Jacksonian democracy characteristic of his times: "When I spoke or speak of the democratic element I do not mean that ill thing vain & loud which writes lying newspapers, spouts at caucuses, & sells its lies for gold, but that spirit of love for the General good whose name this assumes. There is nothing of the true democratic element in what is called Democracy; it must fall, being wholly commercial" (*JMN* 5: 203). It is tempting – but misleading – to think of these two variants of democracy as really existing versus ideal democracy. In that case, actually existing democracy would always differ from the ideal, the "democratic element" would never unfold, and the two axes of universalization would always remain at cross-purposes. Such an ultimately conservative idealism is quite the opposite of what Emerson envisions: His belief is that the thoroughly commercial, selfish, nonspiritual democracy he perceives around himself will make way for a democracy in which individuals come to understand, feel, and live the metaphysical equality of all people in a political and social system that elevates "common people" to the plane of universality. Self-enlargement in this new world will pertain both to the individual and the collective.

## Representativeness

Emerson did not merely postulate the desirability of an enlarged self – individual and collective – but also articulated a more or less concrete idea about how one could get there. He frequently used political, indeed democratic, terms to describe this path. A key term in this regard is the "representative." Particularly in his book *Representative Men*, from 1850, Emerson put the "representative" in place of the "hero" and thus displaced an aristocratic notion of greatness with one that emphasized the essential equality between the representative and the represented. "But also the constituency determines the vote of the representative. He is not only representative but participant. Like can only be known by like. The reason why he knows about them, is that he is of them: he has just come out of nature, or from being a part of that thing" (CW 4: 7).

Employing the language of democracy was Emerson's way of marking out the difference between himself and his friend Thomas Carlyle, whose *On Heroes, Hero-Worship, and the Heroic in History* (1841) promulgated a more traditional Romantic notion of greatness. The very title of his opening chapter – "The Uses of Great Men" – makes abundantly clear that Emerson cared little for marveling at anyone's greatness for long but rather asked how others could profit from that greatness. Judith Shklar aptly summarizes

Emerson's position: "The masses of humanity certainly do not exist in order to allow a great person to emerge from their depth to lead and mold them. The great person serves them. And that service is described in the language of democratic politics."[17]

The idea of the representative had grown in Emerson's thinking ever since his early days as a Unitarian minister. In Sermon 62, from January 1830, for instance, Emerson preaches on the theme of friendship, and he turns to two Unitarian staples, divine benevolence and the importance of self-culture. The former makes it possible, and the latter necessitates, that we relate to Jesus not as a superior, divine being, but as "a friend." Thus, if the believer has a "feeling of friendship to Christ," it will make him "more and more like him, and so continually more capable of estimating him." As a result, the virtuous mind "should perceive the power of indefinite expansion to which God had appointed it by making it in his image" (CS 2: 120).

An early version of the concept of "representative" also informs his early lectures on biography. In 1834, while planning his first series of public lectures, *Biography*, delivered in early 1835, he reflects in his journal on what it is that attracts us to that genre. "Is there not always a silent comparison between the intellectual & moral endowments portrayed & those of which we are conscious? The reason why the Luther, the Newton, the Bonaparte concerning whom we read, was made the subject of panegyric, is, that in the writer's opinion, in some one respect this particular man represented the idea of Man. And as far as we accord with his judgment, we take the picture for a standard Man, and so let every line accuse or approve our own ways of thinking & living by comparison" (*JMN* 4: 256). In placing his emphasis on the comparison between the self and the famed subjects of biography, the distinctly democratic idea of seeing the great man as the provider of a public service is not fully fleshed out yet. But already, Emerson here elaborates on one crucial component of the concept of the representative: those portrayed as great are still "particular" men, and they represent "the idea of Man" only "in some respect." It is because of this very partiality that Emerson, in *Representative Men*, would later end each of his portraits by pointing out his subject's deficiencies. Representatives were not intended to be admired as the embodiment of greatness, but rather as road signs pointing to a more encompassing universality that lay beyond themselves.

Emerson's most striking rendition of this idea is found in "The Uses of Great Men": "Each man seeks those of different quality from his own, and such as are good of their kind: that is, he seeks other men, and *the otherest*" (CW 4: 4, emphasis in original). In the notion of *the otherest*, the question of Emerson's idealism becomes pressing yet again. Is *the otherest* ontologically different from what others around us can be – an ideal that cannot be approached in this world? Stanley Cavell, in detailing what he means by "moral perfectionism," suggests the contrary. Emerson, we can infer from Cavell's line of thought, understands *the otherest* as a realm of possibility for both self and other. As Cavell puts it, perfectionism means "expecting oneself to be, making oneself, intelligible as an inhabitant now also of a further realm [...] and to show oneself prepared to recognize others as belonging there; [...] This is not a particular moral demand, but the condition of democratic morality."[18] Democratic morality, in other words, would grant *the otherest* as a horizon of possibility to anyone.

## Democracy as Way of Life

The representative is democratic, then, in the sense of providing a particular service: that of unfolding the democratic element along its two mutually reinforcing axes: the vertical (spiritual) as well as the horizontal (social). In *Representative Men*, however, Emerson also singles out one representative – Napoleon – who illustrates, and stands in for, democracy in its historical manifestation. And while we saw that in his journals, ranging from the early 1830s through the late 1840s, Emerson had hardly a positive thing to say about actually existing democracy – particularly when it came to "Democracy," that is, the Democratic party – the picture he draws of Napoleon is much more nuanced.

Napoleon, to Emerson, is the "incarnate Democrat" because he represents "the class of industry and skill." He embodies "the instinct of active, brave, able men throughout the middle class everywhere," and he has the spirit of the middle class: "that tendency is material, pointing at a sensual success, and employing the richest and most various means to that end" (*CW* 4: 130). These sentences are taken from a passage early on in the essay, and they display a remarkable appreciation of what the middle class, for all its materialism, exhibits at its best: braveness, ability, and ingenuity. But Napoleon and the people he represents do not merely deserve praise for their skills. Napoleon is also presented as a force of democratization, who helped put an end to the feudal elites' pilfering of the common good: "The people felt that no longer the throne was occupied, and the land sucked of all its nourishment by a small class of legitimates secluded from all community with the children of the soil, and holding the ideas and superstitions of a long-forgotten state of society. Instead of that vampire, a man of themselves held, in the Tuilleries, knowledge and ideas like their own, opening, of course, to them and their children all places of power and trust" (*CW* 4: 139).

Yet, at the essay's end, Emerson predictably focuses on Napoleon's and the middle class's severe limitations: Napoleon represents a narrow, selfish materialism that is as impoverished as that of the Jacksonian Party. In his concluding paragraph, Emerson becomes his most ardent anti-materialist self, who rejects the very foundation of the capitalist order, private property: "As long as our civilization is essentially one of property, of fences, of exclusiveness, it will be mocked by delusions. Our riches will leave us sick, there will be bitterness in our laughter, and our wine will burn our mouth. Only that good profits, which we can taste with all doors open, and which serves all men" (CW 4: 148). The essay thus exhibits a divided mind: Emerson the idealist insists that the true unfolding of the democratic element cannot be achieved under the materialist mindset for which Napoleon, the representative of democracy, ultimately stands. Yet, on the other hand, the social world surrounding Emerson cannot simply be rejected altogether for in it Emerson finds the precipitation of a democratizing, de-hierarchizing tendency that displays amiable traits of practical skill and vigor.

For the greatest part of his career as a popular lecturer and essayist, Emerson maintained a fine balance between these two sides. He tended not to mince words about the spiritual impoverishment he saw all around him, and he typically pointed to the shame felt by himself and anyone else who shared his faith in richer possibilities of ordinary life: "Our modes of living are not agreeable to our imagination. [...] In conversation with a wise man, we find ourselves apologizing for our employment; we speak of them with shame," he told his Boston audience in December 1841 (CW 1: 173).

Yet Emerson presented himself – much in line with his own theory of representativeness – as a member of his audience's community. And, rather than limit himself like a Puritan of old to Jeremiads of collective self-critique, he found much to praise about "our modes of living" in nineteenth-century middle-class America (most strikingly perhaps in his 1844 lecture "The Young American," an oddly one-sided paean to Manifest Destiny). More remarkably even, not only does Emerson often speak in an affirmative voice, but, for all the pleasure he takes in spiritual abstraction, he exhibits a remarkably sharp perception of the mundane and everyday. In a study of Emerson's writing style, Robert Richardson aptly remarks that there is a "side of Emerson that is enormously practical, even though the practicality may be masked by humor or drawn out – by fine attention to detail – into astonishing Platonic universals."[19]

A famous example of this style, sometimes brushed aside as an outlier in the Emerson canon[20], is the essay "Manners," from *Essays, Second Series* (1844), in which Emerson turns his attention once again to the dialectics of form discussed earlier. This time, his theoretical point is couched in mundane examples, and what usually sounds Platonic in this instance seems to anticipate Pierre Bourdieu's sociology of symbolic power: "[Manners] aid our dealing and conversation, as a railway aids travelling, by getting rid of all avoidable obstructions of the road, and leaving nothing to be conquered but pure space. These forms very soon become fixed, and a fine sense of propriety is cultivated with the more heed, that it becomes a badge of social and civil distinctions" (CW 3: 75). In this passage, the railroad – so essential to the life of a traveling lecturer – outruns its illustrative and figurative function and takes off as a theme of its own. The metaphor's vehicle becomes a tenor of its own: the centrality of vehicles in a society undergoing a transportation revolution. The railroad thus encapsulates the mode of living shared by Emerson and his listeners. And addressing it, reflecting on it, whether in print or in front of an audience, becomes an element of Emerson's engagement with democracy as a way of life.

The image of the railroad – at once vehicle and tenor – thus characterizes a rhetorical and poetic program of addressing the ordinary, historically specific reality Emerson shared with his contemporaries. A core element of his commitment to what we can call democracy as a way of life, Emerson, throughout his lectures, articulated a conscious program of speaking to the present concerns of his listeners. In his "Introductory Lecture" to his series titled "Lectures of the Times" (delivered at Boston's Masonic Temple in 1841–42), he states: "But the subject of the Times is not an abstract question. We talk of the world, but we mean a few men and women. If you speak of the age, you mean your own platoon of people" (CW 1: 168). In 1855, he put it even more bluntly: "Whatever is popular, is important, and shows the spontaneous sense of the hour" (LL 2: 29). The choice of material, however, goes only halfway in understanding how Emerson's writerly and speakerly practice became itself part and parcel of the democratic way of life.

Emerson understood that writing and speaking offered more than topical and thematic means of "embrac[ing] the common, [...] explor[ing] and sit[ting] at the feet of the familiar, the low," as he had phrased it in "The American Scholar" (CW 1: 67). Conversation, dialogue, and interaction – these were the modes in which Emerson, the essayist and lecturer, inserted himself into the everyday practice of an egalitarian, democratic culture. About Montaigne's essays, he famously wrote, "Cut these words, and they would bleed; they are vascular and alive" (CW 4: 95). But it is the lines before this oft-quoted sentence that reveal that, to Emerson's mind, Montaigne's words feel alive because they seem embedded in conversation: "I know not anywhere the book that seems less written. It is the language of conversation transferred to a book" (CW 4: 95).

Remarkably, the conversational feel also seems to have been pronounced in Emerson's lecturing style. Many attendees of his lectures pointed out that Emerson's delivery was often halting. He thumbed through his manuscript pages, often getting lost therein; he frequently paused as if lost in thought. And yet he is described as a decidedly captivating speaker. James Russell Lowell explained this seeming paradox by pointing to the oratorical technique by which Emerson drew in his listeners: "how artfully (for Emerson is a long-studied artist in these things) does the deliberate utterance, that seems waiting for the fit word, appear to admit us partners in the labor of thought and make us feel as if the glance of humor were a sudden suggestion, as if the perfect phrase lying written there on the desk were as unexpected to him as to us!"[21] Turning listeners into "partners in the labor of thought": herein lies the essence of Emerson's democratic oratorical style.

## Activism In and Beyond Democracy

For Emerson, however, democracy as a way of life entailed more than participating in a mode of living that granted special authority to the common and ordinary. As we already saw, democracy in his conception had a perfectionist slant and involved the unfolding of the democratic element and the gradual emergence of the individual and collective *otherest*.

Nonetheless, for a long time Emerson remained reluctant to become involved in the social reform movements of his day. Some of his earliest biographers, particularly Oliver Wendell Holmes, conveyed the false impression that Emerson "had never been identified with the abolitionists,"[22] although it was generally known that Emerson committed himself to action during the heated decade before the Civil War, when the Compromise of 1850 and its Fugitive Slave Law pushed many reluctant New Englanders into the abolitionist fold. However, over the last three decades, many scholars, following the lead of Len Gougeon, have corrected the image of Emerson the anti-activist. They have painstakingly demonstrated that Emerson not only was a key figure of the radical abolitionism of the 1850s but was also politically engaged at earlier times. Indeed, he delivered abolitionist addresses regularly before the 1850s: in 1837, 1844, 1845, 1846, and 1849, to be exact.[23] Moreover, in 1838, he addressed a Concord audience with an "Appeal for the Cherokees" and wrote a public letter of protest to President Martin Van Buren in response to the forced removal of the Cherokee from their lands.

But even his most radical lectures, ranging from his 1844 "Address Delivered ... on the Anniversary of the Emancipation of the Negroes in the British West Indies" to his address on "The Fugitive Slave Law," from 1854, begin with quiet notes of protest about having had to leave the scholar's desk in order to "speak to public questions" (*AW* 73). And at times his public comments, delivered expressly in support of reform causes, left listeners with the impression that Emerson wavered in his commitment.

In their reports of his 1855 address to the Women's Rights Convention in Boston, some newspapers even wondered, as Caroline Healey Dall noted after the event, "whether you were for us or against us" (quoted in *LL* 2: 15). Surrounded by feminists in his immediate circle of family and friends – chiefly including his aunt Mary Moody Emerson, his wife Lidian, and his close friend Margaret Fuller – Emerson soaked up an atmosphere of reformist urgency, yet for most of his career he let it cool down in transit from his dinner table to the rocking chair of his study.[24]

What made him shift gears after the Compromise of 1850 was the faltering of his belief, still visible in his 1844 address on the Emancipation in the West Indies, that the progressive course of history would do away with slavery on its own accord. The events he commemorated in 1844 initially bolstered his conviction that the long arc of history bent toward justice. He found confirmation in the fact that the former slaves had arisen from their bondage by their own power and demonstrated their full membership (as he thought of it) in the human race: "Here is the anti-slave: here is man," he rejoiced. "[A]nd if you have man, black or white is an insignificance" (*CW* 10: 325). So powerful a sign of universal progress was the display of self-reliance among Toussaint L'Ouverture and the Haitian revolutionaries that he believed the efforts of white abolitionists to have been revealed as "a poor squeamishness and nervousness" (*CW* 10: 325), dreadfully coupled with inflated self-importance.

With the Fugitive Slave Law of 1850, which forced Northerners to assist Southerners in returning fugitives back into slavery, Emerson all but lost his confidence that history was still on its right track. As Peter S. Field aptly assesses, Emerson, "convinced that the stirring, malevolent power maintaining the peculiar institution was driving out the forces of right, [...] reasoned that he had no choice but to join the ranks of those fighting to abolish it."[25] Joining the ranks of the abolitionists for good, Emerson held on to his time-proven rhetorical arsenal, in particular to the concept of the "representative." But whether his democratic language still matched his new field of engagement became increasingly uncertain. After John Brown's raid on Harpers Ferry, Emerson came out as a public defender of Brown's violent abolitionism, stating that "[Brown] was happily a representative of the American republic" (*CW* 10: 387) and "the rarest of heroes, a pure idealist, with no by-ends of his own" (387–88). Similarly, when he gave an address at a memorial service in Concord after Abraham Lincoln's assassination, he called Lincoln (in the version of the address arranged by his literary executor James Eliot Cabot) "the true representative of this continent; an entirely public man; father of his country, the pulse of twenty millions throbbing in his heart, the thought of their minds articulated by his tongue" (*W* 11: 335).

What he celebrated about both Brown and Lincoln was not merely their principled opposition to slavery but their willingness to act on their principles (though it took Lincoln some time to overcome his reluctance, not unlike Emerson himself). Action had been an element of self-reliance in Emerson's conception before, but up to this point, he had usually suggested that action never quite coincided with the thought driving it. But in John Brown's religiously and morally motivated violence, he saw higher principle and action become fully commensurate. "I said John Brown was an idealist. He believed in his ideas to that extent, that he existed to put them all into action; he said 'he did not believe in moral suasion; – he believed in putting the thing through'" (CW 10: 389).

Len Gougeon speaks of "Emerson's transcendental politics" in order to demonstrate that there was an intimate link between his transcendental philosophy and his reform politics.[26] While the phrase itself is felicitous, the question emerges whether Emerson's politics at this point can still be called democratic. On the one hand, the ideals he promoted clearly remained in line with the democratic ideal of equality. Yet if democracy as a way of life entailed receptiveness to the view of others, to dialogue and interaction, and if democracy as a political system relied on the observance of procedures and norms as well as respect of institutions, Emerson was having none of it. "In this national crisis, it is not argument that we want, but that rare courage which dares commit itself to a principle, believing that Nature is its ally, and will create the instruments it requires," he wrote in "American Civilization," an essay that appeared in *The Atlantic Monthly* in April 1862, as the Civil War entered its second year (CW 10: 405). Indeed, he went so far as to praise Lincoln's declaration of martial law and the suspension of the right to writs of habeas corpus, which together effectively imposed a wartime state of exception: "Government must not be a parish clerk, a justice of the peace. It has of necessity in any crisis of the state the absolute powers of a Dictator" (CW 10: 406).

As we saw earlier, Emerson had always prioritized morality over historical forms – including forms of government. As long as he didn't praise dictatorial rule, there never seemed to be a fundamental conflict between the idea and ideals of democracy and the actual instantiation of the "democratic element." Indeed, because of the mutual reinforcement of the spiritual and the social axis of universalizing enlargement, the moral idea of democracy and actually existing democracy had seemed to depend on each other. Now, however, as his moral convictions dictated uncompromising struggle in the name of justice, the relation between justice and democracy became unstable. Emerson himself couldn't have been more explicit on this point: "The end of all political struggle is to establish morality as the basis of all legislation. It is not free institutions, 'tis not a republic, 'tis not a democracy, that is the end, no, but only the means. Morality is the object of government" (*CW* 10: 409).

It may be for this reason that Emerson sometimes preferred the terms culture and civilization over democracy. While democracy posed the problem of how to encapsulate plurality, interaction, and contingency under one moral principle, civilization and culture defined the collective by a moral standard that could be fought for with means that were – if necessary – violent and, at their most radical, even undemocratic. Nor was this a view Emerson only entertained once he became a committed activist. In his 1849 essay "War," which is based on a lecture given in 1838, he described war as "a temporary and preparatory state [that] does actively forward the culture of man. War educates the senses, calls into action the will, perfects the physical constitution, brings men into such swift and close collision in critical moments that man measures man" (*CW* 10: 352). To Emerson, the means of justice could vary so greatly that sometimes violence and war – even *"religious wars"* (*CW* 10: 351) – seemed better suited than the means of democracy.

Are we, then, ultimately mistaken in taking Emerson to be a thinker of democracy? Some scholars, notably Neal Dolan and Daniel Malachuk, have put forward this very argument.[27] In their view, Emerson's entire body of writing is oriented around a set of metaphysical and even religious values, which he aimed to realize with varying means and powers. And while equality – based on humans' divine nature – belongs to these values, democracy does not. Emerson, on this reading, is a foundationalist who treats a clearly defined, transcendentally authorized conception of the good as the normative yardstick for political action.

Such critical efforts aiming to "retranscendentalize" and effectively de-democratize Emerson miss the complexity of how social and spiritual universalization are interwoven in his thought, however. Emerson's commitment to the – if necessary violent – defense of his principles was logically also a defense of democracy, even if he thought he could downgrade democracy to the level of means. "[War] does not suit us. We are advanced some ages on the war-state, – to trade, art, and general cultivation," Emerson noted in "American Civilization" (*CW* 10: 407). Violence, even divinely sanctioned violence, was legitimate and necessary in the moment of crisis, when anti-democratic forces of oppression were poised to win. But such violence was merely a transitional stage bent on reinstating a mode of living in which the process of collective perfectionist unfolding could continue.

That process, in Emerson's transcendental imagination, did not consist in putting into action a catalog of moral ideals clearly discerned and deciphered. Rather, the aim of overcoming the slave power consisted of collectively finding ever new instantiations, indeed, revelations, of what the moral law – which could only be intuited and which exceeded precept and word – could mean, and this process of finding was not least a poetic process. As William James put it on the occasion of Emerson's centenary, "thoughts which would be trivial expressed otherwise are important through the nouns and verbs to which he married them."[28]

For Emerson, the vanquishing of slavery was achieved with Lincoln's Emancipation Proclamation. It was a moment that he could only describe as "a poetic act and record" (CW 10: 432), and that did not only promise to bring former slaves into the political community of the United States but also reinstate his dialogical approach to democracy as a way of life.

It is no coincidence that in searching for the perfect analogy for the visceral effect that the Emancipation Proclamation had on him, he thought of his happiest moments on the lecture platform. "At such times, it appears as if a new public were created to greet the new event. It is as when an orator, having ended the compliments and pleasantries with which he conciliated attention … suddenly lending himself to some happy inspiration, announces with vibrating voice the grand human principles involved, – the bravoes and wits who greeted him loudly thus far, are surprised and overawed, a new audience is found in the heart of the assembly, an audience hitherto passive and unconcerned, now at last so searched and kindled, that they come forward every one a representative of mankind, standing for all nationalities" (CW 10: 432–33). Every single member of his audience having become a representative of a world community of liberated equals, the victory over slavery would usher in a future world pervaded by the poetry of democracy. Emerson's vision of the future of America was the vision of a future democracy, a democracy in which the social and spiritual axis of the universal worked together, coming to represent all nationalities. Consisting of a new public that has been awakened by spiritual surprise and wonder, his democracy of the future far exceeds the limitation of a particular political form. No longer one of many, democracy becomes *the* way of life. In his essay "Circles," from 1841, he had famously glossed it: "The way of life is wonderful: it is by abandonment" (CW 2: 190). As Emerson also knew, however, and as we have continued to witness since his day, what makes democracy as a way of life so tenuous is the ease with which we abandon abandonment.

## Notes

This chapter is dedicated to the memory of Herwig Friedl (1944–2022).

1. John Dewey, "Emerson – The Philosopher of Democracy [1903]," in *The Essential Dewey*, Vol. 2, ed. Larry Hickman and Thomas Alexander (Bloomington, IN: Indiana University Press, 1998), 366–70.

2. See Judith Shklar, "Emerson and the Inhibitions of Democracy," in *A Political Companion to Ralph Waldo Emerson*, ed. Alan M. Levine and Daniel S. Malachuk (Lexington: University of Kentucky Press, 2011); George Kateb, *Emerson and Self-Reliance* (Thousand Oaks: Sage, 1995); Cornel West, *The American Evasion of Philosophy: A Genealogy of Pragmatism* (Madison: University of Wisconsin Press, 1989); and Stanley Cavell, "Aversive Thinking," in *Emerson's Transcendental Etudes*, ed. David Justin Hodge (Stanford: Stanford University Press, 2003).

3. See Vernon Louis Parrington, *Main Currents in American Thought: An Interpretation of American Literature From the Beginnings to 1920* (New York: Harcourt Brace, 1927–1930); F. O. Matthiessen, *The American Renaissance: Art and Expression in the Age of Emerson and Whitman* (New York: Oxford University Press, 1941); Daniel Aaron, *Men of Good Hope: A Story of American Progressives* (New York: Oxford University Press, 1951); Richard Poirier, *The Renewal of Literature: Emersonian Reflections* (New York: Random House, 1987); Len Gougeon, *Virtue's Hero: Emerson, Anti-Slavery, and Reform* (Athens: University of Georgia Press, 1990); Lawrence Buell, *Emerson* (Cambridge, MA: Harvard University Press, 2003); Herwig Friedl, *Thinking in Search of a Language* (New York: Bloomsbury, 2019); Donald E. Pease, "'Experience,' Antislavery, and the Crisis of Emersonianism," *Boundary* 234:2 (2007): 71–103; and Branka Arsić, *On Leaving: A Reading in Emerson* (Cambridge, MA: Harvard University Press, 2010).

4. George Santayana, "The Genteel Tradition in American Philosophy," in *Winds of Doctrine and Platonism and the Spiritual Life [1913]* (Gloucester, MA: Peter Smith, 1971), 199.

5. George Santayana, "The Genteel Tradition in American Philosophy"; 193. See also Van Wyck Brooks, *America's Coming of Age*.

6. Sacvan Bercovitch, *The Rites of Assent: Transformations in the Symbolic Construction of America* (New York: Routledge, 1993); Quentin Anderson, *The Imperial Self: An Essay in American Literary and Cultural History* (New York: Knopf, 1971); Christopher Newfield, *The Emerson Effect: Individualism and Submission in America* (Chicago: University of Chicago Press, 1996).

7. Perry Miller, "Emersonian Genius and the American Democracy," in *Critical Essays on Ralph Waldo Emerson*, ed. Robert Burkholder and Joel Myerson (Boston: G.K. Hall, 1983), 288.

8. Perry Miller, "Emersonian Genius and the American Democracy"; Benjamin Park, "Transcendental Democracy: Ralph Waldo Emerson's Political Thought, the Legacy of Federalism, and the Ironies of America's Democratic Tradition," *Journal of American Studies* 48:2 (2014); Neal Dolan, *Emerson's Liberalism* (Madison: University of Wisconsin Press, 2009); Daniel S. Malachuk, "Emerson's Politics, Retranscendentalized," in *A Political Companion to Ralph Waldo Emerson*, ed. Alan M. Levine and Daniel S. Malachuk (Lexington: University of Kentucky Press, 2011), 265–304.

9. John Dewey, "Creative Democracy – The Task Before Us [1939]," in *The Essential Dewey, Vol. 1*, ed. Larry Hickman and Thomas Alexander (Bloomington, IN: Indiana University Press, 1998), 341.

10. Roberto Frega, *Pragmatism and the Wide View of Democracy* (Cham: Palgrave Macmillan, 2019), 2.

11. Miller, "Emersonian Genius and the American Democracy," 278.

12. Dolan, *Emerson's Liberalism*, 305–25.

13. See Alexis de Tocqueville, *Democracy in America*, vol. 1 (New York: Landley, 1841), 288–89.

14. Alexis de Tocqueville, *Democracy in America*, vol. 1 (New York: Landley, 1841), 286; for Adorno and Horkheimer's excerpt, see *Dialectic* 105–6.

15. The linkages between Emerson and Adorno's critical theory have recently begun to be studied by Shannon Mariotti. On the complicated relationship between Frankfurt critical theorists and the New York intellectuals, see Wheatland.

16. Jacques Rancière, *Aisthesis: Scenes from the Aesthetic Regime of Art* (New York: Verso, 2013), 64.

17. Shklar, "Emerson and the Inhibitions of Democracy," 60.

18. Stanley Cavell, *Conditions Handsome and Unhandsome: The Constitution of Emersonian Perfectionism* (Chicago: University of Chicago Press, 1990), 125.

19. Robert Richardson, *First We Read, Then We Write: Emerson on the Creative Process* (Iowa City: University of Iowa Press, 2009), 22.

20. See Kateb, who writes, "I believe this essay is aberrant." in *George Kateb, Emerson and Self-Reliance* (Thousand Oaks: Sage, 1995), 174.

21. James Russell Lowell, *My Study Window [1871]* (Boston: Houghton Mifflin, 1899), 383. On Emerson as lecturer, see Ronald Bosco's and Joel Myerson's Historical and Textual Introduction to *The Later Lectures* (LL 1: xvii–lxii), Peter S. Field, *Ralph Waldo Emerson: The Making of a Democratic Intellectual* (Lanham: Rowman and Littlefield, 2003), ch. 5; Johannes Voelz, *Transcendental Resistance: The New Americanists and Emerson's Challenge* (Hanover: University Press of New England, 2010), ch. 2; and R. Jackson Wilson, "Emerson as Lecturer: Man Thinking, Man Saying," in *The Cambridge Companion to Ralph Waldo Emerson*, ed. Joel Porte and Saundra Morris (New York: Cambridge University Press, 1999).

22. Oliver Wendell Holmes, *Ralph Waldo Emerson* (Boston: Houghton Mifflin, 1884), 304.

23. Gougeon, *Virtue's Hero: Emerson, Anti-Slavery, and Reform*, 2.

24. See Phyllis Cole for a fine-grained analysis of the domestic debates on reform among Mary, Lidian, and Waldo.

25. Field, *Ralph Waldo Emerson: The Making of a Democratic Intellectual*, 167.

26. Len Gougeon, "Emerson, Self-Reliance, and the Politics of Democracy," in *A Political Companion to Ralph Waldo Emerson*, ed. Alan M. Levine and Daniel S. Malachuk (Lexington, KY: University of Kentucky Press, 2011), 190.

27. See Dolan, *Emerson's Liberalism*, Introduction, and Malachuk, "Emerson's Politics," where he states apodictically: "All of Emerson's significant political positions stemmed from his fundamental belief that our equality as human beings is based upon our shared transcendental essence, a belief here called 'transcendental equality'" (265).

28. William James, "Address at the Centenary of Ralph Waldo Emerson, May 25, 1903," in *William James: Writings 1902–1910* (New York: Library of America, 1987), 1120.

# 10

## DAVID LAROCCA

# Characterizing *English Traits*

Compared with the voluminous engagement Ralph Waldo Emerson's well-known and influential work has received, his 1856 book *English Traits* has drawn relatively scant scholarly attention.[1] Nevertheless, the compact volume, which was among the most widely read and celebrated during his lifetime, offers the contemporary reader much insight into the more popular and durable elements of his oeuvre and into his intellectual and historical moment. It brims with vivid observations and trenchant critiques of Victorian manners; a cultural, topographical, literary and one might even say "biographical" history of England (and by refraction, its near-term descendent, America); a transatlantic travel narrative; interspersed notes on archaeology, architecture, modern institutions, reform movements, natural science, industrial capitalism, and colonialism; and, if problematically, unstable theorizations of race and nationality. Even as Emerson marshals his prodigious energies along these varied vectors, *English Traits* presents a natural history of the English language, in particular, an extended meditation on metaphor and metonymy; it is a volume that teems with genealogical and generative tropes – blood, birth, plants, parents, family, names, and race – and affords an exploration of how natural scientific metaphors are especially salient for their moral import and effects.

In this chapter, I reintroduce Emerson's "anomalous" book and seek to situate it within the context of Emerson's transatlanticism from "The American Scholar" to *Representative Men*, "Fate," and, crucially, his decades-in-the-making series "Natural History of Intellect." Befitting *English Trait's* ongoing pertinence – in cultural matters as well as scholarly ones – I analyze and contextualize Emerson's comments on race in relation to the formation of national mythologies (British and, referentially by way of lineage, also American). The prevailing object of Emerson's inquiry is England (not Wales, Scotland, or Ireland), and the dominant metaphor of his investigation (viz., traits) places his thought in a matrix of natural history and evolutionary sensibilities (hence the continuity that would have a book entitled *English Traits* meaningfully illuminate American traits). Meanwhile, the syntagma "English traits" should have us rightly thinking about deep time and the coursings of people across a specific spot of land, in this case, an island (and, in due course, a subsequent dissemination across the Atlantic). Yet the phrase also compellingly invokes a much smaller scale: the prehistory of Emerson's own descent.

### Pedigrees of Influence

In the wake of his first visit to Europe and England in 1833 and his first book *Nature* (1836), Emerson began presenting what might be deemed "anti-influence" addresses (anticipating Harold Bloom's twentieth-century formulation[2]), most conspicuously "An Address" (July 1837) and "The American Scholar" (August 1837), both delivered at Harvard. Returning from a transatlantic passage in 1834, Emerson achieved a fresh take on the status of his birth country and the country that gave birth to it, England – and with it, the British Empire. In "The American Scholar," Emerson proclaims, "Our day of dependence, our long apprenticeship to the learning of other lands, draws to a close" (CW 1: 52). During lectures, addresses, and essays over the next few years, Emerson's heterodox formulations were perceived by others to be dangerous, as he sounded clarion calls to individual liberty, anti-colonial intellectual emancipation, and the formation of a national identity (and the pride to go with it). In large measure, this early Emerson is the Emerson of the current popular imagination – the patron saint of "rugged individualism," "boot-strap" empowerment, and, upon further study, other problematic expropriations and cultivated mythologies (such as that of the "self-made man").

In "Literary Ethics," he issued advice to scholars, to laborers of all kinds, in fact, to take up the rich possibilities of life in a "new" land, where "the perpetual admonition of nature to us, is, 'The world is new, untried [...].'" He heralded an optimistic guess at what will become of thinking – its letters and its laws – given the attention of passionate minds. "I pass now to consider the task offered to the intellect of this country. [...]," he says to his audience in 1838, "To be as good a scholar as Englishmen are; to have as much learning as our contemporaries; to have written a book that is read; satisfies us" (CW 1: 105). Six years later, in "The Young American" (1844), Emerson reminded his readers that they are part of a young nation, one constituted differently from antique if auspicious models: democracy is the adolescent nation's gift against the tyranny of tradition. "The English have many virtues, many advantages, and the proudest history of the world; but they need all and more than all the resources of the past to indemnify a heroic gentleman in that country for the mortifications prepared for him by the system of society, and which seem to impose the alternative to resist or to avoid it." As such, monarchy and the English class "system is an invasion of the sentiment of justice and the native rights of men, which, however decorated, must lessen the value of English citizenship" (*CW* 1: 244). By contrast, Emerson assured his New England listeners, "we only say, Let us live in America, too thankful for our want of feudal institutions. Our houses and towns are like mosses and lichens, so slight and new; but youth is a fault of which we shall daily mend."

A decade after Emerson's anti-influence addresses, he headed abroad again – this time mainly to England for an extended visit, having been invited to give a series of lectures by Alexander Ireland. From October 1847 to July 1848, Emerson visited twenty-six cities and delivered seventy-four formal lectures. He was no longer a twenty-nine-year-old unemployed widower and ex-preacher but a marquee name in American letters. And, following a series of grave personal losses, the euphoric pronouncements of radical liberty propounded in "Self-Reliance" and "Circles" (1841) had given way to the sober stock-taking of "Experience" (1844) and the inaugural, book-defining statement of *The Conduct of Life*, "Fate" (1860). At the same time, Emerson had become more attuned to the implications of scientific, philosophical, and Romantic thought arriving from Europe and England (whether from Michael Faraday or Thomas Carlyle, Robert Chambers or Richard Owen, Charles Lyell or Adam Sedgwick – all of whom he visited with in 1848). To be sure, Emerson's first visit to Europe and England supercharged his nascent interest in the natural sciences. In 1833, while visiting the Jardin des Plantes in Paris, the ex-minister resolved "I will be a naturalist" (*JMN* 4: 200).[3] If Emerson had become a student of nature while not aspiring to be a scientist per se, he would have woven its varied outlook – where its techniques become tropes and its preoccupations and marvels an analog – for his literary, philosophical, and spiritual writing.[4] Like his views on race, Emerson was unburdened by strict disciplinary boundaries. In *English Traits*, as in so much other work, he presents himself as an amalgamation of philosopher of science, ethnographer, metaphysician, man of letters, and taxonomist (Carl Linnaeus was another touchstone). With such an inventive, eclectic sensibility for combination and arrangement, we should be surprised neither by the novelty of his observations nor their occasional mystifications.

While Emerson was fascinated by the natural history museums of his first voyage to Europe, he was, upon his return visit fourteen years later, celebrity enough to meet with the scientific heroes whose work he read, whose empirical ideas refracted off his own conceptual ones in fields such as geology, anthropology, mathematics, zoology, chemistry, and magnetism. By the time Emerson published *English Traits* in 1856, he had developed a more nuanced, if world-weary, appreciation of the life-shaping vicissitudes of cause and effect – the fate of embodiment. He had turned away from his stumping for boundless, unobstructed freedom and dismissal of inherited authority and patrimony, and turned toward a disciplined, patient advocacy for contingency, limitation, and, yes, influence. *English Traits* was Emerson's Declaration of Dependence. He was, alas, bound to England – to its history, people, ideas, and even to its natural history – and happily, proudly so. He was intrigued by *his* English traits.

## Currents of Relation

Perhaps the shortest possible summary of *English Traits* is also its title: what do we mean by "English," and how do these differ from Welsh, Scottish, Irish, British, and conglomerations such as the United Kingdom, Great Britain, and the still more expansive "European," not forgetting, before them all – Celt, Angle, Saxon, Viking, and so on? How would one identify "English" traits in exclusivity from the rest – or does the definition, instead, depend on their inclusion? Thus, "English" is not a precipitate but an accumulation and admits of its "composite character" (*CW* 5: 27). Moreover, what do we mean by "Traits": for instance, taken up figuratively and embodied in history, culture, language, topography, and so on; and/or as literal descriptions of physical characteristics of the human body, progeny, and genotype (e.g., as blood, family, race, genetic inheritance, and related)? As noted, Emerson's two major visits to England occurred in the heyday of the British Empire, and so his relationship to England – despite the American Revolution – nevertheless has the cast one would expect from a citizen of the Commonwealth: deferential at times, defensive at others, and curious about what links one land to another – and what differentiates origination points from their offspring. We can understand why. Emerson was born when Thomas Jefferson was president, in 1803, a mere fourteen years after the US Constitution was ratified. With the revolutionary pedigree of his New England ancestors haunting the streets (and some denizens still alive to share their stories with him), and calling to the significance of a place called *New* England – even if Emerson was, himself, many generations removed from England itself.

In his correspondence with Alexander Ireland about the prospect of his return to England, moments of unguarded confession suggest Emerson's despondent frame of mind along with his still-precarious professional situation (only 500 copies of the revised edition of *Essays: First Series* were issued). At the outset of 1847, he wrote, "I am not young enough now to have any projects of literary propagandism there, and do not wish to collect an audience with pains, or that others should for me. [...] As I manage now, I who have never done anything, never shall do anything."[5] Later in the year, as he prepared for his departure to England – or rather, didn't – he related to his brother, William, that after being tasked with other duties, "I came to the preparation of lectures for England [...] too late & am sadly fretted with miscellaneous parts."[6] (Upon arrival, he would end up reading mainly from lectures that later appeared in *Representative Men* in 1850; "Shakespeare" and "Napoleon" went into heavy rotation).

Though Emerson would extensively develop and revise the content that would become *English Traits* for the better part of the decade to come, it is instructive to hold in mind the metaphor of "miscellaneous parts." The pasted-together, patchwork quality of the book is a function of its charm – providing a space for the amalgamation of diverse genres (e.g., autobiographical private journal, anthropological study, travelogue, political tract, natural science notebook, philosophical commentary, etc.) and, along with those genres, prose exhibiting varied moods, tones, and styles (the poetic, the political, dispassionate scientism, stump-speech rhetoric). Contemporaneous reviews of the finished book were largely favorable, arguably making *English Traits* Emerson's "wittiest,"[7] most well-reviewed, and positively appreciated volume of his lifetime.[8]

Structurally, there are nineteen chapters of *English Traits*, the first two being drawn extensively from Emerson's letters and journals – no novel innovation for him, since the methodology of selecting and adapting from private notebooks was familiar to his established writings and lectures. Chapters 1 and 2 amount to autobiographical travelogues, the first chapter about his first voyage, and the second chapter from his second transatlantic venture. Chapters 3 to 15 follow, each marked by a bold single word: a discernable topic (such as Land, Race, Manners, Character, Aristocracy, Universities, etc.) that, in turn, reveals its interconnectedness with the others. Chapters 16 to 18 return to the more explicitly first-person, including a memorable account of visiting Stonehenge with Thomas Carlyle. While fielding Carlyle's curmudgeonly musings, Emerson freely admits his admiration for the English; yet he also knows that upon returning to Massachusetts, to America, "that there and not here is the seat and centre of the British race." Emerson concludes, in the company of a stalwart Scotsman, that England, "an old and exhausted island, must one day be contented, like other parents, to be strong only in her children" (*CW* 5: 155).

In these moods of awe at English actualities and renewed confidence in American potentialities, Emerson offers some lessons gleaned from decades of study and travel, but especially from his 1847–48 visit, morals that Emerson calls "Result," the title of his penultimate chapter, among them that while "England is the best of actual nations," it doesn't provide an "ideal framework" for imitation by young admirers, including nascent nations (*CW* 5: 169). The book concludes in yet another register – with a speech given at Manchester – a mode of address that occasions the public declaration of private reflections (e.g., asking aloud what "lures a solitary American in the woods with the wish to see England," the "island from which my forefathers came," the "mother of nations") (*CW* 5: 177). In Manchester, he announces his Americanness as the sort of earthly characteristic that would draw a person to investigate origins, to ask after the common currents that circulate through families, peoples, nations – to justify a legitimate interest in England, its history, and its nature.

Emerson was not given to writing monographs but instead preferred essayistic dispatches on a range of philosophical, religious, poetic, and political topics. Thus, we get "essays" that arrive in a "series." So even while *English Traits* appears to declare a single, uniform topic (or, at best, two in the form of a single noun phrase), as *Nature* did two decades earlier, the singularity, once again, veils a multitude. Emerson's philosophical methodology is akin to the natural scientist who observes, writes, and in that writing *tests* (Fr. *essais*); who collects specimens, labels, and then comments on them – looking for their lines of affinity or differentiation, asking after their origins but also after their present-day relation. As a poet-philosopher with a keen interest in the natural sciences and natural history – and the phenomena that animate those studies – his reports, not surprisingly, teem with organic metaphors (blood, soil, gardens) and tropes of human descent and relationality (family, inheritance, race). Like a clever entomologist or discerning anthropologist, Emerson looked to his appointed subject and wanted to find a reply to the question "Why England is England?" (*CW* 5: 18). The baldness of the copula may strike contemporary readers as metaphysically antiquated – admitting a search, as it were, for essences. But Emerson was intellectually savvy enough to know that his single object was, in fact, multiform, and for that reason, indeterminate – endlessly complex, like the natural forms he marveled at. And yet, under the umbrella of "English traits," he explores and describes the proliferating forces and their effects, which could travel under this single name, or network of interconnected things, events, and the descriptions we give to them.

*English Traits* builds. After the first two chapters, we arrive on *terra firma* with a meditation on Land. Here topography and terrain occasion consideration of the mythical origins of any people, such as they emerge from a specific place – and its determining climates, flora, fauna, and limit situations (fertile, arable soil; favorable bays for fishing and trade; a rugged coastline for defense; and so on). "What are the elements of that power which the English hold over other nations?" Emerson asks and hazards an answer: "If there be one test of national genius universally accepted, it is success; and if there be one successful country in the universe for the last millennium, that country is England" (*CW* 5: 19). Emerson vacillates between acquiescence to "a civilization already settled and overpowering" and reassurance that "[t]he American is only the continuation of the English genius into new conditions, more or less propitious." The parent/child dynamic Emerson argues for us to acknowledge encodes familiar (and familial) structures: rebellion in one instance, claims to legitimate descent in another. Emerson's take on American identity is necessarily mixed with the broad and indomitable history of its forebears.

Emerson's obsessive interest in "all things English" may strike modern readers as a variant of Anglophilia – indeed, Howard Mumford Jones said that "Emerson was an Anglophile from a characteristically Anglophilic portion of the United States and therefore a sympathetic observer."[9] Emerson's adoration is, as noted, nonetheless often layered with concern and critique. In *Anglophilia: Deference, Devotion, and Antebellum America*, Elisa Tamarkin provides a broad context in which to test the widespread "imperial nostalgia" present in American culture – and not just in American social life and notions of class, but also in American higher education (in academic life, in qualities of intellectualism). Despite the defeat of Great Britain in the Revolutionary War, and the founding of a new democracy, Americans retained – and cultivated – an ongoing, anachronistic attachment to the English that "makes an art out of colonial vicariousness,"[10] and that precedes today's "special relationship" and the perennial interest in the Royal Family. Tamarkin's study complements Emerson's insofar as both pursue an inquiry into "Englishness" – the ongoing pursuit of what the "state of being English" might mean, contain, or imply.[11] Tamarkin notes that "the English in *English Traits* already know the lessons of 'Experience': that life, as Emerson puts it, is not 'intellectual or critical, but sturdy'; that 'to fill the hour' is the greatest happiness; and that the 'practical wisdom' that lets us fill the hour however we can [...] 'infers an indifferency' from objections to the futility of our doing it."[12] Tracking traits of Englishness (and what she calls elsewhere "Englishy English" – "some pure essence of England, and echoic moment of sheer, elicitory English"[13]), Tamarkin concludes that "there is nothing for Emerson that is more characteristically English than being satisfied and engrossed with the present moment as it comes to be."[14] Tamarkin, in turn, helps us consider the ways in which Emerson, in fact, operates in an English "mode of thought."[15] Such a "mode" would have us consider the *Englishness* of this now-iconic American thinker – the extent to which, from the further temporal distance that we occupy, Emerson can't help but appear proximate to, indeed continuous with, the English models and influences he studied and, in a constitutional sense (i.e., in matters of familial descent, inherited cultural habits, and idiosyncratic personal and temperamental interests), he embodied.

Given that Emerson was impressed *and* horrified by what he saw first-hand in England – the ingenuity, wealth, and influence of cutting-edge industrial capitalism as it made white sheep black from coal dust while also covering-over a decidedly impoverished underclass – perhaps caustic, often indirect commentary was the best he could manage given the constraints of decorum. If a visitor will be forgiven for adulation, how much can the same visitor insult his hosts, audience, and ancestors? In his final appointment with the author of *The French Revolution*, Emerson was not shy to tell Carlyle (himself an active critic of Chartism and an anti-Black racist) that England "has reached its zenith, and will begin to dwindle, and that America is the future of the English race" (*JMN* 10: 335–36). Encounters with other "great men," including among the aristocracy, "I saw only as spectacles," he writes late in his travels, "theirs is a bread that ends in the using, & no seed" (*L* 4: 62, April 25, 1848). Mark Twain is known for his satire, like Swift before him, but Emerson's often-lacerating sketches also regularly provide that rare double gift of comedy: the revelation of a truth coupled with a bit of estranging the familiar. Who better to make a study of England than a quintessential American? Just as Alexis de Tocqueville, whom Emerson met in Paris, had in the previous decade delivered his own version of "American traits" from the perspective of a visiting Frenchman (viz., *Democracy in America*), so Emerson brought his postcolonial disposition back for a tour and a distinctly American – such as that term was itself under development – reading of England.

## English Traits and Race

Writing from antebellum America, or from an England that abolished slavery in 1833, Emerson was keenly aware of the valences of race as they related to "Caucasian" (then a relatively new term) and "African." In the spirit of a poetically inclined student of nature, he asks after the literal and figurative genealogy of the English and how their genotype and phenotype express themselves to a mid-century American tourist who can claim some remote ancestry from the place. A word like "race," then, doesn't age well in the context of *English Traits*, along with phrases such as "natural genius of the British mind" (*CW* 5: 19). In terms of Emerson's possible senses and allusions, his methods, and temperament, "race" is shorthand for the groups of people who, like him, trace their origins to this island plot in the middle of the North Atlantic. In other words, race and nation are near synonyms – conceptual cousins. Whether we take it as a fault or feature, "race" for Emerson is an anthropological, political, and poetic catch-all for the traits, characteristics, and embodied practices that collectively make a people recognizable (especially in relation to another group – for instance, when he visits Paris during its revolutionary May 1848, he refers to the French as "the most joyous race" and notes how "[t]heir universal good breeding is a great convenience" (*L* 4: 76)). In his context-based deployment of the term, Emerson proceeds to identify features of "race" with praise and protest, admiring what he can and calling out what seems problematical in turn "France is, by its natural contrast, a kind of blackboard on which English character draws its own traits in chalk" (*CW* 5: 82). Concluding not long after: "I am afraid that English nature is so rank and aggressive as to be a little incompatible with every other" (*CW* 5: 83). Given such invocations of character and nature, what then is our best cognate for Emerson's "race"? —Cultural milieu? National sensibilities? Ethnographic particularities? Simply the political entity we call a nation (thus, "French race" and "French nation" as cognates)? In any case, he is far from our contemporary understandings of race and their combustible politics of the status of "whiteness" as a racial category. Rather, as befits his prismatic study, and with a hobby-naturalist's interest in the liability of evolution as well as its gifts, along with a maven-like interest in many seemingly unrelated facts and features, Emerson comments: "But nature makes nothing in vain, and this little superfluity of self-regard in the English brain, is one of the secrets of their power and history. For, it sets every man on being and doing what he really is and can" (*CW* 5: 83). Even these few lines provide an indication of Emerson's approach to biology, genetics, ontology, and social arrangements. As he is freely inclined to speak of the French as a race and imagines an "English brain," we pick up his postulates of a fatalistic essentialism (viz., "being and doing what he really is and can").

In *America's England: Antebellum Literature and Atlantic Sectionalism*, Christopher Hanlon devotes a chapter to "Transatlantic Bloodlines and English Traits." Hanlon argues that "it makes sense to think of the book as one expression of the wider culture's wavering outlook on England."[16] On this reading, Anglophilia meets ambivalence. One of the more fertile debates among scholars is whether *English Traits* is "really" about England and the English, but instead hides (somehow) that "Emerson's true subject is America and the racially determined American character."[17] Such a debate, Hanlon notes, "intimates the solipsism of *English Traits*." Yet, befitting the ambivalence – and thus double status of the book – there is a project of "ethnic dissociation" (a phrase borrowed from Werner Sollors) that, according to Hanlon, "rests upon the use of British history as a kind of typology for the domestic situation unfolding in America at the mid-century."[18] Ethnic dissociation is, on this reading, essential to the creation of nationhood – that is, as a formulation that aims to reconcile location, people, their tendencies, time, cultural ephemera, and the rest, in a bid for a coherent, if evolving, identity.

Despite being the title of a single chapter, Hanlon claims emphatically that "[r]ace is, of course, everywhere in *English Traits*,"[19] and so, perhaps despite Emerson's intentions, "[t]he book is embroiled [...] in a form of Atlantic sectionalism: rather than charting an escape from the cisatlantic conflict, Emerson understands questions about English constitution and character [and 'temperament,' 'genius,' etc.] to have everything to do with questions concerning U.S. sectional strife."[20] Just as Tamarkin alerts us to a lingering (and in some circles robust) "nostalgia" for Englishness, Hanlon traces several modes of race theorizing as they coexisted and sometimes overlapped at mid-century (often with science and politics drawn together, not unlike today). The question, indeed the challenge, for readers coming to *English Traits* is discerning which debates, if any, Emerson was participating in, and whether and to what extent he was making a claim to them (e.g., their truth or falsity, or neither). Hanlon helpfully rehearses passages from *English Traits* in conversation with their sources and points of influence, including controversial racial theorists such as Robert Knox, author of *The Races of Men: A Fragment* (1850, reissued in 1862 as *The Races of Men: A Philosophical Enquiry into the Influence of Race over the Destinies of Nations*). Knox's race theories were unconvincing to Emerson since his postulations appeared unscientific, implausible, and compromised by motivated rhetoric.

Emerson begins his chapter devoted to race with a head-on confrontation with Knox. Though Knox may try to "prove that races are imperishable," it turns out Emerson defiantly counters by way of caution and correction, "nations are pliant political constructions, easily changed or destroyed." Here "race" and "nation" are used interchangeably. And, precisely because Emerson "slips" between *race* and *nation*, we can track his lack of confidence in the term race altogether. "Race" in Emerson's hands, activates and informs profound philosophical lessons, among them that "you cannot draw the line where a race begins or ends" (*CW* 5: 24). To make sure we catch the drift of Emerson's contempt, cited prominently in the chapter's first sentence, he adds that Knox "did not found his assumed races on any necessary law, disclosing the ideal or metaphysical necessity; nor did he, on the other hand, count with precision the existing races, and settle the true bounds" (*CW* 5: 24). Emerson calls Knox's approach caustically "a point of nicety, and the popular test of the theory," which is to say no test at all. What we find time and again in Emerson's uptake of the term "race" is a radically fluid ontology. Then again, the radicality – including in the etymological senses of the word that would get us closer to *origins* and *roots* – is a function of the age, in a word: one poised to process the world-changing, concept-altering theory of evolution already in the air – and soon to crest the horizon.

Hanlon underlines that "[a]gainst Knox's warnings that miscegenation leads to degeneration and sterility, Emerson [...] insists that the English belie taxonomical analysis precisely because they instantiate a successful fusion of types."[21] As Emerson wrote, the English do not "appear to be of one stem; but collectively a better race than any from which they are derived." (*CW* 5: 28). And he pursues the crucial point about the mythology of origins, beginnings, and purity that haunt racial division: "Nor is it easy to trace it home to its original seats. Who can call by right name what races are in Britain? Who can trace them historically? Who can discriminate them anatomically, or metaphysically" (*CW* 5: 28)? Notice the sense of "discriminate" here – what used to be understood as judgment, a variant of taste. And moreover, Emerson doubts the discovery of some "right name" by which one clan, tribe, or lineage might be delineated from another. Emerson suggests, rather, "the impossibility of arriving at satisfaction on the historical question of race," admitting, "I fancied I could leave quite aside the choice of a tribe as [the Englishman's] lineal progenitors" (*CW* 5: 28). In fitting Emersonian fashion, *English Traits* is Janus-faced, for if "[r]ace is, of course, everywhere in *English Traits*," it is also persistently resistant to a final definition or a fixed theory; it remains an historically volatile and indeterminate category, given to the productive flux and mercurial metamorphoses that characterize Emerson's thought more generally.

In *Fleshing Out America: Race, Gender, and the Politics of the Body in American Literature, 1833–1879*, Carolyn Sorisio reminds us that Emerson wrote, in the years before his second voyage to England, "what is arguably his most radical declaration of the possible equality and future success of the 'negro' race" in "An Address ... on ... the Emancipation of the Negroes in the British West Indies" (1844) and a year later, "Anniversary of the West Indian Emancipation" (1845).[22] As Sorisio puts it, "none of his later writings matches the zeal with which Emerson sets about demonstrating how the British emancipation in the West Indies signifies the 'annihilation of the old indecent nonsense about the nature of the negro.'"[23] Emerson's anti-slavery writings and speeches reveal his frame of mind upon his second visit to England. He was a committed and vigorous abolitionist – outspoken, unyielding, filled with the fervor of a righteous cause – during the composition of *English Traits*, and not just politically but philosophically as well. He declaimed eloquently, marshalling moral suasion and scientific reasoning to demolish any prevailing faith in the separation or separability of races (in our contemporary sense of chromatics). If he admired the English for liberating enslaved people in the West Indies, he was celebrating not just their freedom from physical constraint and unjust infringements of freedom, but also their moral imagination in recognizing spiritual facts that all humans share. Understandably, his esteem for these faraway visionaries was turned, at home, into reasons for shame: "Whilst I have read of England, I have thought of New England" (*AW* 23). The "civility of no race can be perfect, whilst another race is degraded. It is a doctrine alike of the oldest, and of the newest philosophy, that, man is one, and that you cannot injure any member, without a sympathetic injury to all the members."[24] Humankind is of one kind.

Despite the prominence, explicitness, and duration of Emerson's commitment to the emancipation of enslaved peoples, Sorisio, like other contemporary critics, directs our attention to Emerson's contradictions. She says, for instance, that "Emerson cannot escape language that undercuts his calls for equality and tentatively works toward the racialized national identity that *English Traits*, 'The President's Proclamation,' and 'Fortune of the Republic,' explicitly formulate."[25] Sorisio's marshaled evidence "suggest that as much as Emerson proclaims the future success and possible equality of emancipated slaves, he fills his essay with language establishing racial difference and white superiority."[26] Sorisio turns to *English Traits* to "examine further Emerson's conflicting descriptions of race" and emphasizes a crucial fact about the 1856 book: "Here Emerson does not concern himself explicitly with Africans or African Americans."[27]

In his focus, instead, on the English and the American "races" (we modern readers may be helped, as suggested earlier, to add a term such as nationality as a useful cognate), Emerson's interest was, in part, personal. He made *English Traits* a public statement that justified questions about his family tree and, in a larger domain, the way that New England was formed and informed by England, even while he pursued a broader view of human history – of whatever vintage – as inseparable from natural history. Emerson already spoke in "The Young American" (1844) of "amelioration in nature." In turn, he was particularly influenced by the pre-Darwinian hypothesizing of Robert Chambers in his *Vestiges of the Natural History of Creation* (also from 1844, but which Emerson read later in an 1845 printing), a speculative piece of natural history and philosophy. As part of his English tour, in 1848, Emerson had met Chambers in London, and in his thinking about race, he seems to braid intimations from Chambers (a monogenesist) with strains of Plotinus and Swedenborg; note the marvelous hybridity of such thinking. Later, in *English Traits*, he sustains a belief that "the barriers of races are not so firm" – and so "we see the rudiments of tiger and baboon in our human form" (CW 5: 27). *Our* human form is, again, a shared status among all *homo sapiens*. And though Sorisio claims that Emerson's critique of Knox at the outset of the "Race" chapter was "an attack that signified Emerson's rejection of racial determinism as an adequate framework with which to interpret history and culture," she pursues seemingly contradictory statements, even those Emerson himself admits "I cannot reconcile" (CW 5: 27). But if Knox's logic was faulty, how could it be reconciled? If the natural science of the day was insufficient, irreconcilable claims would persist. Where Emerson's *scientific* defeat of race theory may have understandably faltered, he compensated with sufficient appeals to ethical principles, the dignity of individuals, and the rights of man (as citizens of nations and of the shared world).

In *The History of White People*, Nell Irwin Painter includes a few chapters on Emerson, including one devoted to *English Traits*, which fits within her capacious view of whiteness from the Greeks and Scythians to contemporary America. Painter begins boldly and without equivocation that Emerson should be understood as "the philosopher King of American white race theory."[28] Painter draws Emerson into company with Carlyle – a conspicuously committed racist and classist – as being devoted to an "heroic figuration of what they termed the Saxon race," and she glosses *English Traits* as "an entire book [dedicated] to the subject."[29] She notes how in reading Sharon Turner's *The History of the Anglo-Saxons* (1799, seventh ed. 1852), Emerson "eagerly absorbed its Saxon chauvinism."[30] "Emerson saw himself as a New Englander," Painter writes uncontroversially, then goes further, "virtually as an Englishman, and therefore as a 'Saxon.'"[31] In Emerson's five-part lecture series on New England (1843), he shares a saying, not his own, that "the Yankee is double distilled English" (LL, 40), which Painter reads as meaning that for Emerson "New Englanders [are] even more English than the English."[32] Painter begrudges Emerson's antislavery efforts, despite the moral revolt contained in his serial expressions, marking him "no radical abolitionist"[33] – and this despite, for example, Len Gougeon's painstaking and, for many, convincing proof of commendable labors in *Virtue's Hero: Emerson, Antislavery, and Reform* (1990), a celebrated investigation that goes unacknowledged in *The History of White People*.[34] As if picking up the mantle from Painter, in *Medieval America* (2020), Robert Yusef Rabiee counters that "Gougeon's reluctance to accept the evidence at hand concerning Emerson's stiffening racial vision may owe more to one scholar's adoration of 'virtue's hero' than it does an accurate account of Emerson's social doctrines."[35] For her part, Painter concludes that "The Anglo-Saxon myth of racial superiority now permeated concepts of race in the United States and virtually through the English-speaking world. To be *American* was to be *Saxon*."[36] It is with this preamble of claims and approaches that Painter devotes a subsequent chapter to *English Traits*.

Painter describes "Race" as "[t]he core chapter of *English Traits*." Consider this assessment an intensification of Hanlon's "Race is, of course, everywhere in *English Traits*."[37] The first claim brackets Chapter 4 as the heart of the book, while the second suggests a thematic that permeates the entire text. By contrast, if a reader picks up the titular "traits" as a master term instead of "race," and looks to its location in the conversation of natural science, one becomes attuned more to *species*-level categories. Emerson, like Thoreau, is more likely to analogize across the full zoological spectrum (and even reach out to the scale of the cosmos) than to dwell solely on a compare-and-contrast with his fellow *homo sapiens*. From our vantage, Emerson's troping of race – especially in the guise of traits – can prove not just murky and unsystematic but also, as noted, draw alarm and censure. Though Emerson addresses one race – the human race – his sense of traits that appear among some groups of humans and not others (distracted, at times, by now-discredited subfields such as phrenology) appears to function not only as a means for considering fitness (viz., those attributes worthy of our awe and admiration) but also as aids to reflection on how such qualities may affect cultural evolution, including philosophy, literature, religion, and the built environment.

## Conclusion

Emerson was, like so many, perplexed by the nature of inheritance, legacy, and patrimony – in biological, cultural, and political senses. His enthusiasm for the natural sciences, however, especially in their methods of observation, experimentation, description, and drawing morals from the process, prompted him over many decades to formulate, or at least make strides toward, what he called "a natural history of intellect," a project that occupied much of his later writing and thinking and yet remained largely unrealized if not out of reach for him. *English Traits* brings a similar spirit to writing an ethnography of the English people, one devoted to facts as he found them, even if those "facts" might now seem to be conceptually and morally muddled. Despite the antiquated moments, there is much to recommend in *English Traits* in the present day: not just Emerson's wit but also his eclectic commonplacing of those aspects of Victorian-era British life that he deemed worthy of reflection, ones that hardly feel exhausted, but instead remain vital and central, and as they were for Emerson, continually and productively vexing.

In *English Traits*, as elsewhere, Emerson doesn't pursue racial theorizing (in terms of whiteness or otherwise); instead, the topic of race is largely continuous with what may be styled his interest in the biography of nations: how they form over time and are conceived and reconceived by the people of "mixed origin" who inhabit them, who come to be their own representatives (*CW* 5: 27; see, for example, "The National Characteristics of the Six Northern States of America"), or, more emphatically, how they behave when facing troubling political and social unrest, for instance, the evolving conditions of antebellum, Civil War-era, and postbellum America. Rather, Emerson's cannily titled and fittingly capacious "Mind and Manners in the Nineteenth Century" ties together a pair of realms (mind, manners) to Emerson's interest in the natural history of human behavior, especially as it expresses itself intellectually, but also practically. Thus, we may abandon, as Emerson did, the apparent pursuit of some rarefied, hegemonic "English traits," and still find the book *English Traits* a nineteenth-century document exhibiting Emerson at the height of his intellectual powers, poised and curious about the world he inhabited, and wonderfully able to marshal orientation to its variety – both its order and its chaos, its ready revelations and its resident contradictions.

## Notes

1. A half-century elapsed between Philip L. Nicoloff's monograph, *Emerson on Race and History: An Examination of* English Traits (New York: Columbia, 1961) and more recent critical interventions on the book, such as Daniel Koch's *Ralph Waldo Emerson: Class, Race, and Revolution in the Making of an American Thinker* (London: I. B. Tauris, 2012), and my *Emerson's* English Traits *and the Natural History of Metaphor* (London: Bloomsbury, 2013).
2. See Harold Bloom, "Emerson and Influence (1975)," in *Estimating Emerson: An Anthology of Criticism from Carlyle to Cavell*, ed. David LaRocca (New York: Bloomsbury, 2013), 507–18.
3. Emerson, *JMN* 4: 199–200.
4. In *Emerson's Life in Science: The Culture of Truth* (2003), Laura Dassow Walls explores the depth of his research in scientific matters; Lee Rust Brown accounts in *The Emerson Museum: Practical Romanticism and the Pursuit of the Whole* (1997) for the influence of natural scientific methods on the development of Romanticism in its American incarnation.
5. February 28, 1847 (*L* 3: 379–81; and see *L* 8: 108–9).

6. *L* 3: 416–17.
7. Wallace E. Williams, "Historical Introduction" (*CW*: 4: xlix).
8. This included some headline-grabbing (and thus book-selling) controversy: Daniel Koch devoted a chapter – "Emerson Mania" – to its British reception. In addition to Koch's *Ralph Waldo Emerson: Class, Race, and Revolution in the Making of an American Thinker* (esp. Chapter 2), see also Moncure Daniel Conway's *Emerson at Home and Abroad* (1882), Townsend Scudder III's *The Lonely, Wayfaring Man: Ralph Waldo Emerson and Some Englishmen* (1936), William Sowder's *Emerson's Impact on the British Isles and Canada* (1966), and Larry J. Reynolds' *European Revolutions and the American Literary Renaissance* (1988).
9. Howard Mumford Jones, "Introduction," in Ralph Waldo Emerson, *English Traits*, ed. Howard Mumford Jones (Cambridge, MA: Harvard University Press, 1966), ix.
10. Elisa Tamarkin, *Anglophilia: Deference, Devotion, and Antebellum America* (Chicago: The University of Chicago Press, 2008), xxv.
11. Ibid., 272.
12. Ibid., 281.
13. Ibid., 179.
14. Ibid., 281.
15. Ibid., 282. Tamarkin has "Experience" in mind.
16. Christopher Hanlon, *America's England: Antebellum Literature and Atlantic Sectionalism* (New York: Oxford University Press, 2013), 19.
17. Dana Philips, "Nineteenth-Century Racial Thought and Whitman's 'Democratic Ethnology of the Future,'" *Nineteenth-Century Literature* 49:3 (December 1994), 298.
18. Hanlon, *America's England*, 21–22.
19. Ibid., 22.
20. Ibid.
21. Ibid., 36.
22. Carolyn Sorisio, *Fleshing Out America: Race, Gender, and the Politics of the Body in American Literature, 1833–1879*, 125. See also *Emerson's Antislavery Writings*, ed. Len Gougeon and Joel Myerson (New Haven: Yale University Press, 1995).
23. Sorisio, *Fleshing Out America*, 125.
24. Ibid., 32.
25. Ibid., 127.
26. Ibid., 128.
27. Ibid.,130.
28. Nell Irvin Painter, *The History of White People* (New York: W. W. Norton, 2010), 152.
29. Ibid., 158.
30. Ibid., 158–59.
31. Ibid., 162.
32. Ibid.
33. Ibid., 163.
34. See also Len Gougeon, "Race,"in *Ralph Waldo Emerson in Context*, ed. Wesley T. Mott (Cambridge: Cambridge University Press, 2014), 196–203.

35. Robert Yusef Rabiee, *Medieval America: Feudalism and Liberalism in Nineteenth-Century U.S. Culture* (Athens: University of Georgia Press, 2020), 209, n.32. For more in this line of approach, see Susan Castillo, "The Best of Nations? Race and Imperial Destinies in *English Traits*," *Yearbook of English Studies*, 34 (2004), 100–11; and Nell Irvin Painter's "Ralph Waldo Emerson's Saxons," *Journal of American History*, 94:4 (March 2009), 977–85. See also Nicoloff, *Emerson on Race and History*, 120.

36. Painter, *The History of White People*, 164; italics in original.

37. Hanlon, *America's England*, 22.

# 11

## DANIELLE FOLLETT

# "Numbers Wild"
## *Emerson's Poetry and Metaphysics*

He renders all his lore
In numbers wild as dreams ...
"May-Day" (1867) (CW 9: 327)

Emerson's poetry has long mystified readers, who have been puzzled by the fact that a writer of such masterful prose has produced what may seem very uneven poetry. Generations of critics have found his poems, with notable exceptions, to be thematically opaque and stylistically unwieldy.[1] As a condensation of his philosophy, they may seem impenetrable; as they adopt and then balk recognizable meters, they make readers stumble. They often resist a regular rhythmic flow, they are laced with slant rhymes, they change meters midstream, and they twist the syntax. They maintain enough obedience to the rules of meter and rhyme to establish patterns, only to blithely rebel. A general conclusion among the majority of both the admirers and detractors of Emerson's poetry is that he was incapable of writing "better" verse. The admirers focus on the philosophical content, admitting but excusing the flaws in versification, while the detractors list the defects. Both approaches have yielded waves of astonishment that a single author could write such faltering poetry and yet such powerful prose, and conclude in unison that Emerson's "real poetry" is in his prose.

Emerson's own low opinion of his own poetic output has tended to fuel these views. His poetic production was considerable: more than 200 poems were published during his lifetime, fragments of verse are scattered through his journals, and hundreds of drafts are left unfinished in his manuscripts. However, he did not express any clear satisfaction with its quality, even to himself in his journal. The *Poetry Notebooks* witness a certain struggle with composition and record the reworkings and rewrites of his material, even after its first publication.[2] In 1835 he wrote to Lydia Jackson before their marriage: "I am born a poet, of a low class without doubt, yet a poet" (*L* 1: 435). In an unpublished fragment he wrote in the same year:

> Bard or dunce is blest, but hard
> Is it to be half a bard. (*PN* 46)

And in 1862, after decades of poetic composition: "I am a bard least of bards" (*JMN* 15: 308). Emerson considered poetry to be the noblest form of human expression, and did not feel that he arrived at the height of his ideals. Despite his frustrations, he never abandoned poetic work and devoted much of his time in his later years to the preparation of his poetry collection. Emerson was aware that writing poetry was, at least for him, more difficult than writing prose. Although he did not consider himself a good poet, he was faithful to the vocation.

Without taking a stand on the question of quality, we may relativize his laments and allow him the humility and dissatisfaction to which all artists are entitled. Putting Emerson's own opinion of his work aside, it seems that the critics' confusion, though not necessarily their condemnation, is justified. The mixture of regularity and freedom, conventionality and license, provokes perplexity and merits attention. The question of the quality of the poetry, surprisingly central in the reception, is arguably a distraction to its interpretation. The general conclusion that Emerson was incapable of writing "better" verse is predicated upon the assumption that he intended to do otherwise but somehow couldn't. Rather, in this chapter I will take as a starting point the thesis that even if he was dissatisfied, what Emerson wrote was what he intended to write, that his irregularities are not accidents, and that his dissonances, however jarring, were not bloopers or infelicities. I'll focus on the style, rhetoric, and prosody of his poems, then relate this to his metaphysics.

## The Anti-Jingle

Part of the confusion experienced by critics may be due to the fact that Emerson's dissonances may be perceived as not jarring enough. He did not make the leap into free verse and remained solidly attached to certain poetic conventions well after reading Whitman. His poetry has neither the radically unmetered cadences of Whitman, nor the simple regularity of the fireside poets, nor the polished sonority of Poe. Rather, his poetic style offers an idiosyncratic mixture of tradition and innovation and is difficult to classify. An example among many is "Each and All" (1847), which he liked enough to place second in both *Poems* (1847) and *Selected Poems* (1876), just after the opening keynote poem "The Sphinx." Like many of his poems, it is composed in variable iambic tetrameter. Irregularities abound: the many anapests, spondees, headless lines, and extra syllables modulate the meter such that no lines are alike. As Gay Wilson Allen observed about this poem: "The regular-beat line occurs with barely sufficient frequency to keep the pattern from being utterly lost."[3]

> Little thinks, in the field, yon red-cloaked clown,
> Of thee from the hill-top looking down;
> The heifer that lows in the upland farm,
> Far-heard, lows not thine ear to charm;
> The sexton, tolling his bell at noon,
> Deems not that great Napoleon
> Stops his horse, and lists with delight,
> Whilst his files sweep round yon Alpine height;
> Nor knowest thou what argument
> Thy life to thy neighbor's creed has lent.
>
> (CW 9:14, lines 1–10)

Our contemporary ear, accustomed to the irregular rhythms of free verse, cannot easily hear how uneven these lines would have sounded in Emerson's time. The spondees and awkward syntax of the fourth line are characteristic of Emerson's poetry, and the anapest that opens the eighth line (if it is an anapest) is not immediately identifiable. The interrupted rhythm of the headless seventh line mimics the stopping of the horse, but headless lines recur, such as "Beauty is unripe childhood's cheat" (line 38). The poem has fifty-one lines; line nineteen is unrhymed. The many spondees slow the rhythm just as the many anapests hurry it, resulting in a somewhat bumpy and rugged tetrameter, or a patchy regularity. The content is similarly odd and unwelcoming. The voice is disembodied and the archaisms contribute to the vatic tone. The seemingly unrelated detail of the red cloak adds to the unsettled feeling. The inverted syntax of the first line does not facilitate the entrance. And rather than feeling included through the direct address, the reader feels interpolated and perhaps belittled, wondering why they are being told that the clown does not think of them and that their life may not figure in their neighbor's creed. The overall effect is somewhat alienating.

Alongside the opaque opening poem "The Sphinx," this is hardly a warm welcome into the collection. Indeed, the poet is explicit about this refusal to ease the reader's entrance: the heifer "lows not thine ear to charm," perhaps like the speaker, who seems as distant and as elevated as the heifer and the red-clad figure. A certain humor and humility may accompany the hinted link of poet to cow and clown. This militant indifference to the reader, almost explicitly acknowledged, seems to serve as a signpost of what is to come; and this acknowledgment may indicate that the ruggedness of the poetry is not unintentional. And yet, despite this unsympathetic opening, the poem abruptly shifts in the next lines:

> All are needed by each one;
> Nothing is fair or good alone.
>
> (lines 11–12)

Abruptly the alienation and separation yield to correlation and connection. The missing transition might be a "despite all this" or a "still": despite the estrangement and the ignorance of kinship, relation prevails. The simultaneity of particularity and unity, aloneness and togetherness, is at the heart of the poem and Emerson's thought. The voice is unsentimental, impersonal, and brusque, yet recognizes an intimate connection with the unfamiliar neighbor, the distant sexton, and, by implication, the alienated reader.

This frosty welcome to the reader has often been reciprocated in the critical reception. The characteristic ruggedness of Emerson's poetry, well displayed in "Each and All," provoked remarks such as that of James Russell Lowell (1883):

> As for Emerson's verse (though he has written some as exquisite as any in the language) I suppose we must give it up. That he had a sense of the higher harmonies of language no one that ever heard him lecture can doubt. The structure of his prose, as one listened to it, was as nobly metrical as the King James version of the Old Testament, and this made it all the more puzzling that he should have been absolutely insensitive to the harmony of verse.[4]

Similar judgments can be found among many other critics: Oliver Wendell Holmes spoke in 1885 of "the palpable defects of his verse," stating that "Emerson experienced a difficulty in the mechanical part of metrical composition.... He made desperate work now and then with rhyme and rhythm, showing that though a born poet, he was not a born singer.... He is a careless versifier and rhymer."[5] In the same year, Edmund Clarence Stedman spoke of the "awkwardness of Emerson's verse" and "the discords of Emerson's song."[6] In 1896 Brander Matthews called his verse-making "careless" and "slovenly."[7] Julian W. Abernethy, a few years later, agreed: "His poetic expression was imperfect; he lacked skill in managing the technique of verse. His ear was defective, betraying him frequently into halting and struggling rhythms, and rhymes that are sometimes cases of 'actual verbicide.'"[8] But overly regular lines annoyed as well; William P. Trent wrote in 1903: "His ever-recurring and often faulty octosyllabic couplets soon become wearisome."[9] Emerson both mangles the meter and indulges in overly repetitive scansion. O. W. Firkins stated in 1915: "There can be no question as to the frequent and flagrant badness of Emerson's versification."[10]

Fueling the exasperation of critics is the fact that at times, Emerson produced perfectly conventional versification, proving that he could "do" conventional elegance when he tried. Richard Garnett, after lamenting that "the poems offend continually by lame and unscannable lines, and clumsinesses and obscurities of expression," wrote in 1888 that "some few of his poems are actual models of perfection, as, for instance, the lines in the dedication of the Concord monument."[11] "Concord Hymn" is often portrayed as the summit of Emerson's poetic art, as its octosyllabic quatrains presumably contain the right number of irregularities to make the poem neither wearisome nor slovenly. Consistent meters exist in other poems, such as "Musketaquid," a Wordsworthian lyric in gentle iambic pentameter, and "The Rhodora." The fact that very few of his poems follow the various conventions of his day seems to indicate that he tried them and moved on. Difficult to classify, Emerson's poetic production can be understood as experimental for his time; he experimented with both conventional and less conventional forms.

With the modernist revolution in poetics, Emerson's prosodic irregularities raised fewer eyebrows, but the philosophical content of his poems also attracted fewer acolytes. As Hyatt Waggoner wrote in his helpful history of the poems' reception, "To the more perceptive critics [at this time], it gradually became apparent that Emerson's 'faults' as a verse writer would have to be reconsidered. At the same time, the characteristic thought patterns of the twenties were increasingly hostile to Emerson's brand of idealism."[12] Despite this, Emerson's poetry continued to attract readers who were drawn to the philosophy and undeterred by the metric anomalies. Robert Frost praised Emerson's poetry highly, appreciating it for its "freedom" and calling "Uriel" "the best Western poem yet."[13] The New Critics generally ignored Emerson, and by mid-century, Emerson's poetry, never generally acclaimed, fell distinctly out of fashion. It has remained so, as it does not fit easily into the various academic trends of the past decades. The renewal of interest in Emerson as a philosopher since the late 1970s has largely bypassed his quite inescapably metaphysical poetry.[14]

While the earlier critics saw slovenly carelessness in Emerson's poems, the record of the painstaking revisions of the poems certainly suggests that he weighed every detail and chose the elements of his poetry deliberately.[15] And although it is impossible to ascertain an artist's intention, the texts themselves tend to support the thesis that Emerson intentionally warped and stretched his prosody. A number of his poems contain elements of an *ars poetica*; for example, "The House" (1847):

> There is no architect
> Can build as the Muse can;
> She is skilful to select
> Materials for her plan;
>
> (CW 9: 240, lines 1–4)

This may have been one of the poems that exasperated earlier critics. The form and content seem to contradict one another: While the poem speaks directly about poetic skill, the second line breaks from the perfect iambic trimeter of the first and either wrenches the accent or ruptures the rhythm altogether, with its iamb, pyrrhic, and spondee. The poem also evokes conscious deliberation of action. Critics have been swifter to conclude that Emerson was a bungler with no ear for music than to entertain the idea that the skillful Muse could choose such awkward materials, and that her music could willfully incorporate dissonance. The rest of this twenty-four-line poem contains no other striking irregularities, proving that the author is capable of regularity. The first two lines thus seem to offer a subtle and slightly disconcerting wink, saying that even discord should be considered skillful and harmonious, and that it is deliberate.

Some critics have granted that the poems reflect deliberate action but read this calculated dissonance as petulance: Brander Matthews wrote that "Emerson cared too little for form often to write so perfect a poem [as "Concord Hymn"]. The bonds of rime and meter irked him and he broke them willfully."[16] More helpful are the thoughts of Franklin B. Sanborn, who knew Emerson personally:

> He lamented his imperfect use of the metrical faculty, which he felt all the more keenly in contrast with the melodious thoughts he had to utter, and the fitting words in which he could clothe these thoughts. He would have written much more in verse if he had been content with his own metrical expression as constantly as he was delighted with it sometimes. But it is also true that he purposely roughened his verse, and threw in superfluous lines and ill-matched rhymes, as a kind of protest against the smoothness and jingle of what he called "poetry to put round frosted cake."[17]

Sanborn highlights Emerson's dissatisfaction with his poetry, but it is important not to confuse the author's own subjective dissatisfaction and the critics' judgment that he was unable to write better poems. If he deliberately defied the conventions of his time, then he was not measuring his poetic performance against those standards but against some other ideal. Sanborn does not give evidence of the claim that "he purposely roughened his verse," but he was an acquaintance of Emerson's, and it is plausible. The key word in Sanborn's passage is "protest." In 1847, during a time when prosody was a widely discussed art, and during the period of Longfellow and Poe, what did it mean to write "There is no architect/Can build as the Muse can ...."? The lines state more or less explicitly that the muse wrenches accents and/or throws regular rhythm to the wind – and, implicitly, this is how it should be. This minor, almost inconspicuous rebellion is a commentary that is similar to though more subtle than the snub that Emerson reportedly gave to Poe when he called him "the jingle man."[18]

Indeed, Emerson seems, at least to some degree, to want to throw convention to the wind. He elaborates on this aesthetic in "Merlin I":

> Thy trivial harp will never please
> Or fill my craving ear;
> Its chords should ring as blows the breeze,
> Free, peremptory, clear.
> No jingling serenader's art,
> Nor tinkle of piano strings,
> Can make the wild blood start
> In its mystic springs.
> The kingly bard
> Must smite the chords rudely and hard
> As with hammer or with mace ...
>
> (CW 9: 223, lines 1–11)

This anti-jingle manifesto claiming the right to poetic wildness ironically begins in something close to ballad meter, though it soon adopts Emerson's characteristic rhythms including variable line length, spondees and headless lines. The speaker later explicitly defends the position that a poet need not heed any regular meter:

> He shall not his brain encumber
> With the coil of rhythm and number
> But, leaving rule and pale forethought,
> He shall aye climb
> For his rhyme.
>
> (CW 9: 224, lines 29–33)

The poem elucidates Emerson's poetic intentions and the awkwardness of his poems in general. Emerson desired art to follow nature – and nature is not always soft and regular. His favored natural artisan was the wind, which is spontaneous, powerful, "free," and often chaotic. As another *ars poetica*, "Merlin I" reinforces the idea that the ruggedness is intentional.

Emerson develops the idea of powerful poetry in his journal:

> It seems to me often as if a little concentration perchance within the power of circumstances, – mountains, war, danger, or love, might give me that faculty of daring rhyme. I would gladly exchange my languid life for this drumbeat. [...] Rhyme; not tinkling rhyme but grand Pindaric strokes as firm as the tread of a horse. Rhyme that vindicates itself as an art, the stroke of the bell of a cathedral. Rhyme which knocks at prose & dulness with the stroke of a cannon ball. Rhyme which builds out into Chaos & Old night

a splendid architecture to bridge the impassable, & call aloud on all the children of morning that the Creation is recommencing. I wish to write such rhymes as shall not suggest a restraint but contrariwise the wildest freedom. (*JMN* 7: 218, 219)

When Emerson speaks of "rhyme," he uses an expansive definition of the term, which includes meter and poetry itself. This statement should be seen in light of Emerson's particular relationship to the concept of power, understood as an immanent natural and metaphysical force that imbues the world and (he hopes) his poetry with life and intensity.

The excerpt from "Merlin I" states the poet's desire to create works that break the bounds of convention and to wield words as tools or weapons, upsetting any regular running rhythm. This may help explain Emerson's predilection for spondees – one may imagine him slamming his fist on the podium, as was his habit when speaking – and may shed light on lines that provoked the consternation of critics, such as:

Of thine eye I am eyebeam.
("The Sphinx," *CW* 9: 8, line 112)

About this line, Firkins wrote that it would be difficult "to find an appropriate dust-heap on which to cast so dissonant a combination of vowels."[19] The unscannable rhythm is as unconventional as the assonance, and the reader is obliged to slow the pace of reading as each word is emphasized, giving more attention and power to each particle. As Elizabeth Luther Cary wrote, "Surprise is a characteristic element in the larger number of the poems. It piques the imagination and startles the indolent mind.... This perhaps is to be expected in the work of a writer bent upon discarding outworn formulas and the conventions of prosy civilisations."[20] But beyond the desire to throw out conventions, a central tenet of Emerson's philosophy, the frequency of spondees in Emerson's poetry was clearly motivated by his personal taste. He was attracted by early Anglo-Saxon poetry, which, Ralph Yoder explains, provided him with an appreciation for lines containing two strong accents but a variable number of syllables, as well as for alliteration and irregular rhyme. Yoder writes: "From one of his sources, Sharon Turner's *History of the Anglo-Saxons*, Emerson would have learned that abrupt transitions, clipped syntax, periphrasis, and repeated epithets were all characteristic devices of the ancient bards, and that they used no rules for meter."[21] Emerson was a great explorer of distant poetry, removed from him both in time and space, and integrated into his experiments certain elements of foreign sounds. The famous awkwardness of his verse followed the dictates of his own ear, and "Far-heard, lows not thine ear to charm."

In exploring the rough edges of meter and the frontier between convention and poetic wildness, Emerson created an idiosyncratic style that has largely failed to attract readers both during his own time and ours. Even now, readers generally expect either metered or free verse; rhythms should be either regular and scannable, or if meter is to be broken, this should be done thoroughly. But Emerson broke the meter partly – enough to annoy, but not enough to revolutionize. He is neither Wordsworth nor Whitman, but somewhere in between, in a niche of his own. Situated in its historical context, Emerson's poetry reveals the crumbling of meter that led to the modernist revolution and free verse. It shows that poetic style did not suddenly jump from Longfellow to Whitman, but rather that meter was stretched and strained before breaking.

## Quaking in Rhyme

The question then arises: Why did this anti-conventional poet continue to struggle with meter and not discard it altogether, even after reading and highly appreciating Whitman's *Leaves of Grass*? Some of his unpublished poems and first drafts are in free verse. What motivated his choice to play with but ultimately preserve meter? The answer to these questions should be sought in his metaphysical views. For Emerson, nature is the model and the source of art – art should arise from the same natural sources and flow with the same dynamic energy as life; it should be a product of nature's own creative metamorphosis. And although nature is chaotic and "free," it is also marked by regularity, repetition, and "rhyme." Nature works in cycles, variations, and iterations, as well as chaotic surprises. Similarly, according to Emerson, should poetry operate.

> A rhyme in one of our sonnets should not be less pleasing than the iterated nodes of a sea-shell, or the resembling difference of a group of flowers. The pairing of the birds is an idyl, not tedious as our idyls are; a tempest is a rough ode without falsehood or rant; a summer, with its harvest sown, reaped, and stored, is an epic song, subordinating how many admirably executed parts. Why should not the symmetry and truth that modulate these, glide into our spirits, and we participate the invention of nature? (CW 3: 15).

Emerson describes the natural and aesthetic principle of "resembling differ-ence," or variation, based upon his metaphysics of a simultaneity of identity and multiplicity.[22] This Neoplatonic doctrine conceives of the multifarious variety of the universe as emanating from a single divine source or cause. All is related, and all is different. Hence, variation, and not radical alterity or heterogeneity, is the principle that governs both nature and art. The variability found within Emerson's rhyme and meter is more bold and "wild" than Longfellow's, for example, but it nonetheless adheres to the principle of resembling difference. "Modulation" and "iteration," appearing in the citation above, are other favorite terms for this dynamic balance of variety and unity. Yet another is "rhyme," whose scope extends into metaphysics. Since all of nature is a song, for Emerson, its variations are appropriately considered rhymes.

In the epigraph to "Beauty," Emerson writes:

> The quaking earth did quake in rhyme,
> Seas ebbed and flowed in epic chime. (CW 6: 149)

And the epigraph to the essay "The Poet" states that the bard

> Saw the dance of nature forward far;
> Through worlds, and races, and terms and times,
> Saw musical order, and pairing rhymes.
>
> (CW 3: 1, lines 8–10)

Rhymes include not only visible or audible similarities but also analogies of all sorts, as well as correspondences between physical and metaphysical entities. In the following passage in the *Topical Notebooks* under the rubric "Symmetry," Emerson states:

> In the poorest landscape, a little water relieves the monotony. Tis no matter what objects are near it, – a grey rock, a little grass, an elder [sic] bush, a stake, – they instantly become beautiful by being reflected. It is rhyme to the eye, & explains the charm of rhyme to the ear, & suggests the deeper rhyme or translation of every natural object to its spiritual sphere (*TN* 108)[23]

The "deeper rhyme or translation" refers to the Neoplatonic doctrine of reflection and correspondences, which Emerson imbibed from Swedenborg; the visible world is the "dial plate" of the invisible, and every object is the emblem of a moral counterpart.[24] The universe is made up of regularities, relations, polarities, balancing, "compensations" and echoes, and beauty results from these forms of repetition.[25] A poet whose metaphysical philosophy is grounded upon the concept of rhyme and repetition would be unlikely to turn to free verse.

Appropriately, then, Emerson's poem "Merlin I," devoted to reckless poetics, is accompanied by its pair, "Merlin II," which is an ode to rhyme. According to the editors of the *Poetry Notebooks*, "it is probable that 'Merlin II' was written first" (*PN* 858–59).

> The rhyme of the poet
> Modulates the king's affairs;
> Balance-loving Nature
> Made all things in pairs.
>
> (CW 9: 228, lines 1–4)

"The king" could be a reference to the central divine source or cause of all phenomena, personified here just as the poet is a personification of Nature. The sonorous repetitions of rhyme are naturally accompanied by rhythmic regularities. Odd, therefore, is the first line, which has a substantially different rhythm than what follows. Its two amphibrachs (or iamb, anapest, and feminine ending) and ternary rhythm sharply contrast with the binary trochaic meter of the next lines. In this quatrain which praises pairing, one line is evidently anomalous. The poem continues on the topic of feet, clearly referring to meter:

> To every foot its antipode;
> Each color with its counter glowed;
> To every tone beat answering tones,
> Higher or graver;
>
> (CW 9: 228, lines 5–8)

The sudden switch from a trochaic to an iambic rhythm in line five illustrates the content of the line: The iamb is the antipode of the trochee. We have then three lines of regular iambic tetrameter catalectic before the meter breaks down again and we stumble on line 8. But perhaps the ternary rhythm of the eighth line makes it the faraway pair of the first. The assonance between these two lines seems to support that idea, and we can thus see a reflectional symmetry between the two quatrains, which resolves the apparent rhythmic oddities. Reflectional symmetry abounds in nature, and it is appropriate that Emerson find a place for it in a poem that celebrates balance. We may witness again Emerson's subtle humor: The poem gives an argument for unity and symmetry underlying the apparent incongruity and dissonance.

The poem continues by evoking pairs as well as feet, and we see that line 8 is matched not only with line 1 in its meter but also with line 9 in its rhyme:

> Flavor gladly blends with flavor;
> Leaf answers leaf upon the bough;
> And match the paired cotyledons.
> Hands to hands, and feet to feet,
> In one body grooms and brides;
> Eldest rite, two married sides
> In every mortal meet.
>
> (CW 9: 228, lines 9–15)

For a poem whose subject is rhyme, the rhyme scheme is rather unpredictable: In the first fifteen lines, we have A B C B D D E F F G E H I I H. This also reflects Emerson's view of nature: Nature is both regular and irregular; it contains both rhyme and freedom. The pairs it manifests are instances of the relatedness and connectivity that underlie the vastly diverse universe.

Rhyming is linked to justice and to fate: Nemesis and "the Sisters" appear in "Merlin II" as agents of symmetry and periodicity:

> Perfect-paired as eagle's wings,
> Justice is the rhyme of things;
> Trade and counting use
> The self-same tuneful muse;
> And Nemesis,
> Who with even matches odd,
> Who athwart space redresses
> The partial wrong,
> Fills the just period,
> And finishes the song.
>
> (CW 9: 229, lines 37–46)

The necessity of the natural analogies that take the poetic form of rhyme and meter are later explicitly likened to the necessity of destiny: "Subtle rhymes ... sung by the Sisters as they spin" (lines 47, 49). Indeed, the simultaneity of irregularity and regularity in Emerson's poetry may be seen as analogous to the balance he describes between freedom and fate in his late essay, "Fate," where Emerson writes that "fate slides into freedom, and freedom into fate" (CW 6: 20). In this essay, Emerson again links rhyme to destiny: "Some people are made up of rhyme, coincidence, omen, periodicity, and presage: they meet the person they seek" (CW 6: 25). Emerson believed that an element of necessity is found in nature's manner of operation, in keeping with his philosophy that all things spring from the same original cause. This inevitability is manifested in the repetitions and "coincidences" within his poetics.

Emerson thus considers rhyme and meter to be essential elements of the poetics of nature, and it would be inconsistent with his metaphysical philosophy to abandon them. His intention seems to be to manifest the variational metamorphoses of nature in verse, through a mixture of similarity and difference, unity and variety. However, finding a perceptible balance between "rhyme" and freedom is a somewhat delicate endeavor. The question remains whether the aesthetic intention to reflect both nature's regularity and its irregularity is recognizable to the reader. While the concept of a unity of opposites is inspiring in theory, it is not easy to implement in practice; when manifested in the poetic material, regularity and irregularity are a zero-sum game and do not readily overlap. Their simultaneity in poetry creates tension and perhaps confusion. When Emerson pairs the end rhymes "surly bear" and "woodpecker" in an iambic rhyming couplet in "Woodnotes I" (provoking complaints from Oliver Wendell Holmes), the metaphysical grounds for the licence, if such exist in Emerson's intentions, may not be immediately perceptible.[26]

The difficulties of recognizing the aesthetic and metaphysical motivations behind Emerson's rough prosody contribute to the bemused reception it has received. Gay Wilson Allen correctly states that "[His] rhythms should be as free as those of nature – though not, however, altogether "free," since nature obeys laws of her own…. His verse technique is somewhere between the old versification and the new – and, therefore, was perhaps more puzzling to his contemporaries and later critics than the theories and practices of the *vers librists* themselves." The paradox of Emerson's poetic style is well expressed in his poem "May-Day" (1867):

> He renders all his lore
> In numbers wild as dreams…
>
> (CW 9: 327, lines 508–9)

The poem describes a wind harp, a favorite figure for the poet who sings with the voice of nature. In the context of another *ars poetica*, "numbers" possibly refer to meter and rhythm. Or perhaps, for a Platonist, this might evoke the mathematical basis of existence. What are wild numbers? In our usual conception, numbers are regular by definition. The potential meanings of "numbers wild" may evoke the simultaneity of opposites. Whether or not the inconsistencies are comprehensible or the aesthetic intentions perceptible, the result is highly evocative, and the phrase is unforgettable.

Even Oliver Wendell Holmes grants that Emerson's poetic ruggedness is compelling:

> And yet while we note these blemishes, many of us will confess that we like his uncombed verse better, oftentimes, than if it were trimmed more neatly and disposed more nicely. When he is at his best, his lines flow with careless ease, as a mountain stream tumbles, sometimes rough and sometimes smooth, but all the more interesting for the rocks it runs against and the grating of the pebbles it rolls over.[27]

Emerson felt that poetry should both follow "balance-loving Nature" and "ring as blows the breeze"; it should express both symmetry and "the wildest freedom." Hence Emerson's imperfect rhymes and messy meter. As he both denounced "jingles" and refused free verse, he may not have seen any other alternative than to stretch and warp the fabric of prosody, to wander between meters, and to give a liberal license to his rhymes.

## Notes

1. For a lucid history of the reception of Emerson's poetry from its publication until 1974, see Hyatt H. Waggoner, "A Century of Critical Agreements and Disagreements" in *Emerson as Poet* (Princeton: Princeton University Press,

1974) 3–52; for its reception in the nineteenth century, see Sarah Ann Wider, "Contesting the Poet: Emerson in the Nineteenth Century," in *The Critical Reception of Emerson: Unsettling All Things* (Rochester: Camden House, 2000), 53–83.

2. Ralph Waldo Emerson, *The Poetry Notebooks of Ralph Waldo Emerson*, ed. Ralph H. Orth et al. (Columbia: University of Missouri Press, 1986).

3. Gay Wilson Allen, *American Prosody* (New York: American Book Company, 1935), 105.

4. James Russell Lowell, letter to James B. Thayer, December 24, 1883, in *Letters of James Russell Lowell*, ed. Charles Eliot Norton, 2 vols. (New York: Harper and Brothers, 1893), 275.

5. Oliver Wendell Holmes, *American Men of Letters: Ralph Waldo Emerson* (Boston: Houghton, Mifflin and Company, 1885), 311, 327, 329.

6. Edmund Clarence Stedman, *Poets of America* (Boston: Houghton, Mifflin and Company, 1885), 158, 159.

7. Brander Matthews, *An Introduction to the Study of American Literature* (New York: American Book Company, 1896), 102.

8. Julian W. Abernethy, *American Literature* (New York: Charles E. Merrill, 1902), 180.

9. William P. Trent, *A History of American Literature 1607–1865* (New York: D. Appleton and Company, 1903), 332.

10. O. W. Firkins, *Ralph Waldo Emerson* (Boston: Houghton Mifflin Company, 1915), 276.

11. Richard Garnett, *Life of Ralph Waldo Emerson* (London: Walter Scott, 1888), 131.

12. Waggoner, *Emerson as Poet*, 37.

13. Robert Frost, "On Emerson," in *Estimating Emerson: An Anthology of Criticism from Carlyle to Cavell*, ed. David LaRocca (New York and London: Bloomsbury, 2013), 459, 461.

14. Three books on Emerson's poetry have been published, all in the 1970s: Waggoner, *Emerson as Poet*; David Porter, *Emerson and Literary Change* (Cambridge, MA: Harvard University Press, 1978); and Ralph A. Yoder, *Emerson and the Orphic Poet in America* (Berkeley: University of California Press, 1978). Emerson's poetry also figures prominently in Elisa New's study of American poetry and religion: *The Regenerate Lyric: Theology and Innovation in American Poetry* (Cambridge: Cambridge University Press, 1993).

15. See *The Poetry Notebooks of Ralph Waldo Emerson*.

16. Matthews, *Introduction of the Study of American Literature*, 102.

17. Franklin B. Sanborn, "Emerson Among the Poets," in *The Genius and Character of Emerson: Lectures at the Concord School of Philosophy*, ed. Franklin B. Sanborn (Boston: James R. Osgood and Company, 1885), 173–314, 211.

18. Emerson said this during a conversation with William Dean Howells: see Edwin Watts Chubb, *Stories of Authors British and American* (New York: Sturgis and Walton Company, 1910), 285.

19. Firkins, *Ralph Waldo Emerson*, 278.

20. Elizabeth Luther Cary, *Emerson, Poet and Thinker* (New York: G. P. Putnam's Sons, 1904), 211.

21. Yoder, *Emerson and the Orphic Poet in America*, 111–12.

22. See Joseph Urbas, *Emerson's Metaphysics: A Song of Laws and Causes* (Lanham: Lexington, 2016) and *The Philosophy of Ralph Waldo Emerson* (New York: Routledge, 2021).

23. *The Topical Notebooks of Ralph Waldo Emerson*, ed. Ralph H. Orth et al., 3 vol. (Columbia: University of Missouri Press, 1990), 1:108. This passage was taken up later in "Poetry and Imagination," where the final clause about "the deeper rhyme or translation" was omitted CW 8: 24).

24. In the chapter of *Nature*, "Language," Emerson quotes Swedenborg: "The laws of moral nature answer to those of matter as face to face in a glass. 'The visible world and the relation of its parts, is the dial plate of the invisible'" (*CW* 1: 21).

25. See Emerson's essay "Compensation" (*CW* 2: 53–73).

26. See Holmes, *American Men of Letters*, 327.

27. Holmes, 328.

# 12

JOSEPH URBAS

# Writing Emerson into the History of American Philosophy

As Emerson's philosophical rehabilitation enters its fifth decade, the time seems ripe for further reflection on his place in the history of American philosophy. The question that Lawrence Buell raised in a key chapter of his now classic 2003 study – "Emerson as a philosopher?"[1] – has been answered in the affirmative. *Yes*, Emerson *is* a philosopher. Yet there remain a number of unresolved methodological questions for historiography and interpretation – questions raised, moreover, by the rehabilitation process itself as it has unfolded over the last forty-some years, or since Stanley Cavell launched it with his 1978 article "Thinking of Emerson."

## Cavell's Legacy in Emerson's Philosophical Rehabilitation

To give a sense of how Cavell guided the process and defined his own role as philosophical rehabilitator-in-chief. Put simply: Emerson had to be rehabilitated as a founding figure because he, like Thoreau, had been the object of "repression"[2] by an American philosophical tradition extending back to Emerson's own day. Cavell would assume the role of custodian restoring Emerson to his rightful place in the canon, but under terms very different from – and often highly critical of – the prevailing norms of professional philosophy, then and especially now. Cavell was reclaiming Emerson for a new American philosophy. As he asserted in 1983, "there has been no serious move, as far as I know, within the ensuing discipline of American philosophy, to take up Emerson philosophically."[3] That would be Cavell's high mission, which he performed with brio. Emerson studies would never be the same again. Emerson scholars, in philosophy and other fields, owe him an immense debt of gratitude.[4]

The question for us today, however, given the sheer weight of Cavell's name in Emerson scholarship, is the validity of his historical assertion – and above all its rationale. Despite the hedging ("as far as I know"), the gesture seems bold, to say the least. As a matter of historical fact, it is plainly untrue; as one philosopher's *personal* claim to the title of direct heir – which is surely how the line *should* be read – it is breathtaking in its audacity. It is a fine specimen of strong misreading – or rather: an example of *Geistesgechichte*, as Richard Rorty defined the genre of philosophical historiography devoted to canon-revision based on a determination of "which questions" are "*philosophical* questions."[5] Cavell effectively deletes the swathe of history that separates himself from Emerson, eliminating all his predecessors and contemporaries. He redefines philosophy, its problems, and history in a way that reads those figures "out of the canon."[6] The successful philosophical rehabilitation of Emerson under Cavell's aegis fits Rorty's model of canon-revision under the authority of the *Geisteshistoriker*, whose "prerogative" such revision is. Rorty's thesis on the function of *Geistesgeschichte*, that it serves the ends of philosophical "self-justification,"[7] also matches what Cavell is doing in his readings of Emerson – presenting himself as an immediate precursor of his own new way of seeing and doing philosophy.

Let us consider, however, what has been lost in the one-on-one colloquy across time. To give some idea, I propose a non-exhausitve list of American philosophers who worked in "the ensuing discipline" and made "serious" efforts "to take up Emerson philosophically":

William T. Harris (1835–1909)
Anna C. Brackett (1836–1911)
Ellen M. Mitchell (1838–1920)
Charles Sanders Peirce (1839–1914)
William James (1842–1910)
Susan E. Blow (1843–1916)
Josiah Royce (1855–1916)
John Dewey (1859–1952)
Mary Whiton Calkins (1863–1930)
George Santayana (1863–1952)
Ella Lyman Cabot (1866–1934)
W. E. B. Du Bois (1868–1963)
William Ernest Hocking (1873–1966)
Edgar Sheffield Brightman (1884–1953)
Herbert W. Schneider (1892–1984)
John William Miller (1895–1978)
Charles Hartshorne (1897–2000)
Robert C. Pollock (1901–78)
Joseph L. Blau (1909–86)

Henry G. Bugbee, Jr. (1915–99)
[Stanley Cavell (1926–2018)]
John J. McDermott (1932–2018)

Cavell's is but one name at the end of a long and distinguished line of Emerson-influenced philosophers. The term "repression" is thus improper, for Emerson never really left the canon.[8] Even Santayana, whose well-known strictures Cavell cites as the "decisive" moment in the history of Emerson-repression, also called Emerson a "fixed star in the firmament of philosophy," if not of the "first magnitude."[9] That is demotion, to be sure, but hardly an outright exclusion. If evidence were needed of an enduring (if at times discreet) Emersonian presence in the literature, one could point to Hocking's 1929 introduction to *Types of Philosophy*, as well as his contributions to the 1946 textbook and companion-reader *Preface to Philosophy*. Emerson's presence in such classroom texts can be observed at least as far back as 1889 (seven years after his death), with Harris's *Introduction to the Study of Philosophy*, and is notable in introductory works by women philosophers on ethics (Cabot, Calkins) and ancient Greek philosophy (Mitchell).[10]

## Completing the Emersonian Genealogy

I point all this out simply to emphasize that in determining from our present moment how to read Emerson into the history of American philosophy, we must inevitably come to terms with Cavell's legacy. That means questioning his authority where necessary, exercising a *droit d'inventaire* that reviews his various interpretive and historical claims with an eye that is critical rather than "reverential."[11] It means reading back in what he read out, or recovering the rich, complex, and at times fraught history of American philosophical engagements with Emerson up to and including Cavell's generation (the list above) and then forward to the present day (a second list that will emerge as I go along). What I mean by "writing Emerson into the history of American philosophy" is the ongoing scholarly effort to retrace this genealogy in full, which will allow us not only to place Emerson at the head of a largely unbroken succession of philosophical heirs but also – thanks to the neglected figures – to gain a clearer perspective on the kind of philosopher he was and on his particular set of philosophical problems. The work of Emerson-influenced philosophers up to Hocking's day is especially valuable for their proximity to Emerson historically and culturally. The air they breathed was still suffused with Emerson's spirit and – a crucial point to which I shall return – with his *literary* culture. William James's remarks on Emerson's philosophy in *The Varieties of Religious Experience* and his address at the Emerson Centenary, for example, display a rare depth of insight into his religious thought and particularly his concept of the soul.[12] Another striking example is Peirce's description of his own "Schelling-fashioned idealism," whose origins he traced back to his youth "in the neighborhood of Concord, – I mean Cambridge, – at the time when Emerson, Hedge, and their friends were disseminating ideas that they had caught from Schelling."[13] A full sense of the enduring Emersonian presence in the history of American philosophy – including in early, profession-forming initiatives such as the St. Louis Hegelian circle, the Concord School of Philosophy, and Harris's *Journal of Speculative Philosophy* – must reflect such underlying continuities, which are part of a broader rehabilitation. This recovery effort will help us recoup what Douglas Anderson has called the "American loss in Cavell's Emerson." The aim is not to "begrudge Cavell his *own* project"[14] but rather to see it as such – that is, as one philosopher staking a direct personal claim on the Emerson inheritance to further his own conception of philosophy.

Projects that consist in "taking Emerson personally"[15] have certainly produced some of the most original and valuable philosophical engagements to date, but for a complete picture of his thought they require supplementing – and where necessary correcting – by the indispensable work of historical reconstruction and careful textual exegesis backed by a command of the corpus as a whole, and not just of the writings that happen to speak to our present condition.

### Emerson's Legacy in Pragmatism

One effect of Cavell's quarrel with pragmatism – which moved him to the provocation: "What's the Use of Calling Emerson a Pragmatist?" – has been to draw attention away from that tradition's deep continuities with Emerson. Fortunately, however, scholars working in the field have been busy writing that part of the Emerson legacy – and much else besides – back into the history books. John J. McDermott's "Spires of Influence" and Cornel West's *The American Evasion of Philosophy* come to mind, as do Russell Goodman's accounts of Emerson's influence in the thought of Peirce, James, and Dewey, which have explored the same "continuities" in American philosophy.[16] Particularly notable, too, is the massive contribution of Peirce scholars.[17] The magnitude of the Peircean contribution taken as a whole, with the flagship journal *Transactions* consistently serving as one of the best venues for new work on Emerson's philosophy, is something of a curiosity, not to say an enigma. The key is perhaps to be found in Douglas Anderson's hypothesis on the real identity of the American

Scholar – Charles Sanders Peirce![18] Peirce does seem to be a serious contender for the title of "Emerson's greatest philosophical disciple."[19]

The turn away from classical pragmatism's inheritance of Emerson has also had the effect of encouraging present-minded views of his philosophy, which Randy L. Friedman sums up conveniently in "the myth of the Emersonian democrat" – a figure who is "secular, skeptical, relativist, anti-realist, and anti-metaphysical."[20] Not to mention: epistemologizing and language-driven. Where these last two traits are concerned, Deweyan pragmatism – to focus on the particular object of Cavell's aversion – demonstrates its usefulness in shedding retrospective light on Emerson's own project and helping us to avoid anachronisms. Dewey's Emersonian "evasion of epistemology-centered philosophy" (Cornell West) may be found in his critique of "intellectualism," or "the theory that all experience is a mode of knowing" and knowledge "the exclusive avenue of access to what is real."[21] This is what Emerson had already mocked in "Experience" as "intellectual tasting of life," which, like it or not, "will not supersede muscular activity": "If a man should consider the nicety of the passage of a piece of bread down his throat, he would starve" (CW 3: 34). The essay's satirical sketch of "Education-Farm" depicts a world where, as Dewey would later put it, "intellectual experience and its material are taken to be primary," "the cord that binds nature and experience is cut," and the self becomes "an unnaturalized and unnaturalizable alien in the world."[22] Dewey's insistence on the irreducibility of primary, spontaneous experience – "unless there is a breach of historic and natural continuity, cognitive experience must originate within that of a non-cognitive sort"[23] – echoes Emerson's own emphasis in "Circles": "*so to be* is the sole inlet of *so to know*" (CW 2: 189). Dewey's conception of the primary level as "the relatively casual and accidental experience of existence," in contradistinction to the "relatively settled and defined" realm of knowing,[24] also helps avoid misunderstandings about "surprise." Emersonian "casualty" – the "kingdom that cometh without observation," that takes by surprise – does not topple "the kingdom of known cause and effect" (CW 3: 40, 39). Rather, the "newness" points to a basic truth all too easy to forget, that we knowers live in a wide, unpredictable world that brings many an "unlooked-for result" (40). Notwithstanding the exorbitant claims of "epistemology-centered philosophy," knowledge, as Dewey usefully reminds us, "does not encompass the world as a whole."[25]

Neither does language. The linguistic strain of the intellectualism that Emerson criticizes always seeks an "answer in words," even for the kind of question that is properly a "question of things" – of our lived experience of "the facts of to-morrow," for example, which only the incoming "tide of being" can disclose ("The Over-Soul," CW 2: 168). In our preoccupation with language, we tend to disregard such Emersonian reflections on its limits. The eloquent person, Emerson says (echoing Schelling), is not one who "deals in words" but "speaks things."[26] Dewey, as a critic of intellectualism, understood particularly well Emerson's criticism of "chains of discourse" (Dewey's term). He quoted the following lines as evidence: "We have yet to learn, that the thing uttered in words is not therefore affirmed"; "Good as is discourse, silence is better, and shames it"; "If I speak, I confine, and am less.... Silence is a solvent that destroys personality, and gives us leave to be great and universal."[27] To see Emersonian language as omnipotent or relentlessly self-referential is to turn away from things to words. Emerson's ordinary world is then reduced to ordinary language.[28] But it is precisely to things and their relations – "the meal in the firkin; the milk in the pan; the ballad in the street; the news of the boat; the glance of the eye; the form and the gait of the body" ("The American Scholar," CW 1: 67) – that Emerson would redirect our attention, for they are at once the stuff of common experience and the raw material of poetry. If there is evocative power in such images, that is "because this power is in nature" ("Poetry and Imagination," CW 8: 10). In Dewey as in Emerson, the reality of primary experience provides meanings and references with their "existential stuff," since "all meanings intrinsically have reference to natural events."[29] What is characteristic of Emersonian idealism, on Dewey's account, is its reference to "immediate life," to the "facts of the most real world in which all earn their living" – that is, to Emerson's workaday world of "the shop, the plough, and the leger."[30] Dewey of course naturalizes where Emerson spiritualizes the ultimate ground of meaning. But with that distinction in mind, a very Emersonian combination of "piety toward the actual" and "devotion to the ideal" might also describe Dewey's Aristotelian-pragmatist conception of religious faith.[31]

Emerson's influence is also evident in pragmatist aesthetic theory. In *Art as Experience*, for example, Dewey argues for "the emergence of works of art out of ordinary experiences" and for a corresponding theoretical continuity of high and low, just as Emerson had already done in the essay "Art," where he urges that "the distinction between the fine and the useful arts be forgotten" since "we find beauty and holiness in new and necessary facts, in the field and roadside, in the shop and mill."[32] Emerson "anticipated almost all the major themes we identify as pragmatist in Dewey's aesthetics," as Richard Shusterman has shown.[33] Among these, I would cite once again Emerson's "glance of the eye" and "gait of the body," which rematerialize in the "somatic naturalism" of Dewey, James, and Alain Locke[34] – a naturalism that continues in Shusterman's own theory of "somaesthetics." An alternate line of descent in pragmatic aesthetic theory – one with Emersonian ethical implications – takes us from Emerson to Peirce to Hartshorne and to latter-day Peirceans such as Dilworth, Kaag, and Guardiano. On this point, Hartshorne gives us a fine illustration of the usefulness of later philosophers in shedding retrospective light on the Emersonian legacy. In his presentation of the "three normative sciences" (aesthetics, ethics, and logic), Peirce had declared aesthetics to be the "foundation of the doctrine of ethics,"[35] and Hartshorne would later articulate the Peircean position on "the aesthetic basis of ethics,"[36] tracing it back to Emerson's conception of "moral beauty."[37]

### The Centrality of Literature in Cavell's Contribution to Emerson Studies

Two final points on Cavell as *Geisteshistoriker*. On the one hand, I should note an inflection in a late piece on Emerson where he appears somewhat less inclined to dispute pragmatism's rightful share in the inheritance. In his introduction to *Emerson's Transcendental Etudes*, Cavell acknowledges that Emerson was of course "a muse of pragmatism."[38] He even appears ready to reconsider Dewey's case on appeal, as it were – but on one condition: to be declared Emerson's legitimate heir *philosophically*, Dewey has to have made "use of him textually, that is, in the actual detailed work of philosophizing."[39] Presumably that means in a manner very like Cavell's own – and of course very unlike Dewey's. This linguisticizing, self-justificatory, and – where Dewey is concerned – exclusionary criterion remains in place despite the seemingly conciliatory stance.

On the other hand, I would suggest that Cavell's greatest contribution to Emerson studies lies elsewhere, in having posed for historians not the narrowly linguistic but the broadly literary question. The distinction is capital. The first question is irrelevant because anachronistic: Emerson, though "a master of language" both "in poetry and prose," as Hartshorne remarked, quoting from memory a line from the "Ode, Inscribed to W.H. Channing,"[40] is not a philosopher of language in the late twentieth-century sense. The second question is highly pertinent historically inasmuch as it foregrounds the issue of the changed cultural conditions presiding over the later reception and transmission of Emerson's philosophy by the profession – or by distinguished philosophers within it. The real question is: *what if the so-called repression had less to do with Emerson's relation to philosophy than philosophy's relation to literature?* For the simple fact is, in the profession's long historical move toward specialization and away from the wider world of letters – the world of Emerson's American Scholar, after all – it did tend to lose sight of America's greatest poet-philosopher and the culture in which he lived. The list of names I presented as having rightful claims on the Emerson estate is especially noteworthy for being full of philosophers with a broad literary culture – broad enough to accommodate not only the poetic but also the spiritual or religious. The same is often true of contemporary figures working on Emerson, whose philosophy requires a genuine literary sensibility in its commentators – something that, alas, no longer goes without saying in the profession. Cavell, as *Geisteshistoriker*, if not always as a reader of Emerson, deserves the highest praise for having put the *literary* question to philosophy, notably in his ongoing elaboration of a perfectionist canon that reunites the two domains.[41]

## Consequences of the Historical Shift away from Emerson's Literary Culture

I referred just now to the change in cultural conditions of reception and transmission. The philosopher at the end of my list, John McDermott, was keenly aware of the issue, to which his own command of the tradition and personal interest in cultural literacy, together with sufficient historical distance, made him particularly sensitive. In "The American Angle of Vision" (1965), he observed that the "increased sophistication of philosophical discourse ... renders the work of Edwards, Emerson, James, and even Dewey inadequate and infelicitous in expression." This was *not* the case, McDermott remarked, "during the classical phase of American philosophy" up to and including the later work of Dewey, when "the culture and its philosophical tradition shared basic concerns and methods of articulation."[42] Among those methods (*genres* is perhaps a better term for my purposes), I am privileging the *literary* as a shared language and *matière à réflexion*. Peirce took it for granted that his readers or listeners would recognize "the baseless fabric of a vision" as a line from *The Tempest* and "of his eye it is eyebeam" as a reference to Emerson's poem "The Sphinx."[43] Hocking too could count on his readers to identify an apt borrowing from Emerson's "Worship" on the theme of spiritual daring ("I am not afraid of falling into my inkpot") as part of a common cultural heritage.[44] Similarly, William T. Harris's references to George Herbert and Nathaniel Hawthorne were neither strained nor irrelevant to his philosophical arguments. Royce could write perceptively on Shelley and on FitzGerald's *Rubaiyat*; Santayana, on Whitman and Browning; Cabot and Dewey, on Wordsworth and Keats; Hocking and Miller, on Thoreau and Robert Frost; and James, on Whitman and Tennyson. Such references, it is safe to say, were not mere distractions from the real business of philosophy, any more than Susan Blow's studies of

Dante were for readers of the *Journal of Speculative Philosophy*. These were cultivated men and women, and Emerson's literary culture was still theirs, though of course expanded to include new figures and references. Today we perhaps tend to underestimate the formative value of literature for philosophic minds. Charles Hartshorne, one of the great American metaphysicians of the late twentieth century, certainly did not. Consider this:

> Influenced early in my career by Emerson, Wordsworth, and Shelley, who were all more or less Platonists, I have never been able to understand how either materialism or dualism (or atheism) can make sense out of the whole of reality.

> I learned, probably first from Emerson and Wordsworth, and then from Plato, that concern for the good, for value, is involved in all thought, whether we recognize it or not.[45]

Nowhere is the earlier literary sensibility in American philosophy more in evidence – and the contrast with our post-lyrical age in philosophical prose more striking – than in this sort of deep familiarity with Emerson's poetry and the use of it for properly philosophical ends. When William T. Harris gave a lecture on "Emerson's Philosophy of Nature" at the Concord School of Philosophy, he drew heavily, and as a matter of course, on the poetry. Likewise for another lecture he delivered on "Emerson's Orientalism," where "Brahma" was of course given pride of place. "Brahma" is a poem that occurred naturally to Emerson's philosophical heirs: I could also cite Brackett, James, Royce, Hocking, Brightman, Miller, and Hartshorne.[46] "Brahma's" philosophic richness is amply attested by the sheer variety of technical themes these thinkers could discern *in the same lines*: skepticism (Royce), teleology (James), temporality (Miller), absolute idealism (Brightman), freedom versus determinism (Hartshorne), education as discipline of the will (Brackett), and the mind-world relation (Hocking). With the motto to Emerson's essay "History," on the other hand, we can see four philosophers giving very different and self-revealing interpretations of the same theme (i.e., the "one mind common to all individual men"), with Blow seeing the ground of a common faith, Santayana calling it mysticism, Miller seeing in it the American Scholar as "Man of the World," and Du Bois seeing hope for racial progress in the "consciousness of the humanity of all men" – "black and white."[47] Of the philosophical encounters with Emerson's poetry, Peirce's recognition of his own philosophical preoccupations in "The Sphinx" – "firstness" (consciousness as immediate feeling), subject–object identity, and the nature and growth of the symbol – is a topic all by itself.[48] The "poetic ground" of Peirce's own philosophy[49] in the properly aesthetic experience of firstness perhaps also explains why, of contemporary philosophers writing on Emerson, Peirceans (notably Dilworth and Guardiano) distinguish themselves once again, here as exceptions to the prevailing attitude of indifference to Emerson's poetry. This indifference reflects a drastic narrowing of the range of references to the Emerson corpus. Brightman – a major influence on Martin Luther King – could cite Emerson's sermons,[50] Cabot and Hartshorne the *Journals*,[51] and everyone the poetry and essays with equal ease. By contrast, contemporary philosophers, following Cavell's lead, tend to limit themselves to the last, and even then only to a handful. Generally speaking, they are far less familiar with the Emerson *œuvre* than their predecessors. Secularization, as part of the general cultural shift,[52] certainly has something to do with the trend, as shown in the counter-examples of Hocking and Brightman. After them, who among philosophers would bother to give careful consideration to Emerson's essay "Worship"?[53] Who among philosophers could now say, with Cabot, that reading "The Over-Soul," "Self-Reliance," and the Divinity School Address "changed my conception of God"?[54]

## The Stylistic Inheritance

Taking the measure of Emerson's influence on later American philosophers inevitably involves us in the question of *style* – his and theirs – as a substantive philosophical matter and condition of his subsequent reception and transmission. Emerson's diction and phrasing echoed on in the ears and minds of philosophers who came after him. Thus Henry Bugbee, in a momentous passage of his journal where he considers the nature of his work and his commitment to it as a "philosophical exploration": "A sense of what governs this task to which I am held may be suggested by use of a phrase in the manner of Emerson: There is *somewhat absolute* in our experience. All my thinking is haunted by it and bears the burden of thinking it out."[55] Manner is no small matter, philosophically speaking. Like Bugbee after him, Dewey had also refused to separate literary form from philosophical content in Emerson and surmised that if philosophers "extol Emerson's keen calm art and speak with some depreciation of his metaphysic," that was "perhaps because Emerson knew something deeper than our conventional definitions."[56] In any case, it can hardly be accidental that among the most conspicuous Emerson heirs we also find some of the most original American philosophers of the twentieth century – philosophers in whom *style* stands out as consubstantial with their philosophical achievement. After Emerson and James, Hocking is surely one of the finest prose stylists in the American philosophical tradition. In his reflections on education, the Emersonian philosophical and poetic heritage resonates with rare depth and power:

Dealing with growing minds, society perforce domesticates the principle of growth: for self-consciousness is never purely complacent, least of all when its eyes are the critical and questioning eyes of a child, a new vital impulse, unharnassed and unbought.

Youth is metaphysical not because metaphysics is a youthful malady but because youth has metaphysical work to do; it has been attached to the universe through the mental veins of its authorities; now it must win an attachment of its own.[57]

American philosophy formed at the school of Emerson learned the lesson that style at its best is at once the manner and the substance of thinking directly experienced. If Hocking put his personal stamp on the elegant yet unmistakably modern Emersonian period, his student John William Miller would prove himself an accomplished continuator of Emerson's aphoristic style. In "The Scholar as Man of the World," where Miller presents his own philosophy of education, Emerson's living presence makes itself felt not only in the occasion (also a Phi Beta Kappa address), the title (with the obvious allusion to "The American Scholar"), the quotations (e.g., the motto to "History" already mentioned above), and the overall purpose ("to reconcile spontaneity and discipline, as the two elements of education"), but also in the vigor, clarity, and vision of the opening lines: "Education makes us men of the world. It sets before us an ordered totality so that knowledge and action, which are finite and particular, may have a setting in infinity."[58]

## Education: Transmitting the Emersonian Legacy

The list of philosophers I presented at the outset embodies a certain continuity of transmission in the long historical chain of teachers and their students who go on to become teachers in their turn, ready to form the next generation of American scholars up to the present day. Harris mentored Brackett, Mitchell, and Blow; Royce taught Calkins and Cabot; he and James taught Du Bois and Hocking; Hocking taught Hartshorne and Miller; Dewey taught Schneider[59]; Pollock and Blau[60] taught McDermott; and these last three taught the older and younger generations of Emerson-friendly philosophers such as Dilworth and Anderson, whose students now further expand and deepen the legacy. Philosophical writing on Emerson has become with time its own kind of freemasonry, as it gets passed on, often discreetly in a less receptive culture, from generation to generation. This is one of the things that has kept it alive and well as a philosophical tradition – though at times partially submerged – when some imagine it to have disappeared altogether as a result of "repression." The ongoing transmission of a living Emersonian legacy – notably in the pedagogical works and classroom practice of women philosophers[61] – needs to be included as an important chapter in the history books. Given the original minds Emerson has engaged over the years, the chapter might be fittingly subtitled, with a nod to Hartshorne, "Creativity in American Philosophy."

## Notes

1. Lawrence Buell, *Emerson* (Cambridge, MA: Harvard University Press, 2003), 199.
2. Stanley Cavell, "Emerson, Coleridge, Kant (*Terms as Conditions*) [1983]," in *Emerson's Transcendental Etudes*, ed. David Justin Hodge (Stanford: Stanford University Press, 2003), 28; I shall cite Cavell's essays on Emerson in this chapter as *ETE*.
3. Cavell, "The Philosopher in American Life" [1983], *ETE*, 45; see also "Thinking of Emerson" [1978], *ETE*, 12.
4. For a sense of Cavell's influence in philosophy and Emerson studies, notably through his concept of "Emersonian perfectionism," see Richard Eldridge, ed., *Stanley Cavell* (Cambridge: Cambridge University Press, 2003); Russell B. Goodman, ed., *Contending with Stanley Cavell* (Oxford: Oxford University Press, 2005); Alice Crary and Sanford Shieh, eds., *Reading Cavell* (London: Routledge, 2006); Branka Arsić and Cary Wolfe, eds., *The Other Emerson* (Minneapolis: University of Minnesota Press, 2012); and Paul Guyer, "Examples of Perfectionism," *The Journal of Aesthetic Education* 48:3 (Fall 2014): 5–27. On Cavell's influential re-interpretation of the Emersonian "ordinary," see Stephen Mulhall, *Stanley Cavell: Philosophy's Recounting of the Ordinary* (Oxford: Clarendon Press, 1994); and Sandra Laugier, "The Ordinary, Romanticism, and Democracy," *MLN* 130:5 (December 2015): 1040–54.
5. Richard Rorty, "The Historiography of Philosophy: Four Genres," in *Philosophy in History: Essays on the Historiography of Philosophy*, ed. Richard Rorty, J. B. Schneewind, & Quentin Skinner (Cambridge: Cambridge University Press, 1984), 58.
6. Rorty, "The Historiography of Philosophy," 58.
7. On canon-formation as the *Geisteshistoriker*'s "prerogative," see "The Historiography of Philosophy," 60; on *Geistesgeschichte* as "self-justificatory," see 61, 63, 65, 68.
8. I do not refer to Emerson's place in philosophy department curricula, where Cavell's point certainly rings true; but one could say the same thing for other philosophers whose reputations have known a period of eclipse (Hocking comes to mind here).
9. Cavell, "Emerson, Coleridge, Kant (*Terms as Conditions*)," *ETE*, 66. Cavell is referring to Santayana's famous essay "The Genteel Tradition in American Philosophy" (1911). I borrow the Santayana quote from Glenn Tiller, "Emerson, Santayana, and the Two Phases of Transcendentalism: Comments on Beard," *Overheard in Seville: Bulletin of the George Santayana Society* 37 (Fall 2019): 121.
10. William T. Harris, *Introduction to the Study of Philosophy*, ed. Marietta Kies (New York: Appleton, 1889); Mary Whiton Calkins, *The Good Man and the Good: An Introduction to Ethics* (New York: Macmillan, 1918); Ella

Lyman Cabot, *Everyday Ethics* (New York: Henry Holt, 1907); and Ellen M. Mitchell, *A Study in Greek Philosophy* (Chicago: Griggs, 1891). For portraits of the women philosophers on my list (Cabot excepted), see Dorothy Rogers, *America's First Women Philosophers: Transplanting Hegel, 1860–1925* (London: Continuum, 2005); on Cabot, see John J. Kaag, *Idealism, Pragmatism, and Feminism: The Philosophy of Ella Lyman Cabot* (Lanham MD: Lexington Books, 2011).

11. I borrow the term from Joel Porte, "Emerson and Thoreau in France," *The New England Quarterly* 76 (Sept. 2003): 460.

12. William James, "*The Varieties of Religious Experience* and 'Address at the Centenary of Ralph Waldo Emerson, May 25, 1903,'" in *Writings, 1902–1910*, ed. Gerald E. Myers (New York: Library of America, 1992), 36–38, 1119–25.

13. See Charles Sanders Peirce, "The Law of Mind," in *The Essential Peirce: Selected Philosophical Writings, Vol. 1 (1867–1893)*, eds. Nathan Houser & Christian Kloesel (Bloomington: Indiana University Press, 1992), 312–13.

14. Douglas R. Anderson, "American Loss in Cavell's Emerson," in *Philosophy Americana: Making Philosophy at Home in American Culture* (New York: Fordham University Press, 2006), 220.

15. I borrow the phrase from John Lysaker, *Emerson and Self-Culture* (Bloomington: Indiana University Press, 2008), chap. 1.

16. See John J. McDermott, "Spires of Influence: The Importance of Emerson for Classical American Philosophy," in *The Drama of Possibility*, ed. Douglas R. Anderson (New York: Fordham University Press, 2007), 89–105; Cornel West, *The American Evasion of Philosophy: A Genealogy of Pragmatism* (London: Macmillan, 1989), chap. 1 ("The Emersonian Prehistory of American Pragmatism"), 9–41; and Russell B. Goodman, "Epilogue: Some Continuities in American Philosophy," in *American Philosophy before Pragmatism* (Oxford: Oxford University Press, 2015), 234–60, and "Emerson, Romanticism, and Classical American Pragmatism," in *Oxford Handbook of American Philosophy*, ed. Cheryl Misak (Oxford: Oxford University Press, 2008), 19–37.

17. See David A. Dilworth, "Elective Metaphysical Affinities: Emerson's 'Natural History of Intellect' and Peirce's Synechism," *Cognitio: Revista de Filosofia* 11:1 (2010): 22–47; Cheryl Misak, *The American Pragmatists* (Oxford: Oxford University Press, 2013), 10–13; John J. Kaag, "Returning to the Unformed: Emerson and Peirce on the 'Law of Mind,'" *Cognitio: Revista de Filosofia* 14:2 (2013): 189–201; Nicholas. L. Guardiano, *Aesthetic Transcendentalism in Emerson, Peirce, and Nineteenth-Century American Landscape Painting* (Lanham, MD: Lexington, 2017); and Rossella Fabbriches, "Spinoza, Emerson, and Peirce: Re-Thinking the Genealogy of Pragmatism, 2019 Presidential Address," *Transactions of the Charles S. Peirce Society* 55:2 (2019): 103–18.

18. Douglas R. Anderson, "Peirce and Pragmatism: American Connections," in *The Oxford Handbook of American Philosophy*, ed. Cheryl Misak (Oxford: Oxford University Press, 2008), 38–41.

19. I am quoting Dilworth's article on Peirce in Tiffany Wayne, ed. *Critical Companion to Ralph Waldo Emerson: A Literary Reference to His Life and Work* (New York: Facts on File, 2010), 367.

20. Randy L. Friedman, "Traditions of Pragmatism and the Myth of the Emersonian Democrat," *Transactions of the Charles S. Peirce Society* 43:1 (2007): 155–56.
21. Cornel West, 5; John Dewey, *Experience and Nature*, ed. Jo Ann Boydston (Carbondale, IL: Southern Illinois University Press, 1988), 28.
22. Dewey, *Experience and Nature*, 29, 30.
23. Ibid.
24. John Dewey, *The Quest for Certainty: A Study of the Relation of Knowledge and Action*, ed. Jo Ann Boydston (Carbondale: Southern Illinois University Press, 1984), 236.
25. Dewey, *The Quest for Certainty*, 236.
26. Emerson, "Eloquence," *CW* 7: 48 (on Schelling, see *JMN* 3: 398, 6: 195, and 11: 273). The ultimate source of eloquence is not to be found in language but rather in "character" and "the moral sentiment" (*CW* 7: 48–50).
27. John Dewey, "Ralph Waldo Emerson – The Philosopher of Democracy," in *John Dewey, The Middle Works, 1899–1924, Volume 3*, ed. Jo Ann Boydston (Carbondale: Southern Illinois University Press, 1977), 186. Dewey quotes "Spiritual Laws" (*CW* 2: 88–89), "Circles" (*CW* 2: 184), and "Intellect" (*CW* 2: 202–3).
28. For an example of Cavell's linguisticism, see his interpretation of Emerson's claim that "character teaches above our wills" ("Self-Reliance," *CW* 2: 34), which turns the essay's critique of voluntarist ethics into an affair of "writing" and "reading," *A Pitch of Philosophy: Autobiographical Exercises* (Cambridge, MA: Harvard University Press), 150–51. See also Anderson, "American Loss," 219; and Friedman, "Traditions of Pragmatism," 169.
29. Dewey, *Experience and Nature*, 219, 220.
30. Dewey, "Ralph Waldo Emerson," 189; Emerson, "The American Scholar," *CW* 1: 67.
31. Dewey, *The Quest for Certainty*, 306. Dewey's conception of religious faith is based on his pragmatist reworking of Aristotelian potentiality and actuality, with nature providing "potential material for the embodiment of ideals" (p. 302).
32. John Dewey, *Art as Experience*, ed. Jo Ann Boydston (Carbondale: Southern Illinois University Press, 1987), 12; Emerson, "Art," *CW* 2: 218.
33. Richard Shusterman, "Pragmatism," in *Routledge Companion to Aesthetics*, 3rd ed., eds. Berys Gaut & Dominic McGiver Lopes (London: Routledge, 2013), 103; see also "Emerson's Pragmatist Aesthetics," *Revue internationale de philosophie* 53 (1999), 87–99.
34. Shusterman, "Pragmatism," 97–98.
35. Charles S. Peirce, "The Maxim of Pragmatism," in *The Essential Peirce: Selected Philosophical Writings, Vol. 2 (1893–1913)*, ed. Nathan Houser et al. (Bloomington: Indiana University Press, 1998), 143.
36. Charles Hartshorne, *The Zero Fallacy, and Other Essays in Neoclassical Philosophy*, ed. Mohammad Valady (Chicago: Open Court, 1997), 199.
37. Hartshorne, *The Zero Fallacy*, 199–200.
38. Cavell, "Introduction," *ETE*, 7.
39. Cavell, "Introduction," *ETE*, 9, my emphasis.
40. Hartshorne, *The Zero Fallacy*, p. 8. Hartshorne quotes lines 50–51 of the poem: "Things are in the saddle, / And ride mankind" (*CW* 9: 148, ll. 50–51).

41. For an outline of a perfectionist canon, see *ETE*, 223. On Cavell as an often unreliable interpreter of Emerson's words, see my "How Close a Reader of Emerson is Stanley Cavell?" *Journal of Speculative Philosophy* 31.4 (2017): 557–74.

42. McDermott, "The American Angle of Vision, Part 2," in *The Drama of Possibility*, 61, 60.

43. Charles S. Peirce, "Of Reasoning in General," *The Essential Peirce: Selected Philosophical Writings, Vol. 2*, 26. On Peirce's allusion to "The Sphinx," see Nicholas L. Guardiano, "Charles S. Peirce's New England Neighbors and Embrace of Transcendentalism," *Transactions of the Charles S. Peirce Society* 53:2 (2017): 232.

44. Emerson, "Worship," *CW* 6: 107; William Ernest Hocking, *Human Nature and Its Remaking* (1912; New Haven, CT: Yale University Press, 1963), 103.

45. Charles Hartshorne, *The Darkness and the Light: A Philosopher Reflects upon His Fortunate Career and Those Who Made It Possible* (Albany: SUNY Press, 1990), 30, 26.

46. Anna C. Brackett, *The Science of Education* (St. Louis: Jones, 1878), 25; William James, "Remarks on Spencer's Definition of Mind," in *Writings 1878–1899*, ed. Gerald E. Myers (New York: Library of America, 1992), 905; Josiah Royce, *The Spirit of Modern Philosophy, in The Basic Writings of Josiah Royce, Vol. 1: Culture, Philosophy, and Religion*, ed. John J. McDermott (New York: Fordham University Press, 2005), 298; William Ernest Hocking, *Types of Philosophy*, rev. ed. (1929; New York: Scribner's 1939), 277, 374; Edgar Sheffield Brightman, *An Introduction to Philosophy* (New York: Henry Holt, 1925), 244; John William Miller, "Mistrust of Time," in *The Task of Criticism: Essays on Philosophy, History, and Community*, ed. Joseph P. Fell, Vincent Colapietro, & Michael J. McGandy (New York: Norton, 2005), 176; and Charles Hartshorne, *Creativity in American Philosophy* (Albany: SUNY Press, 1984), 48.

47. Emerson, "History," *CW* 2: 1–3; Susan E. Blow, *Symbolic Education: A Commentary on Froebel's "Mother Play"* (New York: Appleton, 1895), 34; George Santayana, "Emerson," in *The Essential Santayana: Selected Writings*, ed. Martin Coleman (Bloomington: Indiana University Press, 2009), 523; Du Bois, quoted in Robert W. Williams, "'The Sacred Unity in All the Diversity': The Text and a Thematic Analysis of W. E. B. Du Bois' 'The Individual and Social Consciousness,'" *Journal of African American Studies* 16:3 (2012): 459, 471; and Miller, "The Scholar as Man of the World," in *The Task of Criticism*, 321.

48. See Peirce, "What Is a Sign?" in *The Essential Peirce: Selected Philosophical Writings, Vol. 2*, 10; *The Charles S. Peirce Papers, Vol. 1*, ed. Charles Hartshorne and Paul Weiss (Cambridge, MA: Harvard University Press, 1931), 310. See also David Dilworth's reading of "The Sphinx" in Wayne, ed., *Critical Companion to Ralph Waldo Emerson*, 246–48.

49. See Ivo A. Ibri, "Reflections on the Poetic Ground in Peirce's Philosophy, *Transactions of the Charles S. Peirce Society* 45:3 (2009): 273–307.

50. Edgar Sheffield Brightman, *A Philosophy of Religion* (New York: Prentice Hall, 1940), 419.

51. Cabot, *Everyday Ethics*, 149; Hartshorne, *The Zero Fallacy*, 200.

52. On secularization as an obstacle to our understanding of Emerson, see Randy L. Friedman, "Religious Self-Reliance," *The Pluralist: The Journal of the Society for the Advancement of American Philosophy* 7:1 (2012): 27–53.

53. See Edgar Sheffield Brightman, *Religious Values* (New York: Abingdon Press, 1925), 174–75, 177–78, 188, 204. Dilworth is an exception here; see his article on "Worship" in Wayne, ed., *Critical Companion to Ralph Waldo Emerson*, 293–95.

54. Quoted in Kaag, *Idealism, Pragmatism, and Feminism*, 25.

55. Henry G. Bugbee, Jr., *The Inward Morning: A Philosophical Exploration in Journal Form* (New York: Harper, 1968), 131; see also 132–35.

56. Dewey, "Ralph Waldo Emerson," 188.

57. Hocking, *Human Nature and Its Remaking*, 253, 275.

58. Miller, "The Scholar as Man of the World," *The Task of Criticism*, 327, 312.

59. See Herbert W. Schneider, "American Transcendentalism's Escape from Phenomenology," in *Transcendentalism and Its Legacy*, ed. Myron Simon & Thornton H. Parsons (Ann Arbor: University of Michigan Press, 1966), 215–28; for a more recent anti-phenomenalist reading of Emerson, see Misak, *The American Pragmatists*, 12.

60. See Robert C. Pollock, "Ralph Waldo Emerson, 1803–1882: The Single Vision," in *American Classics Reconsidered: A Christian Appraisal*, ed. Harold C. Gardiner (New York: Scribner's, 1958), 15–58; and Joseph L. Blau, "Emerson's Transcendentalist Individualism as a Social Philosophy," *The Review of Metaphysics: A Philosophical Quarterly* 31:1 (September 1977): 80–92, and *Men and Movements in American Philosophy* (New York: Prentice Hall, 1952).

61. See for example Anna C. Brackett, ed., *Poetry for Home and School* (New York: Putnam, 1881), with its epigraph from Plato's *Republic*; Susan E. Blow, *Symbolic Education*; Ella Lyman Cabot, *Ethics for Children* (New York: Holt, 1907) and *Our Part in the World* (Boston: Beacon Press, 1918); and Marietta Kies's edition of Harris's *Introduction to the Study of Philosophy*.

# 13

MARK NOBLE

# Emerson and Science

Emerson opens "Beauty," the penultimate essay in his 1860 *The Conduct of Life*, with a strange analogy. "The spiral tendency of vegetation," he opines, "infects education also. Our books approach very slowly the things we most wish to know." The essay's hook proposes that the slowness of books, or the grinding pace of intellectual development, recalls the creeping slowness of plant growth. Emerson appears to be arguing that empirical research becomes tedious when it pursues gradually comprehensive models of the physical world, neglecting to climb for higher truths. Like tangled vines on a forest floor, our scientific pursuits twist and turn. Or, the professional study of nature, charged with disclosing those "secret magnetisms" linking our sensations and insights with cosmic energies, too often falls to "frivolous and skeptical" reductions. "Chemistry takes to pieces," he complains, "but it does not construct" (CW 4: 150).

Emerson's 1860 readers likely recognized the Romantic critique of practical knowledge, framed as impatience with the institutions shaping modern thought. But the rebuke of science that preoccupies the first five paragraphs of "Beauty" stands apart. At times, it borders on invective: "We should go to the ornithologist with a new feeling if he could teach us what the social birds say when they sit in the autumn council, talking together in the trees. The want of sympathy makes his record a dull dictionary. His result is a dead bird" (CW 6: 150). On the one hand, the complaint prefaces a turn to aesthetic theory, the essay's topic, which Emerson hopes "may yet light a conflagration" in the ranks of mid-century empiricists, compelling them to reach for the canopy (CW 6: 152). On the other hand, the attacks on botany and ornithology reflect a complex ambivalence about the history and trajectory of professional science. He claims that we too often isolate natural objects, reducing them to elements in a classificatory system: "The bird is not in its ounces and inches, but in its relations to Nature" (CW 6: 150). And yet, as his readers also knew, Emerson's own efforts to bring those "relations" into view drew frequently and passionately on the revelatory potential of scientific insights.

Scholars have thoroughly documented, for example, Emerson's lifelong fascination with theories and discoveries spanning a wide range of empirical disciplines.[1] Alongside botany and ornithology, he tracked developments in astronomy, chemistry, comparative anatomy, embryology, entomology, geology, hydraulics, optics, meteorology, molecular physics, physiology, and zoology. "Open any recent journal of science," he proposes in *Nature*, "and weigh the problems suggested concerning Light, Heat, Electricity, Magnetism, Physiology, Geology, and judge whether the interest of natural science is likely to be soon exhausted" (*CW* 1: 25). The breadth and depth of Emerson's reading in contemporary natural history, and his fascination with its world-altering power to shape modern life, mean that his interests in empiricism cannot be cleanly separated from his theories of human experience and moral philosophy. So what accounts for the dismissive tone and combative posture with which he opens the 1860 essay? Does it amount to a rhetorical gesture or a substantive critique? As often with Emerson's prose, drawing out answers reveals a knot of ideas and attachments.

### The Unifying Tendency of Botanical Research

Consider that "spiral tendency," for instance. The phrase refers to a speculative turn in Goethe's theory of plant morphology, which Emerson read avidly. Late in his 1790 *Metamorphosis of Plants*, Goethe assigns the shaping and unshaping of vegetal sex organs to what he calls "the spiral vessels." He notes that while they often first appear locked in sap or wrapped in sepals, the coiled, sinuous organs at the hearts of flowers never fail to unpack their stamens and styles. Documenting the transformations of membranes and filaments comprising processes of fructification reveals the ubiquity of "spiral" elements acting, as Goethe puts it, "like elastic springs." Botanical observation, according to Goethe, hopes to glimpse just these sorts of organizing principles – the hidden source code giving rise to natural history. More a formal property than a specific component of flowering and fruiting bodies, "spiral vessels" animate the efflorescence we recognize as vegetal growth.[2]

Goethe returns to this idea in 1830, just a few years before Emerson's own botanical epiphany during an 1833 visit to the Jardin des Plantes at the Paris Muséum national d'Histoire naturelle. In Goethe's later writing, spiral vessels resemble components in a wider "system" comprising "the element that develops, expands, nourishes" as plants take and change shape. Here, the tendency to twist, unfold, and flower both collaborates and contends with a "vertical system" responsible for "the enduring element, the solid, the lasting" components of botanical structures. If the spiral tendency in vegetation governs the convolutions of reproduction, the vertical tendency offers the fibrous material on which so much climbing, branching, and flourishing depend. Together, the two elements create the "lasting unity" characteristic of healthy plants. Wherever one tendency predominates and the systems fall out of balance, we get botanical "monstrosities" that collapse under their own weight or stretch out of proportion.[3]

For Goethe, these sorts of speculative insights demonstrate why the study of morphology should be considered a science in its own right. He contends that studying the growth of plants uncovers features of a unified gestalt, a generative form underlying disparate bodies and linking various species. Botanists, in other words, document patterns of plant metamorphosis while tracing an invisible framework – what Thomas Pfau calls "a phenomenal template" – from which vegetal organisms flow.[4] While taxonomic approaches to botany catalog and distinguish *particulars*, studying the habits of change that traverse classes and categories illustrates the importance of *general* tendencies linking disparate observations. In Goethe's writing, that underlying form looks less like a Platonic ideal, or archetypal plant, and more like an intuitive method for linking patterns of growth and varieties of organic transformation. Morphology thus demonstrates its legitimacy "by drawing together what lies scattered among [other sciences] and establishing a new standpoint from which the things of nature may be readily observed."[5] We need a science of changing shapes, Goethe argues, to witness the coordinating engine of the natural world's dynamism.

Perhaps then it is no surprise that this model of plant development also entails a theory of gender. Goethe's "spiral system," said to govern nourishment and reproduction, unfolds in a series of intricate, ephemeral displays. His "vertical system," conversely, introduces rigidity, stability, and a reliable structure on which to hang so many flowers. The gestalt of vegetal development thus includes a homology linking the tendencies governing botanical transformation to several of the commonplace tropes said to govern heterosexual human relationships. To be clear, Goethe is not saying that the sexed parts of plants inherit the properties of one or the other "system." In 1790, he is explicit that tendencies are not bodies; the organs we call male and female are alike the products of "spiral vessels." He rather means to suggest, however implausibly, that locating a gendered binary in the substructure of every botanical transformation should prompt observers "to conceive of all vegetation as androgynous from the root up."[6] By drawing a primordial, pre-sexed plant into view, Goethe posits botany as a kind of Romantic phenomenology – a wider field of inquiry in which all changes to a body's shape or state are enlivened by careful, intuitive observations of its mechanics.

All of this Goethean backstory only deepens the strangeness of Emerson's comment at the beginning of "Beauty." When he claims that "the spiral tendency in vegetation infects education," Emerson seems to align *all* modern science with just the fruiting, feminine half of Goethe's morphological system. Stranger still, he offers the analogy as an opening move in his widest-ranging and longest-winded critique of scientific disciplines:

> What a parade we make of our science, and how far off and at arm's length it is from its objects! Our botany is all names, not powers: poets and romancers talk of herbs of grace and healing, but what does the botanist know of the virtues of his weeds? The geologist lays bare the strata and can tell them all on his fingers; but does he know what effect passes into the man who builds his house in them? (*CW* 6: 150)

The substance of the complaint is that contemporary scientific disciplines address their objects too narrowly, disregarding Goethe's transdisciplinary approach and setting the study of nature on predictable, unimaginative paths. But this seems an odd point to make by way of analogy to the vital curvature of plant growth. Emerson understood that botany, alongside the emerging discipline of organic chemistry, was in fact unlocking healing powers in plants unimagined by Goethe. And he knew that geologists and natural historians of his own generation were developing ever-richer accounts of the relations linking mineral strata and human lifeways. The combative rhetoric is striking not least because it was so often Emerson's own interest in the history of science, with its accretive turns and twisting paths, that compelled him to essay those "powers" and "virtues."

## The Cabinet of Occult Relations

One way to make sense of Emerson's "spiral tendency" quip would be to locate its place in his wider commentary on the role of scientific inquiry in nineteenth-century culture – a story that begins nearly three decades earlier. Following his return from Europe in 1833, Emerson composed and delivered a sequence of five lectures on contemporary science, each of which reflects his still palpable enthusiasm for the insights generated by the Paris museum encounter. The first of these lectures, "The Uses of Natural History," delivered in November to the Society of Natural History at the Masonic Temple in Boston, draws directly from journal entries recorded during his European trip. In a famous passage, the classification and presentation of diverse specimens in museum cabinets generate an ecstasy so overpowering it compels the speaker, a Unitarian minister already wavering in his faith, to declare a change in profession:

The universe is a more amazing puzzle than ever, as you look along this bewildering series of animated forms, the hazy butterflies, the carved shells, the birds, the beasts, insects, snakes, fish, and the upheaving principle of life every where incipient, in the very rock aping organized forms. Whilst I stand there I am impressed with a singular conviction that not a form so grotesque, so savage, or so beautiful, but is an expression of something in man the observer. We feel that there is an occult relation between the very worm, the crawling scorpions, and man. I am moved by strange sympathies. I say I will listen to this invitation. I will become a naturalist.[7]

But of course Emerson does not become a naturalist – at least not in the vocational sense explored by these early lectures. In the years that coincide with the composition and publication of *Nature*, he instead becomes something more like a cultural theorist and critic of modern science. In "Uses," for instance, he outlines five main benefits of professional science: good health to researchers who spend time outdoors; technological advancements enjoyed by civilization; delight experienced by enthusiasts like himself; intellectual and moral growth sponsored by the delight; and, most importantly, a comprehensive vision of our own "true place in the system of being" (*EL* 1: 23). This final virtue of scientific progress, in which the study of nature can "explain man to himself," would become the central tenet in a career-long effort to illustrate that "occult relation" linking scorpions and persons. "The laws of moral nature," he claims in the lecture's conclusion, "answer to those of matter as face to face in a glass" (*EL* 1: 24).

Just a few weeks later, Emerson delivered "The Relation of Man to the Globe" to another audience in Boston, claiming that contemporary science describes a physical world at once designed for our uses and, crucially, responsible for our delight in "the choral harmony of the whole" (*EL* 1: 49). A few days after that, he presented "Water," an account of the world-shaping promise of discoveries in the emerging disciplines of molecular physics and hydraulics, to the Boston Mechanics Institution. Then in May 1834, he returned to the Boston Society to present "The Naturalist," a culminating reflection on what binds the methods of empirical research to the transformative insights and "strange sympathies" responsible for initiating this flurry of activity. Despite relying on distinctive techniques focused on specific classes of objects, the several fields comprising natural history share a logic of methodological ascension, which compels researchers to climb from particular to general – "to ascend from nomenclature to classification; from arbitrary to natural classes; from natural classes, to primary laws; from these, in an ever narrowing circle, to approach the elemental law, the *causa causans*, the supernatural force." (*EL* 1: 80). To characterize the vocational summons animating modern science, in other words,

Emerson contends that the study of material things must open onto that "great Network of organized beings made of our own flesh and blood with kindred functions and related organs." (*EL* 1: 75).

"The Naturalist" is also distinguished, however, by the introduction of a tension between the ends and the means of scientific discovery. In passages that contrast what he calls the "aids of Science" with the "evils of Science," Emerson begins framing the critique of instrumental empiricism that would recur throughout his writing career. The cutting-edge techniques that make interpreting and connecting natural phenomena so exhilarating also risk drawing attention away from the enlarging, humanizing project. The observer who fixates on the objects of analysis as if they were ends in themselves risks "losing sight of the end of his inquiries in the perfection of his manipulations" (*EL* 1: 79). Of course, such manipulations include the laboratory experiments and museum collections that so thrilled Emerson in the first place. "To this end of furnishing us with hints, intimations of the inward Law of Nature," he admits, "a cabinet is useful." But contemporary science must not confuse the trees for the forest, and the surest method for avoiding such confusion involves constant reminding that science is self-study – that "man is the centre from which all our speculations depart" and, in the end, the principal object of every inquiry (*EL* 1: 81).

In "Humanity of Science," the fifth early lecture, Emerson further develops this account of the continuity linking human experience and the nonhuman elements spanning empirical disciplines. "One can feel that we are brothers of the oak and the grass," he argues, "that the vegetable principle pervades human nature also."[8] Those "strange sympathies" generated by the Paris museum here become the foundation for a theory of human knowledge in which our sensations share a logic with the contours of the material world. Because "nature proceeds from a mind analogous to our own," as Goethe implied by linking vegetal and human sexuality, the several foci comprising modern experience are "pervaded by radical analogies, so that music, optics, mechanics, galvanism, electricity, magnetism are only versions of one law" (*SL* 21). The analogy correlating the mind of the observer to the mind of the world then underwrites two rather striking assertions. First, the increasingly sophisticated instruments that seem to unlock scientific discovery in fact resemble mere prostheses for observing facts elsewhere written "in colossal characters" we are still learning to read: "Our microscopes are not necessary. They are a pretty toy for chamber philosophers, but nature has brought every fact within reach of the unarmed eye somewhere." And second, the measure of such insights reflects "the transference of that trust which is felt in nature's admired arrangements, light, heat, gravity, – to the social and moral order" (*SL* 22). Or, as he puts it in *Nature*, published in

228

September of the same year: "The axioms of physics translate the laws of ethics" (*SL* 24).

In these early lectures, Emerson seems at once enchanted and unnerved by the proliferation of new disciplines reshaping secular knowledge in the first half of the nineteenth century. As scientific inquiries, methods, and discoveries continue to multiply and variegate, introducing a new array of professional avenues for researchers, he assumes a role as the critic who reminds that any study of the parts should envision the whole. Each lecture establishes Emerson's bona fides as a follower of new developments, and then each lecture reminds listeners that while modern science advertises astonishing novelty and diversity, its primary function remains the demonstration of a "common law that pervades nature from the deep centre to the unknown circumference" (*SL* 24). Even as it reflects his exhilaration, the early writing contends with possible disorientation by insisting that what may look like unprecedented increases in the variety and power of empirical disciplines are in fact novel demonstrations of Goethe's thesis that the world consists of one mind:

> The history of science in the last and present age teems with this truth. The multitude of problems; the stimulated curiosity with which they have been pondered and solved, the formation of societies, the expeditions of discovery and the surveys, the gifts which science has made to the domestic arts are signs that the human race is in sympathy with this omnipresent spirit. (*SL* 29)

But we also adhere to this underlying continuity linking disparate breakthroughs, and the analogic method that draws it into view, to ensure that facts do not "usurp the throne of the mind" – to mitigate, in other words, that habit of thought in which "men of detail ... cling to the cadaverous fact until Science becomes a dead catalogue" (*SL* 30).

This ambivalence linking the revelatory potential and disconcerting power of scientific innovation would recur, though less in concentrated ways, throughout Emerson's career. In one of his last major essays, the 1872 "Poetry and Imagination," the conceit of a universal mind once again sponsors a humanizing generalization of nonhuman particulars:

> All multiplicity rushes to be resolved into unity. Anatomy, osteology, exhibit arrested or progressive ascent in each kind; the lower pointing to the higher forms, the higher to the highest, from the fluid in an elastic sack, from radiate, mollusk, articulate, vertebrate, up to man; as if the whole animal world were only a Hunterian museum to exhibit the genesis of mankind. (*CW* 8: 3–4)

Here, the discovery that a "progressive" alignment links corporeal forms leads not just to the merger of bodies in an evolutionary sequence but to a poetic conflation of the museum with its specimens, all of which point to us. A few pages later, however, "Science was false by being unpoetical. It assumed to explain a reptile or mollusk, and isolated it, – which is hunting for life in a graveyard" (*CW* 8: 5).

The complaint with which Emerson opens "Beauty" in 1860 reflects this ongoing negotiation between the techniques and the *telos* governing new research. "Bugs and stamen and spores, on which we lavish so many years, are not finalities," he insists, "and man, when his powers unfold in order, will take Nature along with him, and emit light into all her recesses" (*CW* 6: 150). And yet it remains difficult to discern just how seriously to take his assertion that "our science lacks a human side." When Emerson claims that "[t]he human heart concerns us more than the poring into microscopes," he also reminds just how fascinating he finds those microscopic features of our hearts disclosed by laboratory analysis. When he claims that our individual potential "is larger than can be measured by the pompous figures of the astronomer," he also illustrates the challenges of thinking humanism at an astronomical scale (*CW* 6: 150). Tracing the contours of Emerson's critique of science thus means acknowledging this push and pull between the enervating particulars that drew him to those cabinets in 1833 and his insistence on a "common law" idealism that supersedes the particularity and summarizes the whole. The complaint cannot be divorced, in other words, from his fascination with the "occult relation" said to galvanize the would-be naturalist and compel so many returns to those "pompous figures" on display in contemporary journals.

### Torrents of Experience

A second, related way to make sense of the "spiral tendency" comment would be to read it, somewhat more seriously, as a tacit reference to a Goethean scientific method that also emerges in some of Emerson's most striking prose. Perhaps his claim that the twisting logic of plant reproduction "infects education" amounts not just to a critique of popular science, though one surely does follow. Perhaps the quip also implies that our grasp of the "occult relation" said to inspire naturalists and set natural history on its upward trajectory cannot but twist and turn. What if the infection is, for better or worse, endemic? In this reading, our contamination by the spiral tendency looks less like a detour from than a feature of our effort to understand the natural world. Of course, reading the analogy this way means turning to a rather different set of moments spanning the preceding decades of Emerson's writing life.

Scholars often describe "The Method of Nature," an 1841 lecture, as an early turn in Emerson's thinking.[9] Presented to an audience in Maine, just a few months after the publication of his *First Series* essays, the address returns to the question about the balance between empirical and intuitive methods for comprehending natural phenomena. While the earlier works foreground the necessary continuity underlying disparate observations, the new lecture shifts focus to address the difficulty of reckoning with the material world's incessant discontinuity:

> That rushing stream will not stop to be observed. We can never surprise nature in a corner; never find the end of a thread; never tell where to set the first stone. The bird hastens to lay her egg: the egg hastens to be a bird. The wholeness we admire in the order of the world is the result of infinite distribution. Its smoothness is the smoothness of the pitch of the cataract. Its permanence is a perpetual inchoation. (*CW* 1: 124)

The cyclical paradigm linking birds and eggs in this passage recalls the "every narrowing circle" with which science approaches "elemental law" in "The Naturalist." At the same time, however, this account of "perpetual inchoation" more closely resembles the processional logic described in the essay "Circles," in which we observe "no fixtures in nature" (*CW* 2: 179). In such moments, the effort to capture and classify an "infinite distribution" of particulars looks less like a demonstration of an "upheaving principle of life" and more like standing on the "pitch of the cataract." If Emerson's 1830s lectures offer a "vertical" orientation designed to keep the "wholeness we admire" at the heart of scientific discourse, in other words, this 1841 adjustment seems to witness the pursuit of wholeness going over the falls.

When "The Method of Nature" returns to the conceit of a universal mind, for instance, it likewise contends that natural objects flood perception at a rate so destabilizing we risk losing our grip on the mind:

> Every natural fact is an emanation, and that from which it emanates is an emanation also, and from every emanation is a new emanation. If anything could stand still, it would be crushed and dissipated by the torrent it resisted, and if it were a mind, would be crazed; as insane persons are those who hold fast to one thought and do not flow with the course of nature. Not the cause, but an ever novel effect, nature descends always from above. (*CW* 1: 124)

These torrential metaphors introduce an instability in Emerson's account of the relationship between empirical observation and philosophical intuition, a problem scarcely imaginable in 1833. The earlier emphasis on transparency, as in the claim that physics translates ethics, here gives way to an endless sequence of signifiers with no fixed referent: "This refers to that, and that to the next, and the next to the third, and everything refers." (*CW* 1: 125). Even natural objects themselves, formerly eager to disclose their place in the scheme of our collective consciousness, now betray a troubling psychic instability. "Every star in heaven is discontented and insatiable," Emerson laments, "Gravitation and chemistry cannot content them" (*CW* 1: 131).

Emerson's later writing frequently envisions a material world in constant flux. And this shift in emphasis entails a corresponding shift in his account of the mechanics of scientific observation. In a characteristic early moment from 1836, for instance, he contends that "facts are capable of but one interpretation, as the rings on the tree or on the cow's horn record every year of their age. No leaps, no magic, eternal, tranquil procession of old familiar laws" (*SL* 26). But consider this "tranquil procession" motif alongside a famous moment in "Fate," the arduous opening essay of the 1860 volume, which finds that "[e]very solid in the universe is ready to become fluid on the approach of the mind, and the power to flux it is the measure of the mind" (*CW* 6: 23). These are not contradictory passages exactly. For Emerson, the "one interpretation" governing all facts comes to include this "power to flux" required for genuine insight. But the tension between such moments does reflect the twists in his own effort to develop a method for linking material and mental phenomena – his effort to generate a prose technique, however provisional, for capturing and cataloguing those "strange sympathies" he found so exhilarating in 1833.

Read in this context, the claim that our education in science succumbs to "spiral tendency in vegetation" signals much more than just a complaint about scientists. The comment not only describes a tendency to neglect Goethe's generalizing mission, but it also signals a key feature of Emerson's own effort to rethink thinking. By linking our absorption of new turns in natural history to the curving engine of plant morphology, he reminds that aligning mind and world means acknowledging the fluid, often confounding ways both object and observer tend to twist, turn, and effloresce. In a rather striking sentence from "The Method of Nature," for instance, he seems to make this claim explicitly: "As our soils and rocks lie in strata, concentric strata, so do all men's thinkings run laterally, never vertically" (*CW* 1: 122). For readers of his late prose, this earthbound version of the supreme analogy linking things and thoughts may resemble Emerson's most distinctive contribution to the historiography of modern science.

In his own late writing, Goethe introduces a provocative model for understanding the intimate relation between object and observer that distinguished his botanical writing and so excited Emerson. "There is a delicate empiricism," Goethe argues, "which makes itself utterly identical with the object, thereby becoming true theory. But this enhancement of our mental powers belongs to a highly evolved age."[10] Emerson's accounts on the achievements of nineteenth-century science labor to develop a language for such a "delicate empiricism," offering accounts of our identity with objects that enhance our mental powers by subordinating the parts to the whole. And he clearly does long for that "highly evolved age" in which we adhere to the "vertical tendency," dispensing with the disciplinary silos and separation of cultures dividing empirical from humanistic pursuits. As often, however, Emerson's thought also hews toward something more like what William James would call "radical empiricism" in 1904 – a "mosaic" model of the world in which the relations between things (objects, experiences, and ideas) are no less real than things themselves.[11] The uncommon fluency with which Emerson's prose keeps these alternatives in view – Goethean *identity* and Jamesian *adjacency* – remains the most distinctive feature of his response to natural history.

An extraordinary passage from the 1850 essay "The Uses of Great Men" illustrates that ambivalence:

> A man is a centre for nature, running out threads of relation through every thing, fluid and solid, material and elemental. The earth rolls; every clod and stone comes to the meridian: so every organ, function, acid, crystal, grain of dust, has its relation to the brain. It waits long, but its turn comes. Each plant has its parasite, and each created thing its lover and poet. (*CW* 4: 6)

The mind retains its central vantage; the world unfolds its objects as if for a museum cabinet. But lovers and poets are here analogous to parasites; the unifying theory is postponed. Across decades of writing about modern science, Emerson navigates this tension between the pursuit of higher laws and the "rushing stream" of experience. If these "threads of relation" comprising our intimacy with natural objects also have a tendency to parasitic convolutions, his richest prose as often suggests we let them twist and turn.

## Notes

1. Scholarship on Emerson's interest in science is varied and extensive, beginning with Harry Hayden Clark, "Emerson and Science," *Philological Quarterly* 10 (July 1931): 225–60. In the decades following Clark, many studies focus on the period of Emerson's career leading up to and surrounding the publication of *Nature* in 1836; see especially Sherman Paul, *Emerson's Angle of Vision: Man and Nature in American Experience* (Cambridge, MA: Harvard University Press, 1952), 208–20; Jonathan Bishop, *Emerson on the Soul* (Cambridge, MA: Harvard University Press, 1964), 45–59; Gay Wilson Allen, "A New Look at Emerson and Science," in *Literature and Ideas in America: Essays in Honor of Harry Hayden Clark*, ed. Robert Falk (Athens: Ohio University Press, 1975), 58–78; David Robinson, "Emerson's Natural Theology and the Paris Naturalists: Toward a Theory of Animated Nature," *Journal of the History of Ideas* 41 (1980): 69–88,

and William Rossi, "Emerson, Nature, and Natural Science," in *A Historical Guide to Ralph Waldo Emerson*, ed. Joel Myerson (Oxford: Oxford University Press, 2000), 101–50. For discussions that include commentary on Emerson's later writing, see David Robinson, "British Science, The London Lectures, and Emerson's Philosophical Reorientation," in *Emerson for the Twenty-First Century: Global Perspectives on an American Icon*, ed. Barry Tharaud (Newark: University of Delaware Press, 2010), 285–99; Christopher J. Windolph, *Emerson's Nonlinear Science* (Columbia: University of Missouri Press, 2007); Mark Noble, "Emerson's Atom: The Matter of Suffering" *Nineteenth-Century Literature* 64:1 (2009): 16–46; and Jennifer Baker, "Emerson, Embryology, and Culture," *J19: The Journal of Nineteenth-Century Americanists* 3:1 (2015):15–39. For comprehensive monographs offering broader analyses of Emerson's interest in science writing alongside his cultural commentary, epistemology, and ethics, see Lee Rust Brown, *The Emerson Museum: Practical Romanticism and the Pursuit of the Whole* (Cambridge, MA: Harvard University Press, 1997); Eduardo Cadava, *Emerson and the Climates of History* (Stanford: Stanford University Press, 1997); Eric Wilson, *Emerson's Sublime Science* (New York: St. Martin's Press, 1999); and Laura Dassow Walls, *Emerson's Life in Science: The Culture of Truth* (Ithaca: Cornell University Press, 2003). Brown, Cadava, and Walls are especially useful as introductory accounts that span Emerson's writing life.

2. Johann Wolfgang von Goethe, *The Essential Goethe*, ed. Matthew Bell (Princeton: Princeton University Press, 2015), 926–27.

3. Goethe, *The Essential Goethe*, 996.

4. Pfau, "'All is Leaf': Difference, Metamorphosis and Goethe's Phenomenology of Knowledge," *Studies in Romanticism* 49:1 (Spring 2010): 3–41. On Goethe's botanical writing, see also John Neubauer, "Organic Form in Romantic Theory: The Case of Goethe's Morphology," in *Romanticism Across the Disciplines*, ed. Larry Peer (Lanham: University Press of America, 1998), 207–29; Sabine Mainberger, "'In the vortex of the spiral tendency': Questions of Aesthetics, Literature and Natural Sciences in the Work of Goethe," *Estudos Avançados* 24 (2009): 203–18; Gábor Áron Zemplén, "Structure and Advancement in Goethe's Morphology," in *Marking Time: Romanticism and Evolution*, ed. Joel Faflak (Toronto: University of Toronto Press, 2018), 147–72.

5. Goethe, *The Essential Goethe*, 951.

6. Goethe, *Goethe's Botanical Writings*, trans. Bertha Mueller (Woodbridge: Ox Bow Press, 1989), 145.

7. Emerson, *The Early Lectures of Ralph Waldo Emerson*, ed. Stephen E. Whicher and Robert E. Spiller (Cambridge, MA: Harvard University Press, 1959), vol. 1, 10. Hereafter cited parenthetically as *EL*.

8. Emerson, *The Selected Lectures of Ralph Waldo Emerson*, ed. Ronald A. Bosco and Joel Myerson (Athens: University of Georgia Press, 2005), 29. Hereafter cited parenthetically as *SL*.

9. See especially David Jacobson, *Emerson's Pragmatic Vision: The Dance of the Eye* (University Park: Pennsylvania State University Press, 1993); David Robinson, *Emerson and the Conduct of Life: Pragmatism and Ethical Purpose in the Later Work* (Cambridge: Cambridge University Press, 1993); and Jonathan Levin, *The Poetics of Transition: Emerson, Pragmatism, and American Literary Modernism* (Durham: Duke University Press, 1999).

10. Goethe, *The Essential Goethe*, 1002.
11. For a reading of Emerson as Jamesian "radical empiricist," see Paul Grimstad, "Emerson's Adjacencies: Racial Empiricism in Nature," in *The Other Emerson*, ed. Branka Arsić and Cary Wolfe (Minneapolis: University of Minnesota Press, 2010), 251–70.

# 14

NICHOLAS L. GUARDIANO

# Emerson's Aesthetics
## *The Abiding Life of Beauty*

No matter how one defines aesthetics, its topics are found to pervade Emerson's thinking. Aesthetics may refer to the study of αἴσθησις (*aesthesis*), that is, of sensation or perception and the general structures of experience. It also may refer to philosophical studies of art (fine and practical), beauty, taste, the imagination, and creativity. In Emerson's essays and lectures, these all occur as serious and regular concerns, and they possess additional relevance to his life as a poet. Because his views on these topics overlap and cross-inform, it is necessary to treat them synoptically, yet there is one that stands out among them as a unifying principle. Emerson's love of beauty acts as a central thread running throughout his aesthetics and philosophical career. In the following presentation of his aesthetics, beauty will serve as a useful lens for discerning his unique contributions to the field.

Also important is Emerson's status as a world philosopher engaged with a rich history addressing fundamental questions about the reality of beauty, the constitution of experience, and the nature of the work of art and creativity. Emerson no doubt is a master of literary form; however, it is never mere form that he is after.[1] This is emphatically clear from his severe condemnations of the critic who addresses form over content and style over idea. Likewise, he often demands, in Neoplatonic fashion, that art should prioritize the idea. The fundamental principles of his aesthetics, their systematic connections to his greater philosophy, and their abiding relevance and indeed *truth* are most discernible in the content of Emerson's assertions and their synthesis with form. These are further illuminated by situating Emerson's philosophy in a world-historical perspective that compares his major ideas to archetypal theories of the past, including those that had an immeasurable impact on his worldview. Likewise, we gain by a forward-looking comparison with the American pragmatists and future generations of American artists who were significantly influenced by the Sage of Concord and the greater transcendentalist spirit of New England. These philosophical-historical approaches to Emerson's aesthetics will help sharpen our understanding of its conceptual subtleties and the unique contributions of his positions.

## A Love of Beauty

Beauty holds a central place in Emerson's thought. Across his career, he directly addresses the topic in multiple publications and public lectures, and it is a main concern of the chapter "Beauty" in *Nature* (1836); the essays "The Poet" in *Essays; Second-Series* (1844), "Beauty" in *The Conduct of Life* (1860), and "Poetry and Imagination" in *Letters and Social Aims* (1876); as well as the poems "Each and All" (1847 [1839]), "The Rhodora" (1847 [1839]), "Ode to Beauty" (1847 [1843]), and "May-Day" (1867). These and many more writings further describe the beautiful or attractive appearances of nature, human characters, our ideas, and works of art. Countless poems, for example, illustrate the alluring sights, sounds, and smells of our natural environment. Moreover, Emerson's attention to beauty is not some mere interest in style where beauty becomes a superficial ornamentation of his thought. "[O]utside embellishment is deformity," he writes; "if it is done to be seen, it is mean" (*CW* 6: 155). He lived what he preached. Such important works as *Nature*, "The American Scholar," and "The Divinity School Address" carefully incorporate observations of the scenic landscape into their core arguments and theses, and his major essays on aesthetics "The Poet" and "Beauty" present extended philosophical treatments of the nature of beauty and its greater relevance in our lives.

Indeed, the love of beauty ran deep within Emerson's soul, as his own self-characterizations attest. In 1835 during a highly introspective period in his life when he had resigned from the ministry to ponder his true calling, he confided to his fiancée Lydia Jackson that he believed he was foremost a poet:

> I am born a poet, of a low class without doubt yet a poet. That is my nature & vocation. My singing be sure is very "husky," & is for the most part in prose. Still am I a poet in the sense of a perceiver & dear lover of the harmonies that are in the soul & in matter, & specially of the correspondences between these & those. A sunset, a forest, a snow storm, a certain river-view, are more to me than many friends & do ordinarily divide my day with my books. (*L* 1: 435)

In another letter to Lydia composed several years later while visiting New York City, Emerson continues to measure himself against others by his poetic nature. He confesses that this aspect of his identity sets him apart from his politically minded peers Horace Greeley and Albert Brisbane: "Yet I foresaw in the moment when I encountered these two new friends here, that I cannot content them. They are bent on popular action: I am in all my theory, ethics, & politics a poet and of no more use in their New York than a rainbow or a firefly" (*L* 3: 18). Similar pronouncements about his vocation tacitly occur in his philosophical remarks. In "The Poet," for example, he defines an essential character trait of the poet-class – and thus also of himself – claiming: the poet is "the man of Beauty" (*CW* 3: 4). The poet is Emerson's highest class of thinker who stands out as an exemplar of the race by a boundless love for the world and joy in celebrating it – something he found evident in his favorite historical poets Shakespeare, Homer, Chaucer, Sa'di, and Hafiz.[2] Likewise, in "The Transcendentalist" where he grapples with what might unify the group of like-minded thinkers to which he was the acknowledged spokesperson, he suggests that it is in part their (and his) absolute devotion to beauty: "But this class are not sufficiently characterized, if we omit to add that they are lovers and worshippers of Beauty. In the eternal trinity of Truth, Goodness, and Beauty, each in its perfection including the three, they prefer to make Beauty the sign and head" (*CW* 1: 214). That is to say that while we find transcendentalists engaged in a broad range of affairs, including philosophy, spiritual leadership, social reform, and more, Beauty is the common ideal that governs their various pursuits.

Emerson would have recognized that this aesthetic sentiment set apart him and his peers from certain caustic cultural trends in New England, which omit or even show a distaste for beauty. Notably, there were the early nineteenth-century religious attitudes born from the stock of Calvinism that dwelled on the terrors and solitudes of the American wilderness, as well as on the "depraved" condition of the human race. The conservative Unitarian leaders around Cambridge were not much better with their austere rationalism and abstract historicism that had little or no use for the presence of beauty. One would think the burgeoning literary and arts movements of the United States fared better in an appreciation for beauty. However, as was apparent in the different periodicals circulating around Boston and New England, Emerson found these movements infected with the cant of critics. Critics he laments at the opening of "The Poet" were only, even when at their best, pedants obsessed with rules and forms of technique; they thus profess a "shallowness of the doctrine of beauty" (*CW* 3: 3). Finally, there was the contemptible materialistic drive of the growing republic with its bent toward material progress and economic gain. Where was a love of beauty in all this?

The concept of beauty and its correlate poetry, thus are a central topics in the study of Emerson's philosophy in general, and his aesthetics in particular. The centrality given to beauty, moreover, is not simply a matter of personal preference or taste but possesses a theoretical and metaphysical primacy for Emerson. Before considering how that plays out, we must first better understand what is meant by beauty. Although Emerson will come to define it in multiple ways throughout his career, there is one sense that is quite basic. It is the attractive or pleasing appearance of the world, or as he explains in the third chapter on the topic in *Nature*, it is the "delight *in and for themselves*" (CW 1: 12) of things when they meet the senses. Simply put, it is the wonderful spectacle of the κόσμος: The Greek term Emerson prefers for describing the universe as a whole, over the English *kinde* or Latin *natura*, precisely because of its connotations with beauty or "that power which seems to work for beauty alone" (CW 7: 87).[3] We will see that this immediate impression of the world will have significant ramifications for Emerson's philosophy – as it did for his favorite philosopher Plato who expressed the like feeling in the *Timaeus*: "the cosmos is the most beautiful of things born and its craftsman the best of causes" (ὁ μὲν γὰρ κάλλιστος τῶν γεγενημένος, ὁ δ᾽ ἄριστος τῶν αἰτίων).[4]

We further gain an understanding of Emerson's sense of beauty when he contrasts beauty to "commodity" or the material usefulness of things. Beauty, rather, is that modality or dimension of nature that cannot be bought, bargained, or traded for. It thus appears in that charming aspect of the landscape to which men's "warranty-deeds give no title" (CW 1: 9). In other words, "Beauty is its own excuse for being," as the poem "The Rhodora" states about a precious wildflower hidden away in the woods and in response to the dull-witted "sages" who "ask thee why / This charm is wasted on the earth and sky" (CW 9: 79).[5] We do not need to address the practical purpose of beauty because, unlike a hammer, wagon, or toaster oven, it is not that sort of thing. Emerson's sense of beauty as that which has value in itself shares a family resemblance to Plato's good in itself (*contra* good for its benefits) and to Immanuel Kant's aesthetic judgment of beauty as a "disinterested pleasure" (*contra* an interested pleasure connected to desire).[6] Emerson never tired of appreciating this sacrosanct aesthetic aspect of our lives that always remains transcendent of economics and the material desires of humankind. He continues to express this sentiment in the late lecture about his hometown, "Country Life (Concord)":

> When I bought my farm, I did not know what a bargain I had in the blue-birds, bobolinks, and thrushes, which were not charged in the bill: as little did I guess what sublime mornings and sunsets I was buying, – what reaches of landscape, and what fields and lanes for a tramp. Neither did I fully consider what an indescribable luxury is our Indian river, the Musketaquid ... where a skiff or a dory gives you, all summer, access to enchantments, new every day, and, all winter, to miles of ice for the skater. (*LL* 2: 37)

In Emerson's ironic play on the trope of "buying" beauty, the economic mindset runs aground, revealing its limitations precisely in the domain of aesthetics. Beauty is not charged in the bill, because it cannot be directly purchased and thus remains an inadvertent consequence of the sale.

Beauty thus is an irreducible, pervasive feature of the world. Its wide scope extends across, at least, the domains of material nature, moral virtue, and art – three aesthetic domains Emerson identifies in *Nature* while drawing on the tripartite roughly outlined by Plotinus in his treatise on the subject.[7] It thus contributes to an aesthetic pluralism characterizing the universe in its qualitative and creative multitudinousness.[8] Yet, Emerson – never the blind romantic – wisely recognizes that this feature is not something always given or easily attained at will. It frequently happens that "[w]e are immersed in beauty, but our eyes have no clear vision" (*CW* 2: 210). His poems, so often paeans to natural beauty with a philosophical upshot, teach this important lesson. For instance, "Each and All" contemplates the distasteful phenomenon of enthusiastically finding and then inadvertently losing beauty. Luminous seashells once so colorful on the sunny shorelines are no longer once they are taken indoors, and a most beloved and endearing girl loses her charm the moment she becomes a wife. A similar chord is struck in "Ode to Beauty" that "features the Transcendental paradox that the beautiful is ever present and yet ever receding."[9] Beauty is like an all-consuming bright flash of "lightning through the storm, / Somewhat not to be possessed, / Somewhat not to be caressed" (*CW* 9: 175).

Our tentative relationship with beauty is the aesthetic fallout of Emerson's sober romanticism, which Stanley Cavell, followed by Russell Goodman and others, has explored in terms of an "epistemology of moods." In essays like "Circles" and "Experience," Emerson discerns the way our varying moods or emotions cannot help but subjectively mediate our perceptions of the world. An idea drawing on the legacy of Kant's Copernican Turn, the self and world are intimately linked in their co-configurations, even at the level of our temperamental evaluations that each insist on excluding the other. Yet, Emerson's epistemology of moods, despite acknowledging the ephemerality of our deeper insights and aesthetic appreciations, does not result in a relativistic or nihilistic worldview.[10] In the narrative twists of "Each and All," the poet throws up his hands swearing off beauty as "unripe childhood's cheat," yet only to discover:

> As I spoke, beneath my feet
> The ground-pine curled its pretty wreath,
> Running over the club-moss burrs;
> I inhaled the violet's breath;
> Around me stood the oaks and firs;

Pine-cones and acorns lay on the ground;
Over me soared the eternal sky,
Full of light and of deity;
Again I saw, again I heard,
The rolling river, the morning bird; –
Beauty through my senses stole;
I yielded myself to the perfect whole. (CW 9: 15)

Give up on beauty and it seizes you nonetheless. For Emerson, the insistence of beauty is a sign of its persistence, that is, its reality. It is equally a sign of its sovereignty. Beauty neither answers to our willful attempts to possess it nor tolerates our overt denials of its existence. Yet, it does conditionally permit us to approach it through our attitudes of respect, gratitude, patience, love, and piety. Such temperaments welcome things on their own terms, acknowledging that which is other or more than the self.

## Experiential Life

Beauty's power to seize hold of us exemplifies the way experience in general involves a relational self that is situated even absorbed in deep folds of meaning. This naturally leads to a discussion of Emerson's greater views on the fundamental structures of experience (or αἴσθησις or "aisthesis") and its value in the conduct of life. Some of the more unforgettable moments in Emerson's writings are his outspoken remarks that prioritize experience over the habits of bookworms, formal study, and the literary life, which he critiques for stifling our own original thoughts and for distracting us from our own personal surroundings. He trumpets to the Harvard graduates in his "The American Scholar" address: "Only so much do I know, as I have lived. Instantly we know whose words are loaded with life, and whose not" (CW 1: 59). But in what does living or experiencing consist?

First and foremost, as we find in his firsthand experiential descriptions of the everyday and his more direct theorizing on the topic of experience, Emerson reveals a concern with the lived experience of immediate consciousness. His well-known 1844 essay "Experience" is far from a traditional empiricist treatise on the preconscious causes and laws governing over passively given sense-impressions, but rather is a down-to-earth meditation on a directly felt sense of the human condition in all its complexity. This includes those "unhandsome" (CW 3: 29) parts of our condition, like the emptiness of grief and the unavoidableness of disillusionment, which Emerson does so well to illustrate with heartfelt sincerity. This humanistic understanding of experience as a value-rich field would impact the next generation of American philosophers, including Charles Sanders Peirce with his triadic phenomenology, William James with his radical empiricism, and John Dewey with his naturalistic empiricism.[11] In Dewey's account, our everyday experience consists of processes of action and "undergoing." We exist in a state of *experiencing*, rather than as an isolated subject receiving bulks of sense-data or *experienced* content. "Like its congeners, life and history, it [experience] includes *what* men do and suffer, *what* they strive for, love, believe and endure, and also *how* men act and are acted upon, the ways in which they do and suffer, desire and enjoy, see, believe, imagine – in short, processes of *experiencing*."[12]

We should further add that, for Emerson, experience contains not only the "what" and the "how" but also the "may" or "might." That is, it contains possibilities or "prospects" – to use a favorite word of his – that suggestively intimate new meanings. One way to understand this aspect is in view of his remarks on the representational or symbolic status of experience and nature.[13] Peirce who later formalizes a theory of signs that follows up on the transcendentalist legacy in this regard helps us understand the implications. His semeiotic explains that signs by their very referential nature stand for some object while standing to some interpreter. Under this triadic framework of the sign/object/interpreter, the interpreter completes the determination of a given sign while further projecting forth its meaning in the form of a new sign, and therefore advancing an ever-expanding horizon of interpretive possibilities. I return to this prospective semeiotic of Emerson's aesthetics in the following sections.

The Emersonian experience, thus, is not the simple given of raw impressions, as described by modern empiricism. Those impressions amounted to things in themselves mechanistically imprinting onto a subject who was little invested in its surroundings. Also, at the opposite extreme, Emersonian experience is not a phenomenal flux of appearances that would forever imprison the self in an illusory world.[14] On this point, we should carefully notice that although Emerson uses the tropes of "illusions," "surfaces," and "succession," he consistently turns the tables on the easy conclusion of subjective idealism that nature or the external world is thoroughly a construct of the human mind. For instance, at a crucial turning point in his essay "Illusions," he keenly observes that if "life seems a succession of dreams, yet poetic justice is done in dreams also" (*CW* 6: 172). There is also Emerson's crucial move made at the end of his chapter "Idealism" in *Nature* that rejects the hypothesis of subject idealism for a metaphysics of spirit, which is taken up in the following chapter of his book.[15] Moreover, for Emerson, there is phenomenological evidence for real otherness – and thus for something more than the ego as an ingredient in the constitution of experience – in the unpredictability of events. We might live among "surfaces" of our own making, but, despite ourselves, life presents "a series of surprises" (*CW* 3: 35, 39), such as when natural beauty steals in through our senses during our less than beautiful moods. The upshot is that while Illusion and other "Lords of Life" prove that we can and often do get stuck in our experience, nevertheless, it is not necessary that we must remain there.

In addition, the phenomenalist presupposition that draws a radical divide between the ontological domains of the subject and object or mind and nature is simply incompatible with Emerson's transcendentalist philosophy. In his Schellingian and equally Neoplatonic, Spinozistic, and Swedenborgian metaphysics of ideal-realism, or objective idealism, the mind and nature are organically related, connatural, and consanguineous. The same is true of his religious outlook unifying spirit and nature, whereby the divine immanently resides in both material nature and the human soul. These are all parts of Emerson's "single" or "synoptic vision," as Robert Pollock keenly observes, that gives equal value to the traditionally polarized pairs.[16] The transcendentalist metaphysics also accounts for those poetic "intimations and suggestions which permeate man's experiences of the natural world," as experience emerges from the connatural intertwining and interplay of the subject and object or mind and nature.[17]

This synechistic metaphysics – to use Peirce's term for "continuity," whose metaphysics follows the same historical line – informs Emerson's theory of "intuition," a commonly discussed aspect of his transcendentalist philosophy relevant to his aesthetics. These deeper insights about the self and world are *intellectual observations* that depend on a sympathetic feeling for one's subject matter or a disposition whereby like knows like.[18] For Emerson, it is the poets who among humankind possess an expertise of intuition, and this skill corresponds to the first half of the binary defining the artistic co-powers of reception and expression. Hence, Shakespeare is the "representative poet" because he possesses "a heart in unison with his time and country" (*CW* 4: 109), which makes him sensitive to discerning the general habits, interests, practices, and traditions of the English people. These intuitions become the experiential resources for constructing his artistic creations. Thus wise, the artistic self becomes attuned to the meanings that pervade experience, which are later deployed as resources toward its creative achievements.

## The Aesthetic Ideal

I return now to the centrality of beauty for Emerson in order to better understand in what that centrality consists theoretically. To return to "The Transcendentalist" where Emerson elects Beauty as "the sign and head" (*CW* 1: 214) of the three transcendentals, we are provided with the following justification:

> Something of the same taste [for beauty] is observable in all the moral movements of the time, in the religious and benevolent enterprises. They have a liberal, even an aesthetic spirit. A reference to Beauty in action sounds, to be sure, a little hollow and ridiculous in the ears of the old church. In politics, it has often sufficed, when they treated of justice, if they kept the bounds of selfish calculation. If they granted restitution, it was prudence which granted it. But the justice which is now claimed for the black, and the pauper, and the drunkard, is for Beauty – is for a necessity to the soul of the agent, not of the beneficiary.... We call the Beautiful the highest, because it appears to us the golden mean, escaping the dowdiness of the good, and the heartlessness of the true. (*CW* 1: 214)[19]

Here we come to see that a "reason why the beautiful holds such a central place in Emerson's texts is because it is his ground for any claim to ethical authenticity and political authority."[20] Emerson insightfully discerns that Beauty – unlike its otherwise equals the morally Good and Truth – may stand as a kind of ultimate ideal of human conduct and thought. Being that which is revered in itself, it can serve as a sort of main beacon (i.e., sign), goal, or source of inspiration for our highest endeavors, whether those be intellectual, spiritual, or artistic. Moreover, because of its autonomy as an absolute principle, its draw on us takes the form of a general appeal rather than a specific mandate. On the contrary, the Good in its susceptibility to corrupt appropriations through selfish and political means, and Truth in its proneness to an abstract and insipid state of existing, both fail in this regard. Consequently, Beauty alone has the potential to jointly engage our minds *and* hearts, and thus to invigorate the human soul in its fullness. In these ways Emerson's primacy of Beauty anticipates Peirce's triadic division of the Normative Sciences that similarly prioritizes Esthetics over Ethics and Logic. Esthetics Peirce defines as the science of beautiful or "admirable" ideals in themselves without reference to how they might be realized in the world. Theoretically, it subtends Ethics and Logic, which treat the *particular* ideals of the morally Good and Truth, respectively, and insofar as these exist as ends of conduct to be attained.[21]

Beauty's function as "sign and head" comes into even sharper focus when we consider how a concrete love of beauty accompanies our speculative interests. Just months after returning from Europe in 1833, where in Paris he had enthusiastically studied the natural history cabinets at the Jardin des Plantes and listened to lectures on science at the Sorbonne, Emerson reflected on the lessons learned in his first public lecture outside the ministry, "The Uses of Natural History":

*The beauty of the world is a perpetual invitation to the study of the world.*
Sunrise and sunset; fire; flowers; shells; the sea – in all its shades, from indigo
to green and gray, by the light of day, and phosphorescent under the ship's
keel at night; the airy inaccessible mountain; the sparry cavern; the glaring
colours of the soil of the volcano; the forms of vegetables; and all the elegant and majestic figures of the creatures that fly, climb, or creep upon the
earth – all, *by their beauty*, work upon our curiosity and court our attention.
The earth is a museum, and the five senses a philosophical apparatus of such
perfection, that the pleasure we obtain from the aids with which we arm them,
is trifling, compared with their natural information. (*EL* 1: 6; my emphasis)

Emerson returns to the same point later in life in his essay "Beauty" in *The
Conduct of Life*. In contrast to the analytical methods of natural science
that render nature "a dull dictionary," he discerns: "Beauty is the form
under which the intellect prefers to study the world. All privilege is that of
beauty; for there are many beauties; as, of general nature, of the human face
and form, of manners, of Brain, or method, moral beauty, or beauty of the
soul" (*CW* 6: 150, 153). In line with his theory of experience as "prospective" and symbolically suggestive, Emerson proposes that our appreciation
for beauty motivates our intellects in our more deliberate studies. Like an
open doorway into the unknown, the aesthetic spectacle that is the κόσμος
draws forth its admirers into interpretive explorations of its greater possible
meanings.[22] The poem "Monadnoc" captures in a nutshell the intellectual
draw of nature as a beautiful symbol. Listen as the sublime New Hampshire
mountain peak visible on the distant horizon in Concord calls forth the
lowland poet to explore its deeper reality:

> Up! – If thou knew'st who calls
> To twilight parks of beech and pine,
> High over the river intervals,
> Above the ploughman's highest line,
> Over the owner's farthest walls!
> ....
> Read the celestial sign!
> Lo! the south answers to the north;
> Bookworm, break this sloth urbane;
> A greater spirit bids thee forth
> Than the gray dreams which thee detain. (*CW* 9: 120–21)

The sight of the distant peak quite literally drew Emerson and his fellow
transcendentalists to explore it. Emerson sought to build a house with a
clear view of Monadnoc and made multiple excursions to the mountain
over the course of his lifetime.[23] Emerson's aesthetic ideal has special relevance today regarding the historically unprecedented destruction of the

Earth's species and natural environments. The loss of each animal and plant species, each wilderness landscape and balanced ecosystem, is a loss of a beautiful ideal to compel our better selves into the future.

By no means mere poetic musings, then, Emerson's experiential descriptions of the beauty of the world play a serious role in his philosophy. It has been said with good reason that Emerson is "a hard-headed empiricist," who should be grouped with other empirically minded philosophers, including the American pragmatists.[24] In fact, he often secures his own speculative inquiries by submitting an observational account of natural beauty as the first premise to his arguments. For example, Chapter 1 of *Nature* invokes the sublimity of the starry night sky with its "envoys of beauty" that "awaken a certain reverence" for nature (*CW* 1: 9). Likewise, "The Divinity School Address" begins with an ode to "this refulgent summer" where the "grass grows, the buds burst, [and] the meadow is spotted with fire and gold in the tint of flowers" (*CW* 1: 76) – beauties that environ lecturer and audience outside the walls of Divinity Hall in July 1838. These sights are not window-dressing but serious empirical support for Emerson's conclusions about the general ends of nature and the reality of the religious sentiment.[25]

## Neoplatonic Metaphysics of Beauty

Emerson's aesthetics comes into full focus when we attend to its connections with his metaphysical worldview. Aesthetic appreciation, artistic creativity, the imagination, and beauty depend upon deeper structures and causes of being.[26] With regard to beauty, as we have seen, Emerson makes explicit its metaphysical status in its existence as one of the three eternal transcendentals, and he continues to lay out a greater metaphysics of beauty in his essays "The Over-Soul," "The Poet," and "Beauty." His monism of the Over-Soul features that absolute being encompassing the complete variety of phenomena – both natural and human, subject and object – and that furthermore is "*the universal beauty*, to which every part and particle is equally related; the eternal One … whose beatitude is all accessible to us" (*CW* 2: 160; my emphasis). Existing as the universal beauty, the Over-Soul is the primordial ontological ground of all particular beauties. As Emerson says in his essay "Beauty" when returning to the subject in his later writings, it is the "cosmical quality" that "constitutes a thing beautiful" (*CW* 6: 161). Further spelling out the metaphysics of beauty is "The Poet," which presents an aesthetic cosmogenesis. It affirms that "the world is not painted, or adorned, but is *from the beginning beautiful*; and God has not made some beautiful things, but *Beauty is the creator of the universe*" (*CW* 3: 5; my emphasis). In other words, a primeval form of "poetry was all written before time was, and whenever we are so finely organized that we can penetrate into that region where the air is music, we hear those primal warblings" (CW 3: 5–6). The inner self like the outer world is equally an effect of this aboriginal creator. In his journal entry that would become the infamous Transparent Eyeball passage in *Nature*, Emerson states: "I am the heir of uncontained beauty & power" (J 5: 18). Emerson thus appoints an absolute form of beauty as the originating first cause, further adding a causal or dynamic dimension to the metaphysical monism of beauty. All embodied instances of beauty, all perceivers of beauty, and all creative processes tending toward beauty that have, do, and might appear in the world derive their aesthetic existence from this preeminent form of beauty. As a consequence, the aesthetic qualities of everyday things are in no way superficial or assigned from without, but possess integrity at their ontological core. Such metaphysical hypotheses contribute to the justification of a love of beauty for the aesthetic pluralism pervasive throughout nature and society.

In historical context, Emerson's metaphysically informed aesthetics blazes a path not typical of the one followed by earlier Enlightenment thinkers. David Hume, who was skeptical of all things metaphysical, settled for a psychological analysis of the general sentiments of human taste. His well-known essay "On the Standard of Taste" makes such non-Emersonian claims as, "Beauty is no quality in things themselves: it exists merely in the mind which contemplates them; and each mind perceives a different beauty."[27] Kant, although turning to the critical method of focusing on the a priori in order to establish the objectivity of knowledge, follows Hume's lead insofar as he takes the rightful topic of aesthetics to be our feelings of appreciation.[28] Emerson's metaphysically informed aesthetics, however, does not share an elective affinity with these modern thinkers, but rather with the ancient Platonic philosophers.[29] Plato and his intellectual heirs show a mutual concern for establishing beauty as a fundamental reality. An originating text of this tradition is the *Symposium* and the oracular words spoken by Diotima about a Platonic form of beauty, which serves as the eternal archetype in which all sensuous manifestations of beauty participate.[30] Advancing Plato's ideas, Plotinus features them in his dynamic emanation philosophy. In his widely influential treatise "On Beauty," beauty is identified with the One – that pinnacle or first cause of all beings and essences – whose diffusive reality emanates downward into the other two hypostases of the Intellect and Soul, eventually terminating in the sense world of nature.

Emerson's enthusiasm for Plato and Plotinus – fellow lovers and contemplators of beauty – no doubt contributed to his own take on a cosmic form of beauty and his dynamic vision of its outwardly creative processes.

Vivian Hopkins's book on Emerson's aesthetics, *Spires of Form*, finds Plotinian emanation at the heart of Emerson's vision of upward ascending cycles of creative processes. Emerson, however, upgrades Plato's and Plotinus's theories by rejecting any hierarchy of aesthetic being or downward trajectory of aesthetic degradation. In Plotinus's cosmogony, nature (including the human body), due to its distance from the One and from the forms of the Intellect, is inherently ugly, not beautiful. In its materiality, it exists in a state of ontological fragmentation, intellectual depravity, and sensuous repulsiveness. Any glimmer of beauty that nature might reveal exclusively depends on the forms of the Intellect, which serve to unify the inherent disorder of its material being.[31] The transcendentalist metaphysics of Bronson Alcott – Emerson's close friend with whom he sometimes was in healthy disagreement – also shares this vestige of an austere Platonism in its negative assessments of nature as the "sepulcher of the risen soul" and "the fair corpse of spirit."[32] Emerson, on the contrary, consistently promotes the beauty of nature while providing a more truly comprehensive aesthetics of being. All existing things, whether high or low, grand or ordinary, possess an unassailable aesthetic nobility, each positively participating in a world replete with poetic immediacies to enjoy. Plotinus would have been baffled by Emerson's deep attraction for such things as the "noonday darkness of the American forest, the deep, echoing, aboriginal woods ... the pines, bearded with savage moss ... the broad, cold lowland ... haggard and desert beauty, which the sun and the moon, the snow and the rain repaint and vary" (*CW* 1: 106–7). Such proclamations as "the standard of beauty is the entire circuit of natural forms, – the totality of nature" (*CW* 1: 17) would have appeared as corrupt inversions of the emanation philosophy. And Plotinus would have utterly shuddered at Emerson's belief that "[e]ven the corpse hath its own beauty" (*CW* 1: 13). Nevertheless, Emerson blazes his own American aesthetics, and one that is systematically consistent with his metaphysics, as well as his ethical and religious views. For Emerson, just as each individual soul possesses an unmediated access to the divine spirit, each particle of nature however small or seemingly insignificant fully embodies that "universal beauty ... whose beatitude is all accessible to us" (*CW* 2: 160).

The ontological grounding of variety in unity, each in all, or conditional beauty in absolute beauty also informs Emerson's views on art. His synoptic vision features artistic acts and artistic works as connatural manifestations of *natura naturans* (nature naturing) and *natura naturata* (nature natured), respectively. Art is thereby a tributary of the one outward-flowing spirit energizing the world. "Thus is Art, a nature passed through the alembic of man. Thus in art, does nature work through the will of a man filled with the beauty of her first works" (*CW* 1: 17). The upshot for art is that it is metaphysically equipped with the full powers of nature, as well as a participant in the absolute beauty that is the creator of the universe.

One way Emerson promotes art as connaturally grounded in primordial beauty is by arguing for the greater symbolic registers of everyday objects. By sharing in the universal form of beauty, any particular may be selected out for artistic celebration and made representative of a bigger issue. Thus, "A squirrel leaping from bough to bough, and making the wood but one wide tree for his pleasure, fills the eye not less than a lion, – is beautiful, self-sufficing, and stands then and there for nature." Likewise, the neighbor's dog and farmer's piglets carry an artistic excellence "not less than the frescoes of Angelo" (*CW* 2: 211–12). Art is thus set free from any outside standard that might restrict its subject matter or means of expression. Emily Dickinson got the message: "I dwell in Possibility."[33] Her simple lifestyle and domestic world provided ample materials for her "Wild Nights!" of poetic reverie.[34] The Hudson River School artists and other American painters of the nineteenth century, including John James Audubon, Asher Durand, Thomas Cole, William Sidney Mount, John Kensett, Frederic Church, and Winslow Homer, also got the message. Their depictions of the local natural scenery and everyday life not only portray new artistic subjects but also elevate them to transcendentalist heights.[35] This expansive sense of art in the boundless appreciation of things further illustrates the autonomy of Beauty qua aesthetic ideal. We bear witness to the same in the poem "Mithridates" that celebrates the aesthetic splendors of the world by featuring the Hellenistic ruler and polyglot joyously indulging in all varieties of food and bodily tinctures, even poison! Emerson's poetic affirmation that rises to embrace even a *beautiful death* implicitly repudiates any logic of good and evil, let alone a practical mindset of commodity. Rather, it proclaims Beauty as an unassailable poetic muse. The same plays out in Emerson's ethics when he provides his answer to how we should live in a world determined by "Fate," that principle demarcating our destinies and necessary limitations. We are to positively embrace this formidable reality in order to "build altars to the Beautiful Necessity" and "draw on all its omnipotence" (*CW* 6: 26, 27).

## Metamorphic Art and the Poetic Curve of the Universe

The greater metaphysical implications of Emerson's aesthetics and its relevance to the transformative power of art are further illuminated in his theory of poetic metamorphosis.[36] Emerson's theory combines both a dynamic and symbolic sense of art. He works out its details in "The Poet" while continuing to build upon it in the lengthy, vintage-career essay "Poetry and Imagination." The former would prove to be one of his most influential works upon would-be artists, helping launch the poetic careers of no less than the great American poets Walt Whitman and Emily Dickinson.[37] The latter essay is equally important. Its material was drawn from various lectures Emerson delivered during the second half of his life, including those featured in the 1870 lecture series "Natural History of Intellect," marking his public return to Harvard College after a more than thirty-year hiatus. This capstone work "brings to a head the central thrust of his entire poetical and philosophical output."[38] Moreover, its central claims valorizing the creative life of nature and art would make a significant impact on the worldviews of future generations of American philosophers. For instance, it characterizes Peirce's evolutionary cosmology with its growing universe of signs.

Influenced by Goethe's morphological studies of metamorphosis as a master pattern playing out across natural forms, organic and inorganic, Emerson understands the imaginative use of symbols in art to be one with the equally symbolic and transformative processes of nature. A passage from "Poetry and Imagination" adequately sums up Emerson's considered view:

> Nature itself is a vast trope, and all particular natures are tropes.... All thinking is analogizing, and 'tis the use of life to learn metonymy. The endless passing of one element into new forms, the incessant metamorphosis, explains the rank which the imagination holds in our catalogue of mental powers. The imagination is the reader of these forms. The poet accounts all productions and changes of Nature as the nouns of language, uses them representatively, too well pleased with their ulterior to value much their primary meaning. (CW 8: 7–8)

Artistic works of poetry, literature, painting, architecture, sculpture, dance, and music through their varying mediums symbolically appropriate their environments for their unique expressive purposes. Even when art focuses on representing loss, death, and decay, it positively transforms the world in this way giving it a new lease on life. Likewise, despite the necessary dependency of art upon cultural practices and restrictions of its media, it finds freedom of expression in manipulating these toward original ends. Hence, as Emerson explains in "Shakspeare, or the Poet" and "Art" (1870), any external necessities that would govern art are less determining factors and more preconditions of action. Moreover, as new expressions appropriate old ones in time, these continue to play out on the field of reimaginings or "metamorphoses," thus having a compounding effect. By an internally self-regulating and openly evolving process, art shares in the inter-informing, polyphonic growth of a universe of signs.[39]

This is one of Emerson's most valuable (and underappreciated) contributions to aesthetics, given its consequences for the ongoing appreciation of art by the human race. For one reason, the view that art is symbolic highlights the fact that art has something to communicate and thus something to say and know. On the contrary, overtly sensual forms of art, such as those that aim to merely titillate our senses or satiate our desires, fail to capitalize on art's greater symbolic registers in this regard. Emerson says "it is not metres, but a metre-making argument, that makes a poem.... The poet has a new thought: he has a whole new experience to unfold; he will tell us how it was with him, and all men will be the richer in his fortune" (CW 3: 6–7). Unlike mere meters, that is, mere poetic lyricism, a meter-making argument is *intellectually* expressive, and unlike a mere formal argument, it is *artistically* expressive. We might define it as a beautiful form capable of compelling belief.[40] This is not to say that beauty is to be exploited as a rhetorical ploy to force an issue. Rather, beautiful symbols possess an organic relationship to their messages by exhibiting them qualitatively and sharing in their aesthetic realities.

If art can be intellectually fruitful or possess "*Veracity*" (CW 8: 15), as Emerson likes to say, then it has epistemic potential, and if that is the case, then the long-fraught quarrel between poetry and philosophy has been ill conceived. Indeed, poetry shares the same end as philosophy and science in disclosing truth. However, it may even have an advantage in this regard, since its beautiful and imaginative renderings of the everyday have the added value of producing pleasure and deeply cultivating a concern for habitually overlooked aspects of life. Comparing poetry to philosophy, Emerson argues:

> A happy symbol is a sort of evidence that your thought is just. I had rather have a good symbol of my thought, or a good analogy, than the suffrage of Kant or Plato. If you agree with me, or if Locke or Montesquieu agree, I may yet be wrong; but if the elm-tree thinks the same thing, if running water, if burning coal, if crystals, if alkalies, in their several fashions, say what I say, it must be true. Thus, a good symbol is the best argument, and is a missionary to persuade thousands. (CW 8: 6–7)

The epistemic dimension of art is another illustration of the primacy-cum-unity of Beauty in its relationship to Truth and Goodness. In our admiration of its "happy symbols" lies the potential to learn new things and to grow as better persons by indulging in the beautiful radiance of existence.[41] Second, Emerson's metamorphic theory justifies why we continually find art fresh and relevant to our lives. By its symbolic reimaginings of new ideas in new forms for new interpretive possibilities, we trust art has a future, and a beautiful one at that. Paralleling reflections made in essays like "The Method of Nature" and "Circles" on the ecstatic growth of nature, Emerson sketches a progressive view of art that follows a reflexively elevating and creatively expansive trajectory in the ongoing multiplication of beauty. Hence, the "poet's fidelity to his office of announcement and affirming" secures "the beauty of things, which becomes a *new*, and *higher* beauty, when expressed" (*CW* 3: 8; my emphasis). In this way, the poet contributes to "the poetic curve of nature" that tracks the "*arrested and progressive development*" of an open universe (*CW* 8: 3). The poetic curve shapes the progressively ramifying symbols of art throughout history, and it is axiomatic to any artistic effort that strives to realize novel creative works.

Emerson's aesthetics thus provides us with an expansive vision of art that is metaphysically grounded in the real beauties of a symbolically expressive cosmic *poiesis*. As such, it challenges recent theories of art that would proclaim the death of art under a historically deterministic worldview or deflate its spiritual import through positivistic and nominalistic accounts. Nourished by a love of beauty, Emerson's affirmative poetic sense recognizes the value-rich and suggestive intimations of lived experience. It pledges a commitment to Beauty as an autonomous aesthetic ideal capable of drawing us forth into the world.

## Notes

1. For a study of Emerson's aesthetics focusing on the literary forms of his texts – the shape of their narratives, word semantics, or use of personas – see Lawrence Buell, *Emerson* (Cambridge: Belknap Press, 2003), chap. 3.
2. See, for example, *CW* 4: 123 in "Shakespeare, or the Poet," and the poems "Mithridates," "Bacchus," and "Saadi," which all portray the celebratory aspect of the poet.
3. Also see the opening of the chapter "Beauty" in *Nature* where Emerson equates the κόσμος with beauty *simpliciter* (*CW* 1: 12).
4. Plato, *Plato's Timaeus*, trans. Peter Kalkavage (Newburyport: Focus Publishing, 2001), 59 (29a). Emerson frequently refers to the *Timaeus* in his writings.
5. For a thoughtful reading of this poem in connection to Kant's aesthetics, see Harold Schweizer, "Are We Not Beautiful?" *Nineteenth-Century Prose* 40:2 (2013): 217–26. Schweizer shows how Emerson's short poem encapsulates numerous aspects of his aesthetic position.
6. See Plato, *Republic*, Book 2, and Immanuel Kant, *Critique of Judgment*, "First Moment" in the "Analytic of the Beautiful."
7. See *Enneads* 1.6.
8. I explore this aesthetic pluralism of Emerson's philosophy in Nicholas L. Guardiano, *Aesthetic Transcendentalism in Emerson, Peirce, and Nineteenth-Century American Landscape Painting* (Lanham: Lexington Press, 2017), chap. 1.
9. David A. Dilworth, "Ode to Beauty," in *Critical Companion to Ralph Waldo Emerson: A Literary Reference to His Life and Work*, ed. Tiffany K. Wayne (New York: Facts on File, 2010), 203.

10. Cavell, Goodman, and other followers draw from Emerson's epistemology of moods the overly hasty conclusion of perspectivism. Problems with Cavell's and Cavellian interpretations of Emerson are noted in Douglas R. Anderson, "American Loss in Cavell's Emerson," in *Philosophy Americana: Making Philosophy at Home in American Culture* (New York: Fordham University Press, 2006), 206–20, and Joseph Urbas, "How Close a Reader of Emerson is Stanley Cavell," *The Journal of Speculative Philosophy* 31:4 (2017): 557–74.

11. For an insightful discussion of Emerson's doctrine of experience as a central concern of the classical American pragmatists, see John J. McDermott, "Spires of Influence: The Importance of Emerson for Classical American Philosophy," in *New Morning: Emerson in the Twenty-first Century*, ed. Arthur S. Lothstein and Michael Brodrick (Albany: SUNY Press, 2008), 52–58.

12. John Dewey, *Experience and Nature*, vol. 1, *The Later Works, 1925–1953* (Carbondale: Southern Illinois University Press, 2008), 18.

13. See, for example, CW 1: 17–23 and 201–2, and I provide a full exposition of Emerson's semiotic ideas in Nicholas L. Guardiano, "Transcendentalist Encounters with a Universe of Signs," *The American Journal of Semiotics* 37:1–2 (2021): 5–45.

14. Dewey also agrees we need not fall for the conclusions of phenomenalism while we live within a world of everyday experience; see, for example, *Experience and Nature*, 12–13, 17, and 27. And again see Anderson's "American Loss in Cavell's Emerson," which uncovers important links between Emerson and Dewey on the nature of experience. Meanwhile, Vivian Hopkins further provides context with Emerson's contemporaries by explaining how Emerson rejected the phenomenalism of his friend Carlyle with its background in Fichte's philosophy (Vivian C. Hopkins, *Spires of Form: A Study of Emerson's Aesthetic Theory* [Cambridge, MA: Harvard University Press, 1951], 31–32).

15. See CW 1: 35–36.

16. See Robert C. Pollock, "A Reappraisal of Emerson," *Thought: Fordham University Quarterly* 32:124 (1957): 86–132.

17. Ibid., 95.

18. See the essay "Intellect" and its explanation of "intellect receptive" as maintaining a "pious reception" or respectful openness for gaining insight, as opposed to using forcible means (CW 2: 195 and 198).

19. Emerson names the three transcendentals in "The Poet" too where he concludes Beauty possesses a preeminent status (see CW 3: 5). Another valuable reference is Edward Emerson's reminiscence of his late father in his "Biographical Sketch," which opens *The Complete Works of Ralph Waldo Emerson*: "As he was a good citizen of his village and a patriotic American, so he was a happy and trusting soul in the Universe, seeing everywhere, in Protean forms, the inseparable Trinity of Truth, Goodness and Beauty. Mr. Emerson tells us that as a boy he pleased himself as he lay on his bed with the beauty of the Lord's equilibrium in the Universe, instead of shuddering at the terrors of his judgment, – that all was so intelligible and sweet, instead of inscrutable and dire" (Edward Waldo Emerson, "Biographical Sketch," in Ralph Waldo Emerson, *The Complete Works of Ralph Waldo Emerson*, ed. Edward Waldo Emerson, vol. 1 (Boston: Houghton, Mifflin, 1903–1904), xxxix.

20. Schweizer, "Are We Not Beautiful?" 223.
21. See Charles Peirce's "The Three Normative Sciences." Emerson is another candidate for the provenance of Peirce's trichotomic hierarchy of the Normative Sciences, together with Friedrich von Schiller whose *Aesthetic Letters* Peirce read during his college years. On the latter connection, see David A. Dilworth, "Intellectual Gravity and Elective Attractions: The Provenance of Peirce's Categories in Friedrich von Schiller," *Cognitio: Revista de Filosofia* 15, no. 1 (2014): 37–72.
22. I have elsewhere explored this aesthetic draw of nature in terms of its "transcendentalist significance" or inherent semiotic suggestiveness in Nicholas L. Guardiano, "Metaphysical Grounds of Universal Semiosis," *Cognitio: Revista de Filosofia* 21:2 (2020), esp. 11, and Guardiano, "Transcendentalist Encounters with a Universe of Signs," 21, 36, 37, passim.
23. See Albert J. von Frank's headnote to the poem at *CW* 9: 118–20.
24. McDermott, "Spires of Influence," 54.
25. Emerson's predecessor and "representative writer" Johann Wolfgang von Goethe likewise argues that poetry may aid science in the search for truth.
26. For studies of Emerson's aesthetics that attend to its crucial dependence on metaphysics, see Hopkins, *Spires of Form*; Joseph Urbas, *The Philosophy of Ralph Waldo Emerson* (New York: Routledge, 2021), chap. 4, and Guardiano, *Aesthetic Transcendentalism*, chap. 1.
27. David Hume, "On the Standard of Taste," in *Selected Essays*, ed. Stephen Copley and Andrew Edgar (Oxford: Oxford University Press, 2008), 136.
28. See Part One of the *Critique of Judgment*. Of course, Emerson's philosophy is indebted to Kant's Copernican Turn, and there are important affinities between their aesthetics, as I have had occasion to mention.
29. See Frederic Ives Carpenter, *Emerson and Asia* (Cambridge, MA: Harvard University Press, 1930), chaps. 3 and 4, which closely aligns Emerson's ideas with Neoplatonism.
30. See Plato, *Symposium*, 211a–b.
31. See Plotinus, *Enneads*, I.6.2–3 and V.8.1–2.
32. Amos Bronson Alcott, "Orphic Sayings," *The Dial* 1:3 (1840), 361, and *The Dial* 2:4 (1842), 424.
33. Emily Dickinson, *The Complete Poems of Emily Dickinson*, ed. Thomas H. Johnson (New York: Little, Brown and Company, 1961), poem 657.
34. Ibid., poem 249.
35. For more on the philosophy of nineteenth-century American landscape art, see Guardiano, *Aesthetic Transcendentalism*, chaps. 1 and 4.
36. For other interpretations of this aspect of Emerson's aesthetics, see Hopkins, *Spires of Form*, 121–34; Nicholas L. Guardiano, "Metamorphosis in Art and Nature: Emersonian Poetry," *Southwest Philosophical Studies* 33:1 (2011): 2–10, and Urbas, *The Philosophy of Ralph Waldo Emerson*, 167–78.
37. See Chatherine Tufariello, "'The Remembering Wine': Emerson's Influence on Whitman and Dickinson," in *The Cambridge Companion to Ralph Waldo Emerson*, ed. Joel Porte and Saundra Morris (Cambridge: Cambridge University Press, 1999), 162–91.
38. David A. Dilworth, "Elective Affinities: Emerson's 'Poetry and Imagination' as Anticipation of Peirce's Buddhisto-Christian Metaphysics," *Cognitio: Revista de Filosofia* 10:1 (2009): 57.

39. For more on art's participation in natural semiosis, see my "Transcendentalist Encounters," 22–23.

40. Compare Charles Peirce's insightful distinction between "argument" and "argumentation" that pragmatically expands the notion of the argument to any process of thought that compels belief (Charles S. Peirce, "A Neglected Argument for the Reality of God," in *The Essential Peirce: Selected Philosophical Writings*, ed. The Peirce Edition Project, vol. 2 (Indianapolis: Indiana University Press, 1998), 435.

41. The transcendentalist-inspired poet Wallace Stevens similarly promotes the power of poetry to disclose truth while recognizing its superiority over philosophy to this end. See, for example, his poem "Of Modern Poetry" and his essay "The Figure of the Youth as Virile Poet," in *The Necessary Angel: Essays on Reality and the Imagination*.

# 15

SPENCER TRICKER

# Emerson, Asia, and the "Progress of Culture"

In a late-career essay of 1875, Emerson celebrates Persian poetry for its "gnomic verses, [and] rules of life, conveyed in a lively image." "If the poem is long," he adds, "It is only a string of unconnected verses. They use an inconsecutiveness quite alarming to Western logic" (*CW* 8: 127). Ironically, Emerson might have used such phrases to describe his own style of essay writing, honed on the Lyceum circuit, where his "approach was to identify broad domains of inquiry and treat them in sweeping encyclopedic fashion loosely unified by leading ideas," while "depend[ing] on incisive expression to provoke an effect impossible for methodical analysis."[1] Likewise, Emerson's reputation as both a "master of digression" and a "master of the lapidary aphorism" echoes the liberty of association and vibrancy he praised in the Persian poets.[2] His engagement with this body of Asian writing, too, was hardly cursory. Quotations and references to the poet Hafiz, for example, appear in his journals over a period of nearly forty years.[3] That Emerson should specifically extol those stylistic elements of Persian poetry that resonated with the dynamics of his own poetic prose (not to mention his poetry proper) makes his unblinking reiteration of contemporary, standard-issue Orientalist stereotypes, in the very same essay, especially jarring. "Oriental life and society, especially in the Southern nations," he writes, "Stand in violent contrast with the multitudinous detail, the secular stability, and the vast average of comfort of the Western nations" (*CW* 8: 124).

The stark disjuncture between Emerson's characterization of Oriental literature, as something vital and stylistically assimilable, and his dichotomizing segregation of Occidental and Oriental "life and society" in "Persian Poetry" illustrates a larger dynamic at work behind his representations of Asia. John Eperjesi has observed a basic bifurcation in Emerson's conception of Asia: namely, that he seems to distinguish between "a religious-philosophical Asia" and "an economic Asia."[4] I agree with the first of these terms but would revise the second, broadening the economic to encompass a larger, geographical-historical vision. When discussing Asian religion, art, and philosophy, Emerson generally bestows praise and tends toward cosmopolitan, universalist sentiments. Old Asian ideas, especially from Persian, Indian, and Chinese traditions, reinforced his Transcendentalist sense of morality and, especially, his belief in "the infinitude of the private man."[5] In the contexts of geography and history, however, he gravitates toward nationalist, imperialist, and racist views. Here he betrays his vulnerability to some of the ruling ideas of geographical determinism and teleological historicism informing the ideology of manifest destiny. Yet, true to form for a writer who so famously abjured consistency, this basic distinction does not always hold. Therefore, I begin with an examination of Emerson's discrepant Asias before analyzing how – despite this general dichotomy – he was sometimes able to subvert his prevailing tendency and introduce uncommon subtleties.

## "This every man contains within him": Emerson's Religious-Philosophical Asia

Emerson wrote that "the only bond of connection which can traverse the long duration which separates the ends of the world and unites the first people to the knowledge and sympathy of the last people, is religion" (*JMN* 10: 62). Given his background as a former minister, Emerson's espousal of this view is hardly surprising. In the context of religion, he greatly esteemed Asian civilizations, especially Persia, India, and China. Emerson thought that human fulfillment should be sought within and that self-reliance was a prerequisite to communion with nature, the world, and the divine. As he wrote in "The Over-Soul" (1841), "Within man is the soul of the whole; the wise silence; the universal beauty, to which every part and particle is equally related; the eternal ONE" (*CW* 2: 160). This belief resonated strongly with certain ideas he encountered in Asian religion and philosophy, even if this resonance has often gone unheard. As Yoshinobu Hakutani points out, "American interpreters [of Emerson] have long failed to see the globalization and hybridization of American transcendentalism."[6] Importantly, Emerson considered the major texts of Persia, India, and China to be among "the Bibles of the world." Among these, he specifically classified "the Desatir of the Persians, and the Zoroastrian Oracles; the Vedas and Laws of Menu; the Upanishads, the Vishnu Purana, the Bhagavat Geeta of the Hindoos; the books of the Buddhists; [and] the Chinese classic, of four books, containing the wisdom of Confucius and Mencius" as "living characters translatable into every tongue and form of life." "Is there any geography in these things?" he pondered, "We call them Asiatic, we call them primeval; but perhaps that is only optical" (*CW* 7: 110–11). Among the ancient tomes of Asia, Emerson struck some of his most universalist tones.

Compared to other Asian influences, the impact of Persian poetry and Indian religious-philosophical texts on Emerson is well documented.[7] As Arthur Versluis observes, "Emersonian Transcendentalism subordinate[d] poetry and the arts to the religious impulse," and the Persian poetry of Hafiz and Sa'di to which he was so devoted was firmly rooted in Sufism's unorthodox interpretation of the *Qur'an*.[8] Given Emerson's nonconformist views toward organized Christianity and education, Roger Sedarat argues that "like his Sufi predecessors who attempted to break with traditional modes of learning, he tends to favor revealed insight over rational deduction."[9] Beyond Sufism, Sedarat also notes that Emerson "makes more references to [the ancient Iranian prophet] Zoroaster than any other Oriental writer except Plotinus," though he derived his knowledge of Zoroastrianism through "spurious" sources (such as the *Desatir*).[10] Indian spiritual texts also represent significant influences and points of resonance for Emerson's writing. Under the likely influence of his aunt Mary Moody Emerson, he began reading Indian literature in translation as early as the 1820s. It has been observed that his concept of the "'Over-soul' bears many similarities to the *Brahma* of Upanishad philosophy,"[11] while his theory of "compensation" corresponds closely to the concept of *karma* discussed by Arjuna and Krishna in the Bhagavad Gita.[12] Lawrence Buell notes that although Indian scripture was not a major influence on Emerson until the 1840s, it "helped him frame the antidualistic spirituality that increasingly drew him as the hold of Protestantism waned." More specifically, "It helped him fortify his theory of spiritual impersonality and fathom how the material world might be illusory without being nonexistent."[13] Because such correspondences have been well-established, however, I will spend the remainder of this section discussing the less frequently explored link between Emerson and Chinese religious-philosophical literature.

While Emerson rejected most Buddhist ideas, he found inspiration in the primary texts of Confucianism, or more precisely, Neo-Confucianism. As Yoshio Takanashi has shown, several of Emerson's key ideas display remarkable parallels to those of the leading figures in Neo-Confucianism, especially Song Dynasty scholar Zhu Xi. Each of these thinkers, he explains, "developed theories ... of the correspondence and interrelation of universal law and the human mind."[14] Neo-Confucianism heavily emphasized a canon of Confucian texts known as the Four Books (*Analects of Confucius, Great Learning, Doctrine of the Mean,* and *Book of Mencius*), which comprised central subject matter for Chinese civil service examinations from the thirteenth through early twentieth centuries. As compared to the Five Classics, which had been the dominant Confucian texts prior to this period, "The Four Books tend to be less historical, descriptive, and concrete; [and are]

concerned principally with the nature of man, the springs or inner source of his morality, and his relation to the larger cosmos." It was Zhu Xi, chief among others, who raised the "more discursive and abstract" Four Books to prominence in Chinese culture and this legacy directly influenced the earliest published translations of Confucian texts by Christian missionaries during the nineteenth century.[15] Therefore, while Emerson never alludes to Zhu Xi by name, he would have read translations of the Four Books, such as David Collie's (1828) and James Legge's (1861), that were heavily informed by Zhu's commentaries.

Although Emerson directly refers to Confucius and Mencius in well-known essays like "Fate" (1860), as well as other published and unpublished writings from throughout his career, his affinity for Neo-Confucian thought is best grasped not through specific allusions, but in his overall conception of the individual's progress to moral understanding. One of the most recurrent concepts emphasized in the Four Books is the idea that every individual is born good and true, but that this internal goodness and truth is clouded – to varying degrees depending on the individual – by a "psychophysical" substance called $qi$.[16] The task of the individual is to disperse these clouds through self-cultivation. As expressed in one of the Four Books, "The Way of Great Learning lies in letting one's inborn luminous virtue shine forth, in renewing the people, and in coming to rest in perfect goodness."[17] The ethical character of this idea, combined with its emphasis on the individual, resonates profoundly with the Emersonian account of self-cultivation or "culture," as can be seen in his famous passage on the value of books in "The American Scholar" (1837): "The one thing in the world of value," he writes, "is, the active soul, – the soul, free, sovereign, active. This every man is entitled to; this every man contains within him, although in almost all men, obstructed, and as yet unborn" (CW 1: 56). As in the Neo-Confucian texts, we find that Emerson articulates a common inheritance of interior goodness for all humanity, which nonetheless requires a process of cultivation to refine and exemplify in good moral behavior. This ethical dynamic, which also accentuates the indispensable role of the scholar in maintaining a well-ordered society, showcases one of the most underappreciated synergies of American Transcendentalist and east Asian thought.

Emerson's affinity for Neo-Confucianist teachings and other Asian religious and philosophical ideas renders his regular denigration of Asia in geographical and historical discussions both surprising and incongruous. It seems that like "the bulk of mankind," whom he criticized from the position of an enlightened observer in "Fate," Emerson "believe[d] in two gods" when it came to the topic of Asia. Most people, he opines, "are under one dominion here in the house, as friend and parent, in social circles, in letters, in art, in love, in religion: but in mechanics, in dealing with steam and climate, in trade, in politics, they think they come under another; and that it would be a practical blunder to transfer the method and way of working of one sphere, into the other" (*CW* 6: 17). Here, as in so many other areas of his writing, Emerson identified people's failure to grasp the unity of the individual, the world, and the divine, as one of the most pervasive and disabling illusions of nineteenth-century life. Yet, when it came to representing the world's most populous continent and its cultural expressions, his own understanding was fundamentally disunited.

### "In violent contrast": Emerson's Geographical-Historical Asia

Emerson lived in times given (at least in the West) to teleological understandings of history. There was a clear spatial element to these understandings, which framed human history as originating in Asia and moving west, attaining its destiny with Anglo-Saxon achievement in North America. Such historiography can be traced to Jedidiah Morse's 1797 treatise *The American Universal Geography*, which recast "history as geography" and "celebrated the incarnation of the spirit of liberal idealism and of the individualist self in the North American continent."[18] John O'Sullivan, editor of the *Democratic Review*, would famously reiterate these ideas in his formulation of "manifest destiny," which interpreted American westward expansion as a preordained fact of history. Like O'Sullivan, who in 1839 described the United States as "the great nation of futurity,"[19] Emerson firmly believed his homeland to be "the country of the future" (*CW* 1: 230).

Emerson's investment in Eurocentric, geographical determinism – or "the idea that territorial endowment simultaneously substantiates and enables culture" – can be traced to key passages in some of his most influential texts.[20] Take, for example, the following passage from "Experience" (1844), which champions common sense and intuition: "The great gifts are not got by analysis. Everything good is on the highway. The middle region of our being is the temperate zone. We may climb into the thin and cold realm of pure geometry and lifeless science, or sink into that of sensation. Between these extremes is the equator of life, of thought, of spirit, of poetry, – a narrow belt" (*CW* 3: 36). In this passage, democratic sentiments about the accessibility of insight are filtered through a geographical metaphor of the self, wherein the globe becomes a model for the body, comprised of a northerly mind and southerly appetites. Yet, when we compare this to a late essay like "Resources" (1875), we find that the metaphor is no mere metaphor but grounded in a very particular geographical conception that proves compatible with American exceptionalism:

It is in vain to make a paradise but for good men. The tropics are one vast garden; yet man is more miserably fed and conditioned there than in the cold and stingy zones. The healthy, the civil, the industrious, the learned, the moral race, – Nature herself only yields her secret to these. And the resources of America and its future will be immense only to wise and virtuous men. (CW 8: 81)

This juxtaposition of passages showcases that, for Emerson, "the temperate zone" is not simply a figure for intellectual or spiritual balance, but instead constitutes the actual and exclusive geographical terrain in which humanity can attain both moral and material perfection: America.

What Emerson meant by "the temperate zone" does not exactly coincide with how a present-day geographer or climatologist might use this phrase. Instead, the "temperate" represents a blend of English and American politics, climate, and racial character, as exemplified by his description in "Persian Poetry" of the "secular stability, and the vast average of comfort of the Western nations" (CW 8: 124). Assuming this Western temperament as an ideal, Emerson's related notion of "the temperate zone" was not only longitudinal but also latitudinal. In other words, it encompassed Orientalist principles. As famously described by Edward Said, Orientalism is a Western ideology that divides the world into Occidental and Oriental realms, with "the Orient" representing an absolute otherness against which Occidental culture and society can be negatively defined. Importantly, Said understands Orientalism not only as an ideology about Asia but also "as a Western style for dominating, restructuring, and having authority over the Orient."[21] Although Malini Johar Schueller has observed key differences in the patterns of US Orientalisms versus the older European strain analyzed by Said, Emerson's "Persian Poetry" reproduces a classic, insistent view of the Orient as a land of sharp contrasts, oscillating between lazy passivity and impulsive violence; between lush opulence and stark penury.[22] "Life in the East," he states, "Is fierce, short, hazardous, and in extremes. Its elements are few and simple, not exhibiting the long range and undulation of European existence, but rapidly reaching the best and the worst. The rich feed on fruits and game, – the poor, on a watermelon's peel. All or nothing is the genius of Oriental life" (CW 8: 124). Here, Emerson's penchant for aphorism manifests in its most reductive and derivative guise, showcasing that, in many respects, he "accepted his century's 'racism' with enthusiasm."[23]

Emerson had expressed similar opinions earlier in his career, as can be seen in 1847's "The Superlative." As in "Persian Poetry," Emerson's Orientalist pronouncements are couched in terms of geographical and environmental conditions. "The expression of character," he states, "Is, in great degree, a matter of climate." He draws hard distinctions between East and West:

"Whilst [Nature] appoints us to keep within sharp boundaries of form as the condition of our strength [in the West], she creates in the East the uncontrollable yearning to escape from limitation into the vast and boundless" (W 10: 176). He contrasts the East, as that part of the world where riches are easily obtained and extravagantly displayed by the wealthy, and the West, where prosperity has been hard won through diligent industry, epitomized in "the manufacture of iron." "Universally," he declares, "the better gold, the worse man. The political economist defies us to show any goldmine country that is traversed by good roads: or a shore where pearls are found on which good schools are erected" (W 10: 178). Notwithstanding the irony of the California Gold Rush, which would begin just a year after Emerson delivered his speech, "The Superlative" showcases that geographical determinism represented a key component of his Orientalist view of Asia in both the early and late stages of his career.

At times, Emerson did offer nuanced criticisms of his era's so-called race science. This can be seen in "Experience," for example, when he takes aim at phrenologists as "theoretic kidnappers and slave-drivers, [who] esteem each man the victim of another, who winds him round his finger by knowing the law of his being; and, by such cheap signboards as the color of his beard or the slope of his occiput, reads the inventory of his fortunes and character." "The grossest ignorance," he added, "Does not disgust like this impudent knowingness" (CW 3: 31). Yet the bold confidence with which he contrasts Eastern and Western peoples and civilizations in "Persian Poetry" illustrates just how strongly a geographical, if not biological, determinism informed his worldview. It does seem, as Buell has noted, that "despite his belief in a 'universal' mind linking humankind beneath ethnic differences, despite his indignation that slavery was protected under the Constitution and his doubts about race as a viable category, Emerson never ceased to believe that 'the decided preference of the Saxon on the whole for civil liberty is the security of the modern world.'"[24] In other words, his ostensible cosmopolitanism was undermined by deeper investments in race science. Importantly, however, the "negative" or disparaging Orientalism Emerson displays in "Persian Poetry" and "The Superlative" is not exactly the corollary of an alternate, "positive Orientalism" represented by his interest in the wisdom of ancient Asian texts.[25] This is because Emerson rarely approaches such texts with the aim of establishing their essential difference from superior Western ones. Neither does he elevate Asian ideas in a fetishistic manner (despite giving the nickname of "Asia" to his second wife, Lidian). Instead, he consistently intimates the unity of Western and Eastern philosophical traditions.

This is what makes Emerson's bifurcated representations of Asia so puzzling: They do not simply manifest two sides of the same Orientalist coin.

On the one hand, he engaged with ancient Asian ideas in ways that are less Orientalist than many, if not most, of his American contemporaries. He saw these ideas as offering true wisdom and "thanks in good part to his example, Transcendentalism became the first intellectual movement in the United States to take Asian religious thought seriously."[26] On the other hand, his works exhibit flagrant Orientalist stereotypes that denigrate Asia and Asian peoples as they exist in his nineteenth-century present. Emerson's treatment of India is typical in this regard: He displays a marked tendency to "focu[s] on ancient philosophies and scriptures and sacraliz[e] a spiritual India of the past," while obscuring the material reality of India under British colonial rule in his own moment.[27] Such a disunited conception of Asia may result from what Philip Nicoloff has described as Emerson's notion of the "life-cycle of nations," in which "every matured nation was seen to pass" through phases of "birth, flowering, and decline."[28] If Asian civilizations had run their course, there would be no contradiction in celebrating their past achievements while either abhorring or simply ignoring their present-day manifestations.

Another possible explanation might be that Emerson extracts ideas from Asian religious-philosophical traditions in a manner that is more self-serving than reciprocal. Nan Z. Da has recently observed that Emerson's writings on China represent a key example of "intransitive encounter," which she describes as a species of nineteenth century, transnational literary "exchange in which nothing is exchanged" at all. Instead, such an encounter involves a writer from one country making a "minimal (but not insincere) investment" in the literature of a foreign country (in this case China), which serves up "a set of opportunities to make that which did not seem politically, experientially, or rhetorically plausible, plausible."[29] In other words, "intransitive encounters" represent literary occasions when foreign texts prompt a writer to contemplate the present form of their own society, as well as possibilities for reform in the future. Such meetings of text and reader, in Da's view, occurred regularly among American and Chinese writers during the nineteenth century but have become hard to articulate due to present-day conceptions of literary exchange – informed by the history of globalization – as necessarily resulting in reciprocal transformation among the parties involved.

For Da, Emerson's writings never indicate "any kind of sustained interest in China or cross-cultural literary exchange." Instead, he approached writings about China – in the geographical-historical sense, I would add – "within the genre of China thinking as domestic reform."[30] Notably, Emerson delivered a *pro forma* banquet address to members of an 1868 Chinese embassy in Boston and was closely involved with key shapers of

US foreign policy. Among these figures were Secretary of State William Henry Seward and Ambassador Anson Burlingame, who in 1868 negotiated a treaty that opened emigration between China and the US for a brief but significant period, before domestic anti-Chinese sentiment (especially on the West Coast) led to formal restriction through laws like the Page Act (1875) and Chinese Exclusion Act (1882). Importantly, however, Da notes that Seward and Burlingame's Sino-American policy rhetoric was largely "romantic" and, rather than being committed to serious international cooperation, was mostly "advertised as a boon for domestic infrastructure," such as the transcontinental railroad.[31] If Emerson, too, encountered China in largely "intransitive" terms premised on US development and reforms, rather than any consequential intercultural exchange, this might help to explain why he characterized Asia in such divergent terms. But what about all those years of reading and writing about Persian, Indian, and Chinese religious-philosophical literature? While Da's argument is compelling in the immediate context of Sino-American diplomatic affairs, Emerson's multi-decade immersion in a broader array of Asian texts surely represents something more than a minimal, if sincere, investment in the ideas they expressed: It was, as many scholars have shown, a sustained reading that left indelible marks on his articulation of Transcendentalism. Ultimately, then, the reasoning behind Emerson's discrepant Asias – celebratory in the religious-philosophical sense, derogatory in the geographical-historical – remains hard to explain, even if this basic pattern holds for most of his career.

## Repudiating Progress in "Progress of Culture"

One of the occasions in which Emerson manages to subvert this dynamic is the essay "Progress of Culture," first delivered in 1867 as a Phi Beta Kappa address at Harvard and later reprinted in 1875's *Letters and Social Aims*. Once seen as "a signal of the beginning of [Emerson's] decline as the leading American intellectual," because of his evident struggles at the podium, the text itself represents an important "means for understanding and reclaiming 'late Emerson' as useful and valuable ground."[32] Before discussing this essay, however, it is important to note that Emerson typically uses the word "culture" to signify "a general process of intellectual, spiritual and aesthetic development," as in the sense of "self-cultivation," rather than as a name for "a particular way of life, whether of a people, a period or a group" or as an "independent and abstract noun which describes the works and practices of intellectual and especially artistic activity."[33]

Seven years earlier he had asserted that "culture" (again, as a process of self-development) enables one to "modulate the violence of any master-tones that have a drowning preponderance in his scale, and succor him against himself. Culture redresses his balance, puts him among his equals and superiors, revives his delicious sense of sympathy, and warns him of the dangers of solitude and repulsion" (CW 6: 72). In relation to Neo-Confucian thought, earlier described, Emersonian culture can thus be understood as that which brings the individual into harmony (noting the passage's musical metaphor) with his inner potential for moral rectitude and unity of the self, the world, and the divine. At the end of "Culture," Emerson turns to geology to highlight the continuing need for culture in a world in which people are still incomplete. "The fossil strata," he says, "Shows us that Nature began with rudimental forms, and rose to the more complex, as fast as the earth was fit for their dwelling-place; and that the lower perish, as the higher appear. Very few of our race can be said to be finished men." Culture, he goes on to say, affords the key to man's future completion. "Half-engaged in the soil, pawing to get free, man needs all the music that can be brought to disengage him ... Man's culture can spare nothing, wants all the material. He is to convert all impediments into instruments, all enemies into power" (CW 6: 88). Emerson's allusion to the soil evinces his sense of "culture" as individual cultivation, while the reference to "[un]finished men" betrays his investment in notions of teleological progression from the simple to the complex.

This viewpoint becomes more complicated in the later "Progress of Culture." In this lecture, Emerson returns to the subject of geology. However, in confronting the sublime magnitude of geologic deep time, Emerson implies that the triumphalist teleology of geographic determinism is an insufficient model for understanding world history.

> Geology, a science of forty or fifty summers, has had the effect to throw an air of novelty and mushroom speed over entire history. The oldest empires, – what we called venerable antiquity,--now that we have true measures of duration, – show like creations of yesterday ... The old six thousand years of chronology become a kitchen-clock, – no more a measure of time than an hour-glass or an egg-glass,--since the duration of geologic periods has come into view.... Nothing is old but the mind. (CW 8: 111)

This moment witnesses Emerson's temporary subversion of both geographical determinism and older stadialist models of the rise and fall of republics. While he could not fully extricate himself from a narrative of progress as "the inevitable fulfillment of a preexisting transcendent order," the essay nonetheless demonstrates considerable divergence from this "deterministic theory."[34] More importantly, for present purposes, "Progress of Culture" profoundly adjusts the frame through which Orientalism, premised on the fallen achievement of an ancient Asia, usually operates. Emerson accentuates this alternate view by positing "also a certain equivalence of the ages of history ... it were ignorance not to see that each nation and period has done its full part to make up the result of existing civility ... The world is always equal to itself" (*CW* 8: 111). Interestingly, Emerson had occasionally broached this view in past works, such as "Self-Reliance," in which he writes that "Society never advances. It recedes as fast on one side as it gains on the other. It undergoes continual changes; it is barbarous, it is civilized, it is Christianized, it is rich, it is scientific; but this change is not amelioration" (*CW* 2: 48). In "Progress of Culture," he returned to this assessment, but with a direct reflection on Asia.

As in other works, "Progress of Culture" includes a specific list of Asian writers and thinkers that had become commonplace to Emerson at this stage in his career. As in "Books," where he celebrated them as "living characters translatable into every tongue and form of life," he again extols figures such as Zoroaster and Confucius, while also celebrating "the grand scriptures, only recently known to western nations, of the Indian Vedas, the Institutes of Menu, the Puranas, the poems of the Mahabarat and the Ramayana." More interesting, however, is the fact that Emerson goes on to observe resonances between Asian and North American material forms in the geopolitical present, noting that "the war-proa of the Malays in the Japanese waters struck Commodore Perry by its close resemblance to the yacht America" (a sailing vessel that won the first America's Cup in 1851) (*CW* 8: 112). Although Emerson partly echoes representations of Malays found in the works of earlier Romantic writers (like Thomas de Quincey), as well as contemporary authors (like Herman Melville), by prefacing this comparison with a broader reference to "the races that we still call savage, or semi-savage," his willingness to enfold Malays within the human family stands out from a more common practice of representing Southeast Asian peoples as nonhuman beings.[35] In "Self-Reliance" (1841), Emerson had handled such comparisons differently. "What a contrast," he continues, "between the well-clad, reading, writing, thinking American ... and the naked New Zealander, whose property is a club, a spear, a mat, and an undivided twentieth of a shed to sleep under. But compare the health of the two men, and you shall see that his aboriginal strength the white man has lost" (*CW* 2: 48). By taking the resemblance between the Malay proa and the yacht *America* as signs of a world "always equal to itself," Emerson departs from the stadialist notion behind his earlier discussion of the American and the New Zealander, in which the former's progress toward intellect was indexed precisely by the "aboriginal" stasis of the latter.

In addition to this modification of views, "Progress of Culture" makes room for a cyclical understanding of history and human endeavor that resonates with Indian and Chinese philosophy. At the very least, it unhooks the notion of "progress" from its central place in teleological conceptions of linear history. While the postbellum age was marked by innumerable new technological advances, Emerson does not represent it as dialectically overcoming its predecessor. His statement, at a moment of epochal transition, is to assert that "we find ... a certain equivalence in the ages" (*CW* 8: 111–12). The essay also registers an important "revision of [his] early individualism," by "validating the importance of both cooperative effort and sustaining institutions," which David M. Robinson interprets as being "brought on by the American crisis over slavery" and the Union victory in the Civil War.[36] However, Emerson's emphasis on the relationship of the individual to the health of collectivities and social institutions can also be seen as complementary to Asian religious and philosophical views, such as those outlined in the Neo-Confucian canon, which trace the origins of social harmony to the moral decision-making of leading individuals.

By disrupting the binary between historical treatments of the dynamic West (linear, teleological) and the static East (cyclical), Emerson expressed universalist sentiments in keeping with his Transcendentalism. That philosophy, we recall, conceives of dualistic thinking (so essential to the binaries of Orientalism) as "terms such that, at a deeper or higher level ... are revealed to be really complementary."[37] What is so unusual about "Progress of Culture," however, is its expression of this universalist sensibility, usually reserved for those times when he is discussing religious and philosophical traditions, in the midst of a discussion of geography and history – normally domains in which his representations of Asia tend toward the blatantly Orientalist. Although the essay has been understandably characterized as "an odd, cross-purposed piece that begins with conventional vignettes of cultural progress but pivots to talk about literary history," we might also read it as exhibiting one of the primary advantages of Emerson's essayistic method, which could defy the systematicity of ideological structures like Orientalism, or geographical determinism, by virtue of its innumerable digressions, revisions, and internal contradictions.[38] If, as T. W. Adorno once wrote, a good essay is "something to be taken all the more seriously in that it takes place not systematically but rather as a characteristic of an intention groping its way," we might consider Emerson's erratic representations of Asia as being – at their best – liberatingly indecisive.[39] Reading for these moments of indecision allows us to defamiliarize Emerson, who is often read as a writer fixated on the idea of unity. Disunity, his writings on Asia demonstrate, constitutes another key element of his contribution to nineteenth-century American thought and culture.

# Notes

1. Lawrence Buell, *Emerson* (Cambridge, MA: Harvard University Press, 2003), 26.
2. Catherine Tufariello, "'The Remembering Wine': Emerson's Influence on Whitman and Dickinson," in *The Cambridge Companion to Emerson*, ed. Joel Porte and Saundra Morris (Cambridge: Cambridge University Press, 1999), 189.
3. Wai-Chee Dimock, *Through Other Continents: American Literature across Deep Time* (Princeton: Princeton University Press, 2006), 45.
4. John R. Eperjesi, *The Imperialist Imaginary: Visions of Asia and the Pacific in American Culture* (Hanover, NH: University Press of New England, 2005), 36.
5. Buell, *Emerson*, 59.
6. Yoshinobu Hakutani, *East-West Literary Imagination: Cultural Exchanges from Yeats to Morrison* (Columbia: University of Missouri Press, 2017), 6.
7. Examples of this work include Frederic I. Carpenter, *Emerson and Asia* (Cambridge, MA: Harvard University Press, 1930), and Shanta Acharya, *The Influence of Indian Thought on Ralph Waldo Emerson* (Lewiston, NY: Edwin Mellen Press, 2001).
8. Arthur Versluis, *American Transcendentalism and Asian Religions* (Oxford: Oxford University Press, 1993), 6.
9. Roger Sedarat, *Emerson in Iran: The American Appropriation of Persian Poetry* (Albany: SUNY Press, 2019), 33.
10. Sedarat, *Emerson in Iran*, 38–39.
11. Yoshio Takanashi, *Emerson and Neo-Confucianism: Crossing Paths over the Pacific* (New York: Palgrave MacMillan, 2014), 3.
12. Versluis, *American Transcendentalism*, 58.
13. Buell, *Emerson*, 173.
14. Takanashi, *Emerson and Neo-Confucianism*, 1.
15. Daniel K. Gardner, *The Four Books: The Basic Teachings of the Later Confucian Tradition* (Indianapolis: Hackett, 2007), xxii.
16. Ibid., 133.
17. Ibid., 3.
18. Myra Jehlen, *American Incarnation: The Individual, the Nation, and the Continent* (Cambridge, MA: Harvard University Press, 1986), 9.
19. John O'Sullivan, "The Great Nation of Futurity," *United States Magazine and Democratic Review*, November 1839, 426.
20. Jenine Abboushi Dallal, "American Imperialism UnManifest: Emerson's 'Inquest' and Cultural Regeneration," *American Literature* 73:1 (2001): 58.
21. Edward Said, *Orientalism* (New York: Vintage, 1979), 2–3.
22. Malini Johar Schueller, *U.S. Orientalisms: Race, Nation, and Gender in Literature, 1790–1890* (Ann Arbor: University of Michigan Press, 1998), 9.
23. Philip L. Nicoloff, *Emerson on Race and History: An Examination of English Traits* (New York: Columbia University Press, 1961), 118.
24. Buell, *Emerson*, 262–63.
25. Versluis, *American Transcendentalism and Asian Religions*, 5.
26. Buell, *Emerson*, 172.
27. Schueller, *U.S. Orientalisms*, 157.
28. Nicoloff, *Emerson on Race and History*, 126.

29. Nan Z. Da, *Intransitive Encounter: Sino-U.S. Literatures and the Limits of Exchange* (New York: Columbia University Press, 2018), 1–2.
30. Ibid., 71–72.
31. Ibid., 74.
32. David M. Robinson, "Emerson, American Democracy, and 'Progress of Culture,'" *Nineteenth-Century Prose* 30:1–2 (2003), 285.
33. Raymond Williams, *Keywords: A Vocabulary of Culture and Society* (New York: Oxford University Press, 1976), 80.
34. Robinson, "Emerson, American Democracy, and 'Progress of Culture,'" 293.
35. For discussion of the Malay figure in Melville and antebellum literature, see Spencer Tricker, "'Five Dusky Phantoms': Gothic Form and Cosmopolitan Shipwreck in *Moby-Dick*," *Studies in American Fiction* 44:1 (2017): 1–26.
36. Robinson, "Emerson, American Democracy, and 'Progress of Culture,'" 295.
37. Jehlen, American Incarnation, 82.
38. Da, Intransitive Encounter, 75.
39. Theodor W. Adorno, "The Essay as Form," in *Notes to Literature, Volume One*, ed. Rolf Tiedemann, trans. Shierry Weber Nicholsen (New York: Columbia University Press, 1991), 16.

# 16

SEAN ROSS MEEHAN

# Emerson's Late Styles

A passage from the 1859 lecture "Art and Criticism" provides a useful vantage point for reconsidering the tendency in Emerson studies to disregard Emerson's later work and thought. "Whatever new object we see, we perceive to be only a new version of our familiar experience, and we set about translating it at once into our parallel facts. We have hereby our vocabulary." Discussing the "idealism" by which the poet "regards the world as symbolic, and all these symbols or forms as fugitive and convertible expressions," Emerson repeats a note that echoes back to "The Poet" (1844) and even earlier back to *Nature* (1836). Lecturing nearly a quarter century after his first book, Emerson reiterates a familiar vocabulary of Emersonian expression (W 12: 300).

Where, then, do we find Emerson's later work? How should we distinguish its translations from their earlier, presumably more original versions? Chronologically, we might define the period broadly to include the works that come after *Essays: Second Series* (1844) and extend through the final books published by Emerson, *Letters and Social Aims* (1875) and *Selected Poems* (1876). More narrowly, we could locate late Emerson in the works he delivered or published after *The Conduct of Life* (1860), Emerson's final two decades of work. Delivered near the beginning of that final period, "Art and Criticism" indicates one of the concerns nested in the reception of Emerson's later work: *authorial integrity*. Emerson never published "Art and Criticism" as such, neither as a lecture nor as an essay, in his lifetime. Emerson's son, Edward Waldo Emerson, drawing upon incomplete lecture manuscripts and notebooks, compiled the lecture and published it posthumously in *The Complete Works of Ralph Waldo Emerson* (1903–4), in the final volume titled *Natural History of Intellect and Other Papers*. Edward also recomposed the title piece of that volume as first compiled and published in 1893 by Emerson's literary executor, James Elliot Cabot, adding "Art and Criticism" to the mix. There is, then, a significant element of *mediation* one must reckon with in "Art and Criticism" and throughout the

270

works to follow. This is also the case for the *Natural History of Intellect*, a project that the mature Emerson characterized as his chief intellectual endeavor, delivered in numerous lecture variations between the late 1840s and early 1870s, though never completed or published as a whole by Emerson himself. Some of the later works Emerson did bring to publication in his lifetime, including the essays collected in *Letters and Social Aims*, were not published by Emerson alone, but rather with significant editorial collaboration provided by Cabot and Emerson's daughter Ellen Tucker Emerson, a response to Emerson's weakening mental acuity resulting from a stroke-induced aphasia and the onset of dementia.

But the larger problem that has long underwritten a critical disregard of Emerson's work after the 1850s is not that late Emerson is unfamiliar to readers in his years of declining vitality, as though he had forgotten his place in the middle of reading a lecture. The problem, rather, is that Emerson's thinking on the fugitive symbols of nature seems all too familiar, uncannily so, in its range of repetitions. As Cabot notes in his preface to the volume of *Letters and Social Aims* he republished in the 1893 Riverside edition of Emerson's works, the "loss of memory and of mental grasp" made completing the volume without their editorial collaboration "unlikely": "Sentences, even whole pages, were repeated, and there was a confusion of order beyond what even he would have tolerated" (W 8: x). Cabot provides insight into the challenging circumstances, particularly after 1872, that Emerson's aging and aphasia created for the writing and lecturing that would continue through the rest of the decade. But Cabot's "beyond what even he would have tolerated" should also remind us that Emerson's style of writing was already regarded – by his audience, by his critics, and by Emerson himself – as challenging in terms of its lack of logical coherence and its tendency for repetition.

The disordered condition of the lecture remnants of "Art and Criticism," like the various pieces that remain of the course on *Natural History of Intellect* (delivered at Harvard in 1870 and repeated in 1871), kept both from being included in *The Later Lectures of Ralph Waldo Emerson*, coedited by Ronald A. Bosco and Joel Myerson. But the access now afforded Emerson scholars and readers by the publication of *The Later Lectures* (2001) opens up new vantage points for thinking through Emerson's late works. We can now perceive Emerson "in the laboratory of his composing process," as Bosco and Myerson elucidate the creative significance of Emerson's later lectures in the development of his writing and the shaping of his style. For Bosco and Myerson, apparent disorganization "nevertheless invites the listener or reader to follow the author's own thought processes" (*LL* 1: xx, xxvii). This new vantage is further enhanced by the publication of Emerson's topical and poetry notebooks, antislavery writings, and the publication of the final volumes of the authoritative *Collected Works of Ralph Waldo Emerson*, including *Society and Solitude* (1870) and *Letters and Social Aims*. With these resources in hand, we can responsibly approach the editorial complexities of Emerson's late authorship while also recognizing "Emerson's later intellectual or literary vitality" through the 1860s and into the 1870s (*CW* 7: xxiv).[1] Pathbreaking scholarship by David Robinson, Laura Dassow Walls, Roger Thompson, Joseph Urbas, and others has extended the study of Emerson's engagement in cultural, social, scientific, and philosophical matters into the work beyond the 1850s, warranting the reconsideration of what Robinson calls the "ethical purpose in the later work."[2] We might go further, as Christopher Hanlon does in *Emerson's Memory Loss*, to argue that Emerson's late style of collaborative authorship is part of a continuum that reaches back to earlier work such as "Self-Reliance" (1841), but also unsettles the assertions for originality made famous in that essay. In "Self-Reliance" Emerson warns, "imitation is suicide" (*CW* 2: 27). In "Quotation and Originality," the 1859 lecture published first in 1868 in the *North American Review* and then included in *Letters and Social Aims*, Emerson asserts, "There is imitation, model, and suggestion to the very archangels, if we knew their history" (*CW* 8: 94). For Hanlon, Emerson's later "communal styles of intellection," translating while transfiguring earlier conceptions of Emersonian authorship, are not merely or regrettably something to be cautiously negotiated by readers and editors of late Emerson. Rather, such styles are productively theorized in those works and provide "a way of reading Emerson anew."[3]

The opportunity for reading Emerson anew is to understand how rhetoric for Emerson is a significant concept in, and not just the most relevant context for, the composition and continuing recomposition of the late work. The art of rhetoric or "eloquence" was a popular lecture topic for Emerson, delivered across three decades (1846–75), with distinct essays published from those lectures in both *Society and Solitude* and *Letters and Social Aims*. As Roger Thompson demonstrates in *Emerson and the History of Rhetoric*, Emerson was not just a prominent rhetorical practitioner as a lecturer during these decades; he was also a rhetorical theorist who made "rhetoric as an object of study" central to his aims and office.[4] This does not mean that Emerson was not also actively engaged in philosophy and poetics as well. All three modes of developing ideas engage late Emerson and, indeed, blend together, as is the case most notably in the *Natural History of Intellect* project. But rhetoric, as we will see, names for Emerson not just certain stylistic elements we can track in his writing but also an underlying conception for how thought matters and moves – or in Emersonian vocabulary, how thought circulates, translates, and assimilates – among new perceptions and familiar, older experiences. I have in mind three aspects of style, interrelated in Emerson's vocabulary, that speak to these rhetorical matters: metonymy, analogy, and translation. Yet another word Emerson offers and repeats in his late work to characterize this dynamic, rhetorical relation of thinking across topics and time is "recomposition." Emerson's rhetoric of recomposition mediates among the various ideas and texts of mental and moral philosophy, the natural sciences, poetry, the arts, and cultural and social criticism that captivated Emerson as a reader and which he sought to continue to translate for his readers.

## "A Low Idealism"

To the "modern" topic of "Art and Criticism," defined as the art of writing and the capacity of literature "to make words pass for things," Emerson applies the older, classical "name of Rhetoric" (W 12: 283). In the 1859 lecture, at least as recomposed by Edward Emerson, but also with substantial correlating passages legible in his journals and topical notebooks, Emerson names three characteristic rules of rhetoric: "Low Style," "Compression," and "what the books call *Metonomy* [sic]," the last of which he calls a "principal power of rhetoric" and then renames "a low Idealism" (W 12: 299–300). In fact, the passage on the "new version of our familiar experience" with which I began is set amidst Emerson's articulation of metonymy's significance in his rhetoric. Metonymy (from the Greek, "change of name") names the rhetorical figure for representing something by way of another thing proximally, contiguously, or contextually associated with it. The figure often works by linguistic compression or condensation – Emerson is astute in this regard. The poet Lyn Hejinian defines metonymy simply as "a condensation of its context."[5] However, Emerson greatly expands the figure in describing it as a "principal power of rhetoric." For Emerson, rhetoric does not just employ the figure of metonymic compression as one among many stylistic techniques, including more familiar figures such as metaphor. Rather, rhetoric operates fundamentally through metonymy: rhetoric is a condensation of its context. Emerson thus collapses all of rhetoric into this one figure when he asserts, "All conversation, as all literature, appears to me the pleasure of rhetoric, or, I may say, of metonomy. 'To make of motes mountains, and of mountains motes,' Isocrates said, 'was the orator's office.' Well, that is what poetry and thinking do" (W 12: 300). Characterizing Emerson's "associative style" as "metonymic," Johannes Voelz aligns the transformational potential of Emerson's rhetoric with its "performative," oratorical contexts.[6] In "Art and Criticism," invoking Isocrates, Emerson performs rhetoric's power of transmutation (to make mountains into motes) by transforming the mote of metonymy into a mountainous figure for poetry and all literature, for conversation, and for the act of thinking itself.

Emerson's readers and critics might consider these expansive claims for metonymy in his later work as hyperbole or worse, a confusion and condition of his decline. Emerson (perhaps) really means "metaphor," which is the more familiar trope for the fluency of symbolic expression he uses as early as 1836, where "the whole of nature is a metaphor of the human mind" (CW 1: 21). To regard these later iterations of metonymy in this way is to follow a well-worn path in the critical tradition. With a few exceptions, including studies by Branka Arsić and David LaRocca, critics have tended to ignore the significance of metonymy in Emerson's work and thought.[7] Metaphor, of course, remains a familiar figure in Emerson's poetics. But the conceptual and stylistic presence of metonymy in late works such as "Art and Criticism" and "Poetry and Imagination," where the word "metaphor" does not appear, reinforces Barbara Packer's insight that Emerson's theory of poetry shifts after "The Poet" to "metonymy, the trope of association, not of likeness – as a way out of metaphor's petrifying powers."[8] The rhetoric of metonymy articulates in late Emerson an evolution from metaphor to metamorphosis, from the static "doctrine of Correspondence" (CW 4: 60) that Emerson initially learned from Swedenborg to the "doctrine of the correlation of forces" that Emerson learned from nineteenth-century sciences (LL 2: 377).

We can recognize some implications of this metamorphic metonymy in the dynamics of rhetoric that Emerson names "eloquence." In the "Eloquence" chapter published in Society and Solitude, Emerson emphasizes the democratic potential of oratory, from Demosthenes to the nineteenth-century culture of American oratory in which he played a leading part. Emerson premises the essay on the idea of rhetoric's universal access, that "probably, every man is eloquent once in his life," but then directly complicates the matter by turning attention from the powers of the individual orator to the power that resides in the audience. Emerson writes, "But because every man is an orator, how long soever he may have been a mute, an assembly of men is so much more susceptible." Of such susceptibility Emerson continues, "The eloquence of one stimulates all the rest, some up to the speaking point, and all others to a degree that makes them good receivers and conductors" (CW 7: 30). Emerson offers a complex figuring of the relation between orator and audience, one in which the orator's power to persuade the audience depends upon a correlative force, the audience's responsive power of receptivity. The latent metaphor in the pun of the audience as good "conductors" is revealed shortly when Emerson characterizes the "energy" of oratory in this way: "An audience is not a simple addition of the individuals that compose it. Their sympathy gives them a certain social organism, which fills each member, in his own degree, and, most of all, the orator, as a jar in a battery is charged with the whole electricity of the battery" (CW 7: 31). In the later "Eloquence" chapter published in *Letters and Social Aims*, Emerson once again figures oratorical power as "electricity of action" and further complicates the matter by locating that power not in the individual orator but in the collaboration and "counterbalance" located in the surrounding "auditory." "I must feel that the speaker compromises himself to his auditory," Emerson writes, compressing the orator's ethos and the argument's logos into a pathos that resides in the audience (CW 8: 61).

Emerson "embraced as his intellectual collaborators" the lecture audiences he addressed, as Bosco argues, a collaboration by which he developed his essays for publication, drawing authority "from the approval of his auditors" (CW 7: xxi). The "Eloquence" essays emerge from that collaborative process, but they also theorize the discomposing implications of this rhetorical power, unsettling the conventions of individual, authoritative composition. Emerson uses vivid and familiar metaphors from electromagnetism and biology to figure out an ecology of persuasion. But the underlying power lies in the metonymic compression or "compromise," the promising together, of orator and audience, writer and reader, into an "auditory" that collapses the place and production of eloquence onto the time and event of its reception. It is no surprise that James Crosswhite quotes Emerson's "auditory" and "compromise" as a model for the composite philosophical reason and rhetorical communication that he theorizes in *Deep Rhetoric*.[9] Following Eric Wilson, we might characterize these rhetorical currents and ecological feedback loops as facets of Emerson's metaleptic style, where figures of metalepsis (or "transumption" from the Latin, the compressed quotation or translation of older tropes within a new trope), which Wilson aligns with Emerson's metonymy, compress and mix with other figures. These rhetorical figures foreground and extend their own vital figuration; they are condensations of their own rhetorical contexts. For Wilson, the figurative actions of Emerson's "electric words" thus "stimulate similar activities in readers," much as Emerson envisions the audience as a creative participant in the actions of eloquence.[10]

In "Quotation and Originality," Emerson provides additional vocabulary for rethinking authorship by way of its contexts. There, all composition turns out to be a matter of "recomposition," to invoke the last word of the essay. That is ostensibly a lesson from the natural sciences that Emerson traced across his work, including in "The Progress of Culture," the very next essay in *Letters and Social Aims*, where "continual decomposition and recomposition" is learned from geology and chemistry and applied to intellectual culture. The lesson: "Nothing is old but the mind" (*CW* 8: 111). Though it sounds as though Emerson is asserting that everything is new, this is in fact another way of Emerson arguing that nothing is new since all depends on the mind, which, like nature, relates and recomposes everything it perceives and reads. Thus, in "Quotation and Originality": "All minds quote. Old and new make the warp and woof of every moment" and "[t]he originals are not original" (*CW* 8: 94). Emerson argues for the citational substrate of all invention, both natural and cultural, real and rhetorical. Originality or "original power" relies on origins elsewhere, powers received and cultivated first by what Emerson calls "assimilating power" (*CW* 8: 100). The typewriter is one new "Patent-Office" technology Emerson might have in mind in this late revisioning of originality. But any technology, new or old, would serve as well, to the extent that all technologies and tools are for Emerson "extensions" of the human. That's the claim he makes in "Works and Days," published in *Society and Solitude*, borrowing from Protagoras ("Man is the metre of all things") and circulating a phrase that will later resonate in Marshall McLuhan's *Understanding Media: The Extensions of Man* (*CW* 7: 79). Emerson's rhetoric of recomposition must be shocking to readers more familiar with "Self-Reliance" and its aversions to imitation. But it's a good example of the way Emerson's late style and theory of collaborative authorship, as Christopher Hanlon argues, demands that we reconsider the "privileging of self-reliant, inviolate consciousness as the acme of intellectual integrity."[11]

And yet, the shocking recognition that unoriginality is a vital theory and style in late Emerson should not be entirely surprising. Plato, Shakespeare, Swedenborg, and Goethe all make brief appearances in "Quotation and Originality," but receive extended treatment, each with a chapter, in Emerson's *Representative Men* (1850). Each is fundamentally unoriginal in significant ways that embody the condition of representativeness and the "uses" of greatness in others. As Emerson outlines in the book's opening chapter, relation to the otherness within the individual characterizes the representative: "Other men are lenses through which we read our own minds" (*CW* 4: 4). Each representative author is recomposed by their readers, with Emerson, as author, serving as the most proximate reader and re-composer. We can observe the rhetorical implications of this compression of author and reader in the ways Emerson theorizes the recomposition he undertakes. For example, in "Plato: New Readings," included as a follow-up to the chapter "Plato, or the Philosopher," Emerson locates Plato's intellectual power in his ability to analogize or extend the continuity of thought to its related second and "ulterior senses." Plato's original power rests, therefore,

276

in an assimilating power Emerson calls "expansions or extensions," a power whose organic nature Emerson signals in describing "that law by which in Nature, decomposition is recomposition," and whose rhetorical inheritance Emerson invokes, quite remarkably, by rhyming Plato's philosophy with the same rhetorical powers of Isocrates he will later quote in "Art and Criticism," namely, "his discernment of the little in the large, and the large in the small" (CW 4: 46).

## "All Thinking Is Analogizing"

Emerson's metaleptic recomposition of originality in his "new readings" of Plato makes the representative philosopher an ersatz Isocrates, skilled in the very rhetorical arts Plato dismissed. Perhaps Emerson was reading himself into Plato, or as he writes in "Quotation and Originality," "reading out of it better things than the author wrote: reading, as we say, between the lines" (CW 8: 103). A comparable amalgamation of philosophy and rhetoric would also prove to be problematic for critics of Emerson's philosophical writing and thinking, particularly the unfinished philosophical project on the intellect's natural history. At the same time, this translation between philosophy and rhetoric, which Emerson expands to include poetry, literature, and all thinking, would also prove to be a rich resource for the emergence of philosophical pragmatism among writers, notably William James, who not only read Emerson but, as Joan Richardson argues, learned much from "Emerson's stylistic practice." In *A Natural History of Pragmatism*, Richardson locates "the dramatic effects of [Emerson's] style" of doing philosophy in the transit between Emerson's extensive readings and studies in contemporary nineteenth-century science, or natural philosophy. This includes the developmental theories that anticipate Darwin and Emerson's processes of recomposition, the indexing and re-indexing, and the transcribing and translating of passages from his reading into journals, lectures, and essays. For Richardson, those rhetorical characteristics of compositional and linguistic evolution provide analogues for the emerging philosophy and science of evolution that Emerson actively reads between the lines: "Emerson's imaginative work changed the idea of imagination itself, representing in the formal characteristics of his writing the process of imperfect replication, or mutation, that is the engine of evolutionary change."[12] Emerson's imperfect project on the mind's natural history, as Richardson's own title suggests, assumes greater significance in the very performance of its own editorial, compositional, and intellectual recursiveness.

As we know, Emerson names the characteristic recursiveness of his late style with the rhetorical figure "metonymy," the figure for relational naming. "This metonomy [sic], or seeing the same sense in things so diverse, gives a pure pleasure," Emerson asserts in "Poetry and Imagination." (*CW* 8: 12). This late essay is no mere updating of "The Poet" three decades later. Emerson's argument here for the necessary role of the imagination in science and philosophy – "Science does not know its debt to imagination" and is "false by being unpoetical" – distills, like the "Promethean alembics" it references, the transdisciplinary blending of science, philosophy, poetics, and rhetoric. This blending also informs lecture series such as *Mind and Manners of the Nineteenth Century* (1848), *Natural Method of Mental Philosophy* (1858), *Philosophy for the People* (1866), and the *Natural History of Intellect* courses in philosophy at Harvard. In "Poetry and Imagination," Emerson offers "analogizing" as another name for "this metonomy," asserting, "All thinking is analogizing, and 'tis the use of life to learn metonomy." Here, as elsewhere, Michael Faraday's scientific discoveries of a field theory of electricity provided Emerson analogies for understanding nature itself as fundamentally analogical in its power to convert matter into energy and energy into matter. Faraday lurks in Emerson's characterization of analogy (or metonymy) as the vehicular nature of language and thought: "that the creation is on wheels, in transit, always passing into something else, streaming into something higher" (*CW* 8: 7, 2). As Laura Dassow Walls argues, Emerson turned to the scientist Faraday as an analogue for imagination, choosing him over Plato in his later lectures to conceive of a generalizing, analogizing intellect that could mediate between idealism and materialism, effecting what Walls phrases the "minding of matter."[13]

Across his project on the natural history of intellect, Emerson analogizes, or translates between, the philosophy of nature he was observing (he saw Faraday lecture in England in 1848) and the rhetorical and poetic lessons of the imagination he was producing in his own work. In the manuscript remains of "Imagination," the seventh lecture in the Harvard *Natural History of Intellect* course delivered in May 1870 and repeated in February 1871, we find a compressed version of the lines that will later be published and amplified in "Poetry and Imagination": "All thought is analogizing. Use of life to learn metonomy."[14] To recognize how this matter of metonymic style and analogizing realizes, or, as Richardson proposes, replicates philosophical and scientific principles, consider this passage from "Poetry and Imagination." "Many transfigurations have befallen them," Emerson writes of the "facts of matter" that are "convertible into every other," since the "intellect" reports and reproduces in its actions life's useful lesson in metonymy. The mind reads nature and science imaginatively and finds itself already related, materially located, there. Thus:

> The atoms of the body were once nebulae, then rock, then loam, then corn, then chyme, then chyle, then blood; and now the beholding and co-energizing mind sees the same refining and ascent to the third, the seventh, or the tenth power of the daily accidents which the senses report, and which make the raw material of knowledge. It was sensation; when memory came, it was experience; when mind acted, it was knowledge; when mind acted on it as knowledge, it was thought. (*CW* 8: 12)[15]

Emerson's "beholding and co-energizing mind" replicates the dynamics of the "auditory" and the "assimilating power" that founds original thinking on the rich, quotational texture of experience. Just as the body amalgamates and assimilates, in the physiological senses, the nutrients it recomposes from nature, so the mind assimilates and ameliorates, in the rhetorical senses, the thought it receives and acts upon. Emerson learned from Faraday that all facts and accidents of the material world were radically commensurable, as Mark Noble has argued.[16] In "Poetry and Imagination," Emerson extends that commensurability, by way of metonymy, to the thought circulating through his very writing.

In its demonstration of thought's emergence in the circulation of contiguities, a version of Emerson's passage could have made its way into William James's groundbreaking *Principles of Psychology* and its chapter on the "stream of thought" fifteen years later.[17] James might well have heard, at least indirectly, about Emerson's *Natural History of Intellect* course as he was just then setting out on his career as a psychologist and then philosopher at Harvard in the 1870s. Cabot, who found fault in the disorder and repetition of the essays he helped publish as *Letters and Social Aims*, also contributed a course (on Kant) in the Harvard philosophy series in 1870. Cabot suggests that Emerson's course failed as philosophy due to the unsystematic method of Emerson's analogical style and the project's incompletion – perhaps unfairly, perhaps perceptively, projecting onto Emerson his own words, that "Philosophy is still rude and elementary. It will one day be taught by poets."[18] I would agree with Bosco, who reads an alternative ending to the *Natural History of Intellect*, locating a more successful reception from Emerson's "listeners" beyond the lecture hall, future readers such as James and Dewey.[19] Those readers would be interested, more than Cabot, in the poetics and the rhetoric Emerson brought to the philosophy of mind.

## "The Inconsecutiveness"

Cabot's dismissal of the late project as failed (poetic) philosophy points to a related problem with Emerson's late styles that we are in a better position to reconsider: the philosophy of failure in Emerson's poetics. In "Poetry and Imagination," the imaginative recognition of "this metonymy" and the "charm in the metamorphosis" renders, in the very same paragraph, a potential for misrecognition that Emerson identifies as fundamental to poetry. "When people tell me they do not relish poetry," Emerson counters that "this dislike of the books only proves their liking of poetry": "They like poetry without knowing it as such" (CW 8: 13). Metonymy's "transubstantiation" of natural metamorphosis into thought renders poetry organic, a "poetry which finds its rhymes and cadences in the rhymes and iterations of nature." In this compression of nature into poetic forms, poetry offers another version of "low idealism," a "poetry which tastes the world and reports of it, upbuilding the world again in the thought" (CW 8: 36). But those metonymic iterations and assimilations of nature's "metamorphosis" must not stop with any single form if they are to remain organic. In "bringing poetry back to nature – to the marrying of nature and mind," Emerson conceives a poetics that resists the authority of the poet and poetry's traditional forms, shifting or translating meaning from "actual form" to "possible forms," and from poet to the perception of the poetry's "futurities." Thus, "The poet should rejoice if he has taught us to despise his song," a surprising view that creative authority lies in its rejection. But this perversity should not entirely surprise, as an iteration a few paragraphs later of Emerson's "Circles" should remind the reader: "After the largest circle has been drawn, a larger can be drawn around it" (CW 8: 38, 40, 41). Just as everyone in the audience is a mute orator, so too is every reader in Emerson's vision a sort of poet manqué.

And so too is Emerson. Lawrence Buell argues persuasively for an Emersonian poetics of imperfection in both the poetry and the prose, a "fragment aesthetics" that aimed to be creatively honest about "the inevitable incompletion of any 'final' result." Incompletion and imperfection in this poetics mark a transit between actual and possible forms. Buell points, for example, to the "performance" of failure in the poem "Days," published in May-Day and Other Pieces (1867). He reads in the unfinished, presumably "failed" sonnet of eleven lines "a favorite Emersonian theme of ironic failure to seize the day by giving the appearance of failure to realize itself as a sonnet."[20] In the poem, "the hypocritic Days,/Muffled and dumb, like barefoot dervishes,/And marching single in an endless file" are transfigured into the single file of the lines, but haltingly. As Albert Von Frank suggests, Emerson's own "creative amnesia" may well be the inspiration of the poem and not just the topic (CW 9: 423, 427). The "other pieces" of this late collection of poetry include "Elements," thirteen poems previously published as gnomic epigraphs or mottoes to Emerson's essays, as well as numerous fragmentary quatrains and translations, including a number of Emerson's translations (from the German translation) of favorite Persian poets Hafiz and Saadi, among others. Emerson recollects those translations from his essay "Persian Poetry," first published in the *Atlantic Monthly* in 1858 and later included in *Letters and Social Aims*. In this late interest in translation and fragment aesthetics, Emerson converts the accidents and actions of the "co-energizing mind" into potential forms of poetry.

In "Persian Poetry," Emerson characterizes the epigrammatic and gnomic quality of the verses he translates with a warning to the reader that "They use an inconsecutiveness quite alarming to Western logic" (*CW* 8: 127). He reiterates and celebrates this point in the essay "Saadi," published in 1864 in the *Atlantic*: "Wonderful is the inconsecutiveness of the Persian poets" (*CW* 10: 443). As Paul Kane aptly observes, the warning could just as well apply to Emerson, a concern that Cabot clearly had in mind. In *Emerson in Iran*, Roger Sedarat goes even further, locating in Emerson's translation practices not just a considerable interest in Persian poetry but a paradoxical mirror for locating his own originality in the work of others. For Sedarat, Emerson's translation of Persian poetry extends a rhetorical theory of translational transformation, which relies, like the ghazal poetic form that "[m]uch of Emerson's writing style mirrors," on the relation between originality and quotation. Jan Stievermann argues that these and other facets of Emerson's "translational poetics" – imitation, syncretism, collaboration, and amelioration – underwrite Emerson's transnational cosmopolitanism.[21]

The book on Emerson as an author of "American World Literature," in Stievermann's phrasing, is still being composed by Emerson's readers. The transnational and translational Emerson remain vital areas for new considerations of Emerson inspired by more thoughtful attention to Emerson's late styles. But these poetic, philosophical, and rhetorical lessons in recomposition from Emerson's old age also return us to more fundamental ways Emerson conceived of the workings of thought and writing: "the book's book," as Emerson relates his reader to the streams of universal thought in "Powers of the Mind" (*LL* 2: 76). The iterations of "creative re-composition" and "assimilative creativity" on display in Emerson's late work, including the critically dismissed poetry compilations *Parnassus* (1874) and *Selected Poems* (1876), evince underlying complications with authorial integrity rendered by collaboration and quotation. But such evidence should not be reduced to "a late and regrettable necessity" since it was already "built into his theory and practice of authorship."[22]

Continuing that practice of authorship well into the 1870s, Emerson recomposed and translated from the complex metonymy compressed in his "book's book." Correlating philosophy with the rhetoric of analogizing and science with the transfigurations of poetry, Emerson's late styles risk the kind of criticism leveled by Cabot, an editor well versed in Emerson's inconsecutiveness. And yet, even if we are left in some form with work that remains in need of further composing, that work is also made relevant in the commensuration of its continued reading.

## Notes

1. Bosco's indispensable guidance as scholar and editor of late Emerson can also be consulted in his remarkable "Historical Introduction" to *Letters and Social Aims* (*CW* 8: xix–ccxiii).

2. David M. Robinson, *Emerson and the Conduct of Life: Pragmatism and Ethical Purpose in the Later Work* (New York: Cambridge University Press, 1993); Laura Dassow Walls, *Emerson's Life in Science: The Culture of Truth* (Ithaca: Cornell University Press, 2003); Roger Thompson, *Emerson and the History of Rhetoric* (Carbondale: Southern Illinois University Press, 2017); Joseph Urbas, *The Philosophy of Ralph Waldo Emerson* (New York: Routledge, 2021).

3. Christopher Hanlon, *Emerson's Memory Loss: Originality, Communality, and the Late Style* (New York: Oxford University Press, 2017), 8.

4. Thompson, Emerson and the History of Rhetoric, 2.

5. Lyn Hejinian, *The Language of Inquiry* (Berkeley: University of California Press, 2000), 149.

6. Johannes Voelz, *Transcendental Resistance: The New Americanists and Emerson's Challenge* (Hanover: Dartmouth College Press, 2010), 102–3.

7. Branka Arsić, *On Leaving: A Reading in Emerson* (Cambridge, MA: Harvard University Press, 2010); David LaRocca, *Emerson's English Traits and the Natural History of Metaphor* (New York: Bloomsbury, 2013). See also Sean Ross Meehan, *A Liberal Education in Late Emerson: Readings in the Rhetoric of Mind*, chapter 4, "'Eloquence': Lessons in Emerson's Rhetoric of Metonymy," (Rochester: Camden House, 2019), 93–117.

8. Barbara Packer, "Response to Elisa New's 'Where the Meanings Are,'" *Religion and Literature* 38:1 (Spring 2006), 29.

9. James Crosswhite, *Deep Rhetoric: Philosophy, Reason, Violence, Justice, Wisdom* (Chicago: University of Chicago Press, 2013), 81.

10. Eric Wilson, *Emerson's Sublime Science* (New York: St. Martin's Press, 1999), 122.

11. Hanlon, Emerson's Memory Loss, 23.

12. Joan Richardson, *A Natural History of Pragmatism* (New York: Cambridge University Press, 2007), 8, 15, 43. See also James Albrecht, *Reconstructing Individualism: A Pragmatic Tradition from Emerson to Ellison* (New York: Fordham University Press, 2012).

13. Laura Dassow Walls, "'Every truth tends to become a power': Emerson, Faraday, and the Minding of Matter," in *Emerson for the Twenty-First Century: Global Perspectives on an American Icon*, ed. Barry Tharaud (Newark: University of Delaware Press, 2010), 307.

14. Ralph Waldo Emerson, "Imagination," *Harvard University Lectures, 1870–71*, Ralph Waldo Emerson Lectures and Sermons, bMS Am 1280.212 (7), Ralph Waldo Emerson Memorial Association deposit, Houghton Library, Harvard University.

15. In "The Natural Method of Mental Philosophy," Emerson employs this same digestive metonymy (chyme, chyle, blood) to represent the "circulation" of matter into mind by way of "the eye of analogy" (*LL* 2: 97).
16. Mark Noble, "Emerson's Atom and the Matter of Suffering," *Nineteenth-Century Literature* 64:1 (2009), 29.
17. For further exploration of James' rhetorical and pedagogical relations to Emerson, see Sean Ross Meehan, *A Liberal Education in Late Emerson*, chapter 1, "'Natural Method of Mental Philosophy': William James's Principles of Pedagogy," 21–42.
18. James Eliot Cabot, *A Memoir of Ralph Waldo Emerson*, vol. 2 (New York: AMS Press, 1969), 639.
19. Ronald A. Bosco, "'His Lectures Were Poetry, His Teaching the Music of the Spheres': Annie Adams Fields and Francis Greenwood Peabody on Emerson's 'Natural History of the Intellect' University Lectures at Harvard in 1870," *Harvard Library Bulletin* 8:2 (Summer 1997), 26. Bruce Kuklick describes the flourishing of the Metaphysical Club around 1871–72 in Cambridge after James joined, and connects its "amateur philosophizing" with Emerson's legacy, though he makes no mention of Emerson's Harvard course. Bruce Kuklick, *The Rise of American Philosophy: Cambridge, Massachusetts, 1860–1930* (New Haven: Yale University Press, 1977), 46–47.
20. Lawrence Buell, *Emerson* (Cambridge, MA: The Belknap Press of Harvard University Press, 2003), 109, 113, 138.
21. Paul Kane, "Emerson and Hafiz: The Figure of the Religious Poet," *Religion & Literature* 41.1 (Spring 2009): 111–39; Roger Sedarat, *Emerson in Iran: The American Appropriation of Persian Poetry* (Albany: SUNY Press, 2019), 61; Jan Stievermann, "'We want men...who can open their eyes wider than to a nationality': Ralph Waldo Emerson's Vision of an American World Literature," in *Emerson for the Twenty-First Century: Global Perspectives on an American Icon*, ed. Barry Tharaud (Newark: University of Delaware Press, 2010), 174.
22. Joseph M. Thomas, "Poverty and Power: Revisiting Emerson's Poetics," in *Emerson: Bicentennial Essays*, ed. Ronald A. Bosco and Joel Myerson (Boston: Massachusetts Historical Society, 2006), 237, 238. See also Joseph M. Thomas, "Late Emerson: *Selected Poems* and the 'Emerson Factory'," *ELH* 65:4 (Winter, 1998): 971–94; and Nikhil Bilwakesh, "Emerson's Decomposition: *Parnassus*," *Nineteenth-Century Literature*, 67:4 (March 2013): 520–45.

# 17

PAUL GRIMSTAD

# Emersonian Aesthetics in the Twentieth Century

Emerson's essays are strangely resistant to familiarity. Even after many rereadings, one feels the surprise of an arresting word choice, the charm of an unexpected image, and the vertigo of one assertion swooping diagonally to the next. Dives into what Emerson called the "internal ocean" often bring him back to the surface with exotic curios, as when we learn that individual persons are like a "quincunx of trees," or hear that "time dissipates to shining ether the solid angularity of facts" (*CW* 2: 6). Some have found the prose "over-rich,"[1] as John Bishop put it, referring to the opening lines of his famously indecorous "Divinity School Address," in which Emerson diagnosed what he called the "famine" in the Unitarian church, then went on to inform the graduating class that they were "newborn bards of the Holy Ghost," evidence for which could be found in the "infinite relations" of their own minds (*CW* 1: 90). Others have linked the over-richness to the cliché that Emerson's extravagance is just ornamentation tacked on to a naïve self-help program. Anyone who attributes this sort of shallow optimism to Emerson could not have read much of his work. While one finds tones of reverence everywhere in the *Essays* almost always there is a second move into disavowal, rejection, disappointment, or astonished awe at the ruthlessness of nature. In "Fate" we hear of a natural world that "does not mind drowning a man" and "swallows your ship like a grain of dust" (*CW* 6: 3). The same move happens in the Divinity School Address: after many pages of ravishment before "outrunning laws" and "rapid intrinsic energy" of the soul, we suddenly hear of "a sickness [that] infects and dwarfs the constitution." (*CW* 1: 80). In "Circles" the polarity flips in the space of a single sentence: "I am a God in Nature; I am a weed by the wall." (*CW* 2: 182). And sometimes the mood tilts toward the outlandish, as when, irritated at the unseemliness of groupthink and mass conformism, Emerson imagines the people around him as "a moving cheese, like hills of ants, or of fleas" (*CW* 4: 4).

Whether a volatile mix of plainness and prodigality, merely over-rich, or toggling between reverence and revulsion, Emerson's essays are a new kind of distinctively American art. If, as Perry Miller claimed, Emerson "did not conceive of himself as an artist," that self-appraisal has not deterred poets, novelists, composers, performing musicians, and filmmakers from finding in Emerson's prose a model of the mind at its most imaginatively constructive and free.[2] The cumulative effect of an Emerson essay is not of some cleanly delineated propositional content, nor a demonstration of salon wit or delicacy of judgment, but of an idiosyncratic performance with its own laws and logic. Local assertions become intelligible only in relation to the verbal and conceptual kaleidoscope around them; arguments move in and out of focus and sometimes vanish completely. If, in his *Representative Men*, Emerson does not provide a separate entry for the Artist – Writer and Poet yes, but no Artist – his own writing serves as a constant example of the work of the artist.[3]

By "work of the artist" I mean a certain kind of doing: trying things out, exploring, listening, revising, rearranging, making changes, revising again, looking again, all the while finding judgment shading into feeling and feeling shading into judgment as the process of composition unfolds. Emerson's prose resulted from such a process, as his own sermons, journal entries, and lyceum lectures became the raw stuff from which the *Essays* are built. The compositional activity was so sustained and deliberate it became the underlying principle of his thought. In his first piece of published writing after resigning his pulpit at the Second Church of Boston, the short book *Nature* (1836), Emerson asserts that a theory of nature is also an "approach to [the] idea of creation" (CW 1: 8). In an address he gave at Waterville College in Maine in August 1841, nature is now understood as a "work of *ecstasy*": "All is nascent and infant," he says, "all seems just begun; remote aims are in active accomplishment. We can point nowhere to find anything final; but tendency appears on all hands, planet, system, constellation, total nature is growing like a field of maize in July; is becoming somewhat else; is in rapid metamorphosis" (CW 1: 126).

A few of Emerson's readers extended this art of metamorphosis and "tendency" into their own work. "I am not blind to the worth of the wonderful gift of *Leaves of Grass*," Emerson wrote to a journeyman printer Walter Whitman of Brooklyn, New York, who had sent him a book in the mail. "I find it the most extraordinary piece of wit and wisdom that America has yet contributed ... I give you joy of your free and brave thought. I have great joy in it. I find incomparable things said incomparably well." That Emerson should be not just receptive but so evidently delighted by a strange, DIY volume of mixed prose and verse sent him by a complete stranger tells us something about his belief that anyone might unleash peals of divinity at any time, from any place. It seems likely also that Emerson heard some of his own aphoristic injunctions from "The American Scholar" and "Self-Reliance" weirdly transmuted and intensified in Whitman's prose introduction to *Leaves of Grass*, which advises the reader to, "re-examine all you have been told at school or church or in any book, dismiss whatever insults your own soul."[4]

Some years later a different and in some ways more radical literary art began to germinate in the respectable home of an Amherst lawyer. We don't know if Emily Dickinson ever heard Emerson lecture, though when given the opportunity to meet him socially (he was staying across the street), she declined; a refusal to pay deference to a New England celebrity that might itself be read as an Emersonian act of defiance. A volume of Emerson's poetry was given to her in 1850 as a gift from a young man in her father's law office, her "gentle, yet grave Preceptor" Benjamin Franklin Newton, who had marked in pencil his favorites.[5] If in her verse Dickinson, as David Porter claims, "established the opposite extreme to Emerson and his follower Whitman," it is nevertheless "easy to find passages that might belong to either [Emerson or Dickinson]."[6] Some of her poems indeed seem to echo the *Essays*, as when Emerson's line "the poet should be tipsy with water" seems elaborated in Dickinson's "inebriate of air" and "debauchee of dew" from "I Taste A Liquor Never Brewed"[7] (*CW* 3: 17).

While much more could be said about how these different strains of American art – Whitmanian expansiveness and Dickinsonian severity – can be seen to emerge from Emerson's example, in what follows I want to trace some less well-known tendencies that appear in the twentieth century, with emphasis throughout on music: Marcel Proust's channeling Emersonian idealism in his narrator's hearing passages from Vinteuil's sonata at various points in the *Recherche du temps perdue*; Charles Ives' "Concord" sonata and its accompanying volume of explicitly Emersonian *Essays Before A Sonata*; Ralph Ellison's writings on jazz and the politics of taste in essays on Duke Ellington and Charlie Parker; John Ashbery's poem "The Skaters," his prose poem "The New Spirit," his collaboration with composer Elliott Carter *Syringa*, and his 1968 lecture "The Invisible Avant Garde." In each case we find differently explored and elaborated a principle Emerson returned to throughout his life: That composition is an act of self-reliant experimentation driven by the sheer thrill of putting materials together and, as he put it in "The Poet," "adorn[ing] nature with a new thing"[8] (*CW* 3: 8).

## La musique m'aider à descendre en moi-meme

Scholars who have noted Marcel Proust's love of Emerson are usually quick to point out both how counterintuitive the connection seems – the temperate

Emerson versus the sybarite Proust, the New World provincial versus the cosmopolitan aesthete, Emerson the democrat versus Proust the snob and so on – and how Proust's relation to Emerson (at least in his published writing) is gestural and fleeting at best.[9] Proust's direct engagement with Emerson indeed does not go much beyond quotations in letters and epigraphs (and a single name drop in the *Recherche*); Emerson finds himself in the company of Mallarmé, Thomas à Kempis, Shakespeare, and Baudelaire as a furnisher of epigraphs for the chapters of *Les plaisirs et les jours [Pleasures and Days]* (1896), a collection of sketches gently satirizing haute-bourgeois manners. But the depth of Emerson's importance for Proust comes through most vividly not when he is explicitly mentioned, but in moments in the *Recherche* when the narrator reflects on aesthetic experience. During a brief respite from obsessing over his companion Albertine in *La prisonnière*, Marcel goes to the piano and finds the score of Vinteuil's sonata (a fictional piece by a fictional composer) and starts to play. Almost immediately the sound of the piano becomes indistinguishable from Marcel's inner life; he is "carried back upon the tide of the sound" [*ramené par le flot sonore*] to memories of Combray, an effect that leads him to wonder if there is "in art a more profound reality in which our own true personality [*notre personnalité veritable*] finds an expression that is not afforded it by the activities of life."[10] This then floats him into further reflections, first to the resemblance between the passage he's playing and Wagner's *Tristan*, then into a mode of introspection we might call a musico-literary philosophy of mind.[11] That a passage of music could give us unique access to the depths of our own minds, that it could allow Marcel to "descend into himself" [*"La musique m'aider à descendre en moi-meme"*] (CW 1: 207), is close to what Emerson described in "The Transcendentalist" as the way a certain kind of reflection would give access to "the intuitions of the mind itself." This is made more interesting by the fact that the music does not actually exist. As a novelistic invention we must imagine and, in some basic way, compose ourselves as we read.

The affinity between the experience of hearing a piece of music and a certain strain of idealism is more explicit at an earlier point in the *Recherche*. Hearing *le petite phrase* in the Verdurin's salon, Swann is initially pierced with anguish at memories of Odette, but soon the "sweeping cloak of sound" [*cette apparence sonore*] leads the narrator to reflect on how a "love of music" had opened Swann into the "riches of his own soul" such that "the perspective in which he saw the elements of music" formed an "immeasurable keyboard" [*un clavier incommensurable*]. Far from a reduction to the intervals of diatonic harmony, this ideal keyboard contains all the realities of the soul, "millions of keys of tenderness, of passion, of courage, of serenity [as] discovered by a few great artists who do us the service, when they awaken in us the emotion corresponding to the theme they have discovered, of showing us what richness, what variety lies hidden, unknown to us, in that vast unfathomed and forbidding night of our soul" [*cette grand nuit impénétrée et décourageante de notre ame*].[12] Swann's revelation upon hearing the little phrase is an Emersonian one in that what is unveiled, revealed, and opened by music is the soul's infinity; those "outrunning laws" that become intelligible when the "mind opens and reveals the laws which traverse the universe and make things what they are" (*CW* 1: 78). This ecstatic perception of unrunning laws forms also an isomorphism between reflection upon mental processes and aesthetic ravishment, as with Emerson's account, in "Spiritual Laws" of how, "when reflection takes place in the mind ... we discover that our life is embosomed in beauty" (*CW* 2: 77); Toward the end of "Spiritual Laws," Emerson offers an analogy for this kind of alignment: "We are the photometers, we the irritable goldleaf and tinfoil that measure the accumulations of the subtle element" (*CW* 2: 96). The beauty experienced either outside us or as discovered through inward reflection chimes with Proust's comparison of beautiful sound to unseeable light such that Swann "belonged to a world of ultra-violet light." Swann is a "photometer" in Emerson's sense, sensitive to the ultraviolet frequencies that connect aesthetic experience to inner experience.[13]

## Explore and Explore

Unlike Proust's fleeting and allusive relation to Emerson, Charles Ives modeled his entire aesthetic program after his American precursor. As if to make explicit how the score to the *Concord* sonata was to be thought of in dialogue with the medium Emerson himself composed in, Ives published simultaneously with it an accompanying volume of *Essays Before A Sonata*. If Emerson was, as Ives wrote, "an invader of the unknown, America's deepest explorer of the spiritual immensities,"[14] his choice of the word "explorer" reminds one of Emerson's advising his listeners at an 1838 address at Dartmouth College, later printed as "Literary Ethics" to "explore and explore. Be neither chided nor flattered out of your position of perpetual inquiry. Neither dogmatize yourself nor accept another's dogmatism. Why should you renounce your right to traverse the star-lit deserts of truth?" (*CW* 1: 115) "Exploring" in Emerson's sense is just what occurs for Ives the composer/essayist, who creates a "vision of Emerson to justify his own composing techniques"[15]; an ideal abstraction which licenses exploration in the hands-on work of experiment and revision; the attempts and erasures, grafting and cutting, and the whole flurry of decision and feeling and experiment that constitutes the search of composition. One only has to look at the score drafts of the "Emerson" section of the *Concord* sonata to see just how real that work was for Ives.

To listen to the "Emerson" movement is, for all that, to hang on for dear life as the piano follows a jagged progress across tumultuous and severe harmonies and chord voicings, relentless asymmetries of dynamics and pitch, tempos that warp the metric landscape, snatches of tunes or hymns that are quickly wrenched out of focus, intimations of counterpoint that rapidly dissolve, cascades of sweeping ostinato, and many moments that defy conventional musical vocabulary altogether. It is violently original music, and one that in retrospect constitutes a major strain of American modernism (and which was at the time mostly dismissed as the work of an eccentric dabbler).

Ives' experimental music led to an American modernism attuned not only to the dissonances of the "Emerson" movement of the *Concord Sonata* but to a wholly new kind of complexity. Elliott Carter had spent time at Ives' home listening to music as a teenager, attended concerts with him, and later wrote some of the first criticism of the *Concord Sonata* that was not either outraged dismissal or thoughtless praise for a nebulously invoked originality. He recorded his thoughts of a performance of the *Sonata* he heard at Town Hall in New York in January 1939 and was mostly not taken with the music. Carter hears a "formally weak" piece, "overdressy," "redundant," "unconvincing," full of "confused textures," marred by a "lack of logic which repeated hearings can never clarify" and in which the "much touted dissonances are helter-skelter without great musical sense." The piece was finally "naïve" music that was "more often original than good."[16] However much Carter is lashing out at a musical father, the itemized points of weakness will be just those features of the mature Carter's work that become most striking and conspicuous, such that "in criticizing Ives, Carter was articulating for the first time his own compositional goals"[17] (goals which started to become audible in the *Sonata for Cello and Piano* (1948), the *First String Quartet* (1951) and the *Sonata for Flute, Oboe, Cello & Harpsichord* (1953)). Just as the idealized "Emerson" had been a compositional horizon in relation to which Ives could "explore and explore," so Carter builds an ideal "Ives" as a way forward for his own brand of American modernism. The process bears out the dynamic sketched in Emerson's essay "Circles," in which "the man finishes his story, – how good! How final! How it puts a new face on all things! He fills the sky. Lo! On the other side rises also a man, and draws a circle around the circle we had just pronounced the outline of a sphere" (CW 2: 181). Emerson makes a circle, which Ives redraws and expands, which in turn becomes a circle Carter redraws and expands. Notice how both steps are actualized in the doing of composition: Emerson's essays, Ives' music about the essays, his own essay about the music, Carter's review of the music, and the new music Carter then makes, which takes up and corrects the flaws outlined in the review. These are not so much histories or biographies as aesthetic transactions that allow for new artworks to come into being, new circles to be drawn. Far from blind adulation, the process is a willful and ruthlessly personal taking up of an approach to composition. In the bare timbres of the "Emerson" movement's unaccompanied piano, we hear in x-ray relief the sound of new circles being drawn.

## Swinging and Skating

Extending "Emerson" as an idea to be expanded and redrawn as a new circle happens both more literally and more gesturally in the case of the twentieth-century novelist and critic (and one-time music student at Tuskegee University) Ralph Waldo Ellison.[18] More literally because he is actually named after Emerson, more gesturally in that his writing about another side of American musical modernism, jazz, he extends Emerson's injunction that America has an art and expression of its own, not a mere imitation of Europe. From its gestation in late nineteenth-century New Orleans, to the first recordings by the Original Dixieland Jazz Band some years later, to the emergence in the 1920s of Louis Armstrong as a major stylist, to the swing era of big bands led by Duke Ellington and Count Basie, and on through the self-consciously modern innovations of bebop in the 1940s and post-bop in the 1950s and 1960s, jazz has throughout its evolution been an improvisatory music of imaginative spontaneity. As many commentators have noted, it is even an allegory for American democracy: the collective unity of a band playing together gives space for each individual voice to become salient before the soloist returns to join the collective, all of it held together in swinging rhythm.[19]

In his essay on Duke Ellington, whom Ellison calls "America's greatest composer," what it really means to stop listening to "the courtly muses of Europe" (*CW* 1: 69) is also a complaint about the obtuseness of establishment institutions' failure to recognize what American music actually is.[20] Ostensibly a letter of protest at Ellington's having been passed up for a 1965 Pulitzer Prize, the essay turns into extended praise for the nonimitative art of jazz and of Ellington as one of its greatest stylists. In Ellington's "mastery of form nuance and style" he created both a musical idiom and a way of being, an approach to life, one aligned with the jarring variousness of American experience in the twentieth century.[21] Ellison found "jazz" to mean more than just a particular musical style (about which he was in any case enormously well informed). In what he called the "jazz shaped" aspects of American culture, "jokes, tall tales, even our sports would be lacking in the sudden turns, shocks and swift changes of pace that serve to remind us that the world is ever unexplored, and that while a complete mastery of life is mere illusion, the real secret of the game is to make life swing."[22] It doesn't take too much effort to hear in Ellison's description of "jazz shaped" America, not only the injunction to hearers of "The American Scholar" to stop imitating old world models but also the line from Emerson's darker, stranger essay "Experience" that "we live amid surfaces and the true art of life is to skate well over them." (CW 3: 35). Swinging and skating, attuned to the "real secret of the game," the "true art of life," are words for flexible, improvisatory styles of living, which would, through a kind of ever-modulating tact, skate well through the "jolts" and "sudden turns" of life's contingencies. And it was just this ability, to skate or swing – in music, in attitude, in manners, in style, in adopting complex forms of irony and mockery – that Ellison praises in Ellington.[23] This is not the Dionysian tumult of Ives but a measured Apollonian coolness, such that Ellington's music "reduced the violence and chaos of American life to artistic order."[24]

When it came, however, to further circles to be drawn around the compositional example set by Ellington (and, we might add, by his brilliant arranger and sometime co-composer Billy Strayhorn), Ellison was skeptical. Bebop seems to have struck him as faddish, the myths of its birth in late-night jam sessions at Minton's Playhouse in Harlem mostly fabricated, and the eventual "modernism" of 52nd Street a phony, neurotic hipsterism, the complexity and grace of the music made at Minton's reduced to the "clownish, self-deprecating" word "bop."[25] The most iconic of the bebop virtuosi, Charlie "Yardbird" Parker ("Bird") is described somewhat ungenerously as a "mocking bird" (*Mimus polyglottos*). But Ellison's essay on Bird isn't really about Parker's playing or musical sensibility but the politics of his canonization as the ultimate bebopper.[26] Ellison's cool dismissal of Bird's innovations involves a retelling of Bird's origin story, in which he has a revelation while playing through "Cherokee." Finding that "by using the higher intervals of a chord as a melody line and backing them with appropriately related changes, I could play the thing I'd been hearing"[27] If Bird hit upon a new way of threading a melodic line through chord changes, what is this but the drawing of a new circle around Duke (and to switch the inheritance to Bird's influence—and from alto to tenor—Lester Young and Coleman Hawkins)? Despite Ellison's slightly arch sociology of hipness, his thinking managed to illuminate what it was in Parker's playing that is closest to what Emerson called "the true art of life." The surfaces, for Bird, were scalar and intervallic. When Ellison grudgingly calls him a "most gifted innovator," the faint praise (emphasis on "innovation" meaning, apparently, whatever the new thing is), he refers to Parker's example of real-time invention on the bandstand, in many ways the most dazzling example of swinging, skating, and exploring to be found on record.

Still, Ellison's refusal to uphold the consensus about "bop," or any piece of received wisdom about jazz innovation, is itself evidence of Emersonian commitments. As he put it in his 1964 book *Shadow and Act*, he learned from Emerson to aim for the "broadest range, discovery and articulation of the most exalted values"; and to refuse to "embrace uncritically values which are extended to us by others [which would be] to reject the validity, even the sacredness, of our own experience."[28] That "experience" becomes the freighted word here sends us back to the image of skating taken from Emerson's essay of that title. Here though the "true art of life" will not only be a stylistic mode but also the individual writer's insistence on taking his own measure of the world. Experience here carries the sense of having the courage of one's convictions, the ability to give an "independent genuine verdict" (*CW* 2: 29), even of the tradition one feels closest to, whether that be the writings of an exalted American writer who happens to be one's namesake or the distinctively American art of jazz.

## Take Apart the Notion of You

John Ashbery's long poem from 1966 "The Skaters" begins with the sound ("decibels") of people skating over a rural pond, a winter scene which quickly thaws to a humid, swampy world, which then becomes a molten pool, then a colored liquid fire as imagined through a childhood science book, among the pyrotechnic effects of which is a "phosphorescent fountain," which in turn becomes a magic lantern projection of a haunting, atomized domesticity and what seem to be scenes of past civilizations, one of which is a Crusoe-like desert island featuring a vision in the distance of a "delicate, transparent" water spout (which later looks like a "three dimensional photograph") and an encounter with an atmospheric character called the Storm Fiend, then a jump from the island to a "cozy warm middle class apartment with a good library and record collection," some golf tips, "anagrams of moonlight" and in a final section a shift of time signature, the seasons speeding up, diurnal rhythms growing more generalized and abstract, until the snow patterns of the first section return projected in a last gigantic lantern slide as the "constellations are rising in perfect order: Taurus, Leo, Gemini."

Skating indeed! The poem's gliding, centrifugal motion, whose diction swerves from American everyday to techno-scientific, parodic romanticism and high "philosophical" registers, extends Emerson's image of skating to one of the first poems of Ashbery's to sound conspicuously "Ashberyian." When asked in an interview if he read much philosophy, Ashbery said he "read philosophy that is close to poetry" citing Plato, Montaigne, Nietzsche, William James, and Wittgenstein. Emerson, who devoted essays to the first two figures, and decisively influenced two out of the last three, seems somehow implied by omission in the response.[29] And by the time he begins work on the follow up to *Rivers and Mountains*, *Three Poems*, he has shifted to an elastic prose poetry close in many ways to the range of registers in Emerson's *Essays*.[30] "The New Spirit" begins with explicit reflection on composition: "I thought that if I could put it all down that would be one way. And next the thought came to me that to leave all out would be another, and truer, way."[31] It's the first of these approaches Ashbery adopts for the rest of "The New Spirit," a long address to a "you" (and a "yourself"); likely an earlier, or an alternate (or possibly a future) version of himself. It turns out the inner workings of this "you" may be casually anatomized, as they appear as "painted wooden components of the Juggernaut ... scattered around the yard." And so "ends the first lesson" of the self: that it "does not dissolve when breathed upon but comes apart neatly, like a watch, and the parts be stocked or stored [...] and with everything sorted and labeled you can keep an eye on it a lot better than if it were again free to assume protean shapes and senses," such that we may "take apart the notion of you."[32] Taking the basic insight of "Self-Reliance" – "the one fact the world hates, that the soul *becomes*" (CW 2: 40) – Ashbery gives that thought a humorous literalness, imagining the self as "painted wood components" which may be sorted and labeled, a futile effort to prevent the onrush of becoming from starting again in all of its "protean shapes and senses." Emersonian "reliance" is here at once a fantasy of sorting out the interior world as if it were an eclectically stocked garage or attic and a way of enacting in the freedom of prose poetry the onslaught of endless becoming. When Emerson says enigmatically elsewhere in "Self-Reliance" that the reader should "absolve you to yourself" (CW 2: 30), we see how he too uses the second person to stage a precarious looking inward, what Ashbery will call in the book after *Three Poems* the making of a "self-portrait in a convex mirror."

One consequence of the genealogy of Emersonian art I've been sketching combines two figures already discussed – Ashbery and Elliott Carter – whose collaboration resulted in the sort of medium blur rejected by a strain of criticism that would see the dissolving of the boundaries between one medium and another (painting and sculpture, say) as becoming something other than art.[33] Written in 1975 and appearing in Ashbery's 1977 collection *Houseboat Days*, "Syringa" was selected by Carter because of its ambitious reimagining of the myth of Orpheus and Eurydice and its focus on the relation of music and poetry.[34] After some stark, unadorned guitar chords (Orpheus perhaps plucking his lyre), Carter brings the ensemble in, as if each piece were "drawn in by the spell of the music."[35] When we get to Ashbery's explicit ruminations on how the Orphic notes "mount straight up out of the well of/Dim noon and rival the tiny, sparkling yellow flowers/growing around the brink of the quarry, and encapsulizes/the different weights of the things," the mezzo soprano's singing *tiny sparkling yellow* bleeds into the decay of the resonating guitar (a jarringly wide-voiced chord), to which are then added flute, English horn, and viola in such a way as to make the music itself seem tiny, sparkling, and yellow.[36] At the same time Carter sets against the soprano a bass voice singing a fragment of Sappho in the original Greek – transliterated as "my voice nothing can say" – pulling the piece away from the verbal register of poetry toward its basis in pure sound, and so toward timbral abstractions of orchestral color. All this happens in the space of a couple seconds, and the effect is of what the poem calls "stellification": a congealing density whereby the materials ignite into an emergent star formation, some new mongrel poly-genre, the music made animate in a refulgent synesthesia. Stellification for Carter and Ashbery depends on an aggressive blurring of media – poetry, melody, orchestral color, translation, song, and classical scholarship – comprising an American modernism that would indeed execute that Emersonian art that "adorns nature with a new thing."

## The Invisible Avant Garde

The description I gave earlier of art as a certain kind of work – of trying things out, revising, rearranging, making further changes, and revising again, all the while finding judgment shading into feeling and feeling shading into judgment as the process unfolds – is experimental in the sense both of testing and trying things out and in the sense of avant-garde aesthetics. In a 1968 lecture, "The Invisible Avant Garde," Ashbery sketched a history in which experimental art-making once had to face total obscurity, even contempt, but which in the current American scene had become all too acceptable. "The artist who wants to experiment," Ashbery writes, "is again faced with a dead end, except that instead of creating a vacuum he is now at the center of a cheering mob."[37] As what I take to be an antidote to this unfortunate situation, he describes "an attitude which neither accepts nor rejects acceptance but is independent of it."[38] That independence would, I think, be one with Emerson's urging in "Self-Reliance" to be averse to conformism, whether the impulse arises in the face of demands from authorities or judges, from institutions or commercial markets, or just the oppressive consensus of middle-class respectability. The new conformist tendencies in the avant-garde of the 1960s meant embracing a situation Ashbery described in his 1970 poem "Soonest Mended" as a "sort of fence sitting/raised to the level of an aesthetic ideal."[39] The fence-sitting is between what Emerson in "The American Scholar" celebrates as "the near, the common, the low" and the extravagant style of his own most reticulated sentences. This is the American art Emerson calls for and inaugurates: between the rude and the complex, the direct and the abstract, the demotic and the avant-garde, and undertaken without the pusillanimous concern for "acceptance." The invisible avant-garde just is this tradition of self-reliant art-making whenever and wherever it occurs.

## Notes

1. John Bishop, *Emerson on the Soul* (Cambridge, MA: Harvard University Press, 1964), 88.
2. Perry Miller, *The Transcendentalists* (Cambridge, MA: Harvard University Press, 1950), 9.
3. Emerson lectured in 1835 at the Concord lyceum on "biography" in which Michelangelo served as the representative "artist"; the lecture did become an essay. For more on these early lecture series, see Robert Gross, *The Transcendentalists and Their World* (New York: Farrar, Straus and Giroux, 2021), 345–47.
4. Whitman, *Poems and Prose* (New York: Library of America, 1982), 11.
5. Jack L. Capps, *Emily Dickinson's Reading* (Cambridge, MA: Harvard University Press, 1966), 113–15.
6. David Porter, *Dickinson: The Modern Idiom* (Cambridge, MA: Harvard University Press, 1981), 257; and George Frisbie Whicher, *This Was A Poet: A Critical Biography of Emily Dickinson* (New York: Scribner's, 1938), 205. For a reading of the connection between Emerson and Dickinson on ecstatic experience, see Paul Grimstad, "Providence and Contingency in Edwards, Emerson and Dickinson," *Amerikastudien/American Studies*, 60:4 (2015): 403–15.
7. Emily, Dickinson, "1861 Fascicles: §207," in *The Poems of Emily Dickinson Variorum Edition*, ed. R. W. Franklin (Cambridge, MA: Harvard University Press, 1998), 237–38.
8. The genealogy of Emersonian poetics would include Robert Frost, who called Emerson's poem "Uriel" "the greatest Western poem yet," and Wallace Stevens, whose poem "Sunday Morning" sums up the thrust of the "Divinity School Address" in a single line: "Divinity must live within herself." The heroine of Henry James' *The Portrait of a Lady* (1881) seems an "Emersonian" figure: Isabel Archer's nonconformism, boldness, imaginative idiosyncrasy, and craving for new experience amount for James to the ironized tragedy of what self-reliant freedom really means for an American at liberty to explore herself in Europe. For Emerson and Frost, see Richard Poirier, *Poetry and*

*Pragmatism* (Cambridge, MA: Harvard University Press, 1992); for Stevens as an Emersonian artist, see Harold Bloom, *The Poems of Our Climate* (Ithaca: Cornell University Press, 1977). For a philosophical account of James' *Prefaces* and Emerson's notion of "experience," see Paul Grimstad, *Experience and Experimental Writing* (Oxford: Oxford University Press, 2013).

9. Stanley Cavell records a "lovely discovery" of Proust's use, in the preface to his translation of Ruskin's *Bible of Amiens*, of a line from Emerson's essay "Civilization": "hitch your wagon to a star." Cavell upends what the phrase is assumed to mean – not so much "aim high" as be attuned, in your humblest activities, to the inherence of the highest, to "receiving high" and "accepting high." See Stanley Cavell, "August 27, 2004," in *Little Did I Know: Excerpts from Memory* (Stanford University Press, 2010), 533. Emerson's prose often "hitches" the plainest items of ordinary life (a wagon) to the grandest possible scale (the stars): two sides of his style. F.O. Firkins noted how Emerson had a "double and equal love of rude plainness and prodigal magnificence." F. O. Firkins, *Ralph Waldo Emerson* (Boston: Houghton Mifflin, 1915), 255.

10. Marcel Proust, *In Search of Lost Time Volume 5: The Captive*, translated by C. K. Scott Moncrieff and Terence Kilmartin, revised by D. J. Enright (New York: Modern Library, 204–5) [*A la recherche du temps perdu III. La prisonniére.* Edition publiée sous la direction de Jean-Yves Tadié, 1988 [1922] 664.]

11. While we can't know what Vinteuil's sonata actually sounded like, the Wagner affinity Marcel notes has more to do with melodic chromaticism than orchestral color, or perhaps with the recurrence of themes as a structural principle, as Wagnerian leitmotif may resemble the *petite phrase*. My thanks to Howard Bloch and Ellen Handler Spitz for an informative exchange on the question of what Vinteuil's fictional sonata might actually sound like.

12. The comparisons in Proust to Wagnerian aesthetics become more interesting here, as one of Wagner's innovations was a movement toward increasing chromaticism; that is, a tendency to emphasize smaller increments (semi-tones, half steps), which, if pursued in the way imagined by the narrator of *Le recherché*, would end up as an infinitely subdivided keyboard of ever finer intervallic units.

13. On Emerson and Proust on "surprise," see Kate Stanley, *Practices of Surprise in American Literature After Emerson* (Cambridge: Cambridge University Press, 2018), 54–57.

14. Charles Ives, *Essays before a Sonata, The Majority, and Other Writings*, ed. Howard Boatwright (New York: W. W. Norton, 1962), 21.

15. Kyle Gann, *Charles Ives' Concord: Essays After A Sonata* (Champaign, IL: University of Illinois Press, 2017), 60. For David Robinson, "the prose *Essays* [are both] Ives's most extensive statement of his musical principles [and] in effect a defense of Transcendentalism." In other words, to write an essay in praise of Emerson's thought and writing is at the same time to create a kind of aesthetic manifesto. David B. Robinson, "Children of the Fire: On Charles Ives on Emerson and Art," in *On Emerson: The Best from American Literature*, ed. Edwin Harrison Cady (Durham, NC: Duke University Press, 1988), 183.

16. Elliott Carter, "The Case of Mr. Ives," *Modern Music* 16:3 (March 1939), in *Collected Essays and Lectures, 1937–1995*, ed. Jonathan W. Bernard (Rochester: University of Rochester Press, 1997), 89.

17. David, Schiff, *The Music of Elliott Carter. Second Edition* (Ithaca: Cornell University Press, 1998), 18. Lawrence Kramer says Carter "gives an organic, formally elegant significance to the raw material of Ives' innovations." See Lawrence Kramer, *Music and Poetry, the Nineteenth Century and After* (Berkeley: University of California Press, 1984), 204. For more on Carter's relation to musical modernism see Paul Grimstad, "Elliott Carter" in *The Yale Review*, Volume 99, No. 4, October 2011

18. On Ellison's being "acutely aware" of Emerson as a precursor see Michael Magee, *Emancipating Pragmatism: Emerson, Jazz, and Experimental Writing* (Tuscaloosa, AL: University of Alabama Press, 2004), 210n2.

19. For a history of jazz as an American art form, see Gunther Schuller, *Early Jazz: Its Roots and Musical Development* (Oxford: Oxford University Press, 1968) and Schuller, *The Swing Era: The Development of Jazz 1930–1945* (Oxford: Oxford University Press, 1989).

20. Ralph Ellison, "Homage to Duke Ellington on his Birthday," *Washington Sunday Star*, April 27, 1969, in *Living with Music: Ralph Ellison's Jazz Writings*, ed. Robert G. O'Meally (New York: Random House, 2001).

21. Ralph Ellison, *The Collected Essays of Ralph Ellison*, ed. John F. Callahan (New York: Modern Library, 2001), 96.

22. Ellison, *The Collected Essays of Ralph Ellison*, 97–98.

23. For a portrait of Duke at the height of his fame coasting through a day in New York City meeting and greeting musicians, manager, chauffeurs, restaurant and club owners, policemen, friends, relatives all with what Ellison called "nuance and style," see Whitney Balliet's short piece "A Day with the Duke," in *The New Yorker*, June 19, 1970.

24. Ellison, "Homage to Duke," 86.

25. Ellison, "The Golden Age, Times Past," in *Living With Music*, 56.

26. For anecdotes detailing Parker's often astonishingly crass behavior off the bandstand, see *Bird: The Legend of Charlie Parker*, ed. Robert Reisner (New York: De Capo Press, 1962).

27. Parker quoted in "On Bird, Bird-watching and Jazz," in *Living With Music*, 73.

28. Ellison, *Shadow and Act*, 166–67.

29. John Ashbery, *John Ashbery in Conversation With Mark Ford* (London: Between the Lines, 2003), 60.

30. In his attentive study of Ashbery's poetry (through 1994's *And the Stars Were Shining*), John Shoptaw doesn't make the connection between *Three Poems* and an Emersonian tradition of poetic prose, nor does David Shapiro in his chapter devoted to *Three Poems*. Ashbery himself seems to have had in mind the prose of Giorgio de Chirico's surrealist novel *Hebdomeros*, a "hypnotic" style composed of "long run on sentences" that allow for a "cinematic freedom of narration," a "fluid medium [in which] trivial images or details can suddenly congeal and take on a greater specific gravity, much as in a de Chirico painting a rubber glove or an artichoke can rival our attention merely through being present." See Ashbery's "Introduction" to *Hebdomeros*.

31. John Ashbery, *Collected Poems 1956–1987*, ed. Mark Ford (New York: Library of America, 2008), 247.

32. Ibid., 258.

33. Forcefully argued by Michael Fried in "Art and Objecthood," in which an evasion of medium specificity becomes a form of "theatricality."

34. Elliott Carter, *Syringa for Mezzo Soprano, Bass and Guitar with Ten Instrumentalists* (New York: Associated Music Publishers, 1978). The recording I refer to here is *Quintets and Voices* (Mode, 2003).

35. Schiff, *The Music of Elliott Carter*, 179.

36. Lawrence Kramer shrewdly notes how the soprano's lines here involve "repetition of adjacent pitches [and so the lines] move smoothly, with suppleness and ease," a narrow intervallic range that contrasts with the comparably wide-voiced guitar chords and the more tortured melodic leaps of the bass. See *Music and Poetry, the Nineteenth Century and After*, 208.

37. Ashbery, "The Invisible Avant Garde" [Lecture given at the Yale School of Art, 1968], *Art in America 1945–1970: Writings from the Age of Abstract Expressionism, Pop Art and Minimalism*, ed. Jed Perl (New York: Penguin Random House, 2014), 828.

38. Ibid., 827.

39. Ashbery, *Collected Poems*, 185.

Emerson's life and work have received consistent biographical attention since his lifetime. This bibliography emphasizes monographs published on Emerson since the previous *Cambridge Companion* to his work in 1999. However, key earlier works and a selection of important critical articles and essential edited collections about him are also included.

## Emerson's Writings

*The Annotated Emerson*. Ed. David Mikics. Cambridge, MA: Harvard University Press, 2021.

*The Collected Works of Ralph Waldo Emerson*. Ed. Robert E. Spiller, Alfred R. Ferguson, et al. 10 vols. Cambridge, MA: Harvard University Press, 1971–2013. [CW]

*The Complete Sermons of Ralph Waldo Emerson*. Ed. Albert von Frank et al. Columbia and London: University of Missouri Press, 4 vols., 1989–93. [CS]

*The Complete Works of Ralph Waldo Emerson*. Ed. Edward Waldo Emerson. Boston, MA: Houghton Mifflin, 12 vols., 1903–4. [W]

*The Correspondence of Emerson and Carlyle*. Ed. Joseph Slater. New York: Columbia University Press, 1964. [CEC]

*The Early Lectures of Ralph Waldo Emerson*. Ed. Stephen E. Whicher, Robert E. Spiller, and Wallace E. Williams, 3 vols. Cambridge, MA: Harvard University Press, 1961–72. [EL]

*Emerson's Antislavery Writings*. Ed. Len Gougeon and Joel Myerson. New Haven: Yale University Press, 1995. [AW]

*Emerson in His Journal*. Ed. Joel Porte. Cambridge, MA: Harvard University Press, 1982.

*Emerson: Political Writings (Cambridge Texts in the History of Political Thought)*. Ed. Kenneth Sacks. Cambridge: Cambridge University Press, 2008. [PW]

*Emerson's Prose and Poetry*. Ed. Joel Porte and Saundra Morris. New York: Norton, 2001.

*The Essential Writings of Ralph Waldo Emerson*. Ed. Brooks Atkinson. New York: The Modern Library, 2000.

*The Journals and Miscellaneous Notebooks of Ralph Waldo Emerson*. Ed. William H. Gilman and Ralph H. Orth, et al., 16 vols. Cambridge, MA: Harvard University Press, 1960–82. [JMN]

*The Journals of Ralph Waldo Emerson.* Ed. Edward Waldo Emerson and Waldo Emerson Forbes, 10 vols. Boston, MA: Houghton Mifflin, 1910–14. [*J*]

*The Later Lectures of Ralph Waldo Emerson.* Ed. Ronald Bosco and Joel Myerson, 2 vols. Athens: University of Georgia Press, 2001. [*LL*]

*The Letters of Ralph Waldo Emerson.* Ed. Ralph L. Rusk and Eleanor M. Tilton, 10 vols. New York: Columbia University Press, 1939, 1990–95. [*L*]

*The Major Prose.* Ralph Waldo Emerson. Ed. Ronald A. Bosco and Joel Myerson. Cambridge, MA: Harvard University Press, 2015.

*Memoirs of Margaret Fuller Ossoli* [1852]. Ralph Waldo Emerson, W. H. Channing, and J. F. Clarke. Boston, MA: Roberts Brothers, 1875.

*The Poetry Notebooks of Ralph Waldo Emerson.* Ed. Ralph H. Orth et al. Columbia and London: University of Missouri Press, 1986. [*PN*]

*The Political Emerson: Essential Writings on Politics and Social Reform.* Ed. David Robinson. Boston, MA: Beacon Press, 2004. [*PE*]

*Ralph Waldo Emerson: Natural History of the Intellect.* Ed. Maurice York and Rick Spaulding. Chicago: Wrightwood Press, 2008.

*The Selected Lectures of Ralph Waldo Emerson.* Ed. Ronald Bosco and Joel Myerson. Athens: University of Georgia Press, 2005. [*SL*]

*The Selected Letters of Ralph Waldo Emerson.* Ed. Joel Myerson. New York. Columbia University Press, 1997.

*The Topical Notebooks of Ralph Waldo Emerson.* Ed. Ralph H. Orth et al., 3 vols. Columbia and London: University of Missouri Press, 1990–94. [*TN*]

## Biographical and Historical Studies

Allen, Gay W. *Waldo Emerson: A Biography.* New York: Viking Press, 1981.

Baker, Carlos. *Emerson among the Eccentrics: A Group Portrait.* New York: Viking Press, 1996.

Bosco, Ronald A., and Joel Myerson, eds. *Emerson in His Own Time: A Biographical Chronicle of His Life, Drawn from Recollections, Interviews, and Memoirs by Family, Friends, and Associates.* Iowa City: University of Iowa Press, 2003.

Bosco, Ronald A., and Joel Myerson, eds. *The Emerson Brothers: A Fraternal Biography in Letters.* Oxford: Oxford University Press, 2006.

Bosco, Ronald A. "'His Lectures Were Poetry, His Teaching the Music of the Spheres': Annie Adams Fields and Francis Greenwood Peabody on Emerson's 'Natural History of the Intellect.'" *Harvard Library Bulletin* 8.2 (Summer 1997).

Bosco, Ronald A. "Historical Introduction." In *The Collected Works of Ralph Waldo Emerson: Letters and Social Aims,* edited by Ronald A. Bosco, Glen M. Johnson, and Joel Myerson, vol. 8. Cambridge, MA: Harvard University Press, 2010, xix–ccxiii.

Buell, Lawrence. *Emerson.* Cambridge, MA: Harvard University Press, 2003.

Elliot Cabot, James. *A Memoir of Ralph Waldo Emerson.* Boston, MA: Houghton Mifflin, 1887.

Emerson, Edward W. *Emerson in Concord: A Memoir.* Boston, MA: Houghton Mifflin, 1888.

Emerson, Ellen T. *The Life of Lidian Jackson,* edited by Dolores B. Carpenter. Boston, MA: Twayne, 1980.

Firkins, Oscar W. *Ralph Waldo Emerson.* Boston, MA: Houghton Mifflin, 1915.

Gross, Robert. *The Transcendentalists and Their World.* New York: Farrar, Straus and Giroux, 2021.

Gura, Phillip. *American Transcendentalism: A History.* New York: Hill and Wang, 2007.

Holmes, Oliver W. *Ralph Waldo Emerson.* Boston, MA: Houghton Mifflin, 1884.

James, Henry. "Emerson." In *Henry James: Literary Criticism,* edited by Leon Edel. New York: The Library of America, 1984.

Marcus, James. *Glad to the Brink of Fear: A Portrait of Ralph Waldo Emerson.* Princeton: Princeton University Press, 2024.

McAleer, John. *Ralph Waldo Emerson: Days of Encounter.* Boston, MA: Little, Brown and Company, 1984.

Myerson, Joel, ed. *A Historical Guide to Ralph Waldo Emerson.* New York: Oxford University Press, 1979.

Myerson, Joel. *Transcendentalism: A Reader.* Oxford: Oxford University Press, 2000.

Packer, Barbara L. *The Transcendentalists.* Athens: University of Georgia Press, 2007.

Porte, Joel. *Representative Man: Ralph Waldo Emerson in His Time.* New York: Oxford University Press, 1979.

Richardson, Robert D. *Emerson: The Mind on Fire.* Berkeley: University of California Press, 1995.

Richardson, Robert D. *Three Roads Back: How Emerson, Thoreau, and William James Responded to the Greatest Losses of Their Lives.* Princeton: Princeton University Press, 2023.

Rusk, Ralph L. *The Life of Ralph Waldo Emerson.* New York: Columbia University Press, 1957.

Sanborn, Franklin B., ed. *The Genius and Character of Emerson: Lectures at the Concord School of Philosophy.* Boston, MA: James R. Osgood and Company, 1885.

Whicher, Stephen. *Freedom and Fate: An Inner Life of Ralph Waldo Emerson.* Philadelphia: University of Pennsylvania Press, 1953.

Whitman, Walt. *Specimen Days: Complete Poetry and Collected Prose.* New York: Library of America, 1982.

Wider, Sahar A. *The Critical Reception of Emerson: Unsettling All Things.* Rochester: Camden House, 2000.

## Edited Collections on Emerson and His Contemporaries

Argersinger, Jana L. and Phyllis Cole, eds. *Toward a Female Genealogy of Transcendentalism.* Athens, GA: University of Georgia Press, 2014.

Arsić, Branka, ed. *American Impersonal: Essays with Sharon Cameron.* New York: Bloomsbury, 2015.

Arsić, Branka and Carey Wolfe, eds. *The Other Emerson.* Minneapolis: University of Minnesota Press, 2010.

Bosco, Ronald A. and Joel Myerson, eds. *Emerson: Bicentennial Essays.* Boston: Massachusetts Historical Society, 2006.

Garvey, T. Gregory, ed. *The Emerson Dilemma: Essays on Emerson and Social Reform.* Athens, GA: University of Georgia, 2001.

Hanlon, Christopher, ed. *The Oxford Handbook of Ralph Waldo Emerson.* Oxford: Oxford University Press, 2024.

LaRocca, David, ed. *Estimating Emerson: An Anthology of Criticism from Carlyle to Cavell*. New York: Bloomsbury, 2013.

Levine, Alan and Daniel Malachuk, eds. *A Political Companion to Ralph Waldo Emerson*. Lexington: University of Kentucky Press, 2014.

Löffler, Philipp, Clemens Spahr, and Jan Stievermann, eds. *The Handbook of American Romanticism*. Berlin: de Gruyter, 2021.

Lothstein, Arthur S. and Michael Brodrick, eds. *New Morning: Emerson in the Twenty-First Century*. Albany: SUNY Press, 2008.

Mott, Wesley T., ed. *Ralph Waldo Emerson in Context*. Cambridge: Cambridge University Press, 2014.

Mott, Wesley T. and Robert E. Burkholder, eds. *Emersonian Circles: Essays in Honor of Joel Myerson*. Rochester: University of Rochester Press, 1997.

Myerson, Joel, Sandra Harbert Petrulionis, and Laura Dassow Walls, eds. *The Oxford Handbook of Transcendentalism*. Oxford: Oxford University Press, 2010.

Porte, Joel and Saundra Morris, eds. *The Cambridge Companion to Ralph Waldo Emerson*. Cambridge: Cambridge University Press, 1999.

Sophie, Laniel-Musitelli and Thomas Constantinesco, eds. *Romanticism and Philosophy: Thinking with Literature*. London: Routledge, 2015.

Tharaud, Barry, ed. *Emerson for the Twenty-First Century: Global Perspectives on an American Icon*. Newark: University of Delaware Press, 2010.

Wayne, Tiffany K., ed. *Critical Companion to Ralph Waldo Emerson: A Literary Reference to His Life and Work*. New York: Facts on File, 2010.

## Criticism

Acharya, Shanta. *The Influence of Indian Thought on Ralph Waldo Emerson*. Lewiston, NY: Edwin Mellen Press, 2001.

Albrecht, James M. *Reconstructing Individualism: A Pragmatic Tradition from Emerson to Ellison*. Fordham University Press, 2012.

Arsić, Branka. *On Leaving: A Reading in Emerson*. Cambridge, MA: Harvard University Press, 2010.

Arsić, Branka. "Poetry as Flowering of Life Forms: Rancière's Reading of Emerson." *Textual Practice* 30:4 (2016): 551–78.

Augst, Thomas. *The Clerk's Tale: Young Men and Moral Life in Nineteenth Century America*. Chicago: University of Chicago Press, 2003.

Baker, Jennifer J. "Emerson, Embryology, and Culture." *J19: The Journal of Nineteenth-Century Americanists* 2:1 (2015): 15–39.

Brown, Lee Rust. *The Emerson Museum: Practical Romanticism and the Pursuit of the Whole*. Cambridge, MA: Harvard University Press, 1997.

Buell, Lawrence. *New England Literary Culture: From Revolution through Renaissance*. Cambridge: Cambridge University Press, 2009.

Cadava, Eduardo. *Emerson and the Climates of History*. Stanford: Stanford University Press, 1997.

Cameron, Sharon. *Impersonality: Seven Essays*. Chicago: University of Chicago Press, 2007.

Cameron, Sharon. *The Likeness of Things Unlike*. Chicago: University of Chicago Press, 2025.

Cavell, Stanley. *Conditions Handsome and Unhandsome: The Constitution of Emersonian Perfectionism*. Chicago: Chicago University Press, 1990.

Cavell, Stanley. *Emerson's Transcendental Etudes*. Stanford: Stanford University Press, 2003.

Cavell, Stanley. *The Senses of Walden: An Expanded Edition*. San Francisco: North Point Press, 1981.

Cavell, Stanley. *This New Yet Unapproachable America*. Albuquerque: Living Batch Press, 1989.

Chai, Leon. *The Romantic Foundations of the American Renaissance*. Ithaca: Cornell University Press, 1987.

Clark, Prentiss. "'Pulse for Pulse in Harmony with the Universal Whole': Hearing 'Self-Reliance' Anew," *Nineteenth Century Literature* 69 (2014): 319–41.

Cole, Phyllis. *Mary Moody Emerson and the Origins of Transcendentalism: A Family History*. New York: Oxford University Press, 2002.

Constantinesco, Thomas. "*The Dial* and the Untimely 'Spirit of the Times.'" *American Periodicals* 28:1 (2018): 21–40.

Constantinesco, Thomas. "Limning New Regions of Thought: Emerson's Abstract Regionalism." *ESQ: A Journal of the American Renaissance* 60 (2014): 285–326.

Constantinesco, Thomas. *Ralph Waldo Emerson: L'Amérique à l'essai*. Paris: Editions Rue d'Ulm, 2012.

Constantinesco, Thomas. *Writing Pain in the Nineteenth-Century United States*. Oxford: Oxford University Press, 2022.

Da, Z. Nan. *Intransitive Encounter: Sino-U.S. Literatures and the Limits of Exchange*. New York: Columbia University Press, 2018.

Davis, Theo. *Formalism, Experience and the Making of American Literature in the Nineteenth Century*. Cambridge: Cambridge University Press, 2007.

de Galzain, Alice. "Rewriting the Life of an 'Ultra-Radical': Margaret Fuller, Ralph Waldo Emerson, and *Memoirs of Margaret Fuller Ossoli* (1852)." Ph.D. diss., University of Edinburgh, 2023.

Dewey, John. "Emerson – The Philosopher of Democracy [1903]." In *The Essential Dewey, Vol. 2*, edited by Larry Hickman and Thomas Alexander. Bloomington: Indiana University Press, 1998, 366–70.

Dolan, Neal. *Emerson's Liberalism*. Madison: Wisconsin University Press, 2009.

Dunston, Susan L. *Emerson's Environmental Ethics*. Lanham, MD: Lexington Books, 2018.

Eckel, Leslie Elizabeth. "Emerson, Reluctant Feminist." In *The Oxford Handbook of Ralph Waldo Emerson*, edited by Christopher Hanlon. Oxford: Oxford University Press, 2024, 589–604.

Follett, Danielle. "The Tension Between Immanence and Dualism in Coleridge and Emerson." In *Romanticism and Philosophy: Thinking with Literature*, edited by Sophie Laniel-Musitelli and Thomas Constantinesco. London: Routledge, 2015, 201–21.

Forster, Sophia. "Peculiar Faculty and Peculiar Institution: Ralph Waldo Emerson on Labor and Slavery," *ESQ: A Journal of the American Renaissance* 60 (2014): 35–73.

Friedl, Herwig. *Thinking in Search of a Language: Essays on American Intellect and Intuition*. New York and London: Bloomsbury, 2019.

Fuller, Randall. *Emerson's Ghosts: Literature, Politics, and the Making of Americanists*. Oxford: Oxford University Press, 2011.

Goodman, Russell B. *American Philosophy before Pragmatism*. Oxford: Oxford University Press, 2015.

Goodman, Russell B. "The Colours of the Spirit: Emerson and Thoreau on Nature and the Self." In *Nature in American Philosophy*, edited by Jean De Groot. Washington: Catholic University of America Press, 2004, 1–18.

Goodman, Russell B. "Emerson, Romanticism, and Classical American Pragmatism." In *The Oxford Handbook of American Philosophy*, edited by Cheryl Misak. Oxford: Oxford University Press, 2008, 19–37.

Goodman, Russell B. *Emerson, the Philosopher of Oppositions*. Cambridge: Cambridge University Press, 2025.

Gougeon, Len. *Virtue's Hero: Emerson, Antislavery, and Reform*. Athens, GA: University of Georgia Press, 1990.

Greenham, David. *Emerson's Transatlantic Romanticism*. New York: Palgrave Macmillan, 2012.

Grimstad, Paul. *Experience and Experimental Writing: Literary Pragmatism from Emerson to the Jameses*. Oxford: Oxford University Press, 2013.

Grossman, Jay. *Reconstituting the American Renaissance: Emerson, Whitman, and the Politics of Representation*. Durham, NC: Duke University Press, 2003.

Guardiano, Nicholas L. *Aesthetic Transcendentalism in Emerson, Peirce, and Nineteenth-Century American Landscape Painting*. Lanham: Lexington Press, 2017.

Guthrie, James. *Above Time: Emerson's and Thoreau's Temporal Revolutions*. Columbia: University of Missouri Press, 2001.

Hanlon, Christopher. *America's England: Antebellum Literature and Atlantic Sectionalism*. New York: Oxford University Press, 2013.

Hanlon, Christopher. *Emerson's Memory Loss: Originality, Communality, and the Late Style*. Oxford: Oxford University Press, 2018.

Hurth, Elisabeth. *Between Faith and Unbelief: American Transcendentalists and the Challenge of Atheism*. Boston: Brill, 2007.

Insko, Jeffrey. *History, Abolition, and the Ever-Present Now in Antebellum American Writing*. Oxford: Oxford University Press, 2018.

James, William. "Address at the Centenary of Ralph Waldo Emerson, May 25, 1903." In *William James: Writings 1902–1910*. New York: Library of America, 1987, 1119–25.

Johnson, Linck C. "'Liberty is Never Cheap': Emerson, 'The Fugitive Slave Law,' and the Antislavery Lecture Series at the Broadway Tabernacle," *New England Quarterly* 76:4 (2003): 550–92.

Kateb, George, *Emerson and Self-Reliance*. Oxford: Rowman and Littlefield, 2002.

Koch, Daniel. *Ralph Waldo Emerson: Class, Race, and Revolution in the Making of an American Thinker*. New York: I. B. Tauris, 2012.

LaRocca, David. *Emerson's English Traits and the Natural History of Metaphor*. New York: Bloomsbury, 2013.

Larson, Kerry. "Emerson's Strange Equality." *Nineteenth-Century Literature* 59:3 (2004): 315–39.

Levin, Jonathan. *The Poetics of Transition: Emerson, Pragmatism, and American Literary Modernism*. Durham, NC: Duke University Press, 1999.

Lopez, Michael. *Emerson and Power: Creative Antagonism in the Nineteenth Century*. DeKalb: North Illinois Press, 1995.

Lysaker, John. *Emerson and Self-Culture.* Indianapolis: Indiana University Press, 2008.

Magee, Michael. *Emancipating Pragmatism: Emerson, Jazz, and Experimental Writing.* Huntsville: University of Alabama Press, 2004.

Matthiessen, F. O. *American Renaissance: Art and Expression in the Age of Emerson and Whitman.* New York: Oxford University Press, 1941.

McMurry, Andrew. *Environmental Renaissance: Emerson, Thoreau, and the Systems of Nature.* Athens, GA: University of Georgia Press, 2003.

Meehan, Sean Ross. *A Liberal Education in Late Emerson: Readings in the Rhetoric of Mind.* Rochester: Camden House, 2019.

Newfield, Christopher. *The Emerson Effect: Individualism and Submission in America.* Chicago: University of Chicago Press, 1996.

Noble, Mark. "Emerson's Atom and the Matter of Suffering," *Nineteenth-Century Literature* 64:1 (2009): 16–47.

O'Neill, Bonnie Carr. "'The Best of Me Is There': Emerson as Lecturer and Celebrity," *American Literature* 80 (2008): 739–67.

Packer, Barbara L. *Emerson's Fall: A New Interpretation of the Major Essays.* New York: Continuum, 1982.

Rancière, Jacques. *Aisthesis: Scenes from the Aesthetic Regime of Art.* Trans. Zakir Paul. New York: Verso, 2013.

Reynolds, Larry J. *Righteous Violence: Revolution, Slavery, and the American Renaissance.* Athens, GA: University of Georgia Press, 2011.

Richardson, Joan. *A Natural History of Pragmatism: The Fact of Feeling from Jonathan Edwards to Gertrude Stein.* New York: Cambridge University Press, 2007.

Richardson, Robert. *First We Read, Then We Write: Emerson on the Creative Process.* Iowa City: University of Iowa Press, 2009.

Richardson, Robert D. "A Perfect Piece of Stoicism," *The Thoreau Society Bulletin,* 153 (Fall 1980): 1–5.

Robinson, David. *Emerson and the Conduct of Life: Pragmatism and Ethical Purpose in the Later Work.* Cambridge: Cambridge University Press, 1993.

Robinson, David. *Transcendent Woman: Margaret Fuller's Art and Achievement.* Amherst: University of Massachusetts, 2025.

Sacks, Kenneth. *Understanding Emerson: "The American Scholar" and His Struggle for Self-Reliance.* Princeton: Princeton University Press, 2003.

Schoolman, Martha. *Abolitionist Geographies.* Minneapolis: University of Minnesota Press, 2014.

Sedarat, Roger. *Emerson in Iran: The American Appropriation of Persian Poetry.* Albany: SUNY Press, 2019.

Sommer, Tim. *Carlyle, Emerson and the Transatlantic Uses of Authority: Literature, Print, Performance.* Edinburgh: Edinburgh University Press, 2021.

Stanley, Kate. *Practices of Surprise in American Literature after Emerson.* Cambridge: Cambridge University Press, 2018.

Takanashi, Yoshio. *Emerson and Neo-Confucianism: Crossing Paths over the Pacific.* New York: Palgrave Macmillan, 2014.

Tamarkin, Elisa. *Anglophilia: Deference, Devotion, and Antebellum America.* Chicago: University of Chicago Press, 2008.

Tamarkin, Elisa. *Apropos of Something: A History of Irrelevance and Relevance.* Chicago: University of Chicago Press, 2022.

Thompson, Roger. *Emerson and the History of Rhetoric*. Carbondale: Southern Illinois University Press, 2017.

Urbas, Joseph. *Emerson's Metaphysics: A Song of Laws and Causes*. Lanham and London: Lexington Books, 2016.

Urbas, Joseph. *The Philosophy of Ralph Waldo Emerson*. New York: Routledge, 2021.

Van Cromphout, Gustaff. *Emerson's Ethics*. Columbia: University of Missouri Press, 1999.

Versluis, Arthur. *American Transcendentalism and Asian Religions*. New York: Oxford University Press, 1993.

Versluis, Arthur. *The Esoteric Origins of the American Renaissance*. New York: Oxford University Press, 2001.

Voelz, Johannes. *Transcendental Resistance: The New Americanists and Emerson's Challenge*. Hanover: Dartmouth College Press, 2010.

Voelz, Johannes. "Transnationalism and Nineteenth-Century Literature." In *The Cambridge Companion to Transnational American Literature*, edited by Yogita Goyal. Cambridge: Cambridge University Press, 2017, 91–106.

Walls, Laura Dassow. *Emerson's Life in Science: The Culture of Truth*. Ithaca: Cornell University Press, 2003.

Walls, Laura Dassow. "'Every Truth Tends to Become a Power': Emerson, Faraday, and the Minding of Matter." In *Emerson for the Twenty-first Century: Global Perspectives on an American Icon*, edited by Barry Tharaud. Newark: University of Delaware Press, 2010, 301–17.

Wilson, Eric G. *Emerson's Sublime Science*. London: Macmillan Press Ltd., 1999.

Windolph, Christopher. *Emerson's Nonlinear Nature*. Missouri: University of Missouri Press, 2007.

Wirzbicki, Peter. *Fighting for the Higher Law: Black and White Transcendentalists against Slavery*. Philadelphia: University of Pennsylvania Press, 2021.

Wright, Tom F. *Lecturing the Atlantic: Speech, Print and an Anglo-American Commons*. Oxford: Oxford University Press, 2017.

Zavatta, Benedetta. *Individuality and Beyond: Nietzsche Reads Emerson*. Trans. Alexander Reynolds. New York: Oxford University Press, 2019.

Ziser, Michael. *Environmental Practice and Early American Literature*. Cambridge: Cambridge University Press, 2013.

Zuber, Devin P. *A Language of Things: Emanuel Swedenborg and the American Environmental Imagination*. Charlottesville: University of Virginia Press, 2019.

Zwarg, Christina. *Feminist Conversations: Fuller, Emerson, and the Play of Reading*. Ithaca: Cornell University Press, 1995.

# INDEX

page numbers followed by "n" refer to endnotes

# Cambridge Companions to ...

## AUTHORS

## TOPICS

For EU product safety concerns, contact us at Calle de José Abascal, 56–1°,
28003 Madrid, Spain or eugpsr@cambridge.org.

www.ingramcontent.com/pod-product-compliance
Ingram Content Group UK Ltd.
Pitfield, Milton Keynes, MK11 3LW, UK
UKHW041830280426
470499UK00011B/239